STATISTICS

AFRICA

Sources for Social, Economic and Market Research

Joan M. Harvey, MA, FLA

Senior Lecturer at the School of Librarianship,
Loughborough Technical College

Edition 2
Revised and enlarged

CBD Research Ltd
Beckenham, Kent, England
Telephone 01 650 7745

First published   1970.

Second edition, revised and enlarged   1978.

Copyright   ©   1976   Joan M Harvey.

I S B N   900246 26 X.

Published by   C.B.D. Research Ltd,
                                          154 High Street, Beckenham, Kent, BR3 1EA, England.
                                          Telephone 01-650 7745.

Printed in Great Britain by
McCorquodale (Newton) Limited
Newton-le-Willows

CONTENTS

INTRODUCTION

1.   Following the precedent set by the third edition of "Statistics Europe" this second edition of "Statistics Africa" has been given wider subject coverage than the first edition in order to make the work not only more useful to market researchers and others who used the first edition, but also to those engaged in broader fields of economic and social research.   Despite the fluctuating political and economic conditions in some African countries, the general trend is towards development and this is accentuated in some areas by the discovery of oil deposits and by the increasing demand for, and increasing value of, other basic commodities and raw materials, leading to increased national wealth and the opportunity for material changes in the economic conditions of the country and the lives of the population.

Most statistical information is collected by governments, development planning calling for accurate and up to date statistics.   However, many African States are still relatively new and statistical offices may still be inadequate to carry out complex statistical analyses and to publish regularly their statistical compilations; shortages of staff, inadequate finances, political unrest and other causes may result in regular publications ceasing to be issued, either permanently or temporarily, without warning.   One of the main difficulties faced when compiling a guide such as this one is to discover whether later issues or editions of a particular title do, in fact, exist.

Not all the information that is collected is published, either because of one or more of the problems mentioned above or because it is considered that there would be insufficient general interest for publication, and in such cases it may be possible for the enquirers to obtain the required data from the organisation responsible for collecting it; some information, however, will not be published because it has been supplied on the understanding that it will be treated as confidential.   Statistical information published by the United Nations and other international organisations is generally supplied by the government of the countries concerned, and is often in a form suitable for national comparisons to be made.

It is important for prospective purchasers of priced publications mentioned in this guide to appreciate that many of the publishers in Africa will not supply copies of priced publications unless the order for the publications required is accompanied by a remittance to cover the cost of both the publications and the postage, preferably in local currency.

2.   ARRANGEMENT

The main body of this guide is arranged by countries in alphabetical order, and each entry, whether for the description of an organisation or of a publication, has been allocated a unique reference number. The list of countries (page xi) indicates the first page number for each country.   A selection on Africa as a whole precedes the individual countries.   Each section contains:

(1)   the name, address and telephone number (if available) of the central statistical office of the country and of other important organisations that collect and publish statistical material; this is followed by some information on the organisation and work of each agency, the facilities it provides, etc.

(2)   the principal libraries in the country where collections of statistical material may be consulted by the public;

(3)   libraries and information services in other countries (particularly English-speaking countries) where the country's statistical publications may be consulted;

(4)   the principal bibliographies of statistics; only reasonably current bibliographies have been included, and sales lists are mentioned because of the general dearth of special bibliographies in the field; national bibliographies are not included, but should not be overlooked as a means of tracing statistical titles.

(5)   the major statistical publications, arranged in the following standard groups:
       ¶   A   General
       ¶   B   Production
            i.   Mines and mining
           ii.   Agriculture, fisheries, forestry, etc
         iii.   Industry
         iv.   Construction
           v.   Energy
       ¶   C   External trade
       ¶   D   Internal distribution and service trades

[continued next page]

2(5), continued

¶   E   Population
¶   F   Social
   i. Standard of living
   ii. Health and welfare
   iii. Education and leisure
   iv. Justice
¶   G   Finance
   i. Banking
   ii. Public finance
   iii. Company finance
   iv. Investment
   v. Insurance
¶   H   Transport and communications
   i. Ships and shipping
   ii. Road
   iii. Rail
   iv. Air
   v. Telecommunications and postal services

3. NOTES ON THE GROUPS

¶   A   Titles listed in group A are useful only for general indications of overall patterns, and are not usually sufficiently detailed for research into a particular or specific subject.

¶   B   Group B includes all production statistics.   It includes reports of censuses, which are usually devoted more to the structure (finance, labour, machinery, power, etc) of the industry, etc, than to the quantity and value of goods produced.

¶   C   The classification schemes used for the tabulation of foreign trade statistics follow closely similar patterns, as they are mainly based on the Brussels Tariff Nomenclature (BTN) or on the United Nations Standard International Trade Classification (SITC), which are now correlated.   Many countries classify their imports and exports in more detail than the BTN or SITC, and a useful key to the detailed classification of each country can be the International Customs Journal (Bulletin International des Douanes), which is obtainable from the International Customs Tariff Bureau, rue de l'Association 38, Bruxelles, Belgium or from sales agents.   It comprises about 200 volumes, each containing the customs tariff of a single country, and is kept up to date by supplements and new editions as required.

¶   D   Group D includes statistics of wholesale and retail trade and of service trades, including tourism.

¶   E   Censuses of population, demographic surveys, population projections, vital statistics and labour statistics are included in Group E.

¶   F   This group in general comprises social statistics.   Cost of living indices, wages and salaries, household budget surveys, etc, are included in F.i.   F.ii. includes statistics on national health services, hospitals, national insurance schemes, social security, social insurance and social welfare. F.iii. includes all aspects of education from primary schools to universities and leisure activities such as entertainment, sport, libraries, etc.   F.iv. includes both judicial and criminal statistics.

¶   G   Group G includes all statistics of a financial nature.   G.i. lists publications with statistics of all types of banking, but does not specifically include publications which are solely devoted to the accounts of a particular bank.   G.ii. includes both national and local government financial statistics. G.iii. includes statistics of all types of companies and corporations, but does not include publications devoted to the accounts of one particular company or corporation.   G.iv. is concerned mainly with industrial investment.   G.v. is concerned with statistics of the business of insurance companies, but not the accounts of individual insurance companies.

3. NOTES ON THE GROUPS, continued

¶ H   Group H covers transport and communications statistics generally. H.i. includes statistics of ships and shipping, sea-borne transport, inland waterway transport, traffic at ports, and passenger and cargo traffic in ships.   H.ii. includes statistics of roads, road traffic, road accidents, and passengers and goods conveyed by road.   H.iii. includes statistics of railways, rolling stock, passenger and goods traffic.   H.iv. includes statistics of airports, aircraft, passenger and goods traffic.   H.v. includes statistics of telephones, telephone and telegraph services, post offices and postal services.

4. FORM OF ENTRY

The entry for each publication comprises:

(1)   serial number;

(2)   title, English translation of title if the original is not in English, and name of responsible organisation;

(3)   name and address of publisher or of other agency or sales office from which the publication can be obtained;

(4)   date when first published (omitted in cases where it is difficult to determine because of changes in title, responsible organisation, etc), date of latest issue seen by compiler (not necessarily the latest published) if published annually or less frequently, price (if ascertainable, and generally given in local currency), number of pages or volumes of the issue seen of an annual or less frequent publication;

(5)   description of contents;

(6)   indication of the lapse of time between the latest data included and the date of publication (as the actual date is seldom cited in the publication and seldom coincides with the normal date of an issue, part or edition, this information has been obtained mainly by observation of dates of receipt in libraries, and should be treated with caution);

(7)   language(s) of the text, indicated by the symbol § followed by international symbols (BS 3862).

5. REFERENCES

References have been made to relevant publications in other groups within each country section, but NOT from individual countries to the general section on Africa as a whole.   It will, therefore, often be worth while to consult the appropriate group in the general section if no suitable material is found in a particular section.

6. CHANGES OF TITLE

Only the latest title of each publication is given, except in cases where confusion might arise or where the change is very recent.   Many statistical publications have a long history of title variations, and it would be impossible to list all the changes.   The librarian, sales agent, or publisher will be able to advise prospective users and purchasers of earlier issues if titles have changed.

7. INDEXES

In addition to the index to titles and the index to organisations, this edition includes a subject index.   Although the grouping of entries under each country provides a ready means of identifying publications in broad classes, it was felt that a subject index was needed to enable the user to locate specialised source material more readily.   It must be emphasised, however, that the subject index is NOT a complete analytical index to all subjects covered by all statistical sources listed in the book.

8.   ACKNOWLEDGEMENTS

The compiler would again like to thank everyone who has helped in the preparation of this volume. She has had the utmost co-operation from most of the statistical offices, libraries and other organisations she has approached, and has appreciated the easy access she has been afforded to the many libraries she has used, particularly the Library of the Institute of Development Studies at the University of Sussex, the Documentation Section of the Centre for Middle Eastern and Islamic Studies at the University of Durham, the Statistics and Market Intelligence Library of the Department of Trade and Industry, the Official Publications Library of the British Library, and the Library of Warwick University, where most of the material has been examined.

DISEWORTH, Derby.
October 1977.

LIST OF COUNTRIES - TABLE DES PAYS - LÄNDERVERZEICHNIS

ABBREVIATIONS & SYMBOLS

§	language(s)
Af	Afrikaans
Ar	Arabic
c	circa
De	German
DOM	Départements d'Outre-mer
ed	edition
EEC	European Economic Community
En	English
Es	Spanish
Fr	French
INSEE	Institut National de la Statistique et des Etudes Economiques
It	Italian
p	pages
Pt	Portuguese
t	telephone number
tg	telegraphic address
tx	telex number
TOM	Territoires d'Outre-Mer
UDEAC	Union Douanière et Economique de l'Afrique Centrale
UN	United Nations
vol	volume
yr	per annum (annual subscription)

Some international organisations publishing statistics

001   United Nations,
        New York, NY, USA.
        t   754 1234.

        The Statistical Office of the United Nations collects and publishes data from as many countries as
        possible in periodic as well as ad hoc publications.   On the basis of these statistics, the Statistical Office
        computes a large number of economic indicators in the form of global and regional aggregates and index
        numbers. It also publishes methodological studies, guides and manuals, and assists governments in
        implementing statistical practice recommended by the Statistical Commission. The Statistical Office is a
        part of the United Nations Department of Economic and Social Affairs.

002   United Nations Economic Commission for Africa,
        P O Box 3001, Addis Ababa, Ethiopia.
        t   Ethiopia 7000.

        Established in 1958 to promote and facilitate concerted action for the economic and social development
        of Africa; to maintain and strengthen the economic relations of African countries and territories; to undertake
        and sponsor investigations, research and studies on economic and technological problems and developments;
        to collect, evaluate and disseminate economic, technological and statistical information; and to assist in the
        formulation and development of coordinated policies in promoting economic and technological developme nt
        in the region.

003   Food and Agriculture Organisation of the United Nations,
        viale delle Terme di Caracalla, 00153 Roma, Italy.
        t   (06) 5797 Ex 61181.

        Created to raise the levels of nutrition and standards of living, to secure improvements in the efficiency
        of production and distribution of all agricultural products, and to better the conditions of rural populations.
        To help achieve these aims, the FAO provides an intelligence service of facts and figures relating to nutrition,
        agriculture, forestry and fisheries, and also appraisals and forecasts of production, distribution, and
        consumption in these industries.

004   European Communities.   Communautés Européennes,
        Bâtiment Berlaymont,   Centre Européen, Kirchberg, Luxembourg,
        200 rue de la Loi, 1049 Bruxelles, Belgium.   and   (BP 1907)   t   47 941
        t   735 80 40.   tx Comeur LU3423.

        The nine countries of the European Communities have bound themselves by three treaties (coal and steel,
        economic, and atomic energy) under which their future activities are to become more and more closely woven.
        African countries associated with the European Communities were originally those which were connected
        colonially or economically with the original six members of the Communities, but 49 states signed the Lomé
        Convention on 1.4.76 (including Benin, Botswana, Burundi, Cameroon, Central African Republic, Chad,
        Congo, Equatorial Guinea, Ethiopia, Gabon, the Gambia, Ghana, Guinea, Guinea-Bissau, Ivory Coast,
        Kenya, Lesotho, Liberia, Madagascar, Malawi, Mali, Mauritania, Mauritius, Niger, Nigeria, Rwanda,
        Senegal, Sierra Leone, Somalia, Sudan, Swaziland, Tanzania, Togo, Uganda, Upper Volta, Zaire, and
        Zambia.   Three more countries, including Seychelles and Comores signed in August and September 1976,
        and three more, including Cape Verde and St Thomas & Prince in March 1977.   Whereas the Statistical
        Office of the European Communities compiled, analysed and published statistics of associated member
        countries in the early days, there have been no such publications recently.

005   UNESCO   (United Nations Educational, Scientific and Cultural Organisation)
        7 place de Fontenoy, 75700 Paris, France.
        t   577 1610.

        Established in 1946 'to contribute to peace and security by promoting collaboration among nations through
        education, science and culture, in order to further universal respect for justice, for the rule of law, and for
        the human rights and fundamental freedoms for all'. The organisation is concerned with education, natural
        science, social science, culture, mass communications, international exchanges, and technical assistance; it
        collects many statistics, some of which are included in its statistical yearbook and in other, mainly textual
        publications.

006   Organisation Commune Africaine, Malgache et Maurice   [Organisation of African States, Madagascar
             and Mauritius]
             BP 437, Yaoundé, Cameroun.

        Established in February 1965 to meet the demand for a broadly based organisation to promote co-operation
between the French-speaking African states and Madagascar in political, social and cultural fields, as well as
in economic development.   There have been several changes in membership over the years and the
organisation now includes Chad, Cameroun, Central African Republic, Gabon, Rwanda, Madagascar and
Mauritius.

Libraries and information services

        Many national, university and public libraries throughout the world are deposit libraries for United
Nations publications (a "List of depository libraries receiving United Nations material" is published as a
separate booklet at intervals and it is also included annually in the Cumulative Index to UNDEX, the United
Nations Documents Index); such libraries should have unrestricted documents and publications available for
reference.   United Nations Information Centres usually have the more recent UN publications available.

        It is usual for the official statistical offices of countries to exchange their publications with other
national statistical offices and these publications are often, but not always, stored in the libraries of the
statistical offices.   These libraries are often accessible to those who wish to consult this type of material,
even when generally closed to the public.

United Kingdom

        The most accessible large collection of the publications referred to in this guide is at the Department of
Trade and Industry's Statistics and Market Intelligence Library, Export House, 50 Ludgate Hill, London
EC4M 7HU (t 01-248 5757, ext 368).   A most comprehensive collection of statistical publications of the
developing countries, including African developing countries, is in the Library of the Institute of Development
Studies at the University of Sussex, Andrew Cohen Building, Falmer, Brighton BN1 9RE (t 0273 66261), and
the Documentation Section of the Centre for Middle Eastern and Islamic Studies at the University of Durham,
Elvet Hill, Durham City DH1 3TR (t 0385 64971 or 64720) has an important collection of statistical
publications of the Islamic countries, including those in north Africa.   Other large but somewhat more limited
collections are in the Official Publications Library of the British Library, Great Russell Street, London
EC1B 3DG (t 01-636 1544, ext 487), Warwick University Library, Coventry (t 0203 24011), and the British
Library of Political and Economic Science, Houghton Street, London WC2A 2AE (t 01-405 7686).

        Many of the larger public libraries are deposit libraries for United Nations publications, and one or two
have collections of statistical yearbooks of overseas countries, but none take the more detailed statistical
publications of individual countries listed in the following pages.

Australia

        The two largest collections of statistical publications, including those of international organisations and
of individual overseas countries, are the National Library of Australia, Canberra, ACT 2600 (t (062) 621111)
and the Australian Bureau of Statistics, Cameron Offices, Belconnen, ACT 2617 (t (062) 527911).

        There are also collections of this type of material in the State libraries, situated in each capital city, and
in some university libraries, particularly the University of Sydney.   The Australian National University Library
at Canberra has a collection of statistical material to support its research in demography.

        The United Nations Information Centre at 77 Kings Street, Sydney, NSW 2000 (t (02) 292151) has a
collection of United Nations publications available for reference, and the Library of the Department of Foreign
Affairs, Administrative Building, Parkes, ACT 2600(t (062) 619111) holds a comprehensive collection of UN
publications to which the public could be allowed access, also for reference only.

Canada

        The Library of Statistics Canada, Ottawa K1A OT6 (t (613) 992 2959) has an extensive collection of
statistical material, including the historical collection of Canadian statistics, publications of international
organisations and of individual countries.   The library is open to the public and materials can be borrowed
via interlibrary loan.

        Many larger Canadian government and university libraries are depositories for United Nations
publications and also receive some publications of the EEC, but the existing collections for individual
countries are neither extensive nor comprehensive.

Libraries and information services,   continued

New Zealand

Both the Library of the Department of Statistics, Aorangi House, Molesworth Street, Wellington (Postal address: Private Bag, Wellington; t 729 119) and the National Library of New Zealand, 44 The Terrace, Wellington (Postal address: Private Bag, Wellington; t 722-101) have large collections of statistical material, including publications of international organisations and of individual overseas countries. Some material is also held in the university libraries, in the public libraries of certain other and secondary cities and in the libraries of certain other government departments such as the Department of Trade and Industry.   Much of the material available in New Zealand is accessible for loan through the country's library interloan system.

USA

The Bureau of the Census Library of the US Department of Commerce, Room 2451, Federal Office Building 3, Suitland, Maryland (mailing address: Washington DC 20233; t (301) 763-5042) maintains a collection of final US Census publications from 1790 to date as well as foreign censuses and statistical publications which may be consulted from 08.00 to 17.00 Monday to Friday.

The Library of Congress in Washington, the Joint International Monetary Fund and International Bank for Reconstruction and Development Library in Washington, and the United Nations Library in New York have extensive statistical collections.

The United Nations Information Center, 2101 L Street NW, Washington DC 20037 (t 202-296-5370) has a collection of United Nations publications.   A large number of university and public libraries throughout the US are deposit libraries for United Nations publications and also have some publications of other international organisations.

Bibliographies

007   UNDEX: United Nations documents index (United Nations)
       Sales Section, United Nations, New York, NY 10017; or from sales agents.
       1950-   monthly   £52.00 or US$80.00 yr.
       Lists all unrestricted documents and publications of the United Nations arranged by issuing departments
          of the UN.   Series A is the subject index; series B the country index; and series C the list of
          documents issued.   An annual cumulative checklist and cumulative subject index are included in
          the subscription, and are issued some time after the end of the year covered.

008   United Nations publications: a reference catalogue   (United Nations)
       Sales Section, United Nations, New York, NY 10017; or from sales agents.
       A comprehensive list of the publications of the UN issued for sale since 1945.   The issue for 1945-1963,
          published in 1964, has been followed by annual volumes.

009   Bibliography of industrial and distributive-trade statistics   (United Nations Statistical Office)
       Sales Section, United Nations, New York 10017; or from sales agents.
             £4.16 or US$8.00.   177p.
       Issued as "Statistical papers: Series M, no 36, rev 4" it lists the data being collected by each reporting
          country, mentioning the publications in which the data is published, if it is published.
       Time factor: the 4th revision of this bibliography was published in 1975.

010   Catalogue of statistical materials of developing countries   (Institute of the Developing Economies, Tokyo)
       Asian Economic Press, 42 Hommura-cho, Ichigaya, Shinjuku-ku, Tokyo 162, Japan.
       6th ed, 1974.   not priced.   250p.
       A catalogue of statistical materials collected by the Statistics Division of the Institute.

Bibliographies,   continued

011   Directory of international statistics   (United Nations Statistical Office).
         Sales Section, United Nations, New York, NY 10017; or from sales agents.
         published in 1975.   £6.50 or US$12.50.   296p.
         Issued as Statistical papers, series M, no 56, the directory is in four parts.   Part 1 lists international
              statistical services; part 2 lists international statistical series by subject, organisation,
              publication and series frequency, and data base; part 3 is devoted to international statistical
              standards; and part 4 deals with computerised international statistics, including an inventory of
              data bases of economic and social statistics, computer installations, and inter-organisational
              computer arrangements.   Reference is only to United Nations and related bodies.

012   International population census bibliography: Africa   (Population Research Center, Department of
              Sociology, University of Texas).
         Bureau of Business Research, University of Texas, Austin, Texas, USA.
         Issued in 1965 as Census Bibliography no. 2, there is also a supplementary volume issued in 1968
         (US$3.00 each volume).

013   Situation des recensements et des enquêtes démographiques dans les états africains at Malgache au 1er
              janvier 1970   [Situation on censuses and demographic surveys in French-speaking Africa at 1st
              January 1970]   (INSEE).
         INSEE, 18 boulevard Adolphe Pinard, 75675 Paris Cedex 14, France.
         published in 1970.   63p.
         §   Fr.

014   La démographie en Afrique d'expression française: bulletin de liaison   [Demography in French-speaking
              Africa; liaison bulletin]   (Institut National d'Etudes Démographiques; INSEE; Office de la
              Recherche Scientifique et Technique Outre-mer; Sécretariat d'Etat aux Affaires Etrangères).
         INED, INSEE, MICOOP, ORSTOM, 18 boulevard Adolphe Pinard, 75675 Paris Cedex 14, France.
         1971-   quarterly.   not priced.
         Lists people working on African demographic research and gives the situation on the progress of new
              censuses and demographic surveys.
         §   Fr.

015   A series of guides to official publications, including statistical ones, of African countries and regions is
              being compiled by the staff of the Library of Congress and published by the Superintendent of Documents,
              US Government Printing Office, Washington DC 20402, USA.   Published so far are the following:-
                   Official publications of British East Africa.   4 vols.   1960-1963.
                   Official publications of Sierra Leone and Gambia.   1963.   US$0.55.
                   Official publications of French Equatorial Africa, French Cameroon, and Togo, 1948-1958.
                        1964.   US$0.50.
                   Madagascar and adjacent islands: a guide to official publications.   1965.   US$0.40.
                   The Rhodesias and Nyasaland: a guide to official publications.   1965.   US$1.50.
                   Nigeria: a guide to official publications.   1966.   US$1.00.
                   French-speaking West Africa: a guide to official publications.   1967.   US$1.25.
                   Portuguese Africa: a guide to official publications.   1967.   US$1.50.
                   Ghana: a guide to official publications, 1872-1968.   1967.   US$1.25.
                   Botswana, Lesotho and Swaziland: a guide to official publications in American libraries.
                        1971.   US$1.00.
                   French-speaking Central Africa; a guide to official publications in American libraries.
                        1971.   US$3.25.
                   Spanish-speaking Africa: a guide to official publications.   1974.   US$1.00.

Statistical publications

¶ A - General

016   Statistical yearbook   (United Nations Statistical Office).
        Sales Section, United Nations, New York, NY 10017; or from sales agents
        1947- 1975.   £27.30 (paper £22.10); $42.00 (paper $34.00).   933p.
        Main sections:

World summary	Communication
Population	Consumption
Manpower	Balance of payments
Agriculture	Wages and prices (including cost of living index)
Forestry	National accounts
Fishing	Finance
Industrial production (index numbers)	Public finance
Mining, quarrying	Development assistance
Manufacturing	Housing
Construction	Health
Energy	Education
Internal trade	Science & technology
External trade	Culture
Transport	

        An annex contains a country nomenclature and information on conversion coefficients and factors.
        Time factor: the 1975 edition, published mid-1976, contains tables with figures for many years up to
           1974 and 1975 (provisional).
        §   En, Fr.

017   Monthly bulletin of statistics   (United Nations Statistical Office).
        Sales Section, United Nations, New York, NY 10017; or from sales agents.
        1947- $7.00 or $70.00 yr;   £4.55 or £45.50 yr.
        Provides monthly statistics on a range of subjects similar to those covered by 016, together with special
           table "Retail price comparisons to determine salary differentials of United Nations officials", which
           indicates the cost of living in various capitals of the world.
        Time factor: most tables include data for about 7 years, and at least the last 12 months to two or three
           months prior to the date of the issue.
        §   En, Fr.

018   World statistics in brief   (United Nations Statistical Office).
        Sales Section, United Nations, New York, NY 10017; or from sales agents.
        1976- 1976.   £2.60 or US$3.95.   253p.
        The first of a new series of annual compilations of basic international statistics issued under the title
           "The Statistical Pocketbook".   In two sections, section 1 gives data on a world-wide basis and
           section 2 on a country basis.   Data includes population, national accounts, agriculture, forestry,
           fisheries, mining and quarrying, manufacturing, consumption, transport and communications,
           international tourist travel, external trade, education, and culture (radio, television).
        Time factor: the 1976 edition has data for 1960, 1965, 1970 and 1973, and was published in 1976.
        §   En.

019   UNESCO statistical yearbook: reference tables, education, science and technology, culture and
           communication   (UNESCO)
        UNESCO, 7 place de Fontenoy, 75700 Paris, France; or from sales agents.
        1963- 1975.   £27.00; FrF 180.   767p.
        Includes data on population, education, libraries, museums, book production, paper consumption,
           films, cinema, radio and television for more than 200 territories.
        Time factor: the 1975 edition, published in 1976, has data for several years to 1973 or 1974 or latest
           available.
        §   En, Fr.

¶ A, continued

020   World tables...from the date files of the World Bank   (World Bank).
        Johns Hopkins University Press, Baltimore and London.
        1971-   2nd, 1976.   £6.75.   558p.
        Time series data for most developing and many industrialised countries of the world (covers over 140
            countries).   Includes (1) national accounts and prices, by country, for 1950, 1955, 1960-73;
            (2) balance of payments and central government finance, by country, for 1967 to 1973; (3)
            comparative economic data for various years to 1973, and (4) social indicators from 1960 to 1970.
        Time factor: the 2nd edition was published in 1976.
        §   En.

021   World Bank atlas: population, per capita product and growth rates   (World Bank).
        World Bank, 1818 H Street NW, Washington DC 20433, USA.
        1966-   1976.   not priced.   28p.
        Contains tables, graphs, maps, etc. of data on the above subjects, by country
        Time factor: the 1976 edition, published in 1976, has data to mid-1974.
        §   En.

022   Trends in developing countries   (World Bank Group).
        World Bank, 1818 H Street NW, Washington DC 20433, USA.
        1968-   1973.   not priced.   no pagination.
        Contains global indicators, data on population and economic growth, social indicators, data on
            international capital flow and external debt, and data on international trade.
        Time factor: the 1973 issue has data to 1970.
        §   En.

023   World economic survey   (United Nations. Department of Economic and Social Affairs).
        Sales Section, United Nations, New York, NY 10017; or from sales agents.
        1964-   1975.   £7.15 or US$11.00.   197p.
        Contains a mid-term review and appraisal of progress in the implementation of the international
            development strategy, and data on current economic developments, including production and trade
            in the developed market economies, in the developing countries, and in the centrally planned
            economies.
        Time factor: the 1975 survey, published in 1976, has data for 1975 (sometimes only provisional) and
            some earlier years.
        §   En.

024   Surveys of African economies   (International Monetary Fund).
        International Monetary Fund, Washington DC 20431; or from sales agents.
                  not priced.   6 vols.
        Contents:
            Vol. 1   Cameroon, Central African Republic, Chad, Congo, Gabon
               2   Kenya, Tanzania, Uganda, Somalia
               3   Dahomey, Ivory Coast, Mauritania, Niger, Senegal, Togo, Upper Volta
               4   Zaire, Malagasy, Malawi, Mauritius, Zambia
               5   Botswana, Lesotho, Swaziland, Burundi, Equatorial Guinea, Rwanda
               6   Gambia, Ghana, Liberia, Nigeria, Sierra Leone
        Each volume includes tables of gross domestic product, national accounts, crop production, mineral
        production, industrial production, consumer price index, employment, government revenue and
        expenditure, government finances, monetary survey, balance of payments, foreign trade, etc.
        Time factor: Vols 1 to 6 were published in 1968, 1969, 1970, 1971, 1973 and 1975 respectively and
            contain the latest data available at time of preparation.
        §   En.

¶   A,   continued

025   Statistical and economic information bulletin for Africa.   Bulletin d'information statistique et économique
         pour l'Afrique   (United Nations Economic Commission for Africa).
      United Nations Economic Commission for Africa, Addis Ababa, Ethiopia.
      No 1, [1972]-   No 7.   not priced.   184p.
      Each issue contains statistical studies on various subjects.
      Time factor: No 7 was published in August 1975.
      §   En, Fr.

      Note: replaces "Quarterly statistical bulletin for Africa", which replaced "African statistics", an
         annex to the "Economic bulletin for Africa".

026   Statistical yearbook.   (United Nations Economic Commission for Africa).
      Sales Section, United Nations, New York, NY 10017; or from sales agents.
      1973-   1974.   not priced.   4 vols.
      Contents:
            Part 1.   North Africa (Algeria, Egypt, Libya, Morocco, Sudan, Tunisia)
                2.   West Africa (Dahomey, Gambia, Ghana, Guinea, Ivory Coast, Liberia, Mali,
                      Mauritania, Niger, Nigeria, Senegal, Sierra Leone, Togo, Upper Volta)
                3.   East Africa (Botswana, Ethiopia, Kenya, Lesotho, Madagascar, Malawi, Mauritius,
                      Somalia, Rhodesia, Swaziland, Tanzania, Uganda, Zambia)
                4.   Central Africa, etc (Angola, Burundi, Cameroon, Chad, Congo, Gabon, Mozambique,
                      Namibia, Rwanda, Zaire)
      Contains data for each country on population and employment; national accounts; agriculture, forestry
         and fishing; industry; transport and communication; foreign trade; prices; finance; and social
         statistics (education, medical).
      Time factor: the 1974 edition, published in 1975, has data for the years 1965 to 1973.
      §   En, Fr.

027   Economic bulletin for Africa   (United Nations Economic Commission for Africa).
      Sales Section, United Nations, New York, NY 10017; or from sales agents.
      1965-   irregular.   £3.00 or $5.00.
      Includes a few tables in the text.
      §   En.

028   A survey of economic conditions in Africa   (United Nations Economic Commission for Africa).
      Sales Section, United Nations, New York, NY 10017; or from sales agents.
      1960/64-   1973   Part 1 £3.96; US$9.00.   2 vols.
                  1971/72 Part 2 £3.60; US$6.00.
      Part 1 includes statistical data on gross national product, agriculture, industry, transport,
         communications, tourism, foreign trade, social trends, and monetary and financial developments.
         Part 2 includes data on population trends, employment, and output growth trends.
      Time factor: the 1973 edition, published late 1974, has data for 1971 to 1973.
      §   En.

029   Le zone franc   [The franc areas]   (Comité Monétaire de la Zone Franc)
      Comité Monétaire de la Zone Franc, 39 rue Croix-des-Petits-Champs, 75049 Paris Cedex 01, France.
      1967-   1975.   not priced.   377p.
      Contains data on trends in production, and on foreign trade, finance and investment, money and credit,
         balance of payments, currency reserves, etc, in the French-speaking and franc CFA countries.
         Tables are included in the text.
      Time factor: the 1975 edition, published early 1977, contains data for 2 or 3 years to 1975.
      §   Fr.

¶   A,   continued

030   Economic survey of Africa   (United Nations Economic Commission for Africa).
         United Nations Economic Commission for Africa, Addis Ababa, Ethiopia.
         Contents:
             Vol.   I   Western sub-region   (US$2.50 or £1.09)
                     II   North Africa sub-region   (US$2.50 or £1.09)
                     III East Africa sub-region   (US$3.50 or £1.33)
         The survey is of economic growth, including physical environment and natural resources, population,
             gross domestic product, capital formation, public finance, money and banking, agriculture,
             livestock, forestry and fishing, industry, services, international economic relations, and
             development plans and economic co-operation.   There are tables in the text, covering various
             periods.
         Time factor: Vol.III was published in 1966, vol.II in 1968 and vol.I in 1971.
         §   En.

031   Summaries of economic data   (United Nations Economic Commission for Africa).
         United Nations Economic Commission for Africa, Addis Ababa, Ethiopia.
         1968-   1973.   not priced.   29 fascicules.
         Each fascicule is a general economic survey with statistical tables of an African country, subjects
             covered including population, finance, production, foreign trade and national accounts.   The
             countries are Algeria, Angola, Botswana, Burundi, Cameroun, Central African Republic, Chad,
             Congo, Egypt, Ethiopia, Gabon, Guinea, Ivory Coast, Kenya, Libya, Malawi, Mauritania,
             Morocco, Namibia (South West Africa), Rhodesia, Senegal, Somalia, South Africa, Sudan,
             Tanzania, Tunisia, Uganda, Upper Volta, and Zambia..
         Time factor: the 1973 summaries were published in 1974 or 1975.
         §   En.

032   Annuaire statistique des EAMA.   Statistical yearbook of the AASM...   (Eurostat).
         Office des Publications Officielles des Communautés Européennes, CP 1003, Luxembourg; or from sales
             agents.
         1965-   1973.   £0.84; FrB 100.   262p.
         Contains data on population, employment, education, health, national accounts, agriculture, crops,
             fisheries, energy, industry, transport, foreign trade, prices and wages, public finance, and the
             European Development Fund.   The data is for the 19 French-speaking African countries associated
             with the French-speaking European Communities countries.
         Time factor: the 1973 edition, published late 1973, has data for various years to 1972.
         §   Fr, En.

033   Données statistiques: Africaines et Malgaches   [Statistical data: Africa and Madagascar]   (INSEE).
         Imprimerie Nationale, 2 rue Paul-Hervieu, 75732 Paris Cedex 15, France.
         1961-   quarterly.
         Included, for the French-speaking countries of Africa and for Madagascar, foreign trade by country
             subdivided by main commodity groups and principal commodities; industrial production, mining,
             electricity; transport (rail, sea, river, air); prices and price indices; money and credit; public
             finance; foreign aid; and population.
         Time factor: the publication ceased with the Oct-Dec 1972 edition.
         §   Fr.

034   The Commonwealth and sterling area: statistical abstract   (Board of Trade).
         HM Stationery Office, PO Box 569, London SE1 9NH.
         1850/63-   1967.   84p.
         Includes statistics of values of imports and exports of each of the Commonwealth and sterling area
             countries, production and consumption of selected commodities, population estimates, and balance
             of payments statistics.
         Time factor: ceased publication with the 1967 edition.
         §   En.

¶ A, continued

035   Bulletin de statistique des départements et territoires d'outre-mer   [Statistical bulletin of the overseas
         departments and territories]   (INSEE).
         Imprimerie Nationale, 2 rue Paul-Hervieu, 75732 Paris Cedex 15, France.
         1959-   quarterly.   FrF 6 or FrF 16 (FrF 20 abroad) yr.
         Gives for each of France's overseas departments and territories detailed statistical data on population,
            industry, transport, prices and wages, external trade, and finances.
         §   Fr.

         Note: superseded "Bulletin mensuel de statistiques d'outre-mer".

036   Inventaire social et économique des territoires d'outre-mer, 1950-1955   [Social and economic inventory .
         of France's overseas territories]   (INSEE).
         INSEE, 18 boulevard Adolphe Pinard, 75675 Paris Cedex 14, France.
            not priced.   467p.
         Contains data on France's overseas territories during that period on political and administrative
            organisations, geography and climate, population, public health, education, scientific
            organisations, justice, agriculture, livestock fisheries, forestry, mining, industry, electricity,
            transport and communications, foreign trade, prices and price indices, employment, money and
            credit, and public finance.
         Time factor: published in 1957.
         §   Fr.

037   Données statistiques sur les activités économiques, culturelles et sociales   [Statistical tables on economic,
         cultural and social activities]   (Ministère de la Cooperation Sous-Direction des Etudes
         Economiques et de la Planification).
         Ministère de la Coopération, 192 rue Lecourbe, 75015 Paris, France.
         1973-   irreg.   not priced.
         Related to the development plans of French-speaking African countries, each issue is devoted to a
            particular African state and includes data on population, production, balance of payments,
            public finance, etc.
         §   Fr.

         Note: title has changed recently from "Dossier d'information économique" and the publication now
            has restricted circulation.

038   Africa south of the Sahara   (Europa Publications Ltd).
         Europa Publications Ltd, 18 Bedford Square, London WC1B 8JN.
         1971-   5th, 1975.   £15.00 or US$56.00.   1163p.
         A directory and survey of economic, political and social developments; includes a statistical survey for
            each country with data on area and population, agriculture, forestry, fisheries, mining, industry,
            finance (budget and national accounts), external trade, transport and communications, and education.
         Time factor: the 1975 edition, published in 1975, has data for three years to 1971 or 1973.
         §   En.

039   The Middle East and North Africa   (Europa Publications Ltd).
         Europa Publications Ltd, 18 Bedford Square, London WC1B 8JN.
         1948-   1976/77.   £13.00.   930p.
         Contains similar information to 038 above for Middle Eastern and African countries, including Algeria,
            Egypt, Libya, Morocco, Sudan, Tunisia, and Western Sahara (Western Sahara, Ceuta and Mellilla).
         Time factor: the 1976-77 edition, published in 1976, contains data for the latest two or three years
            available.
         §   En.

         Note: Volume II of the "Europa year book..." also contains data on African countries and includes
            statistical summary tables on similar topics.

AFRICA, continued

¶   A,   continued

040   Notes d'information et statistiques   [Information and statistics]   (Banque Centrale des Etats de
              l'Afrique de l'Ouest).
           Banque Centrale des Etats de l'Afrique de l'Ouest, 29 rue du Colisée, 75008 Paris, France.
           1953-   monthly.   not priced.
           Each issue is a folder of separate booklets on banks and money, the economy of West Africa, economic
              indicators, monetary statistics, and legislation.
           Time factor: each issue has tables with long runs of annual and monthly figures to about three months
              prior to the date of the issue.
           §   Fr.

041   [Rapport annuel]   [Annual report]   (Banque Centrale des Etats de l'Afrique de l'Ouest).
           Banque Centrale des Etats de l'Afrique de l'Ouest, 29 rue du Colisée, 75008 Paris, France.
           1963-   1974.   not priced.   202p.
           The activities of the Bank cover the monetary union of Ivory Coast, Dahomey (now Benin, Upper Volta,
              Niger, Senegal and Togo.   The report has sections on the economics of the monetary union
              (economic activity, production, foreign exchange, external finance for the development of the
              union, revenues and prices), money and credit, and the activities of the Bank.   Statistics are
              included in the text.
           Time factor: the 1974 report, published in 1976, has data for 1974.
           §   Fr.

042   Etudes et statistiques: bulletin mensuel   [Studies and statistics: monthly bulletin]   (Banque des Etats de
              l'Afrique Centrale).
           Banque des Etats de l'Afrique Centrale, 29 rue du Colisée, 75008 Paris, France.
           1963-   not priced.
           Includes a section of statistical tables on national accounts, banking, money, wholesale and retail
              price indices, etc, for the monetary union and for each country separately (Cameroun, Central
              African Republic, Congo, Gabon and Chad).
           Time factor: each issue includes the latest data available.
           §   Fr.

043   Rapport d'activité...   [Report of activities...]   (Banque des Etats de l'Afrique Centrale).
           Banque des Etats de l'Afrique Centrale, 29 rue du Colisée, 75008 Paris, France.
           1963-   1974/75.   not priced.   164p.
           Includes for each country (Cameroun, Central African Republic, Congo, Gabon and Chad) the
              principal products exported, wholesale and retail price indices, and foreign trade, as well as a
              report of the Bank's activities and monetary data.
           Time factor: the 1974/75 report was published late 1975.
           §   Fr.

044   Etudes et statistiques   [Studies and statistics]   (Organisation Commune Africaine, Malgache et Maurice).
           Organisation Commune Africaine, Malgache et Maurice, BP 437, Yaoundé, Cameroun.
           1971-   quarterly.   CFA Fr 1,000 yr in OCAMM countries;
                                  CFA Fr 1,500 yr elsewhere.
           Contains data for Chad, Cameroun, Central African Republic, Gabon, Rwanda, Madagascar, and
              Mauritius.   Tables are included in the text on economic indicators, agriculture, industry, foreign
              trade, transport, public finance, etc.
           §   Fr.

           Note: "Bulletin statistique" was issued between 1966 and 1971, and dealt with individual subjects
              in each issue.

045   Annual report   (African Development Bank).
          African Development Bank, BP 1387, Abidjan, Ivory Coast.
          1965- 1976. not priced.
          Mainly concerned with the activities of the bank, but also includes data on the balance of payments of
               selected African countries and a statistical annex with data on per capita gross national product of
               member countries of the bank, changes in prices for principal commodities produced in member
               countries, share of principal agricultural commodities and minerals ex export earnings in selected
               member countries, share of developing Africa in world trade, foreign trade of selected African
               countries, and export/import ratio of selected African countries.
          Time factor: the 1976 report, published mid-1977, has data for 1975 and 1976 and some earlier years.
          §   En, Fr.

046   Mémento de l'économie africaine   [Memorandum on the economy of Africa]   (EDIAFRIC).
          EDIAFRIC, 57 avenue d'Iéna, 75783 Paris Cedex 16, France.
                    9th ed, 1977.   FrF 480.   various paginations.
          Contains information, including statistics and statistical tables in the text, on population, economic
               accounts, rural production, livestock and fisheries, forestry, energy, industry, transport, foreign
               trade, finance, overseas trade, etc, for the French-speaking African states (Cameroun, Central
               African Republic, Chad, Congo, Dahomey, Gabon, Ivory Coast, Mali, Mauritania, Niger,
               Senegal, Togo, and Upper Volta).
          Time factor: the 9th edition was published in 1977.
          §   Fr.

          Note: EDIAFRIC also publish "Bulletin de l'Afrique Noire" [Bulletin of black Africa] which is a
               news bulletin with some statistics and statistical tables (FrF 1040 yr; FrF 1100 yr abroad).

047   L'économie africaine   [The African economy]   (Société Africaine d'Edition).
          Société Africaine d'Edition, BP 1877, Dakar, Senegal.
          1971-   5th, 1976.   FrF 130; CFA Fr 7.500.   357 p.
          Contains information, including statistics and statistical tables in the text, on geography and climate,
               population and demography, economy, development plans, public finance, production, transport,
               and tourism, for the French-speaking African countries.
          Time factor: the 5th edition was published in 1976.
          §   Fr.

048   Marchés tropicaux et méditerranéens.
          Marchés Tropicaux et Méditerranéens, 190 boulevard Haussmann, 75008 Paris, France.
          1945-   weekly.   FrF 19 (FrF 21 abroad) each issue; special issues separately priced.
          The weekly journal reviews commercial interests of France and French-speaking countries overseas.
               Special issues of 150-200 pages are devoted to individual countries or regions or themes, some
               recent titles being:-
                    Les produits tropicaux et Méditerranéens   [Tropical and Mediterranean products]
                         (FrF 75 (FrF 80 abroad))
                    L'automobile outre-mer, 1976   [The motor car overseas, 1976]   (FrF 60 (FrF 65 abroad))
                    Cameroun, 1960-1980 (FrF 125 (FrF 135 abroad))
                    La France et l'Afrique (FrF 80 (FrF 90 abroad))
                    Gabon, 1960-1980 (FrF 100 (FrF 110 abroad))
          §   Fr.

049   Europe outremer.
          Europe Outremer, 6 rue de Bassano, 75116 Paris, France.
                    monthly.   FrF 16 in France and 'Zone franc' (FrF 18 abroad);
                         FrF 220 in France, CFA Fr 11,000, and FrF 250 abroad yr.
          Each issue is devoted to a particular country or subject, recent examples being:-
               Mali, Niger, Nigeria, Franco-African military co-operation, investment in Africa.
          §   Fr.

¶ A, continued

050   Syrie & monde arabe: étude économique, politique & statistique   [Syria and the Arab world: economic,
            political and statistical studies]   (Office Arabe de Presse et de Documentation).
        Office Arabe de Presse et de Documentation, 67 place Chahbandar, BP 3550, Damas, Syria.
        1954-   monthly.   not priced.
        Includes some statistics in the text, relating to Algeria, Morocco, Tunisia, Libya, Egypt, Sudan,
            Mauritania and Somalia in Africa.
        §   Fr.

051   Rapport économique arabe   [Arab economic report]   (Office Arabe de Presse et de Documentation).
        Office Arabe de Presse et de Documentation, 67 place Chahbandar, BP 3550, Damas, Syria.
        1954-   1974/75.   not priced.   various paginations.
        Has data for each of the countries listed in 050 above on a variety of economic topics.   In the 1974/75
            issue there is a chapter on Arab statistics compared (population, demography, national income,
            agriculture, fisheries, and petroleum refineries).
        Time factor: the 1974/75 issue has data to 1972 or 1973.
        §   Fr.

052   Allgemeine Statistik des Auslandes: Länderberichte   [General foreign statistics: reports on foreign
            countries]   (Statistisches Bundesamt, Wiesbaden, Germany).
        W Kohlhammer GmbH, 62 Mainz 42 (Postfach 120), Federal Republic of Germany.
        A series of reports, each on a particular country, containing statistics on the climate, population,
            health, education, labour, agriculture, forestry, fisheries production, foreign trade, transport,
            tourism, finance, prices and wages, etc.   The reports are supported by a series of briefer reports:
            "Allgemeine Statistik des Auslandes: Länderkurzberichte".   There are reports, mainly the brief
            versions, for all African countries.
        Time factor: the reports are published at varying intervals and contain the latest data available from
            each country.
        §   De.

053   Internationale Monatzahlen   [International monthly figures]   (Statistisches Bundesamt).
        W Kohlhammer GmbH, 65 Mainz 42 (Postfach 120), Federal Republic of Germany.
        1955-   DM 6.40 or DM 64 yr.
        Contains inter-country comparisons as to selected facts which are of particular importance for the
            foreign trade relations of the FDR.
        §   De.

054   Barclays country reports   (Barclays Bank Ltd).
        Barclays Bank Ltd, 54 Lombard Street, London EC3.
        Free.
        A loose-leaf series of economic reports on individual countries, which contain a few statistical tables.
            Issued at intervals.
        §   En.

055   Economic Report   (Lloyds Bank Ltd).
        Lloyds Bank Ltd, 6 Eastcheap, London EC3.
        Free.
        Lloyds Bank issues at intervals a series of economic reports for each of the countries of the world and
            these contain a few statistical tables.
        §   En.

056   Standard Chartered review   (Standard Chartered Bank Ltd).
        Standard Chartered Bank Ltd, 10 Clements Lane, Lombard Street, London EC4.
        Monthly.   free.
        Contains a feature article; area reports on central Africa (Malawi, Zambia), east Africa (East African
            Community, Kenya), southern Africa (Botswana, Swaziland), and west Africa (Ghana, Nigeria,
            the Gambia); and a report on the world at large (including the Seychelles).   There are some
            figures in the text.
        §   En.

¶ A, continued

057 Overseas business reports (US Department of Commerce: Domestic and International Business Administration).
Publications Sales Branch, Room 1617, US Department of Commerce, Washington, DC 20230, USA.
irregular. US$0.15 or US$36.50 yr, plus US$15 for foreign mailing.
The reports are issued on a variety of subjects, including a sub-series titles "Marketing in...", which
include key economic indicators, principal imports and exports, etc. Recent relevant examples
are "Marketing in Gabon" (OBR 76-20), "Marketing in Nigeria" (OBR 76-26), "Marketing in the
Libyan Arab Republic" (OBR 76-45), "Marketing profiles for Africa" (OBR 76-51), "Marketing in
Ivory Coast" (OBR 76-50), and "Marketing in the Sudan" (OBR 76-56).
§ En.

058 Quarterly economic review of... (Economist Intelligence Unit).
Economist Intelligence Unit, Spencer House, 27 St James's Place, London SW1A 1NT.
1965- annual subscription for each title of 4 issues and annual supplement-
£25.00 or US$66.00, plus postage of £1.50 or by airmail US$6.00.
The statistical tables, using information drawn from official sources, cover economic trends and
indicators of economic activity, including industrial production, construction, employment, retail
trade, wages and prices, money and banking, foreign trade and payments, exchange reserves,
exchange rates, exports and imports (broad commodity classification). African countries for which
there are reviews are: Algeria; Angola, Mozambique; Egypt; Gabon, Congo, Cameroun, Central
African Republic, Chad, Madagascar; Ghana, Sierra Leone, Gambia, Liberia; Ivory Coast, Togo,
Benin, Niger, Upper Volta; Kenya; Libya, Tunisia; Morocco; Nigeria; Rhodesia, Malawi;
Senegal, Mali, Mauritania, Guinea; South Africa; Sudan; Tanzania, Mauritius; Uganda, Ethiopia,
Somalia; Zaire, Rwanda, Burundi; and Zambia.
§ En.

¶ B - Production

i. Mines and mining

059 Statistical summary of the mineral industry: world production, exports and imports (Natural Environment
Research Council. Institute of Geological Sciences, Mineral Resources Division).
HM Stationery Office, PO Box 569, London SE1 9NH.
1913/20- 1967-1971. £1.80. 412p.
Contains data on quantities produced, imported and exported of the following minerals for all countries
so far as the information is available: abrasive, aluminium, antimony, arsenic, asbestos, barium
minerals, bentonite, beryl, bismuth, borates, bromine, cadmium, cement, china clay, chrome ore
and chromium, coal, coke and by-products, cobalt, copper, diamonds, diatomaceous earth,
feldspar, fuller's earth, gold, graphite, gypsum, iodine, iron and steel, lead, lithium, magnesite
and dolomite, manganese, mercury, mica, molybdenum, nickel, nitrogen compounds, petroleum
and allied products, phosphates, platinum, potash minerals, pyrites, rare earth and thorium
minerals, salt, selenium, sillimanite, silver, strontium minerals, sulphur, talc, tantalum and
niobium minerals, tungsten, uranium minerals, vanadium, vermiculite, zinc, zirconium minerals,
other minerals and metals.
Time factor: the 1967-1971 edition, containing data for those years, was published in May 1973.
§ En.

060 Minerals yearbook: volume III - area reports, international (US Bureau of Mines).
Government Printing Office, Washington DC 20402, USA.
1932- 1973. US$15.00. 1201p.
Contains detailed textual and statistical data on the mineral industry in each country of the world.
Time factor: the 1973 edition was published in 1976.
§ En.

¶ B.i, continued

061   Metal statistics   (Metallgesellschaft AG).
         Metallgesellschaft AG, Postfach 3724, Frankfurt (Main), Federal Republic of Germany.
         1913-   1965-1975.   not priced.   370p.
         A world survey of production and consumption of aluminium, lead, copper, zinc, tin, antimony,
            cadmium, magnesium, nickel, mercury and silver.   There are comparisons by continent, and
            detailed surveys of the situation in producing countries.
         Time factor: the 1965-1975 edition, covering the years 1965-1975, was published late 1976.
         §   En, De.

         Note: Similar publications in France and Italy are "Statistiques...cuivre, plomb, zinc, étain, antimoine,
            cadmium, cobalt, nickel, aluminium magnesium, mercure, argent, or" issued annually by
            Minerais et Métaux SA, 61 avenue Hoche, Paris 8; and "Metalli non ferrosi e ferroleghe:
            statistiche" issued by Ammi SpA, via Malise 11, Roma.

062   Metal bulletin handbook   (Metal Bulletin Ltd).
         Metal Bulletin Ltd, Park House, 3 Park Terrace, Worcester Park, Surrey, KT4 7HY, England.
         1913-   1976.   £10.00.   847p.
         Contains data on production, consumption, deliveries, exports, and prices of non-ferrous metals and of
            iron and steel.
         Time factor: the 1976 edition, published late 1976, contains data for several years to 1975.
         §   En.

063   Non-ferrous metal data   (American Bureau of Metal Statistics Inc).
         American Bureau of Metal Statistics Inc, 420 Lexington Avenue, New York, NY 10017.
         1921-   1975.   US$15.00.   143p.
         Includes statistics of mines production, smelter production, consumption, imports and exports, etc, on a
            world-wide basis for copper, lead, zinc, nickel, aluminium, bauxite, gold, silver, tin, antimony,
            cadmium, cobalt, magnesium, molybdenum, platinum, etc.
         Time factor: the 1975 edition, published in 1976, has data for 1975 and also earlier figures in some
            tables.
         §   En.

         Note: prior to 1974 the title was "Yearbook of the American Bureau of Metal Statistics".

064   World metal statistics   (World Bureau of Metal Statistics).
         World Bureau of Metal Statistics, 50 Broadway, New York, NY 10004, USA.
         1948-   monthly.   £150.00 or US$300.00 yr.
         Contains data on production, consumption, trade, stocks, prices, etc, of metals (aluminium, antimony,
            cadmium, copper, lead, nickel, tin and lead).   Gives data by country as well as world-wide totals.
         Time factor: each issue has data to about two months earlier than the month of publication.
         §   En.

065   Survey of world iron ore resources   (United Nations. Department of Economic and Social Affairs).
         Sales Section, United Nations, New York, NY 10017; or from sales agents.
                  US$6.50 or £2.85.   488p.
         Contains a general report, technical papers, and regional appraisals.   There are some statistical tables
            in the text.
         Time factor: published in 1970.
         §   En.

066   The world market for iron ore   (United Nations Economic Commission for Europe).
         Sales Section, United Nations, New York, NY 10017; or from sales agents.
                  US$4.50 or £1.70.   333p.
         Contains data on consumption, supplies, international trade, costs, trends in transport, and iron ore
            requirements for 1970, 1975, and 1980.   Includes some statistical tables.
         Time factor: published in 1968.
         §   En.

¶ B.i, continued

067   Tin statistics   (International Tin Council).
         International Tin Council, Haymarket House, 1 Oxendon Street, London SW1Y 4EQ.
         1963/73-   1965-1975.   £8.00.   60p.
         Contains data on the production, exports, imports, stocks, consumption, trade in manufactures, and
            labour for each country.
         Time factor: the 1965-1975 issue, published in 1976, has data for the years 1965 to 1975.
         §   En.

         Note: replaces "Statistical yearbook: tin, tinplate, canning", issued from 1959.

068   Statistical bulletin   (International Tin Council).
         International Tin Council, Haymarket House, 1 Oxendon Street, London SW1Y 4EQ.
         1959-   monthly.   £2.00 or £24.00 yr.
         Up-dates the information in 067 above.
         §   En.

069   Tin prices   (International Tin Council).
         International Tin Council, Haymarket House, 1 Oxendon Street, London SW1Y 4EQ.
         1973-   1976.   £4.00.   13p.
         Gives a concise, picture of the movement of daily tin prices on the leading international tin markets for
            each quarter of the year.
         Time factor: the 1976 issue, published in 1977, has data for the four quarters of 1976.
         §   En.

         Note: there is also a retrospective volume "Tin prices, 1956-1973, London and Penang" published
            in 1974, price £3.50.

070   Uranium: resources, production and demand   (Organisation for Economic Co-operation and Development).
         OECD, 2 rue André-Pascal, 75775 Paris Cedex 16: or from sales agents.
         New up-dated edition.   £3.10; US$7.00; FrF 28.00.   80p.
         Contains estimates of world uranium resources and probable future demand, with consequent requirements
            for increased production capacity and enrichment services.
         Time factor: the December 1975 edition was published in March 1976.
         §   En.

071   Tungsten statistics: quarterly bulletin of the UNCTAD Committee on Tungsten   (United Nations Conference
         on Trade and Development).
         Sales Section, United Nations, New York, NY 10017; or from sales agents.
         1967-   quarterly.   £1.56 or US$3.00 each issue.
         Contains statistics of prices, production, consumption, trade and stocks of tungsten for reporting countries.
         Time factor: each issue has data for several years and includes the most recent annual and quarterly
            statistics available.
         §   En.

072   Mineral resources of South-Central Africa   (R A Palletier).
         Oxford University Press, Walton Street, Oxford.
                 £3.50.   284p.
         Covers the Republic of South Africa, South West Africa, Bechuanaland, Swaziland and Basuto,
            Moçambique, Rhodesia, Zambia, Malawi, Angola, East Africa, Congo Republic including
            Rwanda-Urundi).
         Time factor: published in 1964, the book includes some tables from 1950 to 1963.
         §   En.

¶   B.i,   continued

073   The mineral resources of Africa   (Nicolas de Kun).
          Elsevier Publishing Co, Jan van Gratenstrasse 335, Amsterdam.
                        £12.00.   766p.
          Contains a few statistics and statistical tables in the text.   Summary information on Africa's share of
               world resources, value of African production, distribution of African output and resources, and the
               history and development of mining, is followed by regional sections with detailed data by country
               of resources, production, etc.
          Time factor: published in 1965.
          §   En.

074   Lead and zinc statistics.   Statistiques du plomb et du zinc   (International Lead and Zinc Study Group).
          International Lead and Zinc Study Group, United Nations, New York, NY 10017.
          1966-   monthly.   US$1.00 or US$10.00 yr.
          Contains statistics of mine production, refined production, foreign trade, and consumption of lead and
               zinc.
          Time factor: each issue has about six years of annual figures and more recent quarterly and monthly
               figures to about three months prior to the date of the issue.
          §   En, Fr.

075   Handbook of world salt resources   (Stanley J Lefond).
          Plenum Press, 227 W 17th Street, New York, NY 10010, USA.
                        US$25.00.   407p.
          Includes some statistics and statistical tables in the text.
          Time factor: published in 1969.
          §   En.

076   The British Sulphur Corporation's statistical supplement...raw materials supply/demand...fertilisers
               supply/demand.
          British Sulphur Corporation, Parnell House, 25 Wilton Road, London SW1V 1NH.
          1970-   half-yearly.   not priced.
          Contains data on world production of sulphur in all forms, by country, consumption, supply and demand;
               world sulphuric acid production, by country, supply and demand; world phosphate rock production
               and consumption, by country; world nitrogen fertiliser production and consumption, by country;
               world phosphate fertiliser production and consumption, by country; and world potash fertiliser
               production and consumption, by country.
          §   En.

077   Annual phosphate rock statistics   (International Superphosphate and Compound Manufacturers' Association).
          International Superphosphate and Compound Manufacturers' Association, 121 Gloucester Place,
               London W1H 3PJ.
          1952-   1973.   not priced.   29p.
          Contains data on world production, deliveries and exports by grade; exports by destination; and exports
               by grade and destination.
          Time factor: the 1973 edition, published in 1974, has data for 1973.
          §   En.

078   Water resources of the world: selected statistics   (Fritz van der Leeden).
          Water Information Center Inc, 44 Sintsink Drive East, Port Washington, New York, NY 11050, USA.
                        US$32.50.   568p.
          Contains data by continent and country on rivers, lakes, reservoirs, wells, dams, rain, etc.   Also on
               hydroelectric and thermal power generating stations.
          Time factor: published in 1975, the statistics included are the latest available at the time of
               compilation.
          §   En.

AFRICA,   continued

¶   B,   continued

ii.   Agriculture, fisheries, forestry, etc.

079   Production yearbook   (Food and Agriculture Organisation of the UN).
         FAO, viale delle Terme di Caracalla, 00153 Roma, Italy; or from sales agents.
         1947-   1974.   £8.00 or $20.00.   2 vols.
         Part 1 is concerned with important aspects of food and agriculture relating to land, population, crops,
            livestock numbers and livestock products, means of production, and index numbers of food and
            agriculture production.   Part 2 has data on prices of agricultural products, prices of certain
            production means, freight rates, farm wages, and index numbers of prices.
         Time factor: the 1974 edition, published late 1975, has data for several years to 1974.
         §   En, Fr, It.

080   Monthly bulletin of agricultural economic and statistics   (Food and Agriculture Organisation of the UN).
         FAO, viale delle Terme di Caracalla, 00153 Roma, Italy; or from sales agents.
         1952-   £0.40 (£3.20 yr); $1.00 ($8.00 yr).
         Each issue contains an article, commodity notes, and statistical tables.   Statistical data include
            production, trade and prices for agricultural, fishery and forest products of reporting countries.
         Time factor: each issue has data for about six years and several months or quarters up to between two
            and six months prior to publication.
         §   En.

081   Census of agriculture   (Food and Agriculture Organisation of the UN).
         FAO, viale delle Terme di Caracalla, 00153 Roma, Italy; or from sales agents.
         1950-   1960.   5 vols in 7.
         Contents:
             Vol.1, part A.   Census results by countries (including Libya, Northern Rhodesia (Zambia),
                               Portuguese Guinea (Guinea-Bissau), Seychelles, Southern Rhodesia (Rhodesia),
                               Tanganyika (Tanzania))   (US$45.00)
                    part B.   Census results by countries (including Central African Republic, Mali, South
                               Africa, South West Africa (Namibia))   (US$9.00)
                    part C.   Census results by countries (including Kenya, Lesotho, Madagascar, Senegal,
                               Tunisia, Uganda, United Arab Republic (Arab Republic of Egypt))   (US$16.50)
             Vol.2. Programme, concepts and scope   (US$12.00)
             Vol.3. Methodology.   (US$10.00)
             Vol.4. Processing and tabulation   (US$4.50)
             Vol.5. Analysis and international comparison of census results   (US$7.50)
         Time factor: published between 1967 and 1971.
         §   En.

         Note: it is planned to take another census in 1980.

082   State of food and agriculture   (Food and Agriculture Organisation of the UN).
         FAO, viale delle Terme di Caracalla, 00153 Roma, Italy; or from sales agents.
         1957-   1974.   £5.60; US$14.00.   196p.
         Includes a world review and a regional review on production of agriculture, fisheries, forestry; foreign
            trade; prices; policies and programmes.
         Time factor: the 1974 edition, published 1975, has data for a number of years to 1972 and some
            preliminary figures for 1973.
         §   En.

083   Agricultural commodities projections for 1975 and 1985   (Food and Agriculture Organisation of the UN).
         FAO, viale delle Terme di Caracalla, 00153 Roma, Italy; or from sales agents.
                              US$3.00; £0.75 each volume.   2 vols.
         Contents:
             Volume I   Part I   Summary and conclusions
                         Part II   General outlook and demand, production and trade
                         Part III   Projections by commodity groups
             Volume II   Methodological notes; Statistical appendix.
         Time factor: published in 1967.
         §   En.

¶   B.ii,   continued

084   L'agriculture africaine   [African agriculture]   (EDIAFRIC).
             EDIAFRIC, 57 avenue d'Iéna, 75783 Paris Cedex 16, France.
             1970-   3rd ed, 1976.   FrF 318.   various paginations.
             Contains information, including statistics in the text, on agriculture in the French-speaking African
                  states (Cameroun, Central African Republic, Chad, Congo, Dahomey, Gabon, Ivory Coast, Mali,
                  Mauritania, Niger, Senegal, Togo and Upper Volta).
             §   Fr.

085   World agricultural production and trade: statistical report   (US Department of Agriculture.   Foreign
                  Agricultural Service).
             Foreign Agricultural Service, Department of Agriculture, Washington DC, USA.
             1964-   monthly.   not priced.
             Contained world agricultural production and trade summaries, several subjects within the agricultural
                  field being dealt with in each issue.
             Time factor: ceased publication with the December 1975 issue.
             §   En.

086   Commodity survey   (UNCTAD).
             Sales Section, United Nations, New York, NY 10017; or from sales agents.
                       3rd, 1968.   US$2.00.   123p.
             Contains a survey of the overall commodity situation and the problems of individual commodities and
                  international commodity action.   Tables are included in the text.
             Time factor: the 1968 report, published in 1968, has data to 1967.
             §   En.

087   Commodity trade and price trends...   (International Bank for Reconstruction and Development and
                  International Development Association).
             World Bank, 1818 H Street NW, Washington, DC 20433, USA.
             1973-   1975.   not priced.   123p.
             Contains data on trade, price and freight rate indices, and prices of agricultural and non-agricultural
                  products.   Values are in US$ for comparison.
             Time factor: the 1975 issue, published in August 1975, has long runs of figures to January/June 1975.
             §   En, Es, Fr.

088   FAO: commodity review and outlook   (Food and Agriculture Organisation of the UN).
             FAO, viale delle Terme di Caracalla, 00153 Roma, Italy; or from sales agents.
             1964-   1975-1976.   £3.60 or US$9.00.   180p.
             Reviews the general commodity situation and outlook, and the situation and outlook by commodities -
                  basic food and feedstuffs, other food and beverage crops, non-food crops (tobacco, pepper),
                  agricultural raw materials (cotton, etc, hides and skins), and fishery products.
             Time factor: data available at May 1976 is included in the 1975/76 edition, which was published in
                  1976.   The figures are mainly runs to 1974 and 1975 preliminary.
             §   En.

089   Study of trends in world supply and demand of major agricultural commodities   (Organisation for Economic
                  Co-operation and Development).
             OECD, 2 rue Andre-Pascal, 75775 Paris Cedex 16, France; or from sales agents.
                       £6.00; US$13.50; FrF 54.00.   349p.
             An assessment of world trends in the grain-livestock sector over the next 10 to 15 years, in terms of
                  factors affecting supply and demand, the market and trade outlook, and the major issues ahead -
                  particularly the instability of the agricultural markets and the food needs of developing countries.
                  A general assessment is followed by regional analyses (including "Africa and the Near East") and
                  commodity analyses.   There are some statistics and a few statistical tables in the text.
             Time factor: published in 1976.
             §   En.

¶   B.ii,   continued

090   World wheat statistics   (International Wheat Council).
      International Wheat Council, 28 Haymarket, London SW1Y 4SS, England.
      1955-   1976.   £2.75; US$5.00.   71p.
      Contains data on area, yield and production; wheat flour production; exports and imports of wheat and
          wheat flour; supplies and stocks of wheat; prices, etc.
      Time factor: the 1976 edition, published in 1976, has long runs of annual and monthly figures to
          1974/75 season.
      §   En, Fr, Es, Ru.

091   Review of the world wheat situation   (International Wheat Council).
      International Wheat Council, 28 Haymarket, London SW1Y 4SS, England.
      1958/59-   1975/76.   not priced.   112p.
      Reviews production, trade, prices and freight rates; development in wheat policies; coarse grain and
          rice; recent trends in wheat consumption; grain economy of the USSR; and includes a survey of
          world wheat development, 1949-1976.
      Time factor: the 1975/76 edition, published late 1976, includes data available up to 1st December 1976.
      §   En, Fr, Es, Ru.

092   Wheat market report   (International Wheat Council).
      International Wheat Council, 28 Haymarket, London SW1Y 4SS, England.
      A press release.
      §   En.

093   Grain crops: a review of production, trade, consumption and prices relating to wheat, wheat flour, maize.
          barley, oats, rye and rice   (Commonwealth Secretariat).
      Commonwealth Secretariat, Marlborough House, Pall Mall, London SW1Y 5HX, England.
      1965/66-   Vol.15, 1973.   £2.25.   127p.
      Time factor: Vol.15, 1973, has data to 1970/71 and some tables to 1971/72.   The review ceased
          publication with that issue.
      §   En.

094   Grain bulletin   (Commonwealth Secretariat).
      Commonwealth Secretariat, Marlborough House, Pall Mall, London SW1Y 5HX, England.
      monthly.   £1.00 or £12.00 yr.
      Time factor: up-dated 093 above until it ceased publication with the December 1976 issue.
      §   En.

095   Rice bulletin   (Commonwealth Secretariat).
      Commonwealth Secretariat, Marlborough House, Pall Mall, London SW1Y 5HX, England.
      monthly.   £0.75 or £9.00 yr.
      Contains a general review, followed by information on area and production, exports, imports, and
          prices.
      Time factor: the bulletin ceased publication with the December 1976 issue.
      §   En.

096   FAO rice report   (Food and Agriculture Organisation of the UN).
      FAO, viale delle Terme di Caracalla, 00153 Roma, Italy; or from sales agents.
      1952-   1974/75.   US$2.00 or £0.80.   27p.
      Contains data on rice crops, stocks, market and trade.
      Time factor: the 1974/75 issue, published in 1975, has data for several years to 1973 and estimates for
          1974.
      §   En.

¶   B.ii,   continued

097   Rice trade intelligence   (Food and Agriculture Organisation of the UN).
         FAO, viale delle Terme di Caracalla, 00153 Roma, Italy; or from sales agents.
         1957-   two-monthly.   not priced.
         Contains data on price index, prices, contracts, exports, imports, stocks, paddy production, etc.
         Time factor: each issue has data for several years and months to one month prior to the date of the issue,
             which is the publication date.
         §   En.

098   Fruit: a review of production and trade relating to fresh, canned, frozen and dried fruit, fruit juices and
             wine   (Commonwealth Secretariat).
         Commonwealth Secretariat, Marlborough House, Pall Mall, London SW1Y 5HX, England.
         1964/65-   Vol.19, 1972.   £3.00.   278p.
         Time factor: Vol.19, 1972, contains data to 1972.   The review ceased publication with that issue.
         §   En.

         Note: the Republic of South Africa is the only African country included in the review.

099   Fruit intelligence   (Commonwealth Secretariat).
         Commonwealth Secretariat, Marlborough House, Pall Mall, London SW1Y 5HX, England.
                 monthly.   £1.67 or £20.00 yr.
         Up-dated 098 above until December 1976 issue, with which it ceased publication.
         §   En.

100   Dairy produce: a review of production, trade, consumption and prices relating to butter, cheese, condensed
             milk, milk powder, casein, eggs, egg products and margarine   (Commonwealth Secretariat).
         Commonwealth Secretariat, Marlborough House, Pall Mall, London SW1Y 5HX, England.
         1966-   Vol.20, 1972.   £2.00.   128p.
         Time factor: Vol.20, 1972, contains data to 1972.   The review ceased publication with that issue.
         §   En.

101   Meat: a review of production, trade, consumption and prices relating to beef, live cattle, mutton and lamb,
             live sheep, bacon and hams, pork, live pigs, canned meat, offal, poultry meat   (Commonwealth
             Secretariat).
         Commonwealth Secretariat, Marlborough House, Pall Mall, London SW1Y 5HX, England.
         1964/66-   Vol.19, 1973.   £2.50.   131p.
         Time factor: Vol.19, 1973, contains data to 1973.   The review ceased publication with that issue.
         §   En.

102   Meat and dairy produce bulletin   (Commonwealth Secretariat).
         Commonwealth Secretariat, Marlborough House, Pall Mall, London SW1Y 5HX, England.
                 monthly.   £1.67 or £20.00 yr.
         Up-dated 100 and 101 above until December 1976 issue, with which it ceased publication.
         §   En.

103   Animal health yearbook   (FAO - WHO - OIE).
         FAO, viale delle Terme di Caracalla, 00153 Roma, Italy; or from sales agents.
         1957-   1975.   £4.00 or US$7.00.   201p.
         Contains data on diseases of mammals, birds, bees, fish, by countries.   Also number of inhabitants,
             livestock and veterinarians.
         Time factor: the 1975 issue, published in 1976, contains data available at 31st December 1975.
         §   En, Fr, Es.

¶   B.ii,   continued

104   Sugar yearbook   (International Sugar Organisation).
            International Sugar Organisation, 28 Haymarket, London SW1Y 4SP, England.
            1947-   1975.   £5.00.   375p.
            Contains statistics of production, imports, exports, consumption, stocks, prices, etc, of sugar.
            Time factor: the 1975 edition, published mid-1976, has data for several years to 1975.
            §   En.

105   Statistical bulletin   (International Sugar Organisation).
            International Sugar Organisation, 28 Haymarket, London SW1Y 4SP, England.
            1947-   monthly.   £2.00; £20.00 yr, plus postage.
            Up-dates the information in the annual issue, 104 above.
            §   En.

106   Weltzuckerstatistik.   World sugar statistics   (F O Licht).
            F O Licht, Ratzeburg, Federal Republic of Germany.
            1938/39-   1975/76.   not priced.   64p.
            Includes world sugar statistics, and statistics of imports, exports, prices, consumtpion, and molasses by
                country.
            Time factor: the 1975/76 issue, published late 1976, has data received by July 1976, long runs of
                annual figures to 1975/76 or 1974/75.
            §   De, En.

107   Cocoa statistics   (Food and Agriculture Organisation of the UN).
            FAO, viale delle Terme di Caracalla, 00153 Roma, Italy; or from sales agents.
            1958-   quarterly with monthly supplements.   £0.40 each quarterly issue.
            Includes data on production, imports and exports of beans, butter, powder, paste, chocolate and
                chocolate products, prices of beans and stocks of beans.   Both producing countries and importing
                countries are named.
            Time factor: the date varies with each table.
            §   En, Fr, Es.

108   Cocoa statistics   (Gill & Duffus Ltd).
            Gill & Duffus Ltd, 23 St Dunstan's Hill, London EC3R 8HR, England.
            (annual).   1975.   not priced.   39p.
            Contains statistics of production and grindings of raw cocoa, imports and exports, supply and demand,
                and market prices.   There is also data for cocoa butter and cocoa powder.
            Time factor: the 1975 issue, published in May 1975, has long runs of figures to 1973.
            §   En.

            Note: Gill & Duffus Ltd also issue a "Cocoa market report" about every two months, which includes
                statistics on supply and demand, raw cocoa grindings, world production and grindings of raw
                cocoa, and world production of cocoa beans.

109   Quarterly bulletin of cocoa statistics   (International Cocoa Organisation).
            International Cocoa Organisation, 22 Berners Street, London W1P 3DB, England.
            1975-   £6.00 yr in Europe; £8.00 yr elsewhere.
            Contains data on the world cocoa bean position, production, grindings, exports by country of cocoa
                beans and products, imports by country, prices, etc.
            Time factor: each issue has the latest data available to six months or more before the date of the issue.
            §   En, Es, Fr, Ru.

110   General statistical document: coffee year...   (International Coffee Organisation).
            International Coffee Organisation, 22 Berners Street, London W1P 3DB, England.
            1968/69-   1975/76.   £1.50.   43p.
            Contains data on imports, exports, re-exports and inventories of coffee, by country.
            Time factor: the 1975/76 issue, published in 1976, has data for the coffee year 1975/76 and about five
                earlier years in some tables.
            §   En.

¶   B.ii,   continued

111   Annual coffee statistics   (Pan American Coffee Bureau).
        Pan American Coffee Bureau, 1350 Avenue of the Americas, New York, NY 10019, USA.
        1934-   1975.   US$5.00.   216p.
        The annual review of coffee statistics, including price movements, world production, world trade, as
            well as foreign exchange rates, barter and compensation agreements.   Information is also given for
            individual countries.
        Time factor: the 1975 issue, published in 1976, has data for 1975 and also earlier years in some tables.
        §   En.

112   Rubber statistical bulletin   (International Rubber Study Group).
        International Rubber Study Group, Brettenham House, 5-6 Lancaster Place, London WC2E 7ET, England.
        1947-   monthly.   £0.50; £5.00 or US$13.25 yr.
        Contains statistics of production, consumption, stocks, exports and imports of natural, synthetic and
            reclaimed rubber, and end products.
        Time factor: each issue has data for about ten years and twelve months to three months prior to the date
            of the issue.
        §   En,

113   World rubber statistics handbook   (International Rubber Study Group).
        International Rubber Study Group, Brettenham House, 5-6 Lancaster Place, London WC2E 7ET, England.
                    Vol.1: 1946-1970. $3.00 or US$7.50.   35p.
        A historical base book to 112 above.
        Time factor: Vol.1 was published in December 1974.
        §   En.

114   Annual bulletin of statistics   (International Tea Committee).
        International Tea Committee, Sir John Lyon House, 5 High Timber Street, Upper Thames Street,
            London EC4V 3NH, England.
        1946-   1976.   £5.00 including supplement (to be £25.00 in 1977).   63p.
        Contains data on area and production, exports, imports and consumption, stocks, auction prices,
            instant tea, etc.
        Time factor: the 1976 edition, published in July 1976, has data for several years to 1975.   The
            supplement was published in December 1976.
        §   En.

115   Monthly statistical summary   (International Tea Committee).
        International Tea Committee, Sir John Lyon House, 5 High Timber Street, Upper Thames Street,
            London EC4V 3NH, England.
        1946-   £15.00 yr in 1977.
        Contains data on planting, production, exports, imports, re-exports, stocks, monthly price quotations,
            consumption, and import duties.
        Time factor: up-dates the above title (114).
        §   En.

116   Edible nut statistics   (Gill & Duffus Ltd).
        Gill & Duffus Ltd, 23 St Dunstan's Hill, London EC3R 8HR, England.
        (quarterly).   not priced.
        Contains statistics of crops, imports, exports, and edible nut kernel prices.
        Time factor: each issue has long runs of annual and monthly figures to the date of issue or the latest
            available, and is published in the month of issue.
        §   En.

        Note: there is also an "Edible nut market report".

¶   B.ii,   continued

117   Hides and skins quarterly   (Commonwealth Secretariat).
        Commonwealth Secretariat, Marlborough House, Pall Mall, London SW1Y 5HX, England.
        Contains data on trade in cattle hides, calfskins, sheepskins, goatskins and leather.
        Time factor: ceased publication with the issue for the 4th quarter 1976.
        §   En.

118   Vegetable oils and oilseeds: a review of production, trade, utilisation and prices relating to groundnuts,
            cottonseed, linseed, soya beans, coconut oil and palm oil products, olive oil, and other oilseeds
            and oils   (Commonwealth Secretariat).
        Commonwealth Secretariat, Marlborough House, Pall Mall, London, SW1Y 5HX, England.
        1965/66-   Vol.21, 1973.   £3.50.   215p.
        Time factor: Vol.21, 1973, contains data to 1973. The review ceased publication with that issue.
        §   En.

119   Annual review of oilseeds, oils, oilcakes, and other commodities   (Frank Fehr & Co Ltd).
        Frank Fehr & Co Ltd, 64 Queen Street, London EC4R 1ER, England.
        (annual)   1975.   not priced.   76p.
        Following a general review, there is data for each of the commodities dealt with by the firm, including
            prices, production, imports, exports, etc.
        Time factor: the 1975 issue, published mid-1976, has data for 1973, 1974 and 1975.
        §   En.

120   World oils and fats statistics   (Economic and Statistics Dept, Unilever Ltd, for the International
            Association of Seed Crushers).
        Unilever Ltd, Unilever House, London EC4P 4BQ, England.
        1966/67-   1972/75.   £5.00.   14p.
        Contains a world summary; world production of types of oils and fats, producing areas, and production
            of oilcake and meat; European vegetable oil supplies; a summary of world exports; and world
            exports.
        Time factor: the 1972/75 issue, with data for those years, was published mid-1976.
        §   En.

121   Plantation crops: a review of production, trade, consumption and prices relating to coffee, cocoa, tea,
            sugar, spices, tobacco and rubber   (Commonwealth Secretariat).
        Commonwealth Secretariat, Marlborough House, Pall Mall, London SW1Y 5HX, England.
        1966-   Vol.14, 1973.   £3.95.   318p.
        Time factor: Vol.14, 1973, contains data to 1973.   The review ceased publication with that issue.
        §   En.

122   Tropical products quarterly   (Commonwealth Secretariat).
        Commonwealth Secretariat, Marlborough House, Pall Mall, London SW1Y 5HX, England.
        1960-   £3.00 or £12.00 yr.
        Includes data on production, crops, imports and exports, trade, stocks, prices, sales, etc. of vegetable
            oils and oilseeds, cocoa, coffee and spices.
        Time factor: up-dated 118 and 121 above until December 1976 issue, with which it ceased publication.
        §   En.

123   Tobacco intelligence   (Commonwealth Secretariat).
        Commonwealth Secretariat, Marlborough House, Pall Mall, London SW1Y 5HX, England.
        quarterly.   £3.00 or £12.00 yr.
        Contains data for unmanufactured tobacco, including a general review and a country review, with
            information on area and production, foreign trade, consumption, sales, prices, etc.
        Time factor: ceased publication with the issue for the 4th quarter 1976.
        §   En.

¶ B.ii, continued

124 Yearbook of fishery statistics: catches and landings (Food and Agriculture Organisation of the UN).
FAO, viale delle Terme di Caracalla, 00153 Roma, Italy; or from sales agents.
1942- Vol.40, 1975. £9.75; US$18.00. 439p.
Contains annual statistics for 1970-1975 on nominal catches on a world-wide basis, with detailed
breakdowns by (a) countries, (b) species, and (c) major fishing areas.
Time factor: the 1975 edition was published late 1976.
§ En, Fr, Es.

125 Yearbook of fishery statistics: fishery commodities (Food and Agriculture Organisation of the UN).
FAO, viale delle Terme di Caracalla, 00153 Roma, Italy; or from sales agents.
1942- Vol.41, 1975. £6.50; US$12.00. 353p.
Relates to production and international trade in fishery commodities.
Time factor: the 1975 edition, published late 1976, has data for 1975 and some earlier years.
§ En, Fr, Es.

126 International whaling statistics (Norske Hvalraad [Committee for Whaling Statistics]).
Norske Hvalraad, Oslo.
1930- 1976. not priced. 21p.
Contains data on whaling results for various countries, including the Republic of South Africa, giving
information on species, size, etc.
Time factor: the 1976 issue, published in 1976, has data for the 1975/76 season.
§ En.

127 Yearbook of forest products (Food and Agriculture Organisation of the UN).
FAO, viale delle Terme di Caracalla, 00153 Roma, Italy; or from sales agents.
1947- 1963-1974. £8.00; US$20.00. 464p.
Contains data on production and trade of all kinds of round-woods, sawnwoods, wood-based panels,
wood-pulp, paper and board, and forest products. Also includes direction of trade data for the
main classes.
Time factor: the 1963-1974 edition, published in 1976, has data for the years 1963 to 1974.
§ En, Fr, Es.

128 World forest inventory (Food and Agriculture Organisation of the UN).
FAO, viale delle Terme di Caracalla, 00153 Roma, Italy; or from sales agents.
1948- 5th, 1963. £0.65; US$2.50. 113p.
Based on the results of censuses taken every five years, the inventories contain data on area, growing
stock, forest per caput, including utilisation and removals.
Time factor: the 1963 inventory was published in 1966.
§ En, Fr, Es.

iii. Industry

129 Yearbook of industrial statistics (United Nations Statistical Office).
Sales Section, United Nations, New York, NY 10017; or from sales agents.
1938/61- 8th, 1974. Vol. I US$30.00; £18.00. 2 vols.
II US$32.00; £19.20.
Formerly titled "Growth of world industry". Vol.I, "General industrial statistics", contains basic
national data for each country, and vol.II, "Commodity production data, 1965-1974", contains
detailed information on world production of individual industrial commodities.
Time factor: the 1974 edition, published in 1976, has data for 1974 in vol.I and for 1965-1974 in
vol.II.
§ En.

130   Les conditions d'installation d'entreprises industrielles dans les états africains et Malgache associés   [The conditions for the setting up of industrial companies in the African countries and Madagascar, associated with the European Communities]   (Communautés Européennes).
       Direction Générale de la Coopération et du Développement, Communautés Européennes, 200 rue de la Loi, 1040 Bruxelles, Belgium.
       1st, 1972-   2nd, 1974.   free.   19 vols.
       Each volume relates to a separate country:-

1. Dahomey	8. Togo	14. Cameroun
2. Upper Volta	9. Burundi	15. Central African Republic
3. Madagascar	10. Rwanda	16. Congo
4. Mali	11. Zaire	17. Gabon
5. Mauritania	12. Mauritius	18. Senegal
6. Niger	13. Somalia	19. Ivory Coast
7. Chad		

       Time factor: the 1974 edition, published in 1974, reflects the situation at mid-1974.
       §   Fr (foreword only in En, De, It, Du, Da).

131   L'industrie africaine   [African industry]   (EDIAFRIC).
       EDIAFRIC, 57 avenue d'Iéna, 75783 Paris Cedex 16, France.
               6th ed, 1976.   FrF 534.   2 vols.
       Contains information, including statistics and statistical tables in the text, on industry for the French-speaking African states (Cameroun, Central African Republic, Chad, Congo, Dahomey, Gabon, Ivory Coast, Mali, Mauritania, Niger, Senegal, Togo, and Upper Volta), including the mining industry, food industry, drink and tobacco, textiles and leather goods, timber industry, paper and cartons and stationery, oils, chemicals, construction materials, metallurgy, mechanical and electrical industries, electrical engineering, and water supply.
       §   Fr.

132   International steel statistics   (British Steel Corporation).
       British Steel Corporation, 12 Addiscombe Road, Croydon CR9 3JH, England.
       1959-   1974.   not priced.
       Currently published as a number of separate booklets, some devoted to one country and some having data for two or three countries, containing statistical data on the production, imports and exports of the various types of iron and steel for every iron and steel producing country.   There is a volume for South Africa, including South Africa, South West Africa, Botswana, Lesotho and Swaziland.
       Time factor: the booklets are issued as and when the information for the relevant country or countries becomes available.
       §   En.

133   World stainless steel statistics   (International Nickel Ltd).
       Metal Bulletin Books Ltd, Park House, 3 Park Terrace, Worcester Park, Surrey KT4 7HY, England.
       1974-   1976.   £28.00.   144p.
       A comprehensive review of stainless steel production (South Africa only of African countries) and international trade in the non-Communist countries of the world.
       Time factor: the 1976 edition, published in 1976, has data for several years to 1975.
       §   En.

134   Wood pulp and fiber statistics   (Pulp, Paper & Raw Materials Group, American Paper Institute Inc).
       American Paper Institute Inc, 260 Madison Avenue, New York, NY 10016, USA.
       1937-   1975.   not priced.   2 vols.
       Book 1 deals with the United States and Canada and Book 2 with other countries.   Information given for each country is production, imports, exports, by type.
       Time factor: the 1975 edition, published in November 1975, has long runs of figures to 1974.
       §   En.

135   Annual fertilizer review.   Rapport annuel sur les Engrais.   (Food and Agriculture Organisation of the UN).
        FAO, viale delle Terme di Caracalla, 00153 Roma, Italy; or from sales agents.
        1951/54-   1975.   £5.60.   205p.
        Contains data on world production, consumption, trade, supply and prices of fertilizers (nitrogenous,
            phosphate, and potash).
        Time factor: the 1975 edition, published in 1976, has long runs of figures to 1974/75.
        §   En; notes and glossary also in Fr & Es.

136   Directory of fertilizer production facilities. Part I: Africa   (United Nations Industrial Development
            Organisation (UNIDO)).
        Sales Section, United Nations, New York, NY 10017; or from sales agents.
                            £1.31 or US$3.00.   271p.
        Includes, for each country, annual consumption and production of fertilizers.
        Time factor: published in 1970, the directory shows data for 1960, 1965, 1970 and 1975, the last two
            years being estimates.
        §   En.

137   Industrial fibres: a review of production, trade and consumption relating to wool, cotton and man-made
            fibres, silk, flax, jute, sizal and other hemps, mohair and kapok   (Commonwealth Secretariat).
        Commonwealth Secretariat, Marlborough House, Pall Mall, London SW1Y 5HX, England.
        1966-67-   Vol.20, 1973.   £3.25.   243p.
        Time factor: Vol.20, 1973, has data to 1971/72 or, in some tables, 1972/73.   The review ceased
            publication with this issue.
        §   En.

138   Information sur les textiles synthétique et cellulosiques   [Information on synthetic textiles]   (CIRFS.
            [International Rayon and Synthetic Fibre Committee]).
        CIRFS, 29 rue de Courcelles, 75008 Paris, France.
        1969-   1975.   not priced.   185p.
        Contains data on production, consumption and foreign trade in man-made fibres; labour; consumer
            expenditure on clothing; per caput national income; population; and customs tariffs, etc.
        Time factor: the 1975 edition, published in 1975, has data for 1974 and also one or two earlier years
            in some tables.
        §   Fr, En, De.

139   Quarterly statistical review   (Textile Statistics Bureau).
        Textile Statistics Bureau, 5th Floor, Royal Exchange, Manchester M2 7ER, England.
        1946-   £3.00 or £10.00 yr.
        Apart from detailed United Kingdom statistics, the review contains figures for world production or yarn
            and cloth, and world imports and exports, including data for Egypt.
        Time factor: each issue includes long runs of figures to the latest available on each subject and country.
        §   En.

140   Wool statistics   (Commonwealth Secretariat; International Wool Textile Organisation; and International
            Wool Study Group).
        Commonwealth Secretariat, Marlborough House, Pall Mall, London SW1Y 5HX, England.
        1947/48-   1975/76.   free to subscribers to "Wool Intelligence".
        Contains the results of the annual wool questionnaire, and includes data on production, supplies, stocks,
            consumption, trade, etc. of raw wool, yarns, products, machinery, etc.   South Africa is the only
            African country included.
        Time factor: the 1976/77 issue has data for several years to 1976/77 and was published mid-1977.
            Publication ceased with that issue.
        §   En.

¶   B.iii,   continued

141   Wool intelligence   (Commonwealth Secretariat).
        Commonwealth Secretariat, Marlborough House, Pall Mall, London SW1Y 5HX, England.
        monthly.   £1.67 or £20.00 yr.
        Contained more recent data than 140 above.
        Time factor: ceased publication with the December 1976 issue.
        §   En.

142   Cotton - world statistics: quarterly bulletin of the International Cotton Advisory Committee.
        International Cotton Advisory Committee, South Agriculture Building, Washington, DC 20250, USA.
        1948-   US$9.00 yr to North American member countries; US$10.00 to other member countries;
              US$50.00 yr to non-member countries.
        Contains world tables and country tables on the supply, distribution, production, consumption, imports
              and exports, stocks, and prices of cotton.   Also production, imports and exports of cotton yarn,
              cotton cloth, and rayon cloth.
        Time factor: the latest figures available for each country are published.
        §   En.

        Note: "Cotton: monthly review of the world situation" is included in the subscription.

143   International cotton industry statistics   (International Federation of Cotton and Allied Textile Industries).
        International Federation of Cotton and Allied Textile Industries, am Schanzengraben 29, Postfach 289,
              8039 Zürich, Switzerland.
        1958-   1974.   not priced.   24p.
        Contains data on numbers of spindles, spindle hours worked, consumption of raw materials, numbers of
              looms, and loom hours worked for each country.
        Time factor: the 1974 edition, published late 1975, has data for several years to 1974.
        §   En.

144   Estimated world requirements of narcotic drugs in... and estimates of world production of opium...
              (United Nations. International Narcotics Control Board).
        Sales Section, United Nations, New York, NY 10017; or from sales agents.
        (annual)   1977.   £3.25 or US$5.00.   67p.
        Time factor: the 1977 edition, published in December 1976, is up-dated during the year by supplements
              as new information becomes available.
        §   En, Fr, Es.

145   Statistics on narcotic drugs   (United Nations. International Narcotics Control Board).
        Sales Section, United Nations, New York, NY 10017; or from sales agents.
        (annual)   1974.   £3.12.   104p.
        Contains data in trends in licit movement of narcotic drugs, including raw materials (opium, poppy,
              morphine, codeine, heroin, etc), cannabis and cannabis resin, coca leaf, cocaine, and 'synthetic'
              drugs, by country.
        Time factor: the 1974 edition, published in 1975, has data for 1970 to 1974.
        §   En.

146   Motor industry of Great Britain   (Society of Motor Manufacturers and Traders).
        SMMT, Forbes House, Halkin Street, London SW1X 7JF, England.
        1947-   1976.   £6.50 to members; £14.50 to non-members.   264p.
        Contains detailed statistics of production of cars, commercial vehicles, tractors, etc, in the United
              Kingdom and overseas, and foreign trade of the United Kingdom and overseas countries.
        Time factor: the 1976 edition, published mid-1976, has data for 1975 and some earlier years.
        §   En.

147   World automotive market   (Automobile International).
        Automobile International, 386 Park Avenue South, New York, NY 10016, USA.
        1966-   1976.   US$8.00.   43p.
        Includes data on vehicle production (including South Africa), registrations of motor cars and of trucks
              and buses by country, and import statistics of individual countries.
        Time factor: the 1976 edition, published in 1976, has data for several years to 1975.
        §   En.

¶ B.iii, continued

148   World motor vehicle data   (Motor Vehicle Manufacturers' Association).
      Motor Vehicle Manufacturers' Association, 320 New Center Building, Detroit, Michigan 48202, USA.
      (annual)   1975.   US$20.00.   160p.
      Contains data on world production, vehicle assembly (including Morocco and South Africa), new
         registrations, imports, sales, etc. (including all African countries).
      Time factor: the 1975 edition, published in 1976, has data for several years to 1975.
      §   En.

149   Economic handbook of the machine tool industry   (National Machine Tool Builders' Association).
      National Machine Tool Builders' Association, 7901 Westpark Drive, McLean, Va 22101, USA.
      1969/70-   1975/76.   US$10.00.   238p.
      Contains data on the national economy and machine tools, the world economy, the machine tool
         industry, machine tool shipments and orders, foreign trade, employment and earnings, finance,
         machine tools in use.
      Time factor: the 1975/76 edition, published in 1975, has data to 1974.
      §   En.

150   World record markets   (E.M.I.)
      Henry Melland Ltd, 23 Ridgmount Street, London WC1E 7AH, England.
      1968-   3rd, 1976.   £2.50.   110p.
      Contains data on the numbers of record companies, recording studios, record labels, retail outlets,
         records manufactured, records imported, radio stations and receivers, television stations and
         receivers, etc. Includes data for Nigeria and South Africa.
      Time factor: the 1976 edition, published in 1976, has data for 1975.
      §   En.

iv. Construction

151   Yearbook of construction statistics   (United Nations Statistical Office).
      Sales Section, United Nations, New York, NY 10017; or from sales agents.
      1963/72-   1965/74.   £11.70; US$18.00.   246p.
      Contains data by country, including data on all buildings, residential buildings, non-residential
         buildings, commercial buildings, other buildings, employment, wages and salaries, value of
         construction, costs, etc.
      Time factor: the 1964/73 edition, published late 1975, has data for the years 1964 to 1973.
      §   En.

v. Energy

152   World energy supplies   (United Nations Statistical Office).
      Sales Section, United Nations, New York, NY 10017; or from sales agents.
      1952-   1950-1974.   Cloth US$38.00; £22.80.   898p.
                    Paper US$30.00.
      A study on energy supplies, which includes statistics on production, trade and consumption of solid
         fuels, petroleum and its products, gas and electricity (thermal, hydro and nuclear) for approximately
         150 countries, with regional and global totals. It up-dates and enlarges on previous annual
         volumes.
      Time factor: the 1950-1974 edition, published in 1976, has data for the years 1950 to 1974.
      §   En.

AFRICA, continued

¶ B.v, continued

153 Energia ed idrocarburi: sommario statistico [Energy and hydrocarbon fuels: statistical summary]
(ENI: Ente Nazionale Idrocarburi).
Ente Nazionale Idrocarburi, Roma, Italy.
1955-1974. not priced. 276p.
Contains data on the international economic situation, the international energy situation, the
international oil and gas industry (reserves and production, consumption, prices), the international
nuclear industry (uranium mineral production, installed capacity, nuclear electrical output, and
orders for nuclear power stations), the Italian economic situation, the Italian energy situation, and
the Italian petroleum industry.
Time factor: the 1955-1974 edition, published in 1975, has data for the years 1955 to 1974.
§ It; separate pamphlet with index and glossary in English.

154 World energy conference: survey of energy resources... (Oak Ridge National Laboratory, US Atomic
Energy Commission).
United States National Committee of the World Energy Conference, 345 East 47th Street, New York,
NY 10017, USA and W.E.C. Central Office, 5 Bury Street, London SW1Y 6AB, England.
1929- 1974. 400p and 7 pages of maps.
Contains statistical data on solid fuels; crude oil, natural gas and natural gas liquids; oil shale and
bituminous sands; hydraulic resources; nuclear resources; and other renewable resources, for each
country.
Time factor: the 1974 edition was published in 1974.
§ En.

155 Annual statistical bulletin (Organisation of the Petroleum Exporting Countries).
OPEC, Dr Karl Lueger-Ring 10, 1010 Wien, Austria.
1973- 1974. öS 100.00. 175p.
Contains data on producing wells and wells completed; production of natural gas and crude oil;
refining, consumption of refined products; OPEC member countries exports of crude oil and refined
products; world trade in natural gas, crude oil and refined products; tanker fleets and tanker fleet
rates; major pipelines in OPEC member countries; posted prices; oil revenues; and the financial
situation of major oil companies.
Time factor: the 1974 edition, published in 1975, has data to 1974.
§ En.

156 Annual statistical report (Organisation of Arab Petroleum Exporting Countries).
OAPEC, P O Box 20501, Safat, Kuwait.
4th, 1976. K.D.1 or US$3.00. c100p.
Contains general tables for member countries on reserves of crude oil and gas, crude oil production,
refinery capacity, exports of crude oil, energy consumption, and oil revenues. Also special tables
for each member country, including Algeria, Libya and Egypt, on balance of trade, production of
crude oil and refined products, exports, and local consumption of refined products.
Time factor: the 1976 edition, published in 1977, has data to 1976.
§ En, Ar.

157 OAPEC news bulletin.
OAPEC, P O Box 20501, Safat, Kuwait.
1975- monthly. not priced.
Includes a few statistics in the text.
§ En.

158 B P Statistical review of the world oil industry (British Petroleum Co Ltd).
British Petroleum Company Ltd, Britannic House, Moor Lane, London EC2Y 9BU, England.
(annual) 1975. not priced. 32p.
Contains data on reserves, production, consumption, trade, refining, tankers and energy.
Time factor: the 1975 edition, published mid-1976, has data for several years to 1975.
§ En.

¶   B.v,   continued

159   Know more about oil: world statistics   (Institute of Petroleum).
             Institute of Petroleum, 61 New Cavendish Street, London W1M 8AR, England.
             (annual)   August, 1976.   £0.10.   10p.
             Contains statistics of production, refining, capacity, consumption, tanker tonnage, etc, of oil by
                 countries.
             Time factor: the August 1976 issue, published in August 1976, has data for several years to 1975.
             §   En.

160   World offshore oil and gas: a review of offshore activity and an assessment of worldwide market prospects for
                 offshore exploration/products equipment and materials   (Scottish Council (Development and Industry)).
             Scottish Council, 15 Union Terrace, Aberdeen AB1 1NJ, Scotland.
                                            £21.50.   210p.
             Pages 107-140 deal with Africa.
             Time factor: published in July 1975.
             §   En.

161   Petroleum economist   (Petroleum Press Bureau Ltd).
             Petroleum Press Bureau Ltd, 5 Pemberton Row, Regent Street, London EC4A 3DP, England.
             1934-   monthly.   £20.00 or US$45.00 yr.
             Some statistical tables are included in the articles, and there are regular tables on world oil production,
                 prices, and oil share quotations.
             §   En, Fr, & Japanese editions.

162   Pétrole...éléments statistiques...activité de l'industrie pétrolière   [Petroleum...statistics...activities of
                 the industry]   (Comité Professionel du Pétrole).
             Comité Professionel du Pétrole, 51 boulevard de Courcelles, 75000 Paris, France.
             1974-   1975.   not priced.   375p.
             Mainly concerned with activities in France, but also has a section on world data (production, consumption,
                 activities, frozen reserves, refining, pipelines, etc) and total figures (not for separate countries) for
                 the overseas departments and territories of France.
             Time factor: the 1975 issue was published mid-1976.
             §   Fr.

163   Statistics   (International Union of Producers and Distributors of Electrical Energy).
             International Union of Producers and Distributors of Electrical Energy, 39 Avenue de Friedland,
                 75008 Paris, France.
             1953-   1975/76.   not individually priced.   c150p.
             Contains detailed statistical data relating to electrical energy generation and consumption.   Published
                 as a special number of the journal "L'économie électrique" (FrF 30 yr).
             §   En, Fr.

¶   C - External trade

164   Yearbook of international trade statistics   (United Nations Statistical Office).
             Sales Section, United Nations, New York, NY 10017; or from sales agents.
             1950-   1975.   US$50.00 or £32.50 for 2 vols.   2 vols.
             Provides the basic information for individual countries' external trade performance in terms of overall
                 trends in current value as well as in volume and price, the importance of trading partners and the
                 significance of individual commodities imports and exports.   Volume I deals with trade by country;
                 Volume II with trade by commodity.
             Time factor: the 1975 edition, published in 1976, has data for 1975.
             §   En.

165 World trade annual. Supplement: trade of the industrialised nations with Eastern Europe and the developing
nations. Vol.III: Africa.   (Walker and Co, by agreement with the United Nations Statistical Office).
Walker & Co, 720 Fifth Avenue, New York, NY 10019, USA.
1964-   1972.   US$75.90.   814p.
The main volumes of "World trade annual" contain statistics of foreign trade in each of 1,312 items of the
SITC as reported by 24 principal countries, the data being arranged in commodity order and
sub-divided by countries of origin and destination.   Five supplementary volumes are also published
dealing with the trade of Eastern Europe and the developing countries.   Volume III of the
supplementary volumes contains detailed foreign trade statistics for individual African countries as
reported by the 24 principal trading countries.   The prime purpose of the supplementary volumes is
to serve those who are interested in individual countries for which the trade statistics are not easily
available in internationally comparable form.   Values are given in US $ and quantities in metric
units.
Time factor: the 1972 edition, published in 1975, contains data for 1972.
§   En.

166 Commodity trade statistics   (United Nations Statistical Office).
Sales Section, United Nations, New York, NY 10017; or from sales agents.
            fortnightly.   £1.32 or £28.16 yr; US$3.00 or US$64.00 yr.
Issued in fascicules of about 250 pages each as quarterly data becomes available from the reporting
countries.   Each country's imports and exports are shown in the 625 sub-groups of the SITC,
sub-divided by countries of origin and destination.   Values in each case are converted to US $,
and quantities are in metric units.   In the front of each fascicule is an index showing in which
issues appeared the latest data for each country.   African reporting countries in 1974 were
Cameroon, Egypt, Ghana, Guinea, Libya, Réunion, Senegal, Sierra Leone, Tunisia, and others
as trading partners.
Time factor: varies for each country.   Data are cumulated January-March, January-June, January-
September and January-December.   January-March is not always published.
§   En.

167 Handbook of international trade and development statistics.   Manuel de statistiques du commerce
international et du développement   (UNCTAD).
Sales Section, United Nations, New York, NY 10017; or from sales agents.
1964-   1976.   US$24.00; £14.40.   673p.
Intended to provide a complete basic collection of statistical data relevant to the analysis of problems of
world trade and development, for the use of UNCTAD, etc.   Contents are:
            Part 1 Value of world trade by regions and countries, 1950-1975
                2 Volume, unit value, and terms of trade index numbers by regions; commodity prices
                3 Network of world trade; summary by selected regions of origin and destination and
                    structure of imports and exports by selected commodity groups
                4 Imports and exports for individual countries by commodity structure, and major exports
                    of developing countries by leading exporters.
                5 Financial flows, aid and balance of payments for developing countries
                6 Some basic indicators of development
                7 Special studies
            Annex A   Network of world exports by selected commodity classes and regions of origin
                    and destination, 1955-1974
            Annex B   Ranking of countries and territories according to per capita GNP
Time factor: the 1976 edition, published in May 1976, generally has data for 1974 and some earlier
years.
§   En, Fr.

168 Review of international trade and development   (UNCTAD).
Sales Section, United Nations, New York, NY 10017; or from sales agents.
1967-   1975.   £3.60; US$6.00.   109p.
Part one of the review provides an analysis of the recent economic experiences of developing countries
in relation to the goals and objectives of the International Development Strategy, while part two
contains a review of the implementation of measures envisaged in the Strategy.   Tables are
included in the text.
§   En.

¶ C, continued

169   Trade in manufactures of developing countries and territories   (UNCTAD).
        Sales Section, United Nations, New York, NY 10017; or from sales agents.
        1968-   1974.   £3.60; US$6.00.   106p.
        Part one is a review of recent trends in trade in manufactures of developing countries and territories.
           Part two deals with trade in textiles of the developing countries in the context of international
           arrangements and of the world energy situation.
        Time factor: the 1974 edition, published in 1976, has data for 1972 and earlier years in some tables.
        §   En.

170   International trade   (General Agreement on Tariffs and Trade).
        GATT, Palais des Nations, 1211 Genève 10, Switzerland.
        (annual)   1975/76.   US$11.00; £7.56; FrF 27.00.   192p.
        The report is concerned with main trends in international trade, trade in commodities, trade in
           industrial areas, trade in non-industrial areas, and trade of the eastern trading areas.   Statistical
           tables in the text.
        Time factor: the 1975/76 edition, published in 1976, covers 1973 to 1975.
        §   En.

171   ACP...yearbook of foreign trade statistics: statistical abstract: 1968-1973   (Eurostat).
        Office des Publications Officielles des Communautés Européennes, CP 1003, Luxembourg; or from sales
           agents.
                        £2.20; US$4.80; FrB 200; DKr 31.50.   94p.
        Summary of trade flows of the Africa, Caribbean and Pacific (ACP) countries, signatories of the Lomé
           convention.   Contents are:
              1.   ACP countries in world trade by economic regions, exports by countries, exports by products
              2.   External trade of the ACP countries (total and imports and exports by major product category
              3.   EUR-9 and the ACP countries.   Total trade, exports by STC sections, imports by main
                  products
        Time factor: published in 1975
        §   En, Fr.

172   Foreign trade statistics of Africa.   Series A: Direction of trade.   Statistiques africaines du commerce
           extérieur.   Série A: Echanges par pays   (United Nations Economic Commission for Africa).
        Sales Section, United Nations, New York, NY 10017; or from sales agents.
        1962-   6-monthly.   £3.12 or US$6.00 each issue.
        Contains trade by country data in US $ for those African countries for which the information is available.
        Time factor: varies country by country, the latest available figures being included in each issue.
        §   En, Fr.

173   Foreign trade statistics of Africa.   Series B: Trade by commodity.   Statistiques africaines du commerce
           extérieur.   Série B: Echanges par produits   (United Nations Economic Commission for Africa).
        Sales Section, United Nations, New York, NY 10017; or from sales agents.
        1961-   6-monthly.   £5.20 or US$10.00 each issue.
        Contains cumulated half-yearly data on African commodity trade according to the SITC, sub-divided
           by regions and countries of provenance and destination, in US $.
        Time factor: data for each country is published as it becomes available.
        §   En, Fr.

174   Compendium des statistiques du commerce extérieur de pays africaines et Malgache   [Compendium of
           statistics of foreign trade of African countries and Madagascar]   (INSEE).
        INSEE, 18 boulevard Adolphe Pinard, 75675 Paris Cedex 14, France.
        1938-   1964.   not priced.   293p.
        Contains detailed statistics of foreign trade arranged by commodity and sub-divided by countries of
           origin and destination, for the French-speaking African countries.
        §   Fr.

    ¶   C,   continued

175   Compendium des statistiques du commerce extérieur   [Compendium of foreign trade statistics]
         (Organisation Commune Africaine et Malgache).
         Organisation Commune Africaine et Malgache, Yaoundé, Cameroun.
         1965-   1967.   not priced.   2 vols.
         Vol. 1 contains data on imports and vol. 2 on exports.
         §   Fr.

176   Trade yearbook   (Food and Agriculture Organisation of the UN).
         FAO, viale delle Terme di Caracalla, 00153 Roma, Italy; or from sales agents.
         1947-   1974.   £6.00; US$15.00.   606p.
         Contains data on imports and exports of agricultural commodities and agricultural requisites, classified
            by SITC, for each reporting country.   Data are in US $ and metric quantities.
         Time factor: the 1974 edition, published mid-1975, contains data for varying periods to 1974.
         §   En, Fr, Es.

177   World grain trade statistics: exports by source and destination   (Food and Agriculture Organisation of the UN).
         FAO, viale delle Terme di Caracalla, 00153 Roma, Italy; or from sales agents.
         1954/56-   1973/74.   £1.60 or US$4.00.   78p.
         Contains data on world trade in grain, grain exports by source and destination, trade in grains of
            centrally planned countries, trade in grains by regions and selected countries, recent international
            grain trade contracts, and world trade in wheat and coarse grains.
         Time factor: the 1973/74 edition, published in 1975, has data for 1973 or for 1973/74 provisionally.
         §   En, Fr, Es.

178   Statistics of world trade in steel   (United Nations Economic Commission for Europe).
         Sales Section, United Nations, New York, NY 10017; or from sales agents.
         1913/59-   1975.   £3.25 or US$5.00.   66p.
         Contains data on the exports of the various semi-finished and finished steel products by regions and
            countries of destination.   Exporting countries include South Africa.
         Time factor: the 1975 edition, published in 1976, has data for 1975.
         §   En, Fr, Ru.

179   Annual bulletin of trade in chemical products   (United Nations).
         Sales Section, United Nations, New York, NY 10017; or from sales agents.
         1973-   1975.   US$16.00; £10.40.   299p.
         Contains detailed breakdown of trade in chemical products, arranged by commodities and sub-divided
            by countries of origin and destination.   African countries are included as trading partners.
         Time factor: the 1975 issue, published in December 1976, has data for 1975.
         §   En, Fr, Ru.

180   Exporters' guide to the textile markets of the world   (National Wool Textile Export Corporation).
         National Wool Textile Export Corporation, Lloyds Bank Chambers, 43 Hustlergate, Bradford BD1 1PE,
            England.
                1975/76.   not priced.   108p.
         Contains data on domestic production, imports and exports of tops, yarn, and cloth for each country.
         Time factor: the 1975/76 edition, published in December 1975, has data for 1972, 1973 and 1974.   A
            supplement, published in December 1976, has data for 1975 so extending the currency of the full
            edition.
         §   En.

181   Direction of trade   (International Monetary Fund <u>and</u> International Bank for Reconstruction and Development).
         International Monetary Fund, Washington, DC 20431, USA; or from sales agents.
         1958/62-   11 monthly issues with annual summary.   £0.42; US$1.00 (£4.17; US$10.00 yr).
         Contains data on the value of trade with other countries in US $, both imports and exports.
         Time factor: up-to-dateness varies from country to country, but each issue contains data for the two
            latest months available and comparative figures for the previous year.
         §   En.

¶   C,   continued

182   World invisible trade   (Committee on Invisible Exports).
           Committee on Invisible Exports, 7th Floor, Stock Exchange, London EC2N 1HP, England.
           1966-   1976.   £2.00.   32p.
           Time factor: the 1976 issue, published in August 1976, has data for 1974 and 1973 and also some
                earlier years.
           §   En.

¶   D - Internal distribution and service trades

183   Fachserie Auslandsstatistik. Reihe 5: Preise und Preisindices im Ausland   [Foreign statistics series.
                Series 5: Prices and price indices in foreign countries]   (Statistisches Bundesamt).
           W Kohlhammer GmbH, Postfach 42 11 20, 6500 Mainz 42, Germany.
                monthly.   DM 3.20; DM 10 yr.
           Time factor: each issue has data for the period of the issue and the current year to date, and also
                averages for the last few years.
           §   De.

184   Economic review of world tourism   (International Union of Official Travel Organisations).
           World Tourism Organisation, avenida del Generalísimo 59, Madrid 16, Spain.
           1966-   1976.   US$20.00.   85p.
           Includes statistical tables in the text on tourism in a changing world economy, travel demand, domestic
                tourism, accommodation, transport, economic profile of tourism in the national economy, tourism
                development planning, and tourism and the economic development of developing countries.
           Time factor: published every two years; the 1976 issue, published in 1976, has data for several years
                to 1973 and 1974.
           §   En.

185   World travel statistics   (World Tourism Organisation).
           World Tourism Organisation, avenida del Generalísimo 59, Madrid 16, Spain.
           1947-   1975.   not priced.   looseleaf.
           Arranged by country, and contains data of visitors and tourists arriving, foreign visitors arriving,
                cruise passengers, by country of residence, length of stay, rooms and hotels, receipts and
                expenditures.
           Time factor: the 1975 edition, published in 1976 (pages added as information becomes available), has
                data for 1975 and 1974.
           §   En, Fr, Es.

           Note: previously "International travel statistics".

186   Worldwide operating statistics of the hotel industry   (Horwath & Horwath International and Laventhol
                Krekstern Horwath & Horwath).
           Laventhol Krekstern Horwath & Horwath, 1845 Walnut Street, Philadelphia, Pa 19103, USA.
           1971-   1974.   not priced.   43p.
           Mainly international figures, but one or two tables are sub-divided into continents.
           Time factor: the 1974 issue, published in 1974, has data for 1973.
           §   En.

187   Advertising expenditures around the world: a survey   (Starch Inra Hooper and International Advertising
                Association).
           Starch Inra Hooper, 566E Boston Post Road, Maroneck, NY 10543, USA.
                        12th, 1976.   US$35.00 (US$25.00 to members).   56p.
           Cover title is "World advertising expenditures".   Contains data on worldwide advertising by media and
                category, per capita advertising expenditure, advertising expenditure as a % of GNP, print
                advertising, television advertising, and radio advertising.
           Time factor: the 1976 issue, published in 1976, has data for 1974 and one or two earlier years.
           §   En.

¶   E - Population

188   Demographic yearbook   (United Nations Statistical Office).
            Sales Section, United Nations, New York, NY 10017; or from sales agents.
            1948-   1974.   £21.84 (paper £17.68); US$42.00 (paper US$34.00).   1118p.
            Includes population figures for about 250 geographic areas of the world, including tables by age and sex,
                the population of capital cities and cities over 100,000 inhabitants, and totals from the latest
                censuses of population.   A different field of demographic statistics receives intensive treatment
                each year (1974 - mortality).
            Time factor: the 1974 edition, published in 1975, contains the latest available information for each
                country.
            §   En, Fr.

189   Population and vital statistics report   (United Nations Statistical Office).
            Sales Section, United Nations, New York, NY 10017; or from sales agents.
                    quarterly.   £1.95 or £6.50 yr; US$3.00 or US$10 yr.
            Contains data from the latest census returns and demographic statistics for all reporting countries.
            §   En.

190   Demographic handbook of Africa   (United Nations Economic Commission for Africa).
            Sales Section, United Nations, New York, NY 10017; or from sales agents.
            1971-   2nd, 1975.   not priced.   130p.
            Contains a world summary; population size, density, distribution, structure and growth; fertility and
                mortality; international migration; economically active population; population projections; and
                rates of increase of gross domestic product and of population.
            Time factor: published in 1975, the 1975 edition contains the latest data available for each country.
            §   En, Fr.

191   World population prospects   (United Nations. Department of Economic and Social Affairs).
            Sales Section, United Nations, New York, NY 10017; or from sales agents.
            1963-   2nd, 1968.   £1.76 or US$4.00.   174p.
            Assess prospects for major areas and regions for 1965 to 2000 and for individual countries for 1965
                to 1985.
            Time factor: the 1968 assessment was published in 1973, as Population Studies No.53.
            §   En.

192   La population active et sa structure.   The working population and its structure.   (P Bairoch).
            Université Libre de Bruxelles, Institut de Sociologie, Bruxelles, Belgium.
                            FrB 360.   236p.
            Issued as "Statistiques Internationales Rétrospectives. International historical statistics" Vol.1, the work
                includes statistics of the economically active population by sex and by percentages of occupation,
                and structure by branch of activity of the active population, all arranged by continent and by
                country.
            Time factor: published in 1968, the periods covered vary.
            §   En, Fr.

193   International statistical yearbook of large towns   (International Statistical Institute).
            International Statistical Institute, 428 Prinses Beatrixlaan, Voorburg, The Hague, Netherlands.
            1961-   Vol.6, 1972.   Fl 50.   488p.
            Contains statistics on population, demography, housing, transport, communications, leisure activities,
                and census results, etc.
            Time factor: the 1972 edition, published in 1976, has the latest data available to 1972.
            §   En, Fr.

¶ E, continued

194   Compendium of housing statistics   (United Nations Statistical Office).
       Sales Section, United Nations, New York, NY 10017; or from sales agents.
       1971-   2nd, 1972-74.   £10.80 or US$18.00.   312p.
       Contains information derived from national housing censuses or from national sample surveys.   Includes
           data on population growth, dwelling construction, the cost of housing, and capital formation in
           housing for 176 countries.   Issued as document ST/ESA/STAT/SER.N/2.
       Time factor: the 2nd edition was published in 1976 and contains data received by the UN during the
           period 1972 to 1974.
       §   En, Fr.

195   World housing survey   (United Nations. Department of Economic and Social Affairs).
       Sales Section, United Nations, New York, NY 10017; or from sales agents.
       1974-   1974.   £5.40 or US$9.00.   200p.
       An overview of the state of housing, building and planning within human settlements.   Includes a
           statistical annex (p.142-190).   Topics dealt with are urbanisation trends, slums and squatters
           settlements, housing conditions and housing requirements, land use and development, housing
           finance, house building industry and materials, human resources, housing and development policy.
       Time factor: the 1974 edition, published in 1976, contains statistical tables relating to a variety of
           years.
       §   En.

196   Yearbook of labour statistics   (International Labour Office).
       Bureau International du Travail, rue de Lausanne 154, CH-1211 Genève, Switzerland.
       1941-   1975.   FrS 95.   892p.
       Contains data on the total and economically active population, employment and unemployment, hours
           of work, labour productivity, wages, consumer prices, industrial accidents, and industrial disputes.
           Indices of consumer prices include general indices, food indices, fuel and light indices, clothing
           indices, and rent indices.
       Time factor: the 1975 edition, published late 1975, contains data for the ten years to 1974.
       §   En, Fr.

197   Bulletin of labour statistics   (International Labour Office).
       Bureau International du Travail, rue de Lausanne 154, CH-1211 Genève, Switzerland.
       1965-   quarterly, with 8 supplements,   FrS 15 or FrS 45 yr.
       Contains monthly or quarterly series of indices of the general level of employment and of unemployment
           in non-agricultural sectors, indices of numbers employed and total hours worked in manufacturing,
           numbers and percentages employed, average number of hours worked in non-agricultural sectors and
           in manufacturing, average earnings or wage-rates in non-agricultural sectors and in manufacturing,
           general indices and food indices of consumer prices.   In addition, the results of the ILO October
           enquiry on hourly wages of adult wage-earners in 41 occupations, monthly salaries and normal
           hours of work per week in selected occupations and on retail prices of selected consumer goods, are
           included in the second quarterly issue each year.
       Time factor: varies with each country.   Tables contain monthly, quarterly and half-yearly data for the
           last three years.
       §   En, Fr, Es.

198   Labour force projections, 1965-1985   (International Labour Office).
       Bureau International du Travail, rue de Lausanne 154, CH-1211 Genève, Switzerland.
       1st ed, 1971.   FrS 6 to FrS 10 a volume.   6 vols.
       Prepared as a joint international effort of the United Nations and specialised agencies, and designed
           to produce a co-ordinated series of comprehensive demographic and related projections.   The
           volumes are:
               I   Asia
               II   Africa
               III   Latin America
               IV   Europe, North America, Oceania and USSR
               V   World summary
               VI   Methodological supplement
       §   Vols I -V are in En, Fr, Es; Vol.VI has separate editions in those languages.

¶   F - Social

199   Report on the world social situation   (United Nations. Department of Economic and Social Affairs).
        Sales Section, United Nations, New York, NY 10017; or from sales agents.
        1952-   8th, 1974.   £5.72; US$11.00.   279p.
        Contents:
            Part 1   Regional developments (chapter 2 on Africa)
            Part 2   Sectoral developments (population; employment, wage and price trends, and social
                        security; food and agriculture; health; education; housing; women, youth, social
                        welfare, crime prevention and criminal justice, and popular participation; children
                        and adolescents; and environment)
        Tables are included in the text.
        Time factor: the 1974 edition, published in November 1975, has data for various periods to 1973.   The
            report is now to be published every 4 years.
        §   En.

i. Standard of living

200   Fachserie 17. Preise. Reihe 10: Internationaler Vergleich der Preise für die Lebenshaltung   [Prices.
            Series 10: International comparison of consumer prices]   (Statistisches Bundesamt).
        W Kohlhammer GmbH, Postfach 42 11 20, 6500 Mainz 42, Germany.
        Monthly issues DM 2.10; annual issues DM 8.
        Compares the cost of living in about 50 countries.
        Time factor: the latest figures published are often those for the month of the issue, depending on the
            subject of the tables and four earlier month's figures are included.
        §   De.

201   Prices and earnings around the globe: a comparison of purchasing power in 41 cities   (Union Bank of
            Switzerland).
        Union Bank of Switzerland, Zürich, Switzerland.
        1971-   3rd, October 1976.   not priced.   50p.
        Johannesburg is the only African city included.
        §   En, De, Es, Fr, It eds.

202   Retail price comparisons for international salary determination   (United Nations Statistical Office).
        Sales Section, United Nations, New York, NY 10017; or from sales agents.
                            £1.95 or US$3.00.   171p.
        Published as "Statistical papers, series M, no.14, rev.1", this is the UN system for equalising
            purchasing power of salaries of employees abroad.   Basically retail price comparisons as indicated
            by the price levels of a 'basket' of goods and services of the kind purchased by international
            officials, it gives the retail prices (November 1969) of foods, beverages and drinks, housing,
            transport, house furnishings, medicines and toilet articles, and cleaning and paper supplies in
            New York and capital cities throughout the world.
        Time factor: published in 1971.
        §   En.

        Note: "Retail price indexes relating to living expenditures of United Nations officials" is published in
            the United Nations' "Monthly Bulletin of statistics" in February and August each year.

203   Guide to expenses for the international businessman   (Financial Times Ltd).
        Financial Times Ltd, Bracken House, 10 Cannon Street, London EC4P 4BY, England.
        1976-   2nd, 1977.   not priced.   154p.
        A guide to short-stay and medium-stay business travel costs in the major business centres of the world,
            including prices of hotel accommodation, meals, drinks, etc; cost of communications and
            entertainment; cost of renting furnished accommodation, wages of domestic servants; and cost of
            food in shops.
        Time factor: the 2nd survey was published in January 1977.
        §   En.

¶   F.i,   continued

204   Household income and expenditure statistics: Africa, Asia, Latin America   (International Labour Office).
           Bureau International du Travail, rue de Lausanne 154, CH-1211 Genève, Switzerland.
           1950/54-   No.2, 1960-1972.   FrS 17.50.   258p.
           Contains data on the level, components and size distribution of household income and expenditure.
               The data are presented for urban and rural sectors, social and occupational groups, and households
               of different sizes.
           Time factor: the 1960-1972 report is based on the results of a survey conducted during the period 1960
               to 1972 and was published in 1974.
           §   En.

           Note: a companion volume for North America, Europe, USSR and Oceania was published in 1976
               (FrS 22.50).

ii.   Health and welfare

205   World health statistics annual   (World Health Organisation).
           World Health Organisation, CH-1211 Genève 27, Switzerland; or from sales agents.
           1939/46-   1973/76   Vol.I   £34.00 or FrS 136.   3 vols.
                       1972   II £6.40 or FrS 32.
                       1972   III £6.40 or FrS 32.
           Volume I contains data on vital statistics and causes of death, volume II on infectious diseases – cases,
               deaths, and vaccinations, and volume III on health personnel and hospital establishments.
           Time factor: the three volumes contain data for the years indicated above; Vol.II was published in
               1975 and Vols.I and III in 1976.
           §   En, Fr.

206   World health statistics report   (World Health Organisation).
           World Health Organisation, CH-1211 Genève 27, Switzerland; or from sales agents.
           1948-   monthly.   £20.00 or FrS 70 – yr; single issues are priced according to the number of pages.
           Up-dates 205 above.
           §   En, Fr.

207   The cost of social security   (International Labour Office).
           Bureau International du Travail, rue de Lausanne 154, CH-1211 Genève, Switzerland.
           1949-   8th, 1967-1971.   FrS 60.   198p.
           The results of an enquiry aimed at establishing a consolidated statement of the financial operations of
               social security schemes existing in various countries, etc.   Includes comparative tables of receipts
               and expenditures, benefits, etc.   Also national accounts data, population data, and consumer
               price indices.
           Time factor: the 8th edition has data for the years 1960 to 1971 or the latest available.
           §   En, Fr, Es.

iii.   Education and leisure

208   Statistics of students abroad   (UNESCO).
           UNESCO, 7 place de Fontenoy, 75700 Paris, France; or from sales agents.
           1962/68-   1969-1973.   £4.80; FrF 26.   345p.
           Arranged in two parts, Part 1 is an analysis of general trends, including an appendix on numbers of
               foreign students by country of study, and Part 2 contains country tables showing for each country,
               the number of students enrolled abroad by country of study.
           Time factor: the 1969-1973 issue, published in 1976, has data for the years 1969 to 1973.
           §   En, Fr.

¶ F.iii, continued

209 Higher education: international trends, 1960-1970 (UNESCO).
UNESCO, 7 place de Fontenoy, 75700 Paris, France; or from sales agents.
£2.80; FrF 26. 254p.
Analyses the main trends in the quantitative development of higher education. Includes statistical data,
by continent and country, of teachers and students by type of institution, distribution of students by
field of study, distribution of graduates by field of study, distribution of graduates by level of degree
or dipoloma, and distribution of graduates by level of degree or diploma and level of study.
Time factor: the report was published in 1975.
§ En and Fr eds.

210 Statistics of newspapers and other periodicals (UNESCO).
UNESCO, 7 place de Fontenoy, Paris 75700, France; or from sales agents.
US$1.00; £0.25; FrF 350. 70p.
Contains statistics by country and by frequency of numbers of newspapers and other periodicals.
Time factor: published in 1959, the report has data for 1956 or 1957.
§ En.

211 International statistics of city libraries (J Eyssen).
Academic Press, 111 5th Avenue, New York, NY 10003, USA.
1969- 2nd, 1974. published in International Library Review, vol.8, no.2, April 1976, p.141-149.
The results of a survey, the report includes for each town (Capetown, Johannesburg and Lagos in Africa)
number of inhabitants, book stock, periodicals, audio-visual media, loans, budget, staff, libraries
and branch libraries.
§ En.

¶ G - Finance

212 International financial statistics (International Monetary Fund).
International Monetary Fund, Washington, DC 20431, USA; or from sales agents.
1948- monthly. £1.30 or £8.50 yr; US$2.00 or US$20.00 yr.
Contains general data on par values and central rates, exchange rates, exchange transactions,
international reserves, use of Fund credit, deposit money bank's foreign assets, interest rates,
major world trade commodities, prices, changes in consumer prices, and world trade. For each
country data are given on exchange rates, international liquidity, banks, monetary survey, finance,
international transactions, interest, prices and production, government finance, national accounts,
etc.
Time factor: varies with the country, but generally the last eight quarters and the last seven months are
given up to about three months prior to the date of the issue.
§ En.

ii. Public finance

213 Yearbook of national accounts statistics (United Nations Statistical Office).
Sales Section, United Nations, New York, NY 10017; or from sales agents.
1957- 1974. £24.96 or US$48.00 for 3 vols. 3 vols.
The detailed statistical data and tables provide comparisons between the situation in the countries and
regions covered. Volumes 1 and 2 have individual country data on gross product by type of
expenditure and industrial origin, national income by distribution shares, finance and composition
of gross domestic capital formation, composition of private consumption expenditure, etc. Volume
3 has international tables, including estimates of total and per capita national income, gross
domestic product and gross national product in US $ for comparison.
Time factor: the 1974 edition, published in 1975, has data for 1960 to 1973.
§ En.

¶   G.ii,   continued

214   Balance of payments yearbook   (International Monetary Fund).
            International Monetary Fund, Washington, DC 20431, USA; or from sales agents.
            1948-   Vol.28, 1976.   £3.12 or US$20.00 yr, Binder £1.52 or US$4.50.   loose-leaf.
            Issued in monthly parts as data are received from over 100 countries.   Data include value of goods,
                services and transfers; capital (excluding reserves and related items; allocation of special drawing
                rights; and reserves and related items.
                §   En.

            Note: a "Balance of payments manual" 3rd ed, was published in 1961.

215   Banque Centrale des Etats de l'Afrique de l'Ouest   [Annual report].
            Banque Centrale des Etats de l'Afrique de l'Ouest, 29 rue du Colisée, 75008 Paris, France; and also
                in the capital towns of each of the countries covered.
            1962-   1975.   not priced.   226p.
            Contains banking and financial statistical data for Benin, Ivory Coast, Upper Volta, Niger, Senegal,
                and Togo.
            Time factor: the 1975 issue, published early 1976, has data for 1974 and some earlier years.
                §   Fr.

216   Notes d'information et statistiques   [Information and statistical notes]   (Banque Centrale des Etats de
                l'Afrique de l'Ouest).
            Banque Centrale des Etats de l'Afrique de l'Ouest, 29 rue du Colisée, 75008, Paris, France.
            1962-   monthly.   not priced.
            Each issue has several fascicules, each dealing with a particular subject, such as banks and money, the
                West African economy, economic indicators, monetary statistics, etc, for Benin, Ivory Coast,
                Upper Volta, Niger, Senegal, and Togo, and also the Union Monétaire Ouest Africaine (UMOA).
                §   Fr.

¶   H - Transport and communications

217   World transport data. Statistiques mondiales de transport   (International Road Transport Union.   Union
                Internationale des Transports Routiers).
            Union Internationale des Transport Routiers, Centre Internationale, 1202 Genève, Switzerland.
                    published in 1973.   not priced.   259p.
            Published as a recognition of 25 years of the Union's existence, the volume covers railway, sea and
                inland waterway transport as well as road transport.
            Time factor: statistics for several years are included, usually up to 1970 but this varies country by
                country.
                §   En, Fr.

i. Ships and shipping

218   Statistical tables   (Lloyds Register of Shipping).
            Lloyds Register of Shipping, 71 Fenchurch Street, London EC3M 4BS, England.
            1955-   1975.   not priced.   73p.
            Contains statistical data on ships registered at Lloyds, including country of registration, size and age,
                type, propulsion. Also numbers and tonnage of ships registered, launched and lost.
            Time factor: the 1975 edition, published late 1975, has data for several years to 1975.
                §   En.

¶   H.i,   continued

219   Annual summary of merchant ships completed in the world during...   (Lloyds Register of Shipping).
         Lloyds Register of Shipping, 71 Fenchurch Street, London EC3M 4BS, England.
         1922-   1975.   not priced.   14p.
         Also includes the annual summary of merchant ships launched in the world during the year under review.
            Data includes type of ship, gross tonnage, countries of registration, when built, and where launched.
         Time factor: the 1975 edition, published early 1976, has data for 1975 and some earlier years for some
            tables.
         §   En.

         Note: Lloyds also publish other titles, including the annual "Statistical summary of merchant ships
            totally lost, broken up, etc" and the quarterly "Merchant shipbuilding return" and "Casualty
            return".

220   Review of maritime transport   (UNCTAD).
         Sales Section, United Nations, New York, NY 10017; or from sales agents.
         1969-   1975.   £3.12 or US$8.00.   c120p.
         A review of current and long-term aspects of maritime transport.   Includes data on the development of
            seaborne trade, world seaborne trade, distribution of world tonnage, cargoes, fleets, etc.
         Time factor: the 1975 review, published in 1977, has data for 1972 to 1974 or 1975.
         §   En.

221   Analysis of world tanker tonnage   (Davies & Newman Ltd).
         Davies & Newman Ltd, Bilbao House, 36-38 New Broad Street, London EC2M 1NH, England.
         1971-   twice a year, in January and July.   not priced.
         Time factor: data are for the situation as at the date of the issue, and is published a month or two later.
         §   En.

222   Shipping statistics.   Statistik der Schiffahrt.   (Institut für Seeverkehrswirtschaft. Institute of Shipping
            Economics).
         Institut für Seeverkehrswirtschaft, Hollerallee 32, 2800 Bremen 1, Germany.
         1956-   1975.   DM 58.   320p.
         Contains facts and figures about shipping, shipbuilding, seaports and sea-borne trade.
         Time factor: the 1975 edition, published in 1975, has data for several years to 1974.
         §   De, En.

223   Shipping statistics.   Statistik der Schiffahrt.   (Institut für Seeverkehrswirtschaft.   Institute of Shipping
            Economics).
         Institut für Seeverkehrswirtschaft, Hollerallee 32, 2800 Bremen 1, Germany.
         1956-   monthly.   DM 10; DM 90 yr, plus postage.
         Contains monthly figures of shipping, shipbuilding, ports and sea trade, including data on the world
            merchant fleet, shipping and sea-borne trade, shipbuilding, and ports and sea canals.
         Time factor: each issue has data for several years and months up to one or two months prior to the date
            of the issue.
         §   De, En.

      ii. Road

224   World road statistics.   Statistiques routières mondiales.   (International Road Federation).
         International Road Federation, 1023 Washington Building, Washington DC, USA and Fédération
            Routière Internationale, 63 rue de Lausanne, Genève, Switzerland.
         1951-   1971-1975.   FrS 100.   215p.
         Contains data on road networks, production and export of motor vehicles, first registration and import
            of motor vehicles, vehicles in use, road traffic, motor fuels, road accidents, rates and basis of
            assessment of road user taxes, examples of average annual taxation, annual receipts from road user
            taxation, and road expenditure.
         Time factor: the 1971-1975 edition, published in September 1976, has data for the years 1971 to 1975.
         §   En, Fr, De.

¶ H, continued

iii. Rail

225 International railway statistics: statistics of individual railways (International Union of Railways).
Union Internationale des Chemins de Fer, 14-16 rue Jean Rey, 75015 Paris, France.
1925- 1975. not priced. 225p.
Contains data on the composition and means of the railway system, technical operating results, financial results, and miscellaneous information (fuels, electricity used, accidents, taxes, etc) for each railway.
Time factor: the 1975 issue, published in 1977, has data mainly for 1975.
§ De, En, Fr.

iv. Air

226 World air transport statistics (International Air Transport Association).
IATA, P O Box 160, 1216 Cointrin, Genève, Switzerland and 1155 Mansfield Street, Montreal 113, Quebec, Canada.
1957- 1974. not priced. 75p.
Contains data on world air transport development; IATA members summary and individual statistics; international, regional and route statistics (international, domestic and total flights, scheduled services, non-scheduled services, passengers, non-revenue flights, operating fleets, and financial results).
Time factor: the 1974 edition, published late 1975, has data for 1974 and some earlier years.
§ En.

227 Digest of statistics (International Civil Aviation Organisation).
I.C.A.O., P O Box 400, Succursale, Montreal, Quebec, Canada; Civil Aviation Authority, Greville House, 37 Gratton Road, Cheltenham, Glos, GL50 2BN, England; or other sales agents.
irregular. various prices.
Each issue of the digest is devoted to a particular topic, some titles being published regularly. Subjects covered include traffic flow, airport traffic, fleet personnel, aircraft on register, financial data, non-scheduled air transport, etc.
§ En.

228 International air charter statistics (Statistics Canada).
Publications Distribution, Statistics Canada, Ottawa K1A OT6, Canada.
1971- quarterly. $1.05; $4.20 yr.
Contains data on air charter company activities and passengers carried on air charter flights, including air charter flights to African countries.
§ En.

229 Civil aviation statistics of the world (International Civil Aviation Organisation).
I.C.A.O., P O Box 400, Succursale, Montreal, Quebec, Canada; Civil Aviation Authority, Greville House, 37 Gratton Road, Cheltenham, Glos, GL50 2BN; England; or other sales agents.
1976- 1976. US$4.75. 130p.
Contains world data on aircraft, safety, fleets, traffic, and financial data; aircraft and airline statistics by region and state; commercial air transport operations; and airports. Mainly summarised and selected data from statistics provided to ICAO by contracting states.
Time factor: the 1976 issue, published early 1977, has data for the years 1974 and 1975.
§ En, Es, Fr, Ru eds.

¶   H,   continued

v.   Telecommunications and postal services

230   Yearbook of common carrier telecommunication statistics and telecommunication statistics.   Annuaire
           statistique des télécommunications du secteur public et statistiques des télécommunications
           (Union Internationale des Télécommunications).
           Union Internationale des Télécommunications, Genève, Switzerland.
           1964/73-   1965-1974.   not priced.   349p.
           In two parts, Part 1 deals with common carrier telecommunications statistics and contains a chronological
               series of statistics from 1965-1974, arranged by country, and including data on population,
               telephone statistics, households, residential telephone stations, telephone calls, telegrams, telex
               connections, telex calls, modems, revenue, investment, maintenance and repairs, and exchange
               rates.   Part 2 deals with telephone statistics by country for the year 1974 with data on general
               telephone statistics, general telegraph statistics, and radiocommunication statistics.
           Time factor: the 1965-1974 edition was published in 1976.
           §   Fr, En, Es.

231   The world's telephones   (American Telephone and Telegraph Company).
           American Telephone and Telegraph Company, 5 World Trade Center, New York, NY 10048, USA.
           1912-   1 January 1976.   not priced.   28p.
           Contains, for the principal cities of the world, the numbers of telephones in use, numbers in each city
               as a percentage of the number in the world, number in each city as a percentage of the population,
               and the number that are automatic.
           Time factor: the 1976 edition was published in December 1976.
           §   En.

232   Statistiques des télécommunications...Telecommunications statistics   (Union Internationale des
           Télécommunications).
           Union Internationale des Télécommunications, Genève, Switzerland.
           1913-   1973.   not priced.   32p.
           Contains data on telegraph statistics (internal and international traffic, subscribers, connections, etc),
               telephone statistics (number of stations, traffic, etc), and radiotelecommunications statistics (coast
               and ship stations, amateurs, traffic).
           Time factor: the 1973 edition, published early 1975, has data for 1973.
           §   Fr, En, Es.

Central statistical office

233   Direction des Statistiques et de la Comptabilité Nationale, [Department of Statistics and National
         Accounts]
       10 rue Desfontaines,
       BP 478, Alger.
       t 78-03-23/27
       tx 52 560 02.

       The statistical office is responsible for the collection, processing, analysing and publication of all
regular statistical information, censuses and surveys, in the fields of agriculture, industry, commerce,
transport, consumption, prices, finance, employment and wages, education, population and health.
Unpublished information may be supplied, provided it is available and is not of a confidential nature.

Another important organisation collecting and publishing statistics

234   Direction des Douanes   [Department of Customs],
       12 Boulevard Mohamed Khémisti, Alger.

       The Statistical Office of the Department is responsible for the collection and publication of statistics of
imports and exports.

Libraries

       There is a library in the Department of Statistics (233 above) where statistical publications may be
consulted.

Libraries and information services abroad

       The principal publications of the Direction des Statistiques are available for reference in Algerian
embassies abroad, including:-
       United Kingdom   Algerian Embassy, 6 Hyde Park Gate, London SW7.   t 01-584 9502.
       Canada   Algerian Embassy, 435 Daly Street, Ottawa.   t 232-9453.
       USA   Algerian Embassy, 2118 Kalorama Road NW, Washington DC.   t 234 7246.

Bibliographies

       The Direction des Statistiques issues a list of its publications from time to time.

Statistical publications

¶   A - General

235   Annuaire statistique de l'Algérie   [Statistical yearbook of Algeria]   (Direction des Statistiques et de la
         Comptabilité Nationale).
       Direction des Statistiques et de la Comptabilité Nationale, BP 478, Alger.
       1926-   1974.   A Din 25.   277p.
       Main sections:
            Area and climate   Posts and telecommunications
            Population   Tourism
            Employment   Foreign trade
            Public health   Prices
            Education   Wages
            Housing   Social security and insurance
            Justice   Consumption
            Agriculture, forestry, fisheries   Public finance
            Industry   Money and credit
            Transport
       Time factor: the 1974 edition, published mid-1975, contains data for 1972 and 1973.
       §   Fr.

¶   A,   continued

236   Bulletin trimestriel de statistiques   [Quarterly bulletin of statistics]   (Direction des Statistiques et de la
          Comptabilité Nationale).
          Direction des Statistiques et de la Comptabilité Nationale, BP 478, Alger.
          1964-   not priced.
          Contains data on climate, migration, health, agriculture, fisheries, energy, industry, industrial
             production indices, transport, posts and telecommunications, internal trade, foreign trade, retail
             prices, industrial production price indices.
          Time factor: each issue has data for the quarter of the issue and earlier figures.
          §   Fr.

237   Algeria in numbers: 1962-1972   (Ministère de l'Information et de la Culture).
          Ministère de l'Information et de la Culture, Direction de la Documentation et des Publications, Alger.
          published in 1973.   not priced.   174p.
          Published to commemorate Algeria's ten years of independence.   Covers population, public finance,
             regional balance, agriculture, industry, posts and telecommunications, transport, foreign trade,
             tourism, education and training, cultural development, public health, housing, social security,
             war veterans, four-year plan, and overall estimates.
          §   En and Fr eds.

238   Tableaux de l'économie algérienne   [The Algerian economy]   (Direction des Statistiques et de la
          Comptabilité Nationale).
          Direction des Statistiques et de la Comptabilité Nationale, BP 478, Alger.
          1969-   4th, 1973.   A Din 10.   312p.
          Contains data on population, health, education, crop production, oil and petroleum, mineral
             resources, transport, foreign trade, consumer price indices, and public finance.
          Time factor: the 1973 edition, published late 1974, has data for 1972 and also for earlier years in
             some tables.
          §   Fr.

239   Quelques indicateurs économiques: Algérie: 1969-1973   [Some economic indicators: Algeria: 1969-1973]
          (Direction des Statistiques et de la Comptabilité Nationale).
          Direction des Statistiques et de la Comptabilité Nationale, BP 478, Alger.
                              not priced.   109p.
          Contains indices of industrial production, consumer prices, industrial production prices, and
             agricultural production prices.
          Time factor: published late 1974.
          §   Fr.

240   1972-1962   (Ministère de l'Information et de la Culture).
          Ministère de l'Information et de la Culture, 119 rue Didouche Mourad, Alger.
                              not priced.   174p.
          Contains data on housing, public finance, agriculture, industry, posts and communications, transport,
             foreign trade, tourism, education, cultural development, public health, social statistics, etc.
          Time factor: data are given for all or a selection of the years 1962 to 1972.   No publication date is
             given, but probably 1972.
          §   Ar.

241   Bulletin mensuel   [Monthly bulletin]   (Banque Nationale d'Algérie).
          Banque Nationale d'Algérie, 8 boulevard Che Guevara, Alger and 9 ave Marceau, 75116 Paris, France.
          1971-   not priced.
          Each issue is devoted to various economic and financial subjects and statistics and statistical tables are
             included in the text.
          §   Fr.

          Note: the Bank also produces an annual "Exercice" which includes text and a few tables on the
             economic situation, but is mainly concerned with the activities of the Bank.

¶ A, continued

242   Situation économique de l'Algerie   [Economic situation of Algeria]   (Chambre de Commerce et
           d'Industrie d'Alger).
           Chambre de Commerce et d'Industrie d'Alger, Palais Consulaire, Place des Martyrs, Alger.
           1963- 1968-69.   not priced.   209p.
           Contains information on industry, agriculture, foreign trade, internal trade, finance, and the
               infrastructure (energy, housing, health, transport, etc).   There are some statistical tables in
               the text.
           Time factor: the 1968-69 issue, published in 1970, has data for 1968/69 or 1967/68.
           §   Fr.

¶ B – Production

243   Industrie: données sur l'industrie algeriénne   [Industry: data on Algerian industry]   (Direction des
           Statistiques).
           Direction des Statistiques, BP 478, Alger.
           1953- 1969.   not priced.   4 vols.
           The results of a survey of enterprises with more than 5 employees in mining and quarrying, manufacturing,
               electricity, gas, water, and construction.   Information includes the character of enterprises, its
               establishments, employment, wages and salaries, expenditure on fixed assets, capacity of installed
               power equipment, consumption of energy and water, cost and receipts of production, value of stocks,
               and value and quantity of commodities produced and consumed.   The first two volumes have detailed
               results of the survey and the other two have analytical results.
           Time factor: the results of the 1969 survey were published in 1971-72.
           §   Fr.

i. Mines and mining

           Refer to 238 and 243.

ii. Agriculture, fisheries, forestry, etc

244   Statistique agricole: superficies et productions   [Agricultural statistics: area and production]
           (Ministère de l'Agriculture et de la Reforme Agraire).
           Ministère de l'Agriculture, 12 boulevard Colonel Amirouche, Alger.
           1967-   1976.   A Din 5 each issue.
           Statistical data on agriculture published in Spring (Series A) and in Autumn (Series B) each year.
               Issued within the overall serial title "Revue statistique agricole".
           Time factor: each issue is published very soon after the end of the season concerned.
           §   Fr.

245   Statistique agricole   [Agricultural statistics]   (Ministère de l'Agriculture et de la Réforme Agraire).
           Ministère de l'Agriculture, 12 boulevard Colonel Amirouche, Alger.
           1966-   quarterly.   A Din 15; A Din 40 yr.
           Each issue is devoted to a different subject within the field of agriculture, and annual figures are
               given in the tables in the text.   Issued within the overall serial title "Revue statistique agricole".
           §   Fr.

           Note: a general census of agriculture was taken in 1975 for which four volumes of methodology and
               summary results have been published (central, west and east regions and national results).
               Further detailed volumes are in preparation.

ALGERIA, continued

¶ B.ii, continued

246   Statistique agricole: l'agriculture algérien à travers des chiffres   [Agricultural statistics: Algerian
            agriculture in figures]   (Ministère de l'Agriculture et de la Réforme Agraire).
        Ministère de l'Agriculture, 12 boulevard Colonel Amirouche, Alger.
        1966-   1973/74.   A Din 15.   93p.
        A pocketbook with data on area, crops, foreign trade, employment, etc.   Published in the general
            series "Revue statistique agricole".
        Time factor: the 1973/74 issue, published in 1976, has data for the crop year 1973/74 and also for
            earlier years.
        §   Fr.

247   Le sucre en Algérie   [Sugar in Algeria]   (Société Nationale de Gestion et de Développement des
            Industries du Sucre).
        Société Nationale de Gestion et de Développement des Industries du Sucre, 8 rue René Tilloy, Alger.
                            not priced.   65p.
        Contains data on production, import, consumption, etc, of sugar, and also on employment.
        Time factor: published in 1973, the volume contains data from 1966 to 1972 and projections to 1975.
        §   Fr.

        Refer also to 235, 236, 237, 238, 239, 240, 242.

    iii. Industry

248   Production industrielles et indices de la production industrielle, 1969-1974   [Industrial production and
            indices of industrial production, 1969-1974]   (Direction des Statistiques).
        Direction des Statistiques, BP 478, Alger.
                            not priced.   50p.
        The production of firms with 20 or more employees in the principal industries.
        Time factor: published in 1976.
        §   Fr.

249   Indices de la production industrielle   [Indices of industrial production]   (Direction des Statistiques).
        Direction des Statistiques, BP 478, Alger.
        1969/73-   1969/74.   not priced.   28p.
        Time factor: the 1969/74 issue, published in 1975, has data for the years 1969 to 1974.
        §   Fr.

250   Les sociétés nationales à caractère industriel   [National organisations of an industrial character]
            (Direction des Statistiques).
        Direction des Statistiques, BP 478, Alger.
        1969-   two a year.   not priced.
        Includes statistical data on production, stocks, sales, labour and taxes.
        §   Fr.

        Refer also to 235, 236, 237, 239, 240, 242, 243.

    iv. Construction

251   Industrie du bâtiment et des travaux publics...données sur le bâtiment et les travaux publics...   [The
            construction industry and public works...figures...]   (Direction des Statistiques).
        Direction des Statistiques, BP 478, Alger.
                    1970.   not priced.   152p.
        Includes data on the structure of the sector, sales of products expertise, value added, and equipment
            and investments.
        Time factor: published in 1972, with data for 1970.
        §   Fr.

        Refer also to 243.

¶   B, continued

v. Energy

252   Données sur l'activité des sociétés pétrolières   [Data on the activities of petroleum companies]
            (Direction des Statistiques).
        Direction des Statistiques, BP 478, Alger.
        1969– 1971.   not priced.   35p.
        Contains data on employment, production and drilling, cost of drilling, etc.
        Time factor: the 1971 issue, published late 1972, has data for 1971.
        §   Fr.

        Refer also to 236, 238, 243.

¶   C – External trade

253   Documents statistiques sur le commerce de l'Algérie   [Statistics of the foreign trade of Algeria]
            (Direction des Douanes).
        Direction des Douanes, 12 boulevard Mohamed Khémisti, Alger.
        1967– 1974.   not priced.   376p.
        Main tables show statistics of imports and exports by commodity, subdivided by countries of origin and
            destination; imports and exports by country of origin and destination subdivided by commodity
            groups; and balance of payments.
        Time factor: the 1974 edition, published late 1975, contains data for 1974.
        §   Fr.

        Note: a quarterly bulletin of foreign trade, "Statistiques trimestrielles du commerce extérieur de
            l'Algérie: importation, exportation; résultats pays – produits" was published also between
            1968 and 1970.

254   Commerce extérieur agricole   [Foreign agricultural trade]   (Ministère de l'Agriculture et de la Réforme
            Agraire).
        Ministère de l'Agriculture, 12 boulevard Colonel Amirouche, Alger.
        1967–   irregular.   A Din 15; A Din 40 yr.
        Includes various ad hoc titles and also, each year, two volumes titled "I. Echanges par pays" and
            "II. Echanges par produits", which have statistical data on agricultural products imported and
            exported arranged by countries of origin and destination and arranged by commodities.   The
            series is a part of the general series "Revue statistique agricole".
        Time factor: the volumes showing detailed foreign trade statistics of agricultural products for 1972–1973
            were published in December 1976.
        §   Fr.

        Refer also to 235, 236, 238, 242.

¶   D – Internal distribution and service trades

255   Mercuriale des prix des principaux matériaux   [Market prices of principal materials]   (Centre National
            d'Etudes et d'Animation de l'Entreprise de Travaux).
        CNAT, 46a rue Bencheneb, Alger.
        There are separate volumes concerned with prices of materials used in particular industries:-
            Gros-oeuvre [Construction] (A Din 15)
            Electricité [Electricity] (A Din 10)
            Menuiserie [Carpentry] (A Din 5)
            Peinture – vitrerie [Painting – glazing] (A Din 5)
            Plomberie – chauffage [Plumbing – heating] (A Din 5)
        Time factor: published in 1976.
        §   Fr.

ALGERIA, continued

¶ D, continued

256 Données sur le commerce de gros privé   [Data on private wholesale trade]   (Direction des Statistiques).
Direction des Statistiques, BP 478, Alger.
1967- 1969.   not priced.   94p.
Contains data by branch of trade and by governorate.
Time factor: the 1969 issue, published in 1970, has data for 1969
§ Fr.

257 Tourisme et statistiques   [Tourism and statistics]   (Ministère du Tourisme).
Ministère du Tourisme, 42 rue Kh. Boukhalfa, Alger.
1968- 1973.   not priced.   74p.
Contains data on numbers of tourists, residents, arrivals and departures, hotels, etc.
Time factor: the 1973 issue, published in December 1974, has data for 1973.
§ Fr.

Refer also to 235, 236, 237, 240.

¶ E - Population

258 Recensement général de la population   [Census of population]   (Direction des Statistiques).
Direction des Statistiques, BP 478, Alger.
1872- 1966.
Contents include:
    Série A.   Population totale par commune, sex et âge   [Total population by commune, sex
        and age]
        Population totale par wilaya, sector urban ou rural, sex et âge   [Total population by
            governorate, urban or rural sector, sex and age]
        Résultats général pour l'ensemble...par wilaya   [General results by governorate]
        Aperçu méthodologique...   [Methodology]
        Population totale par commune, sexe et âge (0-19 ans)   [Total population by commune,
            sex and age (0-19 years)]
        Données supplémentaires sur les structures socio-économiques de la population
            [Supplementary figures on the socio-economic structure of the population]
        Données supplémentaires sur l'habitat   [Supplementary figures on housing]
        Population non-Algérien   [Non-Algerian population]
    Série B.   concerns towns and cities -
        Vol.   I   Population of towns and cities
            II   State and structure of the population of urban and semi-urban towns
            III Housing
            IV   State and structure of households and families
    Série C.   Vol.   I   State and structure of households in Algeria
            II   State and structure of families in Algeria
    Série D.   will contain district maps on population and housing (2 vols)
    Série I.   17 volumes of data for 'wilaya' or governorates, vol.1 being for Algiers and vol.17 to
            the whole of Algeria in two volumes on population and housing.
Time factor: published between 1969 and 1970.
§ Fr.

259 Projections provisoires de la population algérienne de 1970 à 1985   (Direction des Statistiques).
Direction des Statistiques, BP 478, Alger.
            not priced.   54p.
A working document published in 1972.
§ Fr.

¶   E,   continued

260   Etude statistique nationale de la population   [National statistical survey of the population]   (Direction
              des Statistique).
          Direction des Statistique, BP 478, Alger.
          The results are being published in two series.   Series 1 contains 6 volumes on methodology; series 2
              contains the results and published so far are:-
                    Vol. 1   Provisional results
                         3   Analysis of fecundity
                         4   Structure of households, sex, age, marital status, marriages, education, and economic
                             activity
                         5   Movement of population (fecundity, mortality, migration)
          Time factor: the enquiry was made from 1969 to 1971, and the results published from 1974 onwards.
          §   Fr.

261   La situation de l'emploi et des salaires...   [The situation on employment and wages]   (Direction des
              Statistiques).
          Direction des Statistiques, BP 478, Alger.
          1966-   1973.   A Din 10.   43p.
          The results of an annual enquiry on employment and wages of non-agricultural workers.   Includes data
              on the structure of employment, hours of work, and wages.
          Time factor: the 1973 issue, published in 1975, has data to April 1973.
          §   Fr.

          Refer also to 235, 236, 238.

¶   F - Social

i. Standard of living

          Refer to 235, 236, 238.

ii. Health and welfare

          Refer to 235, 236, 238, 240, 242.

iii. Education and leisure

262   Enquête sur les établissements de formation   [Enquiry on establishments of professional education]
              (Direction des Statistiques).
          Direction des Statistiques, BP 478, Alger.
                              not priced.   190p.
          Contains data on students, diplomas, lecturers, number of places.
          Time factor: the first results of the enquiry were published in November 1973 and the final results in
              December 1974.   Data relates to 1973.
          §   Fr.

263   Informations statistiques   [Statistical information]   (Ministère des Enseignements Primaire et Secondaire).
          Ministère des Enseignements Primaire et Secondaire, avenue de Pékin, Alger.
          1962/3-   1972/73.   not priced.   203p.
          Contains data on primary and secondary schools, public and private, including numbers of pupils,
              teachers, schools, etc.   Data for the whole country and each region.
          Time factor: the 1972/73 issue, published in May 1973, has data for the academic year 1972/73.
          §   Fr, Ar.

          Refer also to 235, 237, 238, 240.

¶   F,   continued

iv. Justice

Refer to 235.

¶   G - Finance

264   Statistiques financières   [Financial statistics]   (Direction des Statistiques).
Direction des Statistiques, BP 478, Alger.
1965-   1973.   A Din 15.   156p.
Contains data on state finance, the budget, local finance, social security, money credit, savings,
and insurance.
Time factor: the 1973 issue, with data for 1973, was published mid-1975.
§   Fr, Ar.

ii. Public finance

265   Comptes économiques   [Economic accounts]   (Direction de la Comptabilité Nationale et de la Prévision).
Direction de la Comptabilité Nationale, Alger.
1963-1968.   not priced.   163p.
Time factor: the volume was published in 1970.
§   Fr.

Refer also to 235, 238, 240, 264.

iv. Insurance

Refer to 264.

¶   H - Transport and communications

266   Transports   [Transport]   (Ministère d'Etat Chargé des Transports).
Revue Transports, BP 37, Alger 08.
quarterly.   A Din 50 or US$15 yr.
Mainly textual, but includes a few statistics on rail, sea, air, etc, transport.
§   Fr.

i. Ships and shipping

267   Statistiques   [Statistics]   (Port Autonome d'Alger).
Port Autonome d'Alger, Alger.
1961/64-   1969.   not priced.   138p.
Includes statistics of traffic, imports and exports through the port.
Time factor: the 1969 issue, published in 1971, has data for 1969 and some earlier years.
§   Fr.

Refer also to 235, 236, 238, 240, 266.

¶   H,   continued

ii. Road

268   Immatriculations des véhicules automobiles   [Motor vehicle registrations]   (Direction des Statistiques).
         Direction des Statistiques, BP 478, Alger.
         1971-   quarterly.   not priced.
         Time factor: each issue has cumulated figures for the year to date and is published some months later.
         §   Fr.

269   Parc automobile   [Motor vehicle registration]   (Direction des Statistiques).
         Direction des Statistiques, BP 478, Alger.
         1971-   2nd, 1973.   not priced.   62p.
         Contains data on registrations of cars, vans, lorries, tractors, motor cycles, buses, etc, by make, age, etc.
         Time factor: the 1973 issue, published early 1976, has data for the situation at 31st December 1973.
         §   Fr.

         Refer also to 235, 236, 238, 240, 266.

iii. Rail

270   Compte rendu de gestion   [Report and accounts]   (Société Nationale des Chemins de Fer Algériens).
         Société Nationale des Chemins de Fer Algériens, Alger.
         (annual).   1968.   not priced.   58p.
         Includes statistical tables on passenger and goods traffic, rolling stock, finance, etc.
         Time afctor: the 1968 report covers the year 1968.
         §   Fr.

         Refer also to 235, 236, 238, 240, 266.

iv. Air

         Refer to 235, 236, 238, 240, 266.

v. Telecommunications and postal services

         Refer to 235, 236, 237, 240.

ANGOLA

Central statistical office

271   Direcção dos Serviços de Estatística,   [Department of Statistical Services]
CP 1215, Luanda.
† 72 296.
tg ESTATISTICA.

The Department is responsible for the compilation and publication of current and base statistics, the preparation of censuses and surveys, and statistical research.   Publications have been temporarily suspended from 1973 or 1974.

Libraries

The Direcção dos Serviços de Estatística has a small library in which may be consulted Angolan statistical publications and the principal statistical publications of other countries.

Angolan statistical publications are also available for consultation in the Biblioteca Nacional de Angola [National Library of Angola] at Luanda.

Bibliographies

The Direcção dos Serviços de Estatística issues a duplicated list of its publications from time to time, and this list is also published at the end of each issue of "Boletim mensal de estatística".

Statistical publications

¶   A - General

272   Anuário estatístico   [Statistical yearbook]   (Direcção dos Serviços de Estatística).
Direcção dos Serviços de Estatística, CP 1215, Luanda.
1933-   1972.   not priced.   391p.
Main sections:

Area and climate	Production and consumption
Demography	Property
Public health and assistance	Trade (includes foreign trade,
Insurance	retail trade, prices)
Labour	Transport and communications
Education, culture, recreation, sport	Credit and money
Justice	Public finance

Time factor: the 1972 edition, published late 1973, contains data for 1972 and often runs of figures for up to 10 years.
§   Pt, Fr.

273   Angola: informações estatísticas   [Angola: statistical information]   (Direcção dos Serviços de Estatística).
Direcção dos Serviços de Estatística, CP 1215, Luanda.
1970-   1973.   not priced.   73p.
Contains data on area, climate, population, hotels, education, migration, air transport, sea transport, rail transport, motor vehicles, electricity, water, gas, mineral production, industry, fisheries, companies, commercial establishments, agriculture, foreign trade, banking, balance of payments, public finance, etc.
Time factor: the 1973 issue, published in 1974, has data for 1972 and 1973.
§   Pt.

274   Boletim mensal de estatística   [Monthly bulletin of statistics]   (Direcção dos Serviços de Estatística).
Direcção dos Serviços de Estatística, CP 1215, Luanda.
1945-   Esc 10 or Esc 120 yr.
Contains data on demography, health and assistance, production, foreign trade, internal trade, prices, companies, transport and communications, credit and money, property, finance, etc.
Time factor: each issue has data for the month of the issue, cumulative figures for the year to date, and corresponding cumulation for the previous year.   An issue is published 11 or 12 months after the month covered.
§   Pt.

¶ A, continued

275   Economic and financial survey   (Banco de Angola).
            Banco de Angola, rua da Prata 10, Lisboa 2, Portugal.
            1960-   1973.   not priced.   178p.
            The annual report of the Bank, containing data for Angola on agricultural production, stock breeding
                and animal products, fisheries, mining and quarrying industries, manufacturing industries, building,
                electricity, transport, external trade, credit and currency, prices, public finance, as well as the
                Bank's accounts and details of its activities.
            Time factor: the 1973 edition is the last to be published.
            §   En and Pt eds.

276   Boletim trimestral   [Quarterly bulletin]   (Banco de Angola).
            Banco de Angola, rua da Prata 10, Lisboa 2, Portugal.
            1958-   not priced.
            Contains data for Angola on foreign trade, agriculture and fisheries, industry, communications and
                transport, credit and money, public finance, wages and prices, etc.   Also has a 2-page supplement
                (in English) titled "Angola: economic indicators".
            Time factor: each issue has data for varying periods.   The last issue to be published was the October/
                December 1974 issue.
            §   Pt.

277   Anuárío estatístico, vol.II: Territórios ultramarinos   [Statistical yearbook, vol.II: Overseas territories]
                (Instituto Nacional de Estatística).
            Instituto Nacional de Estatística, Avenida António José de Almeida, Lisboa 1, Portugal.
            1967-   1973.   Esc 100.   264p.
            Main sections:

Area and climate	Manufacturing industry
Demography	Energy
Health	Construction
Labour	Transport and communications
Social security	Tourism
Co-operative organisations	Consumption and internal trade
Education, cultural activities,	Foreign trade
recreation, sport	Wages and prices
Justice	Money and credit
Agriculture, forestry, fisheries	Public finance
Mining industry	

            Covers Angola and other territories that were Portuguese at that time.
            Time factor: the 1973 edition has data for several years to 1971 or 1972.   Publication of volume II
                of the yearbook ceased with this edition.
            §   Pt, Fr.

278   Boletim mensal de estatística   [Monthly bulletin of statistics]   (Instituto Nacional de Estatística).
            Instituto Nacional de Estatística, Avenida António José de Almeida, Lisboa 1, Portugal.
            1929-   Esc 30 (Esc 40 abroad) or Esc 300 (Esc 400 abroad) yr.
            Included data on industrial production, construction, transport and communications, tourism, foreign
                trade, and prices for Angola until it became independent.
            §   Pt, Fr.

¶ B - Production

279   Estatísticas industriais   [Industrial statistics]   (Direcção dos Serviços de Estatística).
            Direcção dos Serviços de Estatística, CP 1215, Luanda.
            1961-   1971.   not priced.   195p.
            Contains data on the mining industry; manufacturing industry; construction and public works; electricity,
                gas, water and sanitary services; and includes data on the fixed capital, production, consumption
                of materials, etc, in those industries.
            Time factor: the 1971 issue, published in 1973, is the latest published at time of going to press.
            §   Pt.

ANGOLA, continued

¶ B, continued

i. Mines and mining

280 Estatística da actividade mineira [Statistics of activities in the mineral industry] (Direcção dos
Serviços de Geologia e Minas).
Direcção dos Serviços de Geologia e Minas, CP 1260-C, Luanda.
(annual). 1973. not priced. 77p.
Main information is concessions, but also includes statistics on labour, wages, minerals extracted,
products produced by treatment of minerals, exports, etc.
Time factor: the 1973 edition, published in 1974, has data for 1973 and is the latest issued at the time
of going to press.
§ Pt.

Refer also to 273, 275, 277, 279.

ii. Agriculture, fisheries, forestry, etc

281 Recenseamento agrícola de Angola [Agricultural census of Angola] (Missão de Inquéritos Agrícolas
de Angola).
Ministério do Ultramar, Avenida de Ilha de Madeira, Lisboa, Portugal.
1963/64. not priced. 12 vols.
§ Pt.

282 Estatísticas agrícolas correntes de Angola, 1970-1971 [Agricultural statistics of Angola, 1970-1971]
(Missão de Inquéritos Agrícolas de Angola).
Missão de Inquéritos Agrícolas de Angola, Luanda.
not priced. 117p.
The report of an enquiry into Angolan agriculture.
§ Pt.

Refer also to 273, 275, 276, 277.

iii. Industry

Refer to 272, 273, 274, 275, 276, 277, 278, 279.

iv. Construction

Refer to 275, 277, 278, 279.

v. Energy

Refer to 273, 275, 277, 279.

¶ C - External trade

283 Estatísticas do comércio externo: vol.1: comércio por mercadorias e países [Foreign trade statistics: vol.1
trade by commodities and countries] (Direcção dos Serviços de Estatística).
Direcção dos Serviços de Estatística, CP 1215, Luanda.
1956- 1972. not priced. 395p.
Contains detailed statistics of foreign trade arranged by commodities and sub-divided by countries of
origin and destination.
Time factor: the 1972 issue is the latest published, at time of going to press.
§ Pt, Fr.

¶   C,   continued

284   Estatísticas do comércio externo: vol.II: comércio por países, territórios e mercadorias   [Foreign trade
            statistics: vol.II: trade by countries, territories and commodities]   (Direcção dos Serviços de
            Estatística).
        Direcção dos Serviços de Estatística, CP 1215, Luanda.
        1956-   1971.   not priced.   477p.
        Contains detailed statistics of foreign trade arranged by countries and territories and sub-divided by
            commodities.
        Time factor: the 1971 issue, published in 1974, is the latest published, at time of going to press.
        §   Pt, Fr.

285   Estatísticas do comércio externo   [Statistics of foreign trade]   (Instituto Nacional de Estatística).
        Instituto Nacional de Estatística, Avenida António José de Almeida, Lisboa 1, Portugal.
        1843-   1967.   2 vols.
        Volume II included a section on the foreign trade of Portugal's overseas provinces, including Angola.
            Arrangement under each overseas province was by commodities.
        Time factor: the 1967 issue was the last to include this section.
        §   Pt, Fr.

        Refer also to 272, 273, 274, 275, 276, 277, 278.

¶   D - Internal distribution and service trades

        Refer to 272, 273, 274, 278.

¶   E - Population

286   Recenseamento geral de população   [Census of population]   (Direcção dos Serviços de Estatística).
        Direcção dos Serviços de Estatística, CP 1215, Luanda.
        1929-   1960.   4 volumes and annex.
        Content:
              I.   Population by ethnic groups, civil status, and ages
             II.   Population by nationality, and by nationality at birth
            III.   Population by religion, by linguistic groups, and by fertility
            IV.   Population by economic activity
        Annex.   Inventory of property and housing
        §   Pt.

        Refer also to 272, 273, 274, 277.

¶   F - Social

i. Standard of living

        Refer to 272, 274, 275, 276, 277, 278.

ii. Health and welfare

        Refer to 272, 274.

ANGOLA,   continued

¶   F,   continued

iii. Education and leisure

287   Estatística da educação   [Education statistics]   (Direcção dos Serviços de Estatística).
         Direcção dos Serviços de Estatística, CP 1215, Luanda.
         1954-   1971/2.   not priced.   121p.
         Contains data on infant, primary, secondary, higher normal, and other education; financial assistance;
             culture; recreation; sport; and numbers of scholars, teachers, schools and classes.
         Time factor: the 1971/72 issue, published in 1973, has data for the academic year 1971/72 and is the
             latest to be issued at time of going to press.
         §   Pt, Fr.

         Refer also to 272, 273.

iv. Justice

         Refer to 272.

¶   G - Finance

i. Banking

         Refer to 273, 275, 276.

ii. Public finance

288   Estatística das contribuições e impostos   [Statistics of taxation]   (Direcção dos Serviços de Estatística).
         Direcção dos Serviços de Estatística, CP 1215, Luanda.
         1951-   1968.   not priced.   155p.
         Contains data on all kinds of taxation.
         Time factor: the 1968 issue, published in 1973, has data for 1968.   This is the latest published at time
             of going to press.
         §   Pt.

         Refer also to 272, 273, 274, 275, 276.

iii. Company finance

         Refer to 272, 274.

v. Insurance

         Refer to 272.

ANGOLA,   continued

¶   H - Transport and communications

i. Ships and shipping

289   Estatística da navegação marítima   [Statistics of maritime shipping]   (Direcção dos Serviços de Estatística).
        Direcção dos Serviços de Estatística, CP 1215, Luanda.
        1950-   1973.   not priced.   86p.
        Contains data on traffic at ports - ships, cargoes, passengers.
        Time factor: the 1973 issue, published in 1974, is the latest published at time of going to press. It has
            data for 1973.
        §   Pt.

        Note: issued both as the title given above and "Navegação marítima".

        Refer also to 272, 273, 275, 276, 277, 278.

ii. Road

290   Estatística dos veículos motorizados   [Statistics of motor vehicles]   (Direcção dos Serviços de Estatística).
        Direcção dos Serviços de Estatística, CP 1215, Luanda.
        1967-   1973.   not priced.   25p.
        Contains data on the numbers of motor vehicles in circulation, number of registrations of motor vehicles,
            road accidents, and miscellaneous items, such as sales of petrol, oils, etc.
        Time factor: the 1973 issue, published in 1974, has data for 1973 and is the last to be published at time
            of going to press.
        §   Pt.

        Refer also to 272, 273, 275, 276, 277, 278.

iii. Rail

        Refer to 272, 273, 275, 276, 277, 278.

iv. Air

        Refer to 272, 273, 275, 276, 277, 278.

v. Telecommunications and postal services

291   Estatística postal   [Postal statistics]   (Direcção dos Serviços dos Correios, Telégrafos e Telefonas).
        Direcção dos Serviços dos Correios, Telégrafos e Telefonas, Luanda.
                1967.   not priced.   285p.
        Time factor: the 1967 issue, published in 1969, has data for 1967.
        §   Pt.

        Refer also to 272, 274, 276, 277, 278.

Central statistical office

292   Institut National de la Statistique et de l'Analyse Economique   [National Institute for Statistics and
          Economic Analysis],
       BP 323, Cotonou.
       † 31 40 81.

       The responsibilities of the office include the collection and publication of general statistics, and
making surveys on such subjects as agriculture, population, and family budgets, as well as special studies
on national accounts and foreign trade statistics.

Libraries

       National and international statistical publications may be consulted in the publications section of the
Institut National de la Statistique.

Libraries and information services abroad

       Copies of statistical publications of the Institut National de la Statistique are available for reference
in Benin's embassies in Paris and Bonn.

Bibliographies

       Lists of the publications of the Institut National de la Statistique are published inside the back cover
of "Annuaire statistique" and "Bulletin statistique".

Statistical publications

¶   A - General

293   Annuaire statistique du Dahomey   [Statistical yearbook of Dahomey]   (Institut National de la Statistique
          et de l'Analyse Economique).
       Institut National de la Statistique et de l'Analyse Economique, BP 323, Cotonou.
       1965-   no 4, 1973.   not priced.   307p.
       Main sections:

Area and climate	Post and telecommunications
Population	Internal trade
Public health	Foreign trade
Agriculture	Money and credit
Crops	Investment, foreign aid and
Fisheries	balance of payments
Water, forests, hunting	State budget
Mines and energy	National accounts
Activities of enterprises	Judiciary
Transport	Education

       Time factor: the 1973 edition, published in 1975, has data for several years to 1970.
       §   Fr.

294   Bulletin de statistique   [Statistical bulletin]   (Institut National de la Statistique et de l'Analyse
          Economique).
       Institut National de la Statistique et de l'Analyse Economique, BP 323, Cotonou.
       1966-   every two months.   not priced.
       Includes data on climate, justice, production, transport, foreign trade, prices, money and credit, and
          public finance.
       Time factor: latest figures are between 4 and 7 months earlier than the date of the issue, which is the
          date of publication.   Most tables include runs of several months' earlier figures, including
          comparative data for the previous year.
       §   Fr.

¶ A, continued

295   Aspects économiques   [Economic aspects]   (Direction des Affaires Economiques).
             Direction des Affaires Economiques, Ministère des Finances, des Affaires Economiques et du Plan,
                  BP 363, Cotonou.
             1962-   1972.   not priced.   81p.
             Main sections:
                  Area   Trade and co-operation
                  Agricultural production   (including foreign trade)
                  Forestry   Banking
                  Animal production   Industrial development
                  Mines and energy   Employment
                  Transport   Public finance
             Time factor: the 1972 edition, published in 1975, has data for several years to 1971.
             §   Fr.

296   Bulletin économique et statistique   [Economic and statistical bulletin]   (Direction des Affaires
                  Economiques, Ministère des Finances, des Affaires Economique et du Plan).
             Direction des Affaires Economiques, BP 363, Cotonou.
             1953-   every 2 months.   not priced.
             Contains data on climate, production (agriculture, livestock, fisheries, water, forests, hunting),
                  commerce (agricultural and foreign trade, licences to import), transport, credit, wholesale price
                  indices, etc.
             Time factor: each issue was published up to a year after the date of its issue and contents; publication
                  now lapsed.
             §   Fr.

297   Rapport d'activité   [Report]   (Banque Dahoméenne de Développement).
             Banque Dahoméenne de Développement, Cotonou.
             1970/71-   1972/73.   not priced.   42p.
             As well as statistics of the activities of the bank, the report includes data on agriculture, industry and
                  transport, foreign trade, money and credit.
             Time factor: the 1972/73 report, published in 1974, has data for 1972/73 and for earlier years.
             §   Fr.

¶   B - Production

i. Mines and mining

          Refer to 293, 295.

ii. Agriculture, fisheries, forestry

          Refer to 293, 295, 296, 297.

iii. Industry

298   Recensement des entreprises, 1965   [Census of enterprises, 1965]   (Direction de la Statistique).
             Institut National de la Statistique, BP 323, Cotonou.
                            not priced.   23p.
             Contains data on the number of enterprises in the country by type of company, nationality, activity;
                  numbers employed and wages; numbers and types of vehicles they have on the road; consumption
                  of power; consumption of raw materials; production; and sales of commercial enterprises.
             Time factor: the census was taken between July and November 1966 on activities of the enterprises in
                  1965, and the results were published in 1967.
             §   Fr.

BENIN, continued

¶   B.iii,   continued

299   Activités des entreprises   [Activities of enterprises]   (Direction de la Statistique).
        Institut National de la Statistique, BP 323, Cotonou.
        1965/66- 1967/72.   not priced.   2 vols.
        Contains data on the enterprises, finances, investment, labour and wages, trade, etc.
        Time factor: the 1967/72 issue and a supplement covering 1969/72 were published in 1974 and relate
            to 1967 and 1969 to 1972.
        §   Fr.

        Refer also to 293, 294, 295, 296, 297.

    v. Energy

        Refer to 293, 295.

¶   C - External trade

300   Statistiques du commerce extérieur: commerce spécial: importations, exportations (produits)   [Statistics of
            foreign trade]   (Institut National de la Statistique).
        Institut National de la Statistique, BP 323, Cotonou.
        1958-   monthly.   not priced.
        Contains detailed statistics of imports and exports arranged by commodities and sub-divided by countries
            of origin and destination.
        Time factor: each issue has data for the month and cumulation for the year to date, and is published
            some considerable time later.
        §   Fr.

301   Associés: commerce extérieur: République du Dahomey: annuaire 1959-1966.   Associates: foreign trade:
            Dahomey Republic: yearbook 1959-1966.   (European Communities).
        Office des Publications Officielles des Communautés Européennes, CP 1003, Luxembourg 1; or from
            sales agents.
                    £0.90 or FrB 100.   128p.
        One of a series of retrospective publications on the foreign trade of African states associated with the
            European Communities.   Main tables show imports and exports arranged by commodity and
            sub-divided by countries of origin and destination.   Values are in US $.
        Time factor: figures are given for each of the years 1959 to 1966 and the volume was published in 1969.
        §   De, En, Fr, It, Nl.

302   Cinq années du commerce extérieur du Dahomey   [Five years of foreign trade of Dahomey]   (Direction
            de la Statistique).
        Institut National de la Statistique, BP 323, Cotonou.
        1961/65- 1965/69.   not priced.   77 pages.
        Retrospective volumes intended to be followed by annual issues.   The 1965/59 issue, with data for
            those years, was published in 1971.
        §   Fr.

303   Dahomey: un an de commerce extérieur   [Dahomey: one year of foreign trade]   (Institut National de la
            Statistique, BP 323, Cotonou.
        1970-   1970.   not priced.   114p.
        Contains details of imports and exports arranged by commodity and sub-divided by countries of origin
            and destination.   Also imports and exports arranged by country or origin and destination, and
            summary tables.
        Time factor: the 1970 issue, published in 1973, has data for 1970.
        §   Fr.

        Refer also to 293, 294, 295, 296, 297.

¶   D - Internal distribution and service trades

Refer to 293, 295, 296.

¶   E - Population

304   Enquête démographique du Dahomey; résultats definitifs   [Demographic survey of Dahomey; final results]
            (Direction de la Statistique, Cotonou, and INSEE, Paris).
        Imprimerie Nationale, 2 rue Paul-Hervieu, 75732 Paris Cedex 15.
        1936-   1961.   Fr 15.   315p.
        Contains statistical data on the population of Dahomey in 1961.
        §   Fr.

305   Recensement de Cotonou, 1964   [Census of Cotonou, 1964]   (Direction de la Statistique).
            Provisional and final results were published in "Bulletin de Statistique" (294), nos. 1 & 2 of 1964.

        Refer also to 293.

¶   F - Social

i. Standard of living

306   Prix-indices des prix et coût de la vie   [Price and cost of living indexes]   (Direction de la Statistique).
            Institut National de la Statistique, BP 323, Cotonou.
            1969-   1970.   not priced.   31p.
            Contains data on a monthly basis for 1970 and also on an annual basis for 1970 and 1969.
            §   Fr.

        Refer also to 294.

ii. Health and welfare

        Refer to 293.

iii. Education and leisure

307   Statistiques scolaires   [Education statistics]   (Ministère de l'Education Nationale).
            Ministère de l'Education Nationale, BP 315, Porto-Novo.
            1965/66-   1974/75.   not priced.   108p.
            Contains data on public and private primary, secondary, normal and higher education.
            Time factor: the 1974/75 issue, published in 1976, has data for the academic year 1974/75.
            §   Fr.

        Refer also to 293.

iv. Justice

        Refer to 293, 294.

BENIN,   continued

¶   G - Finance

i. Banking

Refer to 295, 297.

ii. Public finance

308   Comptes nationaux   [National accounts]   (Direction de la Statistique).
             Institut National de la Statistique, BP 323, Cotonou.
             1964/65/66-   1972.   not priced.   c200p.
             §   Fr.

Refer also to 293, 294, 295.

iii. Company finance

Refer to 293.

iv. Investment

Refer to 293.

¶   H - Transport and communications

i. Ships and shipping

309   Statistiques du trafic   [Traffic statistics]   (Port Autonome de Cotonou).
             Port Autonome de Cotonou, Cotonou.
             1972-   1973.   not priced.   18p.
             Contains data on traffic and trade of the port of Cotonou.
             Time factor: the 1973 issue, published in 1974, has data for the years 1967 to 1973.
             §   Fr.

Refer also to 293, 294, 295, 296, 297.

ii. Road

310   Situation du parc automobile au 30 septembre...   [Motor vehicle registrations at 30th September...]
             (Ministère des Finances. Central Mécanographique).
             Ministère des Finances, Cotonou.
             (annual).   1972.   not priced.   computer print-out.
             §   Fr.

Refer also to 293, 294, 295, 296, 297.

v. Telecommunications and postal services

Refer to 293.

BOPHUTHATSWANA

An independent homeland for the Tswana-speaking people of South Africa. Statistical
data is currently included in South African statistical publications.

Central statistical office

311   Central Statistics Office,
       Private Bag 0024, Gaborone.
       t 5298; 5406 & 7; 5395.
       tg STATISTICS.

The Central Statistics Office was set up in July 1966 under the Ministry of Development Planning and is now under the Ministry of Finance and Development Planning.   The Office is responsible for (1) the collection, analysis and publication of the annual statistical abstract and the statistical bulletin, (2) compiling the national accounts report, (3) the population census, and (4) any other studies of current interest.

Libraries

The only library containing statistical publications and available to the public is the National Library at Gaborone, which is open during normal Government working hours.   The languages spoken by the staff are English and Setswana.

Bibliographies

The Central Statistics Office issues a list of its publications from time to time.

Statistical publications

¶   A - General

312   Statistical abstract   (Central Statistics Office).
       Government Printer, P O Box 87, Gaborone.
       1966-   1974.   R 2.00.   116p.
       Main sections:
           Area and climate   Agriculture, commerce and industry
           Population   Water and electricity statistics
           Education   Transport and communications
           Employment and labour   Tourism
           Health   Public finance and financial institutions
           Judicial statistics   National accounts
           External trade and price indices   Election 1974
       Time factor: the 1974 edition, published in 1975, has data for 1973 or 1972/73 generally, and some
           earlier figures in some tables.
       §   En.

313   Statistical bulletin   (Central Statistics Office).
       Government Printer, P O Box 87, Gaborone.
       June, 1976-   quarterly initially, but to be monthly in due course.   R 1.00 each issue.
       Contains data on gross domestic product, migration (tourism), foreign trade (principal commodities -
           imports and exports, direction of trade), mineral production, government revenue and expenditure,
           banking, railway transport, rainfall, cost of living index, building plans approved, electricity
           generated, Botswana recruited for South African mines.
       Time factor: each issue has data for several years and at least 12 months to various dates between three
           and six months prior to the date of the issue.
       §   En.

       Note: the bulletin replaces the "Statistical Newsletter" (315).

314   Bechuanaland: report for the year   (Information Branch of the Bechuanaland Government).
       H M Stationery Office, P O Box 569, London SE1 9NH, England.
       1965-   1965.   £0.70.   183p.
       Includes an appendix of statistical tables on finance, income tax rates, value of principal imports and
           exports, education, medical and crime statistics, and the results of a livestock census.
       Time factor: the 1965 report, published in 1966, is the last to be issued.
       §   En.

¶   A,   continued

315   Statistical newsletter   (Central Statistics Office).
          Government Printer, P O Box 87, Gaborone.
          no.1, 1972-   No.4, 1975.   R 0.30.   c25p.
          Designed to provide up to date information on a number of subjects based on recently completed studies,
              and released in advance of the annual "Statistical abstract" (312).
          Time factor: the publication ceased with the 4th issue and is replaced by the "Statistical Bulletin" (313).
          §   En.

¶   B - Production

i. Mines and mining

316   Annual report of the Geological Survey and Mines Department.
          Government Printer, P O Box 87, Gaborone.
          1967-   1973.   50 cents.   28p.
          Contains a very few statistics on mining.
          Time factor: the 1973 report was published in 1974.
          §   En.

          Refer also to 313.

ii. Agriculture, fisheries, forestry, etc.

317   Annual report   (Ministry of Agriculture, Division of Cooperative Development).
          Government Printer, P O Box 87, Gaborone.
          1964-   1974.   not priced.   54p.
          Contains comparative statistics of membership, share capital and reserves in co-operative marketing
              societies for the last three years; analysis of sales of livestock, crops and fertilisers by co-operative
              marketing societies; the combined balance sheet of co-operative marketing societies; analysis of
              cattle trade; and average prices for cattle.
          Time factor: the 1974 report, published in 1976, has data for 1974.
          §   En.

318   Agricultural survey   (Central Statistics Office).
          Government Printer, P O Box 87, Gaborone.
          1967/68-   1972/73.   not priced.   76p.
          Contains data on area planted, area harvested, holders, crops, livestock, etc.
          Time factor: the 1972/73 report, published in 1974, has data for the year 1972/73.
          §   En.

          Note: a sample design for the annual agricultural survey was published in 1972.

319   Freehold farm survey   (Central Statistics Office).
          Government Printer, P O Box 87, Gaborone.
          1969/70-   1970/71.   30 cents.   24p.
          "A counterpart of the agricultural survey" (318), it covers the distribution of farmers; crop acreage,
              production and yield; machinery and equipment in use; fertilisers used; livestock owned; numbers
              of cattle; farm labour.
          Time factor: the 1970/71 survey report was published in 1972.
          §   En.

320   Report on the Forest Administration of Botswana.
          Government Printer, P O Box 87, Gaborone.
          1940-   1967-1968.   10 cents.   22p.
          Includes statistical tables on the area planted.
          Time factor: the 1967/68 report was published in 1970.
          §   En.

          Refer also to 312, 314.

¶   B,   continued

iii. Industry

A census of production and distribution was taken in 1973/74, but the results have not been published separately.   See issues of 313 and 315 for data.

Refer also to 312 for data on industry.

iv. Construction

Refer to 313.

v. Energy

Refer to 312, 313.

¶   C - External trade

321   External trade statistics   (Department of Customs and Excise).
Central Statistics Office, Private Bag 0024, Gaborone.
1975-   1975.   not priced.   79p.
Contains tables for annual trade statistics for selected years from 1946/61 to 1962/75, monthly and average comparisons for 1974 and 1975, direction of trade for 1973 to 1975, as well as detailed statistics of imports and exports arranged by commodity for 1973 to 1975, and quarterly less detailed statistics of imports and exports arranged by commodity for 1974 and 1975.
Time factor: the 1975 issue was published late 1976.
§   En.

Refer also to 312, 313, 314.

¶   D - Internal distribution and service trades

322   Tourist statistics   (Central Statistics Office).
Government Printer, P O Box 87, Gaborone.
1974-   1976.   R 1.00.   20p.
Contains data on arrivals by reason, country, and date; money spent by visitors; departures; average length of stay; hotels and rooms, etc.
Time factor: the 1976 issue, published mid-1977, has data for 1976.
§   En.

Refer also to 312, 313.

¶   E - Population

323   Report of the population census   (Central Statistics Office).
Government Printer, P O Box 87, Gaborone.
1904-   1971.   R 3.00.   various paginations.
Time factor: the report was published in 1972.

Note: a "Report on the 1975 population census of Selebi-Pikwe" is to be published.

¶   E,   continued

324   Employment survey   (Central Statistics Office).
         Government Printer, P O Box 87, Gaborone.
         1971-   1974.   R 0.30.   14p.
         Contains data on numbers employed and monthly wage bill total, numbers employed by citizenship and
              sex, numbers employed by salary level and citizenship, numbers of establishments by location and
              economic sector, numbers of establishments by size and economic sector.
         Time factor: the 1974 report, published in 1974, has data for 1973.
         §   En.

         Note: the first report (1971) was the results of a labour census taken in 1967/68.

         Refer also to 312, 313.

¶   F - Social

i. Standard of living

325   Household expenditure survey, 1968/70   (Central Statistics Office).
         Government Printer, P O Box 87, Gaborone.
                             R 1.00.   30p.
         Time factor: the report was published in 1972 for the survey carried out between 1968 and 1970.
         §   En.

326   A social and economic survey of three peri-urban areas, 1974   (Central Statistics Office).
         Central Statistics Office, Private Bag 0024, Gaborone.
                             R 1.50.   110p.
         A survey of the main social, demographic and economic characteristics of typical families living in
              peri-urban areas of Botswana.   Includes data on population characteristics, economic and social
              characteristics, health and fertility, and household incomes.
         Time factor: the report of the survey was published in 1975.
         §   En.

327   1974/75 rural income distribution survey   (Central Statistics Office).
         Central Statistics Office, Private Bag 0024, Gaborone.
                             R 6.00.   311p.
         A survey in rural areas of Botswana to measure the statistical distribution of annual incomes among
              households in rural areas.   Includes data on the main sources of income, income distribution,
              income profiles, household consumption, and distribution of cattle among cattle owning households.
         Time factor: the results of the survey were published in 1976.
         §   En.

         Refer also to 313.

ii. Health and welfare

328   Medical statistics   (Central Statistics Office).
         Central Statistics Office, Private Bag 0024, Gaborone.
         1974-   1974.   R 1.00.
         Time factor: the 1974 issue, published in 1975, has data for 1974.
         §   En.

         Refer also to 312, 314.

¶   F,   continued

iii.   Education and leisure

329   Education statistics   (Educational Statistics Division of the Ministry of Education <u>and</u> Central Statistics
              Office).
              Government Printer, P O Box 87, Gaborone.
              1968-   1975.   R 1.00.   80p.
              Part I has data on schools, pupils, and teachers; part II on examinations, finance and miscellaneous
                  information.
              Time factor: the 1975 issue, published in 1975, has data for Part I for 1975 and for Part II for 1974.
              §   En.

              Note: earlier statistics were published in the "Report of the Education Department" from 1961.

              Refer also to 312, 314.

iv.   Justice

330   Annual report   (Prison Department).
              Government Printer, P O Box 87, Gaborone.
              1966-   1973.   R 1.00.   18p.
              Includes statistical data on commitals, length of sentences, previous convictions, daily average number
                  in prisons by sex, etc.
              Time factor: the 1973 edition has data for 1973.
              §   En.

              Refer also to 312, 314.

¶   G - Finance

i.   Banking

331   Annual report   (Bank of Botswana).
              Bank of Botswana, P O Box 712, Gaborone.
              1975-   1976.   not priced.   52p.
              Includes a statistical appendix on banking; there are also statistics and statistical tables in the text of
                  the report on economic indicators, etc.
              Time factor: the 1976 report, published in 1977, has data for 1976.
              §   En.

              Refer also to 313.

ii.   Public finance

332   National accounts of Botswana   (Central Statistics Office).
              Government Printer, P O Box 87, Gaborone.
              1964/66-   1973/74.   not priced.   no pagination.
              Time factor: the 1973/74 accounts were published late 1976.
              §   En.

333   Botswana national accounts and selected indicators, 1966-1976   (Central Statistics Office).
              Government Printer, P O Box 87, Gaborone.
                                        not priced.   38p.
              A special issue for the 10th anniversary of Botswana, brings together the revised national accounts for
                  1965 to 1973/74 and other selected indicators spanning the period.
              Time factor: published in 1976.
              §   En.

              Refer also to 312, 314.

¶   H - Transport and communications

Refer to 312.

BURUNDI

Central statistical office

334   Département des Etudes et Statistiques   [Department of Research and Statistics]
B P 1156, Bujumbura.

The Department, which is attached to the Ministry of Planning, is responsible for the collection, analysis and publication of economic and social statistics of Burundi.

Statistical publications

¶   A - General

335   Annuaire statistique   [Statistical yearbook]   (Département des Etudes et Statistiques).
Département des Etudes et Statistiques, B P 1156, Bujumbura.
1962-   1975.   FrB 150.00.   90p.
Main sections:

Population	Education
Production	Health
Energy	Labour
Transport	Public finance
Foreign trade	Money and credit
Prices	

Time factor: the 1975 edition, published in 1977 as a supplement to the "Bulletin trimestriel" (336), covers the years 1972 to 1975.
§   Fr.

336   Bulletin trimestriel   [Quarterly bulletin]   (Département des Etudes et Statistiques).
Département des Etudes et Statistiques, B P 1156, Bujumbura.
1966-   FrB 120 each issue; supplements FrB 150 each.
Contains statistical data on production, energy, transport, foreign trade, prices, and finance.
Time factor: each issue has data to about three months prior to the date of publication.
§   Fr.

Note: in the earlier years of the publication supplements were also issued on the results of censuses, vehicle registration statistics, etc; more recently the only supplement is the statistical yearbook (335).

337   Bulletin trimestriel   [Quarterly bulletin]   (Banque de la République du Burundi).
Banque de la République du Burundi, B P 705, Bujumbura.
1964-   250 F Burundi or 1,000 F Burundi yr (in African countries FrB 750 or US$19;
        Europe FrB 800 or US$20; other FrB 900 or US$23).
Includes statistics and graphs on money and credit, public finance, foreign trade, transport, prices (indices), and the coffee economy.
Time factor: each issue has long runs of figures to the latest available.
§   Fr.

Note: the Bank also issues "Rapport annuel", an annual report on the activities of the Bank and a review of economic development in the course of the year under review.

¶   B - Production

338   Recensement des entreprises de Bujumbura (Sept-Oct 1967)   [Census of enterprises in Bujumbura, Sept-Oct 1967)]   (Département de Statistique).
Département des Etudes et Statistiques, B P 1156, Bujumbura.
        Burundi Fr 80.
Contains data on the number of establishments, employees, size, turnover and other financial statistics.
Time factor: the report was published in 1968 as a supplement to "Bulletin de statistique", now titled "Bulletin trimestriel" (336).
§   Fr.

Refer also to 335, 336.

¶ C - External trade

Refer to 335, 336, 337.

¶ E - Population

Censuses of the non-indigenous population were taken in 1952 and 1958. The results of the 1958 census are published in "Bulletin mensuel des statistiques générales du Congo Belge et du Ruanda-Urundi", série spéciale no.1, published in 1969.

339 Enquête démographique Burundi, 1970/71: méthodologie - résultats provisoires [Demographic enquiry of Burundi, 1970/71: methodology - provisional results] (Département des Etudes et Statistiques). Département des Etudes et Statistiques, B P 1156, Bujumbura.
not priced. 70p.
Time factor: published in January 1972.
§ Fr.

Refer also to 335.

¶ F - Social

ii. Health and welfare

Refer to 335.

iii. Education and leisure

Refer to 335.

¶ G - Finance

Refer to 335, 336, 337.

ii. Public finance

340 Comptes économiques du Burundi [Economic accounts of Burundi] (Ministère des Affaires Etrangères et de la Co-opération).
Ministère des Affaires Etrangères et de la Co-opération, Bujumbura.
1970- 1970. not priced. 165p.
Time factor: the 1970 issue, published in 1975, has data for 1970.
§ Fr.

¶ H - Transport and communications

Refer to 335, 336, 337.

CAMEROON - CAMEROUN - KAMERUN

Central statistical office

341   Direction de la Statistique et de la Comptabilité Nationale   [Department of Statistics and National
            Accounts],
        BP 660, Yaoundé.

        The Department was recognised in 1967 and now has five central and three regional services.   The
        central services deal with economic and financial statistics, particularly the study of foreign trade,
        financial and monetary statistics; statistics of production, prices and transport; surveys and social statistics;
        national accounts; and economic synthesis.   The regional services are at Douala, Buéa and Garoua.

Bibliographies

        The Direction de la Statistique issues a list of its publications from time to time.

Statistical publications

¶   A - General

342   Bulletin mensuel de statistique   [Monthly bulletin of statistics]   (Direction de la Statistique et de la
            Comptabilité Nationale).
        Direction de la Statistique, B P 660, Yaoundé.
        1968-   CFA Fr 250; CFA Fr 3,000 yr (CFA Fr 4,500 yr abroad).
        Includes statistical data on agricultural production, prices, foreign trade, finance and money.
        Time factor: each issue contains data for that month and some retrospective figures, and is published
            about three months later.
        §   Fr.

343   Note trimestrielle de statistique   [Quarterly note on statistics]   (Direction de la Statistique).
        Direction de la Statistique, B P 660, Yaoundé.
        1964-   CFA Fr 600 or CFA Fr 2,000 (CFA Fr 3,000 abroad) yr.
        Contains statistical data on foreign trade, production, transport, prices, money and credit, public
            finance, etc.
        Time factor: each issue is published about six months after the date of the issue and contains data for
            varying periods up to the date of the issue, with corresponding figures for the previous year.
        §   Fr.

344   Note annuelle de statistique   [Annual note on statistics]   (Direction de la Statistique).
        Direction de la Statistique, B P 660, Yaoundé.
        1964-   1976.   CFA Fr 3,000.
        Contains similar information to 343 above.
        Time factor: the 1976 issue, published in 1976, has data for 1975 and some earlier years.
        §   Fr.

345   Rapport annuel   [Annual report]   (Chambre de Commerce, d'Industrie et des Mines du Cameroun).
        Chambre de Commerce, d'Industrie et des Mines du Cameroun, B P 4011, Douala.
        1968-   1975.   not priced.
        Statistics and statistical tables are included in the text, which covers public finance, agricultural
            production, forestry, industry, public works and construction, energy, businesses, transport,
            general trade and foreign trade.
        Time factor: the 1975 report, published in 1976, has data for 1974 and 1975.
        §   Fr.

        Note: also published is a monthly bulletin, "Bulletin mensuel".

CAMEROON, continued

¶   A,   continued

346   Rapport sur la situation économique de la République Unie du Cameroun   [Report on the economic
            situation in the United Republic of Cameroun]   (Direction de la Planification; Ministère de
            l'Economie et du Plan).
        Ministère de l'Economie et du Plan, Yaoundé.
        1962-   1973-1974.   not priced.   363p.
        Contains data on population, education, health, agriculture, industry, communications, transport,
            tourism, postal and telegraph services, finance and money, and economic growth.   Tables are
            included in the text.
        Time factor: the 1973-1974 issue, published in October 1975, has data for 1973 and 1974.
        §   Fr.

347   Etudes et enquêtes statistiques   [Statistical studies and surveys]   (Direction de la Statistique).
        Direction de la Statistique, B P 660, Yaoundé.
        1974-   irregular.   not priced.
        Each issue is devoted to a particular subject.   For example, no.4 deals with prices in the
            central-south province and no.5 with employment.
        §   Fr.

348   L'économie camerounaise   [The economy of Cameroun]   (EDIAFRIC).
        EDIAFRIC, 57 avenue d'Iéna, 75783 Paris Cedex 16, France.
        1971-   2nd ed, 1977.   FrF 354.   various paginations.
        Contains information, including statistics and statistical tables, on agriculture, forestry, livestock,
            fisheries, industry, mines, energy, public works, transport, tourism, finance, foreign trade, etc.
        §   Fr.

¶   B - Production

i. Mines and mining

349   Activités minières au Cameroun]..   [Mining activities in the Cameroons]   (Direction des Mines et de la
            Géologie).
        Direction des Mines et de la Géologie, Yaoundé.
        1961-   1975.   not priced.   20p.
        Includes statistical data in the text on production, activities of concessionaries, research, and
            explosives, etc.
        Time factor: the 1975 report, published in 1976, has data for 1975.
        §   Fr.

        Refer also to 348.

ii. Agriculture, fisheries, forestry, etc.

350   Annuaire de statistiques agricoles.   Yearbook of agricultural statistics.   (Ministère de l'Agriculture).
        Ministère de l'Agriculture, Yaoundé.
        1963/64-   1971-1972.   not priced.   64p.
        §   Fr.

        Refer also to 342, 343, 344, 345, 346.

¶   B,   continued

iii. Industry

351   Activités des entreprises du secteur moderne (primaire et secondaire): résultats des recensements industriels
          et commerciaux   [Activities of enterprises in the modern sector (primary and secondary): results of
          industrial and commercial censuses]   (Direction de la Statistique).
          Direction de la Statistique, B P 660, Yaoundé.
          1962/63-   1968/69, 1969/70, 1970/71 and 1971/72.   not priced.   214p.
          The results of industrial and commercial censuses taken in the four years.   Data include financial,
          investment, employment, production, etc.
          §   Fr.

          Refer also to 343, 344, 345, 346.

iv. Construction

          Refer to 345.

v. Energy

          Refer to 345.

¶   C - External trade

352   Commerce extérieur du Cameroun Uni   [Foreign trade of the United Republic of Cameroun]   (Direction
          de la Statistique).
          Direction de la Statistique, B P 660, Yaoundé.
          1968-   1974.   CFA Fr 10,000.
          Main tables show imports and exports arranged by commodities and sub-divided by countries of origin
          and destination.
          Time factor: the 1974 issue, published in 1976, has data for 1974.
          §   Fr.

          Note: from 1946 to 1967 there were separate titles for the East and West Camerouns, but a composite
          volume has been produced (see 353).

353   Statistique du commerce extérieur du Cameroun entre 1950 et 1965   [Foreign trade statistics of Cameroon
          between 1950 and 1965]   (Ministère des Affaires du Plan).
          Ministère des Affaires du Plan, B P 675, Yaoundé.
                              not priced.   53p.
          The statistical data is arranged by commodity.
          §   Fr.

          Refer also to 342, 343, 344, 345.

¶   D - Internal distribution and service trades

          Refer to 345, 346.

CAMEROON, continued

¶ E - Population

354   La population du Cameroun Occidental: résultats de l'enquête démographique de 1964   [Population of the
            Western Cameroons: results of the demographic survey of 1964]   (Institut National de la
            Statistique et des Etudes Economiques).
        INSEE, 18 boulevard Adolphe Pinard, 75675 Paris Cedex 14, France.
                        not priced.   3 vols.
        Contents:
            Vol. 1   Structure of the population, socio-economic data, households and housing, and
                    demography
            Vol. 2   Annexes to Vol.1, and methodology and techniques
            Notes of synthesis.
        Time factor: the results were published in 1969.
        §   Fr.

355   Enquête démographique sur la ville de Yaoundé...résultats principaux   [Demographic survey of the town
            of Yaoundé...principal results]   (Direction de la Statistique).
        Direction de la Statistique, B P 660, Yaoundé.
        1957-   2nd, 1969.   CFA Fr 2,000.   116p.
        Time factor: the results of the 1969 survey were published in 1970.
        §   Fr.

        Note: a general census of population and housing was taken in 1976 and the results are to be published
            by Direction de la Statistique.

356   Evaluations et projections démographiques,1970   [Demographic evaluations and projections]   (Direction
            de la Statistique).
        Direction de la Statistique, B P 660, Yaoundé.
                    CFA Fr 2,000.
        Time factor: published in 1970.
        §   Fr.

        Refer also to 346.

¶ F - Social

i. Standard of living

357   Enquête sur le niveau de vie à Yaoundé, 1964-1966   [Survey of the standard of living at Yaoundé]
            (Direction de la Statistique).
        Direction de la Statistique, B P 660, Yaoundé.
                    not priced.   4 vols.
        Fascicule 1 has general comments and demographic results; Fascicule II has data on household budgets
            of Camerounais; and Fascicule III has complementary data on the standard of living of households.
            The fourth volume is "Note de synthèse".
        Time factor: published in 1967.
        §   Fr.

358   Le niveau de vie des populations de la Zone Cacaoyère du Centre Cameroun: résultats definitifs...1964/65
            [The standard of living of the population of Cacaoyère Zone of Central Cameroon; final results...
            1964/65]   (Société d'Etudes pour le Développement Economique et Social).
        Société d'Etudes pour le Développement Economique et Social, 67 rue de Lille, 75007 Paris, France.
                    not priced.   144p.
        Time factor: published in 1966.
        §   Fr.

¶ . F. i, continued

359   Le niveau de vie des populations de l'Adamaoua: résultats...1963-1964...   [The standard of living of the
           populations of the Adamaoua: results...1963-1964]   (INSEE).
        INSEE, 18 boulevard Adolphe Pinard, 75675 Paris Cedex 14, France.
                        not priced.   199p.
        Time factor: published in 1967.
        §   Fr.

ii. Health and welfare

        Refer to 346.

iii. Education and leisure

360   Annuaire statistique   [Statistical yearbook]   (Ministère de l'Education).
        Ministère de l'Education, Yaoundé.
        1967/68-   1973/74.   not priced.   2 vols.
        Contains data on primary, secondary, higher, vocational, etc, education, including enrolments,
            schools, classes, teachers, finances.
        Time factor: the 1973/74 edition, published late 1974, has data for the academic year 1973/74.
        §   Fr.

        Refer also to 346.

¶   G - Finance

        Refer to 342, 343, 344, 346.

ii. Public finance

361   Comptes nationaux du Cameroun   [National accounts of Cameroun]   (Direction de la Statistique).
        Direction de la Statistique, B P 660, Yaoundé.
        1964/65-   1971/71.   CFA Fr 3,000.
        Time factor: the 1971/72 issue, published in 1973, has data for the financial year 1971/72.
        §   Fr.

        Refer also to 343, 344.

¶   H - Transport and communications

i. Ships and shipping

362   Rapport annuel   [Annual report]   (Office National des Ports du Cameroun).
        Office National des Ports du Cameroun, Yaoundé.
                1974.   not priced.
        Contains data on traffic at ports and financial information.
        Time factor: the 1974 report, published in 1975, has data for 1974.
        §   Fr.

        Refer also to 343, 344, 345, 346.

¶   H,   continued

ii. Road

363   Parc des véhicules nouvellement immatriculés   [New vehicle registrations]   (Direction de la Statistique).
        Direction de la Statistique, B P 660, Yaoundé.
        (annual).   1970.   not priced.
        §   Fr.

        Refer also to 343, 344, 345, 346.

iii. Rail

364   Statistiques   [Statistics]   (Régie Nationale des Chemins de Fer du Cameroun).
        Régie Nationale des Chemins de Fer du Cameroun, B P 304, Douala.
        1965/66-   1975/76.   not priced.   no pagination.
        Part 1 contains the report; part 2 statistics of installations, lines, rails, personnel, traffic (passengers,
            goods), services, receipts, and accidents; and part 3 has graphs and charts.
        Time factor: the 1975/76 issue, published in 1976, has data for the year 1975/76.
        §   Fr.

365   Bulletin trimestriel   [Quarterly bulletin]   (Régie Nationale des Chemins de Fer du Cameroun).
        Régie Nationale des Chemins de Fer du Cameroun, B P 304, Douala.
        1968-   not priced.
        Includes some statistics on traffic, rolling stock, etc.
        §   Fr.

        Refer also to 343, 344, 345, 346.

Central statistical office

366   Serviço Nacional de Estatística   [National Statistical Office],
         C P 116, Praia, Cabo Verde.

         The Office compiles and issues a quarterly bulletin of general statistics.

Statistical publications

¶   A - General

367   Boletim trimestral de estatística   [Quarterly bulletin of statistics]   (Serviço Nacional de Estatística).
         Serviço Nacional de Estatística, C P 116, Praia, Cabo Verde.
         1949- $35.00. each issue.
         Contains data on demography, production and consumption, foreign trade, retail prices and price
             index, communications, credit and money, public finance, and miscellaneous items (i.e.
             radiodiffusion).
         Time factor: each issue has cumulated figures for the year to date and for the corresponding period for
             the previous year, and is published some months later.
         §   Pt.

         Note: a statistical yearbook, "Anuarío estatístico", was published from 1933 to 1952.

368   Anuarío estatístico: vol.II: Territórios ultramarinos   [Statistical yearbook, vol.II: Overseas territories]
             (Instituto Nacional de Estatística).
         Instituto Nacional de Estatística, Avenida António José de Almeida, Lisboa 1, Portugal.
         1967-   1973.   Esc 100.   264p.
         Main sections:-
             Area and climate   Manufacturing industry
             Demography   Energy
             Health   Construction
             Labour   Transport and communications
             Social security   Tourism
             Co-operative organisations   Consumption and internal trade
             Education, cultural activities,   Foreign trade
                         recreation, sport   Wages and prices
             Justice   Money and credit
             Agriculture, forestry, fisheries   Public finance
             Mining industry
         Covers Cape Verde Islands and other territories that were Portuguese at the time.
         Time factor: the 1973 edition has data for several years to 1971 or 1972.   Publication of volume II
             of the yearbook ceased with this edition.
         §   Pt, Fr.

369   Boletim mensal de estatística   [Monthly bulletin of statistics]   (Instituto Nacional de Estatística).
         Instituto Nacional de Estatística, Avenida António José de Almeida, Lisboa 1, Portugal.
         1929-   Esc 30 (Esc 40 abroad) or Esc 300 (Esc 400 abroad) yr.
         Included data on industrial production, construction, transport and communications, tourism, foreign
             trade, and prices for the Cape Verde Islands until they became independent in July 1975.
         §   Pt, Fr.

¶   B - Production

ii,   Agriculture, fisheries, forestry, etc.

370   Recenseamento agrícola de Cabo Verde   [Agricultural census of Cape Verde Islands]   (Ministério do
             Ultramar).
         Ministério do Ultramar, Avenida da Ilha da Madeira, Restélo, Lisboa, Portugal.
         1961/63.   not priced.   no pagination.
         Detailed results of the census of agriculture taken in 1961/63.
         §   Pt.

¶ B.ii, continued

371 Provincia de Cabo Verde: estatística agrícola corrente, 1973 [Province of Cape Verde: current
agricultural statistics, 1973] (Ministerio da Coordenação Interterritorial; Missão de Inquerito
Agrícola de Cabo Verde, Guíné e S.Tomé e Principe).
Ministerio da Coordenação Interterritorial, Lisboa, Portugal.
not priced. 15p.
Contains data on area of cultivation and production of crops.
Time factor: published in 1975.
§ Pt.

Refer also to 368.

iii. Industry

Refer to 367, 368, 369.

iv. Construction

Refer to 368, 369.

¶ C - External trade

372 Estatísticas do comércio externo [Statistics of foreign trade] (Repartição Provincial dos Serviços).
Instituto Nacional de Estatística, Delegação de Cabo Verde, Lisboa, Portugal.
1949- 1968. not priced. 278p.
Main tables show imports and exports arranged by commodities and sub-divided by countries of origin
and destination.
Time factor: the 1968 issue, published in 1974, has data for 1968.
§ Pt.

373 Estatísticas do comércio externo [Statistics of foreign trade] (Instituto Nacional de Estatística).
Instituto Nacional de Estatística, Avenida António José de Almeida, Lisboa 1, Portugal.
1843- 1967. 2 vols.
Volume II included a section on the foreign trade of Portugal's overseas provinces, including Cape
Verde. Arrangement under each overseas province was by commodities.
Time factor: the 1967 issue was the last to include this section.
§ Pt, Fr.

Refer also to 367, 368, 369.

¶ D - Internal distribution and service trades

Refer to 368 and 369 for tourism.

¶ E - Population

374 Recenseamento geral da população [Census of population] (Serviços de Administração Civil;
Secção de Estatística).
Comissão para os Inqueritos Agricolas no Ultramar, Lisboa, Portugal.
1920- 1960. not priced. 219p.
Time factor: the report of the 1960 census was published in 1975.
§ Pt.

Refer also to 367, 368, 369.

¶ G - Finance

Refer to 367.

ii. Public finance

75 Contas da gerência e do exercício... [National accounts...] (Repartição Provincial dos Serviços de Fazenda e Contabilidade).
Repartição Provincial dos Serviços de Fazenda e Contabilidade, Praia, Cabo Verde.
1950- 1970. not priced. 142p.
Time factor: the 1970 issue, published in 1971, has data for 1970.
§ Pt.

Refer also to 367.

¶ H - Transport and communications

Refer to 368, 369.

v. Telecommunications and postal services

Refer to 367, 368, 369.

CENTRAL AFRICAN REPUBLIC - REPUBLIQUE CENTRAFRICAINE - ZENTRALAFRIKANISCHE REPUBLIK -
UBANGI-SHARI

Central statistical office

376   Direction de la Statistique Générale et des Etudes Economiques   [Department of General Statistics
              and Economic Studies],
           B P 679, Bangui.

           The Department is responsible for the collection, analysis and publication of economic and social
           statistics of the country.

Another important organisation collecting and publishing statistics

377   Union Douanière et Economique de l'Afrique Centrale   [Customs and Economic Union of Central Africa],
           B P 1418, Bangui.

           The Statistical Department of the organisation is responsible for collecting, analysing and publishing
           economic statistics, particularly foreign trade statistics, for the member countries, of which the Central
           African Republic is one.   Machine tabulations of foreign trade statistics can be supplied.

Statistical publications

¶   A - General

378   Annuaire statistique   [Statistical yearbook]   (Direction de la Statistique Générale et des Etudes
              Economiques).
           Direction de la Statistique Générale et des Etudes Economiques, B P 679, Bangui.
           1962-   2nd, 1970.   not priced.   205p.
           Main sections:
              Area and climate   Transport
              Population   Prices (and price indices)
              Agriculture, forestry, fisheries   Finance
              Industry   National accounts
           Time factor: the 1970 edition, published in 1975, has data for the years 1963 to 1970.
           §   Fr.

379   Bulletin mensuel de statistique   [Monthly bulletin of statistics]   (Direction de la Statistique Générale
              et des Etudes Economiques).
           Direction de la Statistique Générale et des Etudes Economiques, B P 679, Bangui.
           1952-   CFA Fr 300 or CFA Fr 2,000 yr (CFA Fr 4,000 yr abroad).
           Contains data on climate, foreign trade, internal trade, production, transport, prices, money and
              credit, public finance, and demography.
           Time factor: each issue is published about six months later and contains the most recent information
              available at time of publication.
           §   Fr.

380   Bulletin des statistiques générales   [General statistical bulletin]   (Union Douanière et Economique de
              l'Afrique Centrale).
           Union Douanière et Economique de l'Afrique Centrale, B P 1418, Bangui.
           1947-   quarterly.   CFA Fr 2,000 yr (CFA Fr 2,800 yr in other UDEAC countries;
                                              CFA Fr 3,000 to 4,500 elsewhere).
           Contains data for each of the UDEAC countries on climate, production, transport, foreign trade,
              intercommunity trade, prices, credit and money.
           Time factor: each issue has statistics for two years and several quarters to the date of the issue, and is
              published several months later.
           §   Fr.

381   Etudes statistiques   [Statistical studies]   (Union Douanière et Economique de l'Afrique Centrale).
           Union Douanière et Economique de l'Afrique Centrale, B P 1418, Bangui.
           1967-   quarterly.   not priced.
           Each issue is devoted to a separate subject.
           §   Fr.

¶   B - Production

ii. Agriculture, fisheries, forestry, etc.

382   Enquête agricole en République Centrafricaine, 1960-1961: résultats définitifs   [Agricultural survey of the
               Central African Republic: 1960-1961: final results]   (Institut Nationale de la Statistique et des
               Etudes Economiques, Paris).
          Imprimerie Nationale, 2 rue Paul-Hervieu, 75732 Paris Cedex 15, France.
                              not priced.   269p.
          A detailed inventory of Ubangi agriculture in the western and central regions of the Republic.
          Time factor: published in 1965.
          §   Fr.

          Refer also to 378, 379, 380.

iii. Industry

383   Recensement des entreprises du secteur moderne   [Census of business]   (Direction de la Statistique
               Générales et des Etudes Economiques).
          Direction de la Statistique et des Etudes Economiques, B P 679, Bangui.
          1966-   1971.   not priced.   c100p.
          Includes data on all types of enterprises; employment, wages and salaries, inventories, purchases,
               production, finance, etc.
          Time factor: the report of the 1971 census was published in 1973.
          §   Fr.

          Refer also to 378, 379, 380.

¶   C - External trade

384   Commerce extérieur   [Foreign trade]   (Union Douanière et Economique de l'Afrique Centrale).
          Union Douanière et Economique de l'Afrique Centrale, B P 1418, Bangui.
          1960-   1973.   not priced.   75p.
          Main tables show detailed trade arranged by commodities, for each of the four member countries of
               UDEAC.   Issues for 1972 and 1973 were condensed versions.
          Time factor: the 1973 edition, published in 1975, has data for 1973.
          §   Fr.

385   Le commerce extérieur de la République Centrafricaine   [Foreign trade of the Central African Republic]
               (Direction de la Statistique Générale et des Etudes Economiques).
          Direction de la Statistique Générale et des Etudes Economiques, B P 679, Bangui.
          1963/70-   1963-1970.   not priced.   129p.
          Contains summarised data on trade with UDEAC, and trade with other countries.
          Time factor: the 1963-1970 issue, published in 1972, has data for the years 1963 to 1970.
          §   Fr.

386   Associés: commerce extérieur: République Centrafricaine: annuaire 1959-1966.   Associates: foreign trade:
               Central African Republic: yearbook 1959-1966.   (European Communities).
          Office des Publications Officielles des Communautés Européennes, C P 1003, Luxembourg 1; or from
               sales agents.
                              £0.90 or FrB 100.   112p.
          One of a series of retrospective publications on the foreign trade of African states associated with the
               European Communities.   Main tables show imports and exports arranged by commodity and sub-
               divided by countries of origin and destination.   Values are in US $.
          Time factor: published early 1969.
          §   De, En, Fr, It, Nl.

          Refer also to 379, 380.

¶   D - Internal distribution and service trades

Refer to 379.

¶   E - Population

387   Enquête démographique en République Centrafricaine, 1959-1960: résultats définitifs   [Demographic
       survey of the Central African Republic, 1959-1960: final results]   (Service de la Statistique,
       Bangui, and INSEE, Paris).
       Imprimerie Nationale, 2 rue Paul-Hervieu, 75732 Paris Cedex 15.
                    Fr 20.   262p.
       Contains statistics of the population by sex, ethnic groups, place of birth, matrimonial state, religion,
       occupation, degree of education, and households.
       §   Fr.

Refer also to 378, 379.

¶   G - Finance

Refer to 378, 379, 380.

¶   H - Transport and communications

Refer to 378, 379, 380.

Central statistical office

388   Direction de la Statistique et des Etudes Economiques   [Department of Statistics and Economic Research],
B P 453, Fort-Lamy.

The Department is responsible for the collection, analysis and publication of economic statistics,
including economic indicators, national accounts, foreign trade statistics, and censuses.

Another important organisation collecting and publishing statistics

389   Union Douanière et Economique de l'Afrique Centrale   [Customs and Economic Union of Central Africa],
B P 1418, Bangui,
Central African Republic.

The Statistical Department of the organisation is responsible for collecting, analysing and publishing
economic statistics, particularly foreign trade statistics, for the member countries, of which Chad is one.
Machine tabulations of foreign trade statistics can be supplied.

Statistical publications

¶   A - General

390   Annuaire statistique   [Statistical yearbook]   (Direction de la Statistique).
            Direction de la Statistique, B P 453, Fort-Lamy.
            1966-   1972.   not priced.   3 vols.
            Contains data on demography, agriculture, livestock, foreign trade, education, health, etc.
            Time factor: the 1972 edition, published in 1973, has data for several years to 1972.
            §   Fr.

391   Bulletin de statistique   [Statistical bulletin]   (Direction de la Statistique).
            Direction de la Statistique, B P 453, Fort-Lamy.
            1951-   quarterly.   CFA Fr 2,000 or CFA Fr 4,000 (CFA Fr 8,000 abroad) yr.
            Contains data on climate, demography, production, commerce, transport, prices (consumer and
                consumer price index), and finance.
            Time factor: each issue has data for that quarter and for earlier periods and is published about six
                months later.
            §   Fr.

392   Bulletin des statistiques générales   [General statistical bulletin]   (Union Douanière et Economique de
                l'Afrique Centrale).
            Union Douanière et Economique de l'Afrique Centrale, B P 1418, Bangui, Central African Republic.
            1947-   quarterly.   CFA Fr 2,000 yr (CFA Fr 2,800 yr in other UDEAC countries;
                                                        CFA Fr 3,000 to 4,500 elsewhere).
            Contains data for each of the UDEAC countries on climate, production, transport, foreign trade,
                intercommunity trade, prices, credit and money.
            Time factor: each issue has statistics for two years and several quarters to the date of the issue, and is
                published several months later.
            §   Fr.

393   Etudes statistiques   [Statistical studies]   (Union Douanière et Economique de l'Afrique Centrale).
            Union Douanière et Economique de l'Afrique Centrale, B P 1418, Bangui, Central African Republic.
            1967-   quarterly.   not priced.
            Each issue is devoted to a separate subject.
            §   Fr.

¶   A,   continued

394   Rapport   [Report]   (Conseil National du Crédit).
               Conseil National du Crédit, Fort-Lamy.
               1966-   1975.   not priced.   96p.
               Contains information on factors of production, energy, industry, prices and wages, foreign trade and
                     balance of payments, the evolution of the monetary situation, and the banking system.   Tables
                     are included in the text.
               Time factor: the 1975 report, published in 1976, has data for several years to 1975.
               §   Fr.

395   Enquête socio-économique au Tchad, 1965   [Socio-economic survey on Chad, 1965]   (Service de
                     Statistique Général and INSEE).
               Direction de la Statistique, B P 453, Fort-Lamy.
               Time factor: the report was published in 1969.
               §   Fr.

396   Statistiques et commentaires   [Statistics and commentaries]   (Direction de la Statistique).
               Direction de la Statistique, B P 453, Fort-Lamy.
               1968-   irregular.   CFA Fr 500 each issue.
               Each issue on a separate subject.   No. 3 of 1968 contains the results of the 1967 census of enterprises.
               Time factor: only 3 issues of 1968 have been located.
               §   Fr.

¶   B - Production

ii. Agriculture, fisheries, forestry, etc.

397   Rapport annuel...statistiques   [Annual report...statistics]   (Ministère de l'Elevage, des Eaux-Forêts-
                     Pêches et Chasses; Direction de l'Elevage).
               Ministère de l'Elevage, Fort-Lamy.
               1968-   1972.   not priced.   57p.
               Contains detailed data on livestock, including production, prices, diseases, etc.
               Time factor: the 1972 report, published in 1973, has data for 1972.
               §   Fr.

               Refer also to 390, 391, 392.

iii. Industry

398   Statistiques sur les entreprises du secteur moderne   [Census of business]   (Direction de la Statistique).
               Direction de la Statistique, B P 453, Fort-Lamy.
               1966-   1967.   not priced.   c130p.
               Includes data on structure of industry and commerce, production, employment, wages, profits,
                     investments, value added, etc.
               Time factor: the 1967 report, published in 1969, has data for 1967.
               §   Fr.

               Refer also to 391, 392, 394.

v. Energy

               Refer to 394.

¶   C - External trade

399   Commerce extérieur   [Foreign trade]   (Union Douanière et Economique de l'Afrique Centrale).
        Union Douanière et Economique de l'Afrique Centrale, B P 1418, Bangui, Central African Republic.
        1960- 1973.   not priced.   75p.
        Main tables show detailed trade arranged by commodities, for each of the four member countries of
            UDEAC.   Issues for 1972 and 1973 were condensed versions.
        Time factor: the 1973 edition, published in 1975, has data for 1973.
        §   Fr.

400   Le commerce extérieur controlé   [Foreign trade]   (Direction de la Statistique).
        Direction de la Statistique, B P 453, Fort-Lamy.
        1967- 1972.   not priced.   4 vols.
        Contents:
            Vol. I   Imports, arranged by commodity and sub-divided by countries of origin
                 II   Imports, arranged by countries and sub-divided by commodities
                III   Exports, arranged by commodity and sub-divided by countries of destination
                 IV   Exports, arranged by countries of destination and sub-divided by commodities
        Time factor: the 1972 issues, published in 1973, have data for 1972.
        §   Fr.

401   Commerce extérieur de la République du Tchad   [Foreign trade of the Republic of Chad]   (Direction
            de la Statistique).
        Direction de la Statistique, B P 453, Fort-Lamy.
        1972-   quarterly.
        Issued in four volumes each quarter, dealing with exports (by commodity sub-divided by countries),
            exports (by countries sub-divided by commodities), imports (by commodity sub-divided by countries),
            and imports (by countries sub-divided by commodities).
        §   Fr.

402   Associés: commerce extérieur: République du Tchad: annuaire 1962-1966.   Associates: foreign trade: Chad
            Republic: yearbook 1962-1966.   (European Communities).
        Office des Publications Officielles des Communautés Européennes, C P 1003, Luxembourg 1; or from
            sales agents.
                    £0.90 or Fr B 100.   128p.
        One of a series of retrospective publications on the foreign trade of African states associated with the
            European Communities.   Main tables show imports and exports arranged by commodity and sub-
            divided by countries of origin and destination.   Values are in US $.
        Time factor: published early 1969.
        §   De, En, Fr, It, Nl.

        Refer also to 390, 391, 392.

¶   D - Internal distribution and service trades

        Refer to 391.

¶   E - Population

403   Enquête démographique au Tchad...résultats definitifs   [Demographic survey of Chad...final results]
            (INSEE, Paris and Service de la Statistique, Fort-Lamy).
        Imprimerie Nationale, 2 rue Paul-Hervieu, 75732 Paris Cedex 15, France.
        1946- 1964.   not priced.   2 vols.
        Vol.I contains the analysis of the results and vol.II the detailed statistical tables.   Data includes
            population, sex, age and marital condition, migration, households, etc.
        Time factor: the results of the 1964 survey were published in 1966.
        §   Fr.

        Refer also to 390, 391.

CHAD, continued

¶ F – Social

i. Standard of living

Refer to 391, 394.

ii. Health and welfare

Refer to 390.

iii. Education and leisure

404   Statistiques scolaires   [Education statistics]   (Secrétariat Général de l'Education Nationale).
       Secrétariat Général de l'Education Nationale, Fort-Lamy.
       1966/67–   1969-1970.   not priced.   56p.
       Contains data on pupils; pre-school education; primary and secondary schools, public and private;
           normal schools, technical education, special schools, professional education and education
           obtained overseas; higher education, examinations, etc.
       Time factor: the 1969/70 edition, published in 1971, has data for the academic year 1969/70.
       §   Fr.

       Refer also to 390.

¶ G – Finance

Refer to 391, 392, 394.

ii. Public finance

405   Comptes économiques   [Economic accounts]   (INSEE).
       Imprimerie Nationale, 2 rue Paul-Hervieu, 75732 Paris Cedex 15, France.
       1961/62/63–   1961-1962-1963.   not priced.   95p.
       Time factor: the 1961-1962-1963 issue was published in 1965.
       §   Fr.

       Refer also to 394.

¶ H – Transport and communications

Refer to 390, 392.

ii. Road

406   Le parc automobile de la République de Tchad   [Automobile registrations in Chad]   (Service de la
       Statistique).
       Direction de la Statistique, B P 453, Fort-Lamy.
       1962–   1968.   not priced.   22p.
       Contains data on the registration of all types of vehicles.
       Time factor: data is for the situation at the 1st January of the year of the issue.
       §   Fr.

Central statistical office

The islands of Grande Comore, Anjouan and Mohéli with Mayotte were constituted the Territoire des Comores on 31st December 1975 and so ceased to be a part of France.   There is, as yet, no central statistical office.

Statistical publications

¶   A - General

07   Annuaire statistique des territoires d'outre-mer   [Statistical yearbook for the overseas territories]
          (INSEE, Paris).
      Imprimerie Nationale, 2 rue Paul-Hervieu, 75732 Paris Cedex 15, France.
      1959-   1967/68.   not priced.   255p.
      Main sections:

Physical aspects	Prices, wages, family budgets
Climate	Transport and communications
Demography	Foreign trade
Active population	Money and credit
Health	Public finance
Education	Economic accounts
Production (fisheries, agriculture, industry, electricity)	

      Includes data for the Comoro Islands.
      Time factor: the 1967/68 issue has data for 1967, some 1968 figures, and earlier years.
      §   Fr.

08   Etudes sur les comptes économiques des Territoires des Comores   [Economic statistics for the Comoro
          Islands]   (INSEE, Paris).
      Imprimerie Nationale, 2 rue Paul-Hervieu, 75732 Paris Cedex 15, France.
      1959-   1964-1968.   not priced.   72p.
      Contains statistical data on the economic situation, production, imports, finance and employment, etc.
      Time factor: the 1964-1968 issue, published in 1970, has data for the years 1964 to 1968.
      §   Fr.

09   Enquête socio-économique des Comores   [Socio-economic survey of the Comoro Islands]   (INSEE, Paris).
      Imprimerie Nationale, 2 rue Paul-Hervieu, 75732, Paris Cedex 15, France.
                FrF 3.
      Time factor: published in 1961.
      §   Fr.

¶   B - Production

      Refer to 407, 408.

¶   C - External trade

      Refer to 407, 408.

¶   E - Population

410   Recensement de la population: Comores   [Census of population: Comoro Islands]   (INSEE, Paris).
            Imprimerie Nationale, 2 rue Paul-Hervieu, 75732 Paris Cedex 15, France.
            1840-   1966.   not priced.   2 vols.
            One volume contained the principal results, and the other the statistical results.
            §   Fr.

            Note: a census of population was taken in 1974 and the results are in process of being published.

            Refer also to 407, 408.

¶   F - Social

i.   Standard of living

            Refer to 407.

ii.   Health and welfare

            Refer to 407.

iii.   Education and leisure

            Refer to 407.

¶   G - Finance

            Refer to 407, 408.

¶   H - Transport and communications

            Refer to 407.

Central statistical office

411   Direction de la Statistique et de la Comptabilité Economique   [Department of Statistics and Economic Accounts],
Ministère du Plan [Ministry of Planning],
B P 2031, Brazzaville.
t 20 87.

The activities of the Department include the collection, analysis and publication of current statistics of prices, production, foreign trade, public finance, etc, and the undertaking of specific studies such as budget surveys, salaries, censuses of enterprises, etc.   Unpublished statistical information may be supplied on request.

Another important organisation collecting and publishing statistics

412   Union Douanière et Economique de l'Afrique Centrale   [Customs and Economic Union of Central Africa],
B P 1418, Bangui,
Central African Republic.

The Statistical Department of the organisation is responsible for collecting, analysing and publishing economic statistics, particularly foreign trade statistics, for the member countries, of which Congo is one. Machine tabulations of foreign trade statistics can be supplied.

Libraries

Publications of the Direction de la Statistique may be consulted in the Department (411).

Statistical publications

¶   A - General

413   Annuaire statistique   [Statistical yearbook]   (Direction de la Statistique et de la Comptabilité Economique).
Direction de la Statistique et de la Comptabilité Economique, B P 2031, Brazzaville.
1958/63-   1974.   CFA Fr 2,000 (CFA Fr 3,500 abroad).   330p.
Main sections:

Area and climate	Industry and mines
Population	Transport
Education	Foreign trade
Health	Public finance and credit
Agriculture, crops	Prices and price indices
Forestry	

Time factor: the 1974 edition, published in 1974, contains data for 1972 and some earlier years.   The yearbook is not published every year.
§   Fr.

414   Bulletin mensuel des statistique   [Monthly bulletin of statistics]   (Direction de la Statistique).
Direction de la Statistique, B P 2031, Brazzaville.
1965-   CFA Fr 300 (CFA Fr 800 abroad); CFA Fr 3,000 (CFA Fr 8,000 abroad) yr.
Contains data on climate, health, industrial and mining production, electric energy, transport, money and credit, public finances, and population.
Time factor: each issue has data for several months to the date of the issue and comparative figures for two earlier years, and is published about six months later.
§   Fr.

CONGO, continued

¶   A,   continued

415   Bulletin des statistiques générales   [General statistical bulletin]   (Union Douanière et Economique de
            l'Afrique Centrale).
        Union Douanière et Economique de l'Afrique Centrale, B P 1418, Bangui, Central African Republic.
        1947-   quarterly.   CFA Fr 2,000 yr (CFA Fr 2,800 yr in other UDEAC countries;
                                            CFA Fr 3,000 to 4,500 elsewhere).
        Contains data for each of the UDEAC countries on climate, production, transport, foreign trade,
            intercommunity trade, prices, credit and money.
        Time factor: each issue has statistics for two years and several quarters to the date of the issue, and is
            published several months later.
        §   Fr.

416   Etudes statistiques   [Statistical studies]   (Union Douanière et Economique de l'Afrique Centrale).
        Union Douanière et Economique de l'Afrique Centrale, B P 1418, Bangui, Central African Republic.
        1967-   quarterly.   not priced.
        Each issue is devoted to a separate subject.
        §   Fr.

417   Bulletin trimestriel des statistiques du commerce extérieur et des transports   [Quarterly statistical bulletin
            of foreign trade and transport]   (Direction de la Statistique).
        Direction de la Statistique, B P 2031, Brazzaville.
        1963-   not priced.
        Contains data on sea traffic, river traffic, port traffic, rail transport, air transport, and foreign trade.
        Time factor: each issue has data for several years and quarters up to about 12 months prior to the date
            of the issue.
        §   Fr.

418   Rapport   [Report]   (Conseil National du Crédit).
        Conseil National du Crédit, Brazzaville.
        1972-   1973.   not priced.   54p.
        Contains sections on the economy of Congo (agriculture, livestock, fisheries, forestry, mining,
            petroleum production, industrial production, transport, internal trade, foreign trade, public
            finance), the monetary situation, and the banking system of Congo.
        Time factor: the 1973 report has data for 1973, and was published late 1974.
        §   Fr.

¶   B - Production

i. Mines and mining

        Refer to 413, 414, 418.

ii. Agriculture, fisheries, forestry, etc.

        Refer to 413, 415, 418.

iii. Industry

419   Recensement industriel du Congo   [Industrial census of the Congo]   (Union Douanière et Economique de
            l'Afrique Centrale).
        Union Douanière et Economique de l'Afrique Centrale, B P 245, Brazzaville.
        1966-   1969.   CFA Fr 5,000 (between CFA Fr 5,280 and 6,050 abroad, according to destination).
        Includes data on employment, investment, value of energy consumption, value of materials purchased,
            and value of sales in industrial sectors.
        §   Fr.

        Refer also to 413, 414, 415, 418.

¶   B,   continued

v. Energy

Refer to 414, 418.

¶   C - External trade

420   Bulletin trimestriel des statistiques du commerce extérieur et des transports   [Quarterly bulletin of
                statistics of foreign trade and transport]   (Direction de la Statistique).
           Direction de la Statistique, B P 2031, Brazzaville.
           1963-   not priced.
           Contains data on sea, river and port traffic; rail and air transport; and foreign trade.
           Time factor: each issue has data to about 12 months earlier than the date of publication.
           §   Fr.

421   Associés: commerce extérieur: République du Congo (Brazzaville): annuaire 1959-1966.   Associates:
                foreign trade: Congo (Brazzaville): yearbook 1959-1966.   (European Communities).
           Office des Publications Officielles des Communautés Européennes, C P 1003, Luxembourg 1; or from
                sales agents.
                                £0.90 or FrB 100.   128p.
           One of a series of retrospective publications on the foreign trade of African states associated with the
                European Communities.   Main tables show imports and exports arranged by commodity and sub-
                divided by countries of origin and destination.   Values are in US $.
           Time factor: figures are given for each of the years 1959 to 1966 and the volume was published in 1969.
           §   De, En, Fr, It, Nl.

422   Commerce extérieur   [Foreign trade]   (Union Douanière et Economique de l'Afrique Centrale).
           Union Douanière et Economique de l'Afrique Centrale, B P 1418, Bangui, Central African Republic).
           1960-   1973.   not priced.   75p.
           Main tables show detailed trade arranged by commodities, for each of the four UDEAC countries.
                Issues for 1972 and 1973 were condensed versions.
           Time factor: the 1973 edition, published in 1975, has data for 1973.
           §   Fr.

           Refer also to 413, 415, 417, 418.

¶   D - Internal distribution and service trades

Refer to 418.

¶   E - Population

423   Recensement de Brazzaville, 1961: résultats définitifs   [Census of Brazzaville, 1961: final results]
                (Service de la Statistique, Brazzaville and INSEE, Paris).
           Imprimerie Nationale, 2 rue Paul-Hervieu, 75732 Paris Cedex 15, France.
                                FrF 10.   113p.
           Time factor: published in 1965.
           §   Fr.

424   Enquête démographique, 1960-1961 - Congo: résultats définitifs   [Demographic survey, 1960-1961 -
                Congo: final results]   (Service de la Statistique, Brazzaville and INSEE, Paris).
           Imprimerie Nationale, 2 rue Paul-Hervieu, 75732 Paris Cedex 15, France.
                                FrF 12.   120p.
           §   Fr.

425   Recensement démographique de Pointe-Noire, 1958: résultats définitifs   [Demographic census of
        Pointe-Noire, 1958: final results]   (INSEE, Paris).
        Imprimerie Nationale, 2 rue Paul-Hervieu, 75732 Paris Cedex 15, France.
            FrF 10.   126p.

        Refer also to 413, 414.

¶   F - Social

i. Standard of living

        Refer to 413.

ii. Health and welfare

        Refer to 413.

iii. Education and leisure

        Refer to 413.

¶   G - Finance

        Refer to 413, 414, 415, 418.

ii. Public finance

426   Balance des paiements   [Balance of payments]   (Banque des Etats d'Afrique Centrale).
        Banque des Etats d'Afrique Centrale, 29 rue du Colisée, 75008 Paris, France.
        1973-   half-yearly.   not priced.
        Time factor: each issue refers to a first half or a full year and is published some months later.
        §   Fr.

        Refer also to 413, 414.

¶   H - Transport and communications

        Refer to 413, 414, 415, 417.

i. Ships and shipping

427   Rapport annuel   [Annual report]   (Port de Pointe Noire).
        Port de Point Noire, Point Noire.
        1970-   1971.   not priced.   130p.
        Contains data on the traffic of the port.
        Time factor: the 1971 report, has data for 1970 and 1971.
        §   Fr.

¶ H, continued

ii. Road

428   Situation du parc automobile   [Motor vehicle registrations]   (Direction de la Statistique).
          Direction de la Statistique, B P 2031, Brazzaville.
          (annual).   1972.   not priced.
          §   Fr.

Previously a French territory, Djibouti became independent in July 1977 and there is no statistical office as yet.

Statistical publications

¶   A - General

429   Bulletin de statistique et de documentation   [Bulletin of statistics and documentation]   (Ministère du
              Commerce et du Développement Industriel).
         Ministère du Commerce et du Développement Industriel, Djibouti.
         1970-   quarterly.   not priced.
         Contains data on climate, agriculture and livestock, energy, transport and communications, internal
              trade, external trade, travel, industry and construction, and finance.
         Time factor: each issue has data for several quarters and months to the period of the issue, which is
              published some months later.
         §   Fr.

430   Annuaire statistique des territoires d'outre-mer   [Statistical yearbook for the overseas territories]   (INSEE).
         Imprimerie Nationale, 2 rue Paul-Hervieu, 75732 Paris Cedex 15, France.
         1959-   1967/68.   not priced.   255p.
         Main sections:
              Physical aspects   Prices, wages, family budgets
              Climate   Transport and communications
              Demography   Foreign trade
              Active population   Money and credit
              Health   Public finance
              Education   Economic accounts
              Production (fisheries, agriculture,
                 industry, electricity)
         Includes data for Afars and Issas, now Djibouti.
         Time factor: the 1967/68 issue has data for 1967, some 1968 figures, and earlier years.
         §   Fr.

¶   B - Production

ii. Agriculture, fisheries, forestry, etc.

         Refer to 429, 430.

iii. Industry

         Refer to 429, 430.

iv. Construction

         Refer to 429.

v. Energy

         Refer to 429.

¶ C - External trade

431   Bulletin de statistique et de documentation. No. spécial: Statistiques détaillées du commerce extérieur
          en 1973. 1. Commerce spécial: importations   [Bulletin of statistics and of documentation.
          Special number: detailed statistics of external trade in 1973. 1. Special trade: imports]
          (Ministère du Commerce et du Développement Industriel).
       Ministère du Commerce et du Développement Industriel, Djibouti.
                           not priced.   86p.
       Contains data on imports arranged by commodities and sub-divided by countries of origin.
       Time factor: published late 1975.
       §   Fr.

       Refer also to 429, 430.

¶   D - Internal distribution and service trades

       Refer to 429.

¶   E - Population

432   Recensement de la population de la Côte Française des Somalis (population non-originaire)   [Census of
          population of French Somaliland (non-native population)]   (INSEE).
       Imprimerie Nationale, 2 rue Paul-Hervieu, 75732 Paris Cedex 15, France.
       1946-   1956.   FrF 3.   40p.
       Contains data on sex, age, nationality, matrimonial state, education, occupations, families, etc. of
          the non-native population of the territory of what is now Djibouti.
       §   Fr.

433   Recensement général de la population (décembre 1956): résultats définitifs   [General census of the
          population (December 1956): final results]   (Chargé des Relations de la Coopération avec les Etats
          d'Outre-mer: Service de Statistique, Paris).
       Imprimerie Nationale, 2 rue Paul-Hervieu, 75732 Paris Cedex 15, France.
       1946-   1956.   175p.
       Includes data on the population of what was then French Somaliland, as well as other French overseas
          territories.
       §   Fr.

       Refer also to 430.

¶   F - Social

i. Standard of living

       Refer to 430.

ii. Health and welfare

       Refer to 430.

iii. Education and leisure

       Refer to 430.

DJIBOUTI,   continued

¶   G - Finance

ii. Public finance

434   Comptes économiques du Territoire Français des Afars et des Issas   [Economic accounts of the French
              territory of Afars and Issas]   (INSEE).
         Imprimerie Nationale, 2 rue Paul-Hervieu, 75732 Paris Cedex 15, France.
         1965/68-   1971-72.   FrF 5.00.   c50p.
         Time factor: the 1971-1972 issue, published in 1974, has data for 1971 and 1972.
         §   Fr.

         Refer also to 429, 430.

¶   H - Transport and communications

         Refer to 429, 430.

i. Ships and shipping

435   Statistiques marchandises du port du commerce de Djibouti   [Cargo statistics at the commercial port of
              Djibouti]   (Ministère des Affaires Economiques).
         Ministère des Affaires Economiques, B P 121, Djibouti.
         1966-   1969.   not priced.   90p.
         §   Fr.

Central statistical office

436   Central Agency for Public Mobilisation and Statistics,
Nsar City, P O Box 2086, Cairo.
t 833199.   tx 2395 CAPMAS UN.   cables CAPMAS.

The Agency collects, analyses and publishes the main statistical works in the Republic.   It was
established in 1964 as an independent organisation under the Presidency of the Republic, with responsibility
for emergency planning based on statistics, all statistical operations according to a set 5-year programme,
censuses, EDP operations, the statistical programmes of various ministries, population studies, research, etc.

Libraries

The Central Agency for Public Mobilisation and Statistics (436) has a library where statistical
publications may be consulted.

Bibliographies

437   Catalogue of publications   (Central Agency for Public Mobilisation and Statistics).
January, 1973.   not priced.   93p.
§   Ar & En eds.

Statistical publications

¶   A - General

438   Statistical yearbook: Arab Republic of Egypt   (Central Agency for Public Mobilisation and Statistics).
Central Agency for Public Mobilisation and Statistics, P O Box 2086, Cairo.
1952/65-   1952-1973.   338p.
Main sections:

Demography	Housing
Agriculture, agrarian reform and land reclamation	Education
	Information and tourism
Industry	Economy
Transport and means of communication	The High Dam
Health services	Political information
Social affairs	

Time factor: the 1952-1973 edition, published in October 1974, has data for the years 1952 to 1973.
§   En, Ar, & Fr eds.

439   Yearbook   (Federation of Egyptian Industries).
Federation of Egyptian Industries, P O Box 251, Cairo.
1967-   1975.   not priced.   various paginations.
Contains a section of statistics (71p) on population, agricultural production, the State budget,
industrial production, external trade.
Time factor: the 1975 edition, published in 1975, contains statistical data for several years up to 1974.
§   En.

440   Basic statistics   (Central Agency for Public Mobilisation and Statistics).
Central Agency for Public Mobilisation and Statistics, P O Box 2086, Cairo.
1960-   1964.   not priced.   363p.
Main sections:

General	Transport and communications
Population	Education
Employment and wages	Cultural service
Agriculture	Social services
Industry	Health services
Commerce	International comparisons
National economy	

A concise digest of data that was published in greater detail in other publications.
Time factor: the 1964 issue, published in 1965, has data for 1964 and long runs of earlier figures in
some tables.
§   En, Fr.

¶ A, continued

441   Statistical abstract of the Arab Republic of Egypt   (Central Agency for Public Mobilisation and Statistics).
         Central Agency for Public Mobilisation and Statistics, P O Box 2086, Cairo.
         1951/52-1963/64-   1951/52-1971/1972.   not priced.   182p.
         Contains selected data for brief reference in fields of population, agriculture, industry, economics,
            transport, means of communication, social affairs, health services, education, housing, and
            tourism.   Popular presentation of tables, graphs, illustrations, etc.
         Time factor: the 1951/52-1971/72 edition, published in June 1973, has data for 1951/52 to 1971/72.
         §   En & Ar eds. (not every issue is published in an English edition).

442   Statistical handbook: Arab Republic of Egypt   (Central Agency for Public Mobilisation and Statistics).
         Central Agency for Public Mobilisation and Statistics, P O Box 2086, Cairo.
         1952/64-   1966/67-1971/72.   not priced.   359p.
         Main sections:

Statistical and demographic data	Information and tourism
Agriculture, agrarian reform and land	Economic
reclamation	High Dam
Industry	Political information
Transport and means of communication	Arab Socialist Union
Health services	Useful information
Social affairs	International data
Housing	Diplomatic missions
Education	CAPMAS

         Time factor: the 1966/67-1971/72 edition, published in June 1973, has data for the years 1966/67 to
            1971/72 and also 1951/52 for comparison.
         §   Ar, En & Fr eds.

443   United Arab Republic statistical atlas, 1952-1966   (Central Agency for Public Mobilisation and Statistics).
         Central Agency for Public Mobilisation and Statistics, P O Box 2086, Cairo.
                 not priced.   123p.
         Attempts to portray the U.A.R. in the field of economic, social and cultural activity, and includes
            charts, diagrams and tables on population, employment and wages, national economy, agriculture
            and agrarian reform, industry, foreign trade, transport and communications, education, and service
         Time factor: published in July 1968, the atlas covers the 15 years since the revolution.
         §   Ar & En eds.

444   Economic bulletin   (National Bank of Egypt).
         National Bank of Egypt, 24 Sharia Sherif, Cairo.
         1948-   quarterly.   Free.
         Includes a statistical section with tables on banking (national, central and commercial banks, and
            money supply); foreign trade by main commodity groups; foreign receipts, payments and exchange
            rates; agriculture (general, cotton, cereals and other crops); industry; national accounts; prices;
            population and employment; and international statistics (international trade; petroleum and crude
            oil production, quantity and value of exports).
         Time factor: each issue contains long runs of statistics up to six months prior to the date of publication.
         §   En or Ar eds.

445   Economic review   (Central Bank of Egypt).
         Central Bank of Egypt, Cairo.
         1961-   quarterly.   not priced.
         Includes a statistical section with tables on banking, agriculture, exports of cotton, wholesale price
            indices, consumer price indices, whilst the rest of the publication, dealing with the national
            economy and international developments, also includes some statistics.
         §   En or Ar eds.

         Note: the annual Report of the Directors has statistics of the bank's business.

¶ A, continued

446 Industrial Egypt (Federation of Egyptian Industries).
Federation of Egyptian Industries, P O Box 251, Cairo.
1925- quarterly. £E 0.500; £E 2.000 yr (£E 2.500 abroad).
Includes a statistical section with tables giving annual production and exports for various industries
(spinning and weaving; foodstuffs; chemicals; engineering; metallurgy; electrical; woodworking;
leather; palm leaf, straw and bamboo; building materials and refractories). There is also a
table on industrial output generally.
§ En, Ar.

447 A.R.E. economic indicators (Central Agency for Public Mobilisation and Statistics).
Central Agency for Public Mobilisation and Statistics, P O Box 2086, Cairo.
1952/63- 1961/73. £E 0.600. 20p.
Time factor: the 1961/69 issue, published in December 1974, has data for 1960/61, 1968/69,
1969/70, 1971/72 and 1973.
§ En.

¶ B - Production

ii. Agriculture, fisheries, forestry, etc.

448 [Agricultural census] (Central Agency for Public Mobilisation and Statistics).
Central Agency for Public Mobilisation and Statistics, P O Box 2086, Cairo.
1929- 1960. £E 0.600.
Provides comprehensive information in physical, financial and other terms about the structure,
organisation and operation of the agricultural economy.
§ Ar.

449 [Bulletin of irrigation and water resources] (Central Agency for Public Mobilisation and Statistics).
Central Agency for Public Mobilisation and Statistics, P O Box 2086, Cairo.
1964/65- 1969/70. £E 0.300. 94p.
Time factor: the 1969/70 issue, published in 1972, has data for the year 1969/70.
§ Ar.

450 [Annual report on cultivated lands] (Central Agency for Public Mobilisation and Statistics).
Central Agency for Public Mobilisation and Statistics, P O Box 2086, Cairo.
1965/66- 1969/70. £E 0.150.
Time factor: the 1969/70 report was published in 1972.
§ Ar.

451 [Annual bulletin of land reclamation] (Central Agency for Public Mobilisation and Statistics).
Central Agency for Public Mobilisation and Statistics, P O Box 2086, Cairo.
1964/65- 1969/70. £E 0.100.
Time factor: the 1969/70 bulletin was published in 1973.
§ Ar.

452 [Bulletin of agromechanical machinery] (Central Agency for Public Mobilisation and Statistics).
Central Agency for Public Mobilisation and Statistics, P O Box 2086, Cairo.
1966/67- 1970/71. £E 0.350. 35p.
Time factor: the 1970/71 issue, published in 1974, has data for the year 1970/71.
§ Ar.

453 [Livestock statistics] (Central Agency for Public Mobilisation and Statistics).
Central Agency for Public Mobilisation and Statistics, P O Box 2086, Cairo.
1965/66- 1971/72. £E 0.200. 20p.
Time factor: the 1971/72 issue was published in 1974.
§ Ar.

EGYPT,   continued

454   [Index numbers of the agricultural sector]   (Central Agency for Public Mobilisation and Statistics).
        Central Agency for Public Mobilisation and Statistics, P O Box 2086, Cairo.
        1965/66-   1966/67-1970/71.   £E 0.300.   36p.
        Time factor: the 1966/67-1970/71 issue was published in 1974.
        §   Ar.

455   [Annual bulletin of the co-operative activity in the agricultural sector]   (Central Agency for Public
           Mobilisation and Statistics).
        Central Agency for Public Mobilisation and Statistics, P O Box 2086, Cairo.
        1965-   1969.   £E 0.300.
        Time factor: the 1969 issue was published in 1971.
        §   Ar.

456   [Animal diseases statistics]   (Central Agency for Public Mobilisation and Statistics).
        Central Agency for Public Mobilisation and Statistics, P O Box 2086, Cairo.
        1966-   1970.   £E 0.500.   67p.
        Issued every two years, the 1970 volume was published in 1973.
        §   Ar.

457   [Fishing production statistics in Egypt]   (Central Agency for Public Mobilisation and Statistics).
        Central Agency for Public Mobilisation and Statistics, P O Box 2086, Cairo.
        1962/63-1965/66-   1968/69.   £E 0.300.   c55p.
        Time factor: the 1968/69 issue was published in 1972.
        §   Ar.

        Refer also to 438, 439, 440, 441, 442, 443, 444, 445, 446.

     iii. Industry

458   [Census of industrial establishments]   (Central Agency for Public Mobilisation and Statistics).
        Central Agency for Public Mobilisation and Statistics, P O Box 2086, Cairo.
        1942-   1967.   £E 0.300, and £E 0.150.   2 vols.
        Volume 1 contains general tables; volume 2 data for all governorates, with separate pamphlets for each
           one.   The census, which is taken triennially, covers all establishments operating during the period
           of implementation, in all economic activities, agricultural activities being included only when
           operations are performed inside the establishment.   Data include the number of establishments
           classified by status and sector in each governorate and the number of occupied persons in each
           governorate.
        Time factor: the results of the 1967 census were published between 1967 and 1972.
        §   Ar.

        Note: censuses were taken in 1972 and 1975, but the results have not been published, as yet.

459   [Industrial production census]   (Central Agency for Public Mobilisation and Statistics).
        Central Agency for Public Mobilisation and Statistics, P O Box 2086, Cairo.
        1927-   1966/67.   £E 0.500, each volume.   2 vols.
        Volume I is concerned with establishments with nine employees or less in the private sector, and volume
           II with establishments of 10 employees or more in the private and public sectors.   The reports show
           the chief characteristics and nature of the industrial production of the whole country as well as in
           each of the governorates.   Data include the kind of commodity produced, number of persons
           employed, quantity and value of industrial output and input, fuel and electricity consumed.
        Time factor: the reports were published in 1970 and 1971.   Up to the 1966/67 report, the census was
           taken every five years.
        §   Ar.

¶   B.iii,   continued

460   [Industrial production statistics]   (Central Agency for Public Mobilisation and Statistics).
         Central Agency for Public Mobilisation and Statistics, P O Box 2086, Cairo.
         1942-   1967/68.   £E 0.400.
         Similar subject coverage to the quarterly (461) below.
         Time factor: the 1967/68 issue was published in 1973.
         §   Ar.

461   [Industrial production statistics]   (Central Agency for Public Mobilisation and Statistics).
         Central Agency for Public Mobilisation and Statistics, P O Box 2086, Cairo.
         1964/65-   quarterly.   £E 0.150 each issue.
         Includes establishments with 25 or more persons engaged in the private sector and all establishments in
             the public sector, and covers mining and quarrying and manufacturing industries.   Data includes
             employment, wages and salaries, working days, working hours, raw materials used, packing
             materials, industrial services from others, fuels, electricity, fixed assets, production and services
             rendered.
         Time factor: each issue, with data for that quarter, is published 12 or more months later.
         §   Ar.

462   Cotton monthly bulletin   (Central Agency for Public Mobilisation and Statistics).
         Central Agency for Public Mobilisation and Statistics, P O Box 2086, Cairo.
         1964-   £E 0.150, each issue.
         Contains data on supplies, stocks, distribution, consumption, export, etc.
         Time factor: each issue is published about two months after the month of the issue and contains data for
             the month, cumulated totals for the year to date, and corresponding figures for the previous year.
         §   Ar, En.

         Note: there is also a "Weekly cotton bulletin" (m/ms 2000 yr).

463   [Semi-annual bulletin of industrial products and materials prices]   (Central Agency for Public Mobilisation
             and Statistics).
         Central Agency for Public Mobilisation and Statistics, P O Box 2086, Cairo.
         1964-   £E 0.150.
         Time factor: published in January and July (it was quarterly for the first two years of publication).
         §   Ar.

         Refer also to 438, 439, 440, 441, 442, 443, 444, 446.

   iv. Construction

464   [Construction and building statistics (public sector companies)]   (Central Agency for Public Mobilisation
             and Statistics).
         Central Agency for Public Mobilisation and Statistics, P O Box 2086, Cairo.
         1966/67-   1969/70.   £E 0.400.   40p.
         Time factor: the 1969/70 issue was published in 1972.
         §   Ar.

465   [Municipal services statistics]   (Central Agency for Public Mobilisation and Statistics).
         Central Agency for Public Mobilisation and Statistics, P O Box 2086, Cairo.
         1962/63-   1968/69.   £E 0.150.   28p.
         Mainly concerned with housing.
         Time factor: the 1968/69 issue was published in 1971.
         §   Ar.

         Refer also to 438, 441, 442.

   v. Energy

         Refer to 444.

¶   C - External trade

466   A.R.E. foreign trade according to the Standard International Trade Classification   (Central Agency for
            Public Mobilisation and Statistics).
            Central Agency for Public Mobilisation and Statistics, P O Box 2086, Cairo.
            1960-   1973.   not priced.   356p.
            Includes detailed tables of statistics of imports, exports and re-exports arranged by SITC, and summary
                tables showing the balance of trade and foreign trade by commodity sections.
            Time factor: the 1973 issue, published in November 1974, has data for 1973.
            §   En.

467   Monthly bulletin of foreign trade   (Central Agency for Public Mobilisation and Statistics).
            Central Agency for Public Mobilisation and Statistics, P O Box 2086, Cairo.
            1887-   8 issues per year.   not priced.
            Includes tables showing foreign trade by ports, foreign trade by commodity, foreign trade by country,
                cotton exports by variety, and cotton exports by country of destination.   Both monthly and
                cumulated statistics are included.
            Time factor: each issue appears about 2 months after the end of the period covered.
            §   Ar, En.

468   [Index numbers of foreign trade]   (Central Agency for Public Mobilisation and Statistics).
            Central Agency for Public Mobilisation and Statistics, P O Box 2086, Cairo.
            1952-   1970/71.   £E 0.300.
            Time factor: the 1970/71 issue, published in 1972, has index numbers for 1970/71 and about 5 earlier
                years.
            §   Ar.

469   [Chemical imports statement]   (Central Agency for Public Mobilisation and Statistics).
            Central Agency for Public Mobilisation and Statistics, P O Box 2086, Cairo.
            1961/62-   1970/71.   £E 0.500.
            Time factor: the 1970/71 statement was published in 1972.
            §   Ar.

470   [Import statement of metals and machinery]   (Central Agency for Public Mobilisation and Statistics).
            Central Agency for Public Mobilisation and Statistics, P O Box 2086, Cairo.
            1961/62-   1970/71.   £E 0.500.
            Time factor: the 1970/71 statement was published in 1973.
            §   Ar.

471   [Medicaments and medical preparations imports]   (Central Agency for Public Mobilisation and Statistics).
            Central Agency for Public Mobilisation and Statistics, P O Box 2086, Cairo.
            1967-   1969/70.   £E 0.500.
            Time factor: the 1969/70 issue was published in 1972.
            §   Ar.

            Refer also to 439, 443, 444, 445, 446.

¶   D - Internal distribution and service trades

472   [Wholesale trade in the private sector, excluding joint stock, limited and limited liability companies and
                branches of foreign companies]   (Central Agency for Public Mobilisation and Statistics).
            Central Agency for Public Mobilisation and Statistics, P O Box 2086, Cairo.
            1960/61-   1969/70.   £E 0.400.   29p.
            Time factor: the 1969/70 issue was published in October 1973.
            §   Ar.

¶   D,   continued

473   [Wholesale and retail trade in the public sector, limited and limited liability companies in the private
          sector]   (Central Agency for Public Mobilisation and Statistics).
          Central Agency for Public Mobilisation and Statistics, P O Box 2086, Cairo.
          1960/61-   1969/70.   £E 0.200.   75p.
          Time factor: the 1969/70 issue was published in October 1973.
          §   Ar.

474   Index numbers of wholesale prices   (Central Agency for Public Mobilisation and Statistics).
          Central Agency for Public Mobilisation and Statistics, P O Box 2086, Cairo.
          1939-   monthly.   £E 0.600 each issue.
          §   Ar, En.

475   [Monthly bulletin of selling prices to the consumer (classified)]   (Central Agency of Public Mobilisation
          and Statistics).
          Central Agency for Public Mobilisation and Statistics, P O Box 2086, Cairo.
          1965-   £E 0.150 each issue.
          Time factor: each issue is published some months after the date of the issue.
          §   Ar.

476   [Statistics of the number of firms in the private sector involved in wholesale and retail trade in the UAR]
          (Central Agency for Public Mobilisation and Statistics).
          Central Agency for Public Mobilisation and Statistics, P O Box 2086, Cairo.
                          £E 0.900.   3 vols.
          Time factor: published in 1965.
          §   Ar.

477   [Tourism statistics bulletin]   (Central Agency for Public Mobilisation and Statistics).
          Central Agency for Public Mobilisation and Statistics, P O Box 2086, Cairo.
          1967-   quarterly.   £E 0.100 each issue.
          Time factor: each issue is published two or three months after the end of the period covered.
          §   Ar.

478   Egypt tourist press letter   (Ministry of Tourism. Department of Publicity and Advertising).
          Department of Publicity and Advertising, Ministry of Tourism, Cairo.
          1968-   monthly.   not priced.
          Contains news and brief tourism statistics.
          §   En & Fr eds.

479   [Hotel and boarding house statistics in the public and private sectors in Egypt]   (Central Agency for Public
          Mobilisation and Statistics).
          Central Agency for Public Mobilisation and Statistics, P O Box 2086, Cairo.
          1963/64-   quarterly.   £E 0.100 each issue.
          Time factor: each issue is published some considerable time after the end of the period covered.
          §   Ar.

          Note: annual from 1963/64 to 1968/69.

          Refer also to 440, 442, 445.

¶   E - Population

480   [Final results of the micro census of the population of Egypt]   (Central Agency for Public Mobilisation and
             Statistics).
             Central Agency of Public Mobilisation and Statistics, P O Box 2086, Cairo.
             1882-   1966.   7 vols.
             Contents: Final results –
                     Vol.   I   Stages and methodology   (£E 0.300)
                             II   Summary tables and urban governorates   (£E 0.600)
                             III   Lower Egypt governorates   (£E 1.00)
                             IV   Upper Egypt governorates   (£E 1.00)
                             V   Governorates of frontiers   (£E 0.300)

                     Detailed results –
                     Vol.   I   Population characteristics for each of the governates   (£E 0.400) for each pamphlet
                                       covering one of the governorates
                             II   Population characteristics: summary tables and urban governorates   (£E 0.400)
             Time factor: the volumes were published between 1967 and 1972.
             §   Ar.

             Note: a full census of population was taken in 1960.

481   [Population trends in Egypt: projections to the year 2000]   (Central Agency for Public Mobilisation and
             Statistics).
             Central Agency for Public Mobilisation and Statistics, P O Box 2086, Cairo.
                             £E 0.300.   41p.
             Time factor: published in June 1973.
             §   Ar.

482   Population and development: a study of the population increase and its challenge to development in Egypt
             (Central Agency for Public Mobilisation and Statistics).
             Central Agency for Public Mobilisation and Statistics, P O Box 2086, Cairo.
                             not priced.   315p.
             Deals with demographic elements, the economic factors of problems of over-population, and socio-
                  economic development in relation to population-growth in Egypt.   There are tables in the text.
             Time factor: published in 1973, the tables are for varying periods to 1970.
             §   En.

483   [Statistics for births and deaths]   (Central Agency for Public Mobilisation and Statistics).
             Central Agency for Public Mobilisation and Statistics, P O Box 2086, Cairo.
             1931-   1970.   £E 0.300.   203p.
             Time factor: published in 1972.
             §   Ar.

484   [Marriage and divorce statistics]   (Central Agency of Public Mobilisation and Statistics).
             Central Agency for Public Mobilisation and Statistics, P O Box 2086, Cairo.
             1962-   1971.   £E 0.200.   149p.
             Time factor: the 1971 issue, published in 1973, has data for 1971.
             §   Ar.

485   [Labour force sample survey in Egypt]   (Central Agency for Public Mobilisation and Statistics).
             Central Agency for Public Mobilisation and Statistics, P O Box 2086, Cairo.
             1961-   1970.   £E 0.500.
             §   Ar.

486   [Population movements and migration across UAR frontiers]   (Central Agency for Public Mobilisation and
             Statistics).
             Central Agency for Public Mobilisation and Statistics, P O Box 2086, Cairo.
             1967-   quarterly.   £E 0.300, each issue.
             §   Ar.

             Refer also to 438, 439, 440, 441, 442, 443, 444, 488.

¶   E,   continued

487   [Employment, wages and hours of work statistics]   (Central Agency for Public Mobilisation and Statistics).
        Central Agency for Public Mobilisation and Statistics, P O Box 2086, Cairo.
        1942-   1968.   £E 0.150.   c150p.
        Time factor: the 1968 issue was published in May 1973.
        §   Ar.

¶   F - Social

488   [Social services statistics]   (Central Agency for Public Mobilisation and Statistics).
        Central Agency for Public Mobilisation and Statistics, P O Box 2086, Cairo.
        1962/63-   1968/69.   £E 0.200.   c90p.
        Time factor: the 1968/69 issue was published in 1970.
        §   Ar.

i. Standard of living

489   Monthly bulletin of consumer price index   (Central Agency for Public Mobilisation and Statistics).
        Central Agency for Public Mobilisation and Statistics, P O Box 2086, Cairo.
        1967-   £E 0.150 each issue.
        Time factor: each issue is published two or three months later.
        §   Ar, En.

490   [Family budget survey]   (Central Agency for Public Mobilisation and Statistics).
        Central Agency for Public Mobilisation and Statistics, P O Box 2086, Cairo.
        1955-   1964/65.   £E 0.500.
        §   Ar.

491   [Quarterly return of food stuff prices]   (Central Agency for Public Mobilisation and Statistics).
        Central Agency for Public Mobilisation and Statistics, P O Box 2086, Cairo.
        1964-   £E 0.100.
        Time factor: each issue published several months after the end of the period covered.
        §   Ar.

        Refer also to 440, 443, 444, 445.

ii. Health and welfare

492   [Bulletin of health service statistics]   (Central Agency for Public Mobilisation and Statistics).
        Central Agency for Public Mobilisation and Statistics, P O Box 2086, Cairo.
        1966/67-   1969/70.   £E 0.300.   33p.
        Time factor: the 1969/70 issue was published in 1974.
        §   Ar.

        Note: "Health statistics" was published between 1901 and 1952.

493   [Statistics of general medical aid]   (Central Agency for Public Mobilisation and Statistics).
        Central Agency for Public Mobilisation and Statistics, P O Box 2086, Cairo.
        1964/65-   1970/71.   £E 0.150.   26p.
        Time factor: the 1970/71 issue was published in 1972.
        §   Ar.

¶ F.ii, continued

494   [Statistics of social welfare institutions]   (Central Agency for Public Mobilisation and Statistics).
        Central Agency for Public Mobilisation and Statistics, P O Box 2086, Cairo.
        1966/67-   1967/68.   £E 0.300.
        Time factor: the 1967/68 issue was published in 1969.
        §   Ar.

        Refer also to 438, 440, 441, 442.

   iii.   Education and leisure

495   [Educational trends]   (Ministry of Education).
        Ministry of Education, Cairo.
        1967-   half-yearly.   not priced.
        Time factor: published some months after the period covered.
        §   Ar.

496   [Qualifications and academic degrees in Egypt]   (Central Agency for Public Mobilisation and Statistics).
        Central Agency for Public Mobilisation and Statistics, P O Box 2086, Cairo.
        1966-   separately priced.
        Each issue deals with graduates of a particular faculty.
        §   Ar.

497   [Cultural statistics: broadcasting and press]   (Central Agency for Public Mobilisation and Statistics).
        Central Agency for Public Mobilisation and Statistics, P O Box 2086, Cairo.
        1963/64-   1968/69.   £E 0.200.   c65p.
        Time factor: the 1968/69 issue was published in 1970.
        §   Ar.

498   [Cultural statistics: cinema and theatre]   (Central Agency for Public Mobilisation and Statistics).
        Central Agency for Public Mobilisation and Statistics, P O Box 2086, Cairo.
        1963/64-   1968/69.   £E 0.400.
        Time factor: the 1968/69 issue was published in 1972.
        §   Ar.

499   [Cultural statistics: production of books and libraries]   (Central Agency for Public Mobilisation and Statistics).
        Central Agency for Public Mobilisation and Statistics, P O Box 2086, Cairo.
        1963/64-   1968/69.   £E 0.200.
        Time factor: the 1968/69 issue was published in 1971.
        §   Ar.

500   [Cultural statistics: museums, parks and exhibitions]   (Central Agency for Public Mobilisation and Statistics).
        Central Agency for Public Mobilisation and Statistics, P O Box 2086, Cairo.
        1963/64- 1969/70.   £E 0.200.
        Time factor: the 1969/70 issue was published in 1971.
        §   Ar.

501   [Cultural statistics: cultural centres and associations, and conferences and patents]   (Central Agency for Public Mobilisation and Statistics).
        Central Agency for Public Mobilisation and Statistics, P O Box 2086, Cairo.
        1966/67-   1968/69.   £E 0.200.
        Time factor: the 1968/69 issue was published in 1971.
        §   Ar.

        Refer also to 438, 440, 441, 442, 443.

¶ F, continued

iv. Justice

502 Rapport statistique judiciaire annuel [Annual judicial statistical report] (Ministry of Justice: Department of Statistics).
Ministry of Justice, Cairo.
1965- 1971. not priced. 227p.
Includes statistics of crimes, judgements, the work of tribunals, sentences, suicides, etc.
Time factor: the 1971 report, published in 1972, has data for 1971 and totals only for 1970.
§ Ar, Fr.

¶ G - Finance

Refer to 444, 445.

i. Public finance

503 [National income from agriculture] (Central Agency for Public Mobilisation and Statistics).
Central Agency for Public Mobilisation and Statistics, P O Box 2086, Cairo.
1955/60- 1973. £E 0.400. 56p.
Time factor: the 1973 issue was published in 1975.
§ Ar.

504 [National economic statistics] (Central Agency for Public Mobilisation and Statistics).
Central Agency for Public Mobilisation and Statistics, P O Box 2086, Cairo.
1962/63- 1968/69. £E 0.400. 54p.
Statistics and financial information about the public sector, except banks and insurance companies.
Time factor: the 1968/69 issue was published in 1973.
§ Ar.

¶ H - Transport and communications

505 [Public transport statistics in Egypt (passengers)] (Central Agency for Public Mobilisation and Statistics).
Central Agency for Public Mobilisation and Statistics, P O Box 2086, Cairo.
1965/66- quarterly. £E 0.100 each issue.
Time factor: each issue is published some 18 months after the date of the issue.
§ Ar.

Note: published annually for the first two years, then semi-annually for a year before becoming quarterly.

Refer also to 438, 440, 441, 442, 443.

i. Ships and shipping

506 Annual bulletin of sea-borne traffic (Central Agency for Public Mobilisation and Statistics).
Central Agency for Public Mobilisation and Statistics, P O Box 2086, Cairo.
1880- 1970/71. £E 0.200.
Contains data on motor-vessels sea-borne traffic (number of vessels and registered tonnage, cargo, passengers, coastwise traffic) and sailing vessels sea-borne traffic (external, coastwise, etc).
Time factor: the 1970/71 issue, published in 1973, has data for the year 1970/71.
§ Ar, En.

¶   H.i,   continued

507   Sea-borne traffic   (Central Agency for Public Mobilisation and Statistics).
            Central Agency for Public Mobilisation and Statistics, P O Box 2086, Cairo.
            1965-   quarterly.   £E 0.200 each issue.
            Similar subject coverage to 506 above.
            §   Ar, En.

            Note: prior to 1968 title was "Quarterly bulletin of maritime transport in main ports..." and was
                issued in Arabic only.

508   Suez Canal report   (Suez Canal Authority).
            Suez Canal Authority, Garden City, Cairo.
            1960-   1966.   not priced.   176p.
            Includes a section of statistical tables on traffic through the canal, types of vessels, flags, passengers,
                cargoes, and petroleum products.
            Time factor: the 1966 issue contains data for 1966 and summary data for 1927 to 1966.
            §   En & Ar eds.

509   Monthly report   (Suez Canal Authority).
            Suez Canal Authority, Garden City, Cairo.
            1959-   not priced.
            Similar subject coverage to that in 508 above.
            Time factor: ceased publication with the May 1967 issue.
            §   En & Ar eds.

      iv. Air

510   [Air transport statistics in Egypt]   (Central Agency for Public Mobilisation and Statistics).
            Central Agency for Public Mobilisation and Statistics, P O Box 2086, Cairo.
            1965/66-   1966/67.   £E 0.100.
            Time factor: the 1966/67 issue was published in 1968.
            §   Ar.

      v. Communications

511   [Statistics of postal services in Egypt]   (Central Agency for Public Mobilisation and Statistics).
            Central Agency for Public Mobilisation and Statistics, P O Box 2086, Cairo.
            1964/65-   1969/70.   not priced.
            Time factor: the 1969/70 issue was published in 1971.
            §   Ar.

There is, as yet, no central statistical office for the Republic of Equatorial Guinea, which became independent in 1968 after being Spanish colonies. The Republic consists of Rio Muni on the mainland and adjacent islets, and the island of Macias Nguema (formerly Fernando Poo) on which is the capital, Malabo (formerly Santa Isabel).

Statistical publications

¶   A - General

512   Anuario estadístico de España (edición normal)   [Statistical yearbook of Spain (standard edition)] (Instituto Nacional de Estadística).
Instituto Nacional de Estadística, avenida de Generalísimo 91, Madrid 16, Spain.
1912-   1968.   Ptas 300.   811p.
Contains some statistics, such as population and education, for what is now Equatorial Guinea (then Spanish Guinea).
Time factor: the 1968 edition, published early 1969, contains data for several years to 1967.
§   Es.

¶   E - Population

513   Censo de la población de las viviendas de España, 1960. Tomo 1, cifras generales de habitantes   [Census of population of Spain, 1960. Part 1, general statistics]   (Instituto Nacional de Estadística).
Instituto Nacional de Estadística, avenida de Generalísimo 91, Madrid 16, Spain.
1920-   Ptas 200.   444p.
Includes data for Equatorial Guinea (formerly Spanish Guinea).
§   Es.

Refer also to 512.

¶   F - Social

iii. Education and leisure

Refer to 512.

Central statistical office

514   Central Statistical Office,
         P O Box 1143, Addis Ababa.
         t 113010.

   The Office was established in 1961 as a coordinating body.   Duties include the formulation and
implementation of the statistical programmes; assisting the departmental statistical offices to formulate
and adopt standards, statistical methods and records; collation and analysis of all the economic and
social statistics collected by the various statistical offices; the organisation of censuses, surveys and
other statistical enquiries; the publication of statistical data; and liaison between the government and
external statistical agencies.

Another important organisation collecting and publishing statistics

515   Customs Administration,
         Ministry of Finance,
         Addis Ababa.

   The Statistical Department of Customs Head Office is responsible for the collection and publication of
statistics of foreign trade.

Libraries

   The United Nations Economic Commission for Africa has a library in Addis Ababa (P O Box 3005),
where statistical publications of an economic nature may be consulted.

Statistical publications

¶   A - General

516   Statistical abstract of Ethiopia   (Central Statistical Office).
         Central Statistical Office, P O Box 1143, Addis Ababa.
         1963-   1975.   not priced.   231p.
         Main sections:
            Land and climate   Public finance
            Population   Banking and balance of payments
            Agriculture and livestock   Technical assistance
            Mining   Insurance
            Industry   Prices
            Construction   Health
            Transport and communication   Education
            External trade   Law and order
            National accounts
         Time factor: the 1975 edition, published early 1976, has the latest data available at the time of
            publication.
         §   En, Amharic.

517   Quarterly bulletin   (National Bank of Ethiopia).
         National Bank of Ethiopia, P O Box 5550, Addis Ababa.
         1964-   not priced.
         Contains statistical data on monetary and credit developments, industrial production, price developments
            foreign trade, balance of payments, budget estimates, economic development, etc, in the text.
            There is a statistical annex with tables on monetary statistics, government debt, production and
            sales, foreign trade and payments.
         Time factor: each issue has long runs of annual and monthly figures to the quarter prior to the date of
            the issue.
         §   En.

¶   A,   continued

518   Ethiopia statistical pocket book   (Central Statistical Office).
            Central Statistical Office, P O Box 1143, Addis Ababa.
            1968-   4th, 1972.   not priced.   143p.
            Main sections:

Area and climate	Public finance
Population	Banking
Agriculture	Balance of payments
Mining and industry	Prices
Construction	Health
Transport and communications	Education
External trade	Law and order
National accounts	General information

            Time factor: the 1972 edition, published in 1974, has runs of figures to 1972 or 1971/72.
            §   En.

519   Annual report   (National Bank of Ethiopia).
            National Bank of Ethiopia, P O Box 5550, Addis Ababa.
            1964/65-   1974/75.   not priced.   79p.
            Includes a statistical appendix on the activities of the bank, of other banks, indices of manufacturing
                production and electricity output, capital formation, money supply and quasi-money, domestic
                credit, gold and foreign exchange holdings, balance of payments, value and quantity of major
                exports, value of imports by commodity groups and end-use, production and investment, wholesale
                price indices, retail price indices, and public finance.
            Time factor: the 1974/75 report, published in 1976, has data for 1974/75 and also earlier years in some
                tables.
            §   En.

520   Statistical bulletin   (Central Statistical Office).
            Central Statistical Office, P O Box 1143, Addis Ababa.
            1968-   irregular.   not priced.
            Issues so far include:
                1.   Survey of major towns in Ethiopia.
                2.   Survey of manufacturing and electricity industry, 1964/65-1966/67.
                3.   Major crops and crop seasons in major 13 provinces.
                4.   Local names of diseases and pests.
                5.   General district information in 13 provinces.
                6.   Population of Addis Ababa; National sample survey, 1st round.
                8.   Population of Addis Ababa: results from population sample survey of 1967.
                9.   Urbanisation in Ethiopia.
                10.   Results of the national sample survey, 2nd round (2 vols).
                12.   Results of 1968 population and housing censuses: population and housing characteristics in
                        Asmara.
            §   En.

521   Statistical digest   (Chamber of Commerce, Addis Ababa).
            Chamber of Commerce, Addis Ababa.
            1970-   irregular.   not priced.
            Contains data on industry, electricity, agriculture, building construction, tourism, telecommunications,
                transport (truck, bus, railway, air), port traffic, development finance, foreign transactions, and
                prices.
            Time factor: sometimes two issues a year, but more often only one.   Includes long runs of figures to the
                latest available.
            §   En.

522   Market report   (Commercial Bank of Ethiopia).
            Commercial Bank of Ethiopia, P O Box 255, Addis Ababa.
            1969-   quarterly.   not priced.
            As well as articles, the report contains the retail price index, wholesale price index, data on money
                and banking, and other economic indicators.   Very general.
            §   En.

¶   A,   continued

523   Ethiopia economic review   (Ministry of Commerce and Industry).
            Ministry of Commerce and Industry, Addis Ababa.
            1959-   1968.   Eth$ 2.00.   63p.
            A general review with a few statistics in the text.
            §   En.

524   National sample survey   (Central Statistical Office).
            Central Statistical Office, P O Box 1143, Addis Ababa.
            1963/67-   not priced.
            The survey is multi-purpose in character, being designed to collect information on population, vital
                statistics, agriculture, land tenure, livestock, etc.   The first round was completed in 1963-1967
                and the results have been published in a series of 12 reports, one for each of the 12 provinces.
                The second round of the survey was completed from 1968 to 1970, the results being published in
                two volumes:
                    Vol. I   The demography of Ethiopia, deals with population size and distribution, population
                            characteristics, vital rates, and projections of 1970 estimates to 2000.
                            (published in 1974).
                    Vol. II Deals with all the surveyed areas of all the provinces except Eritrea, which has not
                            been covered in the survey.
            §   En.

¶   B - Production

i. Mines and mining

        Refer to 516, 518.

ii. Agriculture, fisheries, forestry, etc.

525   Coffee statistics handbook   (National Coffee Board of Ethiopia).
            National Coffee Board of Ethiopia, P O Box 3222, Addis Ababa.
            1961/62-   no.5, 1962/63-1971/72.   not priced.   70p.
            Contains detailed statistics on marketing coffee.
            Time factor: the 1962/63-1971/72 issue, published in 1974, has data for the years 1962/63 to 1971/72.
            §   En.

        Note: the Board also publishes "Ethiopian coffee review", which has some statistics.

        Refer also to 516, 518, 520, 521, 524.

iii. Industry

526   Advance report on the 1972/73 rural survey of cottage and handicraft industries   (Central Statistics Office).
            Central Statistics Office, P O Box 1143, Addis Ababa.
                            not priced.   81p.
            Contains results by province and summary tables.
            Time factor: published in April 1975.
            §   En.

        Refer also to 516, 517, 518, 519, 520, 521.

iv. Construction

        Refer to 516, 518, 521.

   ¶   B,   continued

   v. Energy

      Refer to 519, 520, 521.

   ¶   C - External trade

27   Annual external trade statistics   (Customs Head Office).
        Customs Head Office, Ministry of Finance, Addis Ababa.
        1954/55-   1975.   not priced.   256p.
        Main tables show imports, exports and re-exports arranged by commodity and sub-divided by countries
          of origin and destination.   Also included are summary tables, trade relations with some
          neighbouring countries, and trade relations with selected countries.
        Time factor: the 1975 issue, published in 1976, has data for 1975.
        §   En.

28   External trade statistics   (Customs Head Office <u>and</u> Central Statistical Office).
        Customs Head Office, Ministry of Finance, Addis Ababa.
        1967-   monthly.   not priced.
        Main tables show imports and exports arranged by commodity and sub-divided by countries of origin and
          destination.
        Time factor: each issue has data for the month of the issue and cumulated figures for the year to date,
          and is published some months later.
        §   En.

        Refer also to 516, 517, 518, 519, 521.

   ¶   D - Internal distribution and service trades

      Refer to 521, 522.

   ¶   E - Population

29   Urban surveys of Ethiopia   (Central Statistical Office).
        Central Statistical Office, P O Box 1143, Addis Ababa.
        1966-   not priced.   11 vols.
        Contents:

Analysis instruction	Harer
Gondar	Soddo
Bahir Dar	Nazareth
Adwa	Assab
Jima	Desoe
Debrezeyt	

        §   En.

30   Report on the census of population, 10-11 September 1961   (Municipality of Addis Ababa).
        Municipality of Addis Ababa, Addis Ababa.
                 not priced.   66p.
        Time factor: published in 1961.
        §   En.

        Note: the report of the latest full census of population of Ethiopia is included in the Italian census
          of 1931.

¶   E,   continued

531   Addis Ababa employment survey: report for half-year...   (Department of Labour and Employment:
            Employment and Manpower Division).
        Department of Labour and Employment, Addis Ababa.
        1971-   half-yearly.   not priced.
        Includes data on employment trends, demand for personnel, persons seeking work, and shortages of
            manpower.
        §   En.

        Refer also to 516, 518, 520, 524.

¶   F - Social

i. Standard of living

532   Local prices...   (National Bank of Ethiopia).
        National Bank of Ethiopia, Addis Ababa.
        1966-   3rd, 1969.   not priced.   135p.
        Time factor: the 1969 issue, published in June 1970, has data for 1969 and some data for the period
            1957 to 1969.
        §   En.

        Refer also to 516, 517, 518, 519, 521, 522.

ii. Health and welfare

533   Statistics on hospital in-patient discharges: Ethiopia - 1961 E.C. (1968/69 G.C.)   (Ministry of Public
            Health).
        Ministry of Public Health, Addis Ababa.
                        not priced.   15p.
        Time factor: published in 1971.
        §   En.

534   Summary report on hospital discharges, 1962 E.C. (1969/70 G.C.)   (Ministry of Public Health).
        Ministry of Public Health, Addis Ababa.
                        not priced.   57p.
        Time factor: published in 1973.
        §   En.

        Refer also to 516, 518.

iii. Education and leisure

535   School census for Ethiopia: Part 1   (Ministry of Education and Fine Arts).
        Ministry of Education and Fine Arts, Addis Ababa.
        1961/62-   1967/68.   not priced.   93p.
        A statistical survey of schools, teachers, classroom units, students, in primary, secondary and higher
            education.
        §   En.

        Refer also to 516, 518.

¶   G - Finance

        Refer to 516, 517, 518, 519, 521, 522.

ETHIOPIA,   continued

¶   H - Transport and communications

Refer to 516, 517, 521.

GABON - GABUN

Central statistical office

536   Direction Générale de la Statistique et des Etudes Economiques   [General Department of Statistics
            and Economic Studies],
        B P 2081, Libreville.
        t 214 16.

        The Department is responsible for the collection, analysis and publication of official statistics for the
Republic of Gabon.

Another important organisation collecting and publishing statistics

537   Union Douanière et Economique de l'Afrique Centrale   [Customs and Economic Union of Central
            Africa],
        B P 1418, Bangui,
        Central African Republic.

        The Statistical Department of the organisation is responsible for collecting, analysing and publishing
economic statistics, particularly foreign trade statistics, for the member countries, of which Gabon is one.
Machine tabulations of foreign trade statistics can be supplied.

Libraries

        The library of the Centre d'Information, Libreville, may be able to assist members of the public who
require to consult statistical publications in Libreville.

Statistical publications

¶   A - General

538   Annuaire statistique   [Statistical yearbook]   (Direction de la Statistique et des Etudes Economiques).
            Direction Générale de la Statistique, B P 2081, Libreville.
            1964-   2nd, 1968.   not priced.   various paginations.
            Main sections:
                Physical geography   Production (agriculture, livestock, fisheries)
                Climate   Forestry
                Political and administrative organisations Mines, industries, energy
                Population   Transport
                Health   Tourism and hotel business
                Education   Prices
                Social affairs   Money and credit
                Employment   Public finance
                Foreign trade   Economic accounts
            Time factor: the 1968 edition has data for 1968 and some earlier years.
            §   Fr.

539   Bulletin mensuel de la statistique   [Monthly bulletin of statistics]   (Direction Générale de la Statistique).
            Direction Générale de la Statistique, B P 2081, Libreville.
            1959-   CFA Fr 300 (CFA FR 700 abroad) or CFA Fr 3,000 (CFA Fr 7,000) yr.
            Contains statistical data on climate, production, foreign trade, transport, prices, money and credit,
                public finance, etc.
            Time factor: each issue contains data for the month of the issue and cumulations for the year to date;
                also retrospective figures for some tables.   Publication is about 3 months after the date of the issue.
            §   Fr.

118

¶ A, continued

540 Etudes et enquêtes statistiques   [Statistical studies and surveys]   (Direction Générale de la Statistique).
        Direction Générale de la Statistique, B P 2081, Libreville.
        1966-   irregular.   included in the subscription to above.
        Issued as supplements to the "Bulletin mensuel de la statistique", each issue is on a particular subject,
            as indicated below:-
                No.1   Methods of compiling wholesale price indices.
                    3   Provisional results of a survey of roads in Gabon, and results of an enquiry on the traffic
                        in goods on the frontier between Gabon and Congo.
                    4   Study of the economy, population and foreign trade.
                    7   Report on road traffic, 1965 1968.
                    8   Balance of payments.
                    9   Methodology of the census of population, 1969/70.
                   10   Statistics of the pay of civil servants, 1969-1971.
        §   Fr.

541 Situation économique, financière et sociale   [Economic, financial and social situation]   (Direction
            Générale de la Statistique).
        Direction Générale de la Statistique, B P 2081, Libreville.
        1963-   1972.   CFA Fr 4,000 (CFA Fr 4,500 to 6,000 abroad).   176p.
        Contains data on production (forestry, agriculture, mining and industry), foreign trade, transport,
            prices, public finance, employment and wages, money and credit, and social services (health,
            education and assistance).
        Time factor: the 1972 edition, the latest to be published at time of going to press, was issued in 1974
            and has data for several years to 1972.
        §   Fr.

542 Bulletin des statistiques générales   [General statistical bulletin]   (Union Douanière et Economique de
            l'Afrique Centrale).
        Union Douanière et Economique de l'Afrique Centrale, B P 1418, Bangui, Central African Republic.
        1947-   quarterly.   CFA Fr 2,000 yr (CFA Fr 2,800 yr in other UDEAC countries;
                                       CFA Fr 3,000 to 4,500 elsewhere).
        Contains data for each of the UDEAC countries on climate, production, transport, foreign trade,
            intercommodity trade, prices, credit and money.
        Time factor: each issue has statistics for two years and several quarters to the date of the issue, and
            is published several months later.
        §   Fr.

543 Etudes statistiques   [Statistical studies]   (Union Douanière et Economique de l'Afrique Centrale).
        Union Douanière et Economique de l'Afrique Centrale, B P 1418, Bangui, Central African Republic.
        1967-   quarterly.   not priced.
        Each issue is devoted to a separate subject.
        §   Fr.

544 L'économie gabonaise   [The economy of Gabon]   (EDIAFRIC).
        EDIAFRIC, 57 avenue d'Iéna, 75783 Paris Cedex 16, France.
                2nd ed, 1977.   FrF 354.   various paginations.
        Contains information, including statistics and statistical tables, on agriculture, forestry, livestock,
            fisheries, industry, mines, energy, public works, transport, tourism, finance, foreign trade, etc.
        §   Fr.

¶   B - Production

i. Mines and mining

        Refer to 538, 541, 544.

¶   B,   continued

ii. Agriculture, fisheries, forestry, etc.

545   Résultats de l'enquête agricole au Gabon, 1960-1961: résultats définitifs   [Results of an agricultural
            survey of Gabon, 1960-1961: final results]   (INSEE).
        INSEE, 18 boulevard Adolphe Pinard, 75675 Paris Cedex 14, France.
                        not priced.   139p.
        Time factor: the report was published in 1969.
        §   Fr.

        Refer also to 538, 539, 541, 542, 544.

iii. Industry

546   Recensement général des entreprises de type moderne   [General census of business enterprises]   (Service
            National de la Statistique).
        Direction Générale de la Statistique, B P 2081, Libreville.
        Contains data on the characteristics of the enterprises and their establishments, direct and indirect
            taxes, investment, employment, wages and salaries, vehicles, capacity of power equipment, and
            production.   All enterprises are included, including handicrafts.
        Time factor: the results of the 1964 census were published in 1965.
        §   Fr.

547   Statistique industrielle, 1966: République du Gabon   [Industrial statistics, 1966: Republic of Gabon]
            (Union Douanière et Economique de l'Afrique Centrale).
        Union Douanière et Economique de l'Afrique Centrale, B P 1418, Bangui, Central African Republic.
        Contains data on number of establishments, employment, wages and salaries, vulue of output and
            input, investment, etc.
        §   Fr.

        Refer also to 538, 539, 541, 542, 544.

v. Energy

        Refer to 538, 544.

¶   C - External trade

548   Associés: commerce extérieur: République du Gabon: annuaire 1959-1966.   Associates: foreign trade:
            Gabon: annual 1959-1966   (European Communities).
        Office des Publications Officielles des Communautés Européennes, C P 1003, Luxembourg; or from
            sales agents.
                        £0.90 or FrB 100.   134p.
        One of a series of retrospective publications on the foreign trade of African states associated with the
            European Communities.   Main tables show imports and exports arranged by commodity and sub-
            divided by countries of origin and destination.   Other tables show summaries of imports and
            exports arranged by main categories of products, by countries sub-divided by main categories of
            products, and by direction of trade.   Values are in US $.
        Time factor: the volume was published late 1968.
        §   De, En, Fr, It, Nl.

549   Commerce extérieur   [Foreign trade]   (Union Douanière et Economique de l'Afrique Centrale).
        Union Douanière et Economique de l'Afrique Centrale, B P 1418, Bangui, Central African Republic.
        1960- 1973.   not priced.   75p.
        Main tables show detailed trade arranged by commodities, for each of the four member countries of
            UDEAC.   Issues for 1972 and 1973 were condensed versions.
        Time factor: the 1973 edition, published in 1975, has data for 1973.
        §   Fr.

        Refer also to 538, 539, 541, 542, 544.

¶ D - Internal distribution

550 Recensement général des entreprises de type moderne [General census of business enterprises] (Service National de la Statistique).

For description see 546.

551 Enquête sur le commerce de détail dans les régions de l'Estuaire et de l'Ogooué-Maritime, novembre 1964: septembre 1965 [Survey of retail trade in the Estuary and Maritime regions, November 1964, September 1965] (Service National de la Statistique).
Direction Générale de la Statistique, B P 2081, Libreville.
Results of the sample retail trade survey taken in the Estuary region in November 1964 and in the Maritime region in September 1965.
Time factor: the results were published in 1966.
§ Fr.

Refer also to 538, 540, 541, 544.

¶ E - Population

552 Recensement de la population [Census of population] (Service National de la Statistique).
Direction Générale de la Statistique et des Etudes Economiques, B P 2081, Libreville.
1946- 1960-61. CFA Fr 140 each volume. 3 vols.
Vol. 1 contains general tables; volume 2 contains data on the regions of Estuaire, Haut-Ogooué, Moyen-Ogooué, Ngounié and Nyanga; volume 3 the regions of Ogooué-Invido, Ogooué-Loco, Ogooué-Maritime, and Waleu-n'tem.
§ Fr.

553 Recensement de la population de la commune de Libreville...1964 [Census of the population of the town of Libreville...1964] (Service National de la Statistique).
Direction Générale de la Statistique et des Etudes Economiques, B P 2081, Libreville.
not priced. 56p.
§ Fr.

Refer also to 538, 540, 541.

¶ F - Social

i. Standard of living

Refer to 538, 541.

ii. Health and welfare

Refer to 538, 541.

iii. Education and leisure

554 Statistiques de l'enseignement au Gabon [Statistics of education in Gabon] (Ministère de l'Education Nationale).
Ministère de l'Education Nationale, B P 334, Libreville.
1972- 1973. not priced. various paginations.
Contains data on primary, secondary, technical, higher education, including schools, pupils, teachers, examinations, finance, etc.
Time factor: the 1973 issue, which gives the situation at 1st January 1973, was published later that year.
§ Fr.

Refer also to 538, 541.

GABON, continued

¶   G - Finance

   Refer to 538, 539, 541, 542, 544.

ii. Public finance

555   Comptes économiques   [Economic accounts]   (Direction Générales de la Statistique).
      Direction Générale de la Statistique, B P 2081, Libreville.
      1960-   1973.   not priced.   no pagination.
      Time factor: the 1973 edition, published in 1974, has data for 1973.
      §   Fr.

      Refer also to 538, 539, 540, 541.

¶   H - Transport and communications

   Refer to 538, 539, 540, 541, 542, 544.

Central statistical office

556
Central Statistics Division,
Ministry of Economic Planning and Industrial Development,
The Quadrangle, Banjul.
t 636.

The duties and functions of the Statistics Office are to formulate and implement statistical programmes to serve the needs of development, manpower, and physical planning, to assist the statistical sections of the various ministries and departments, to compute the national income accounts, to undertake censuses and surveys, to prepare short- and long-term projections of key socio-economic indicators, to provide data-processing facilities to other departments, to publish statistical data, and to coordinate statistical work of ministries and other departments.

Another important organisation collecting and publishing statistics

557
Central Bank of the Gambia,
Banjul.

The Bank computes and publishes balance of payments statistics.

Libraries

There is a library in the Statistics Office of the Ministry of Economic Planning and Industrial Development where statistical publications of Gambia, a few other countries and international organisations may be consulted. The library is open from 9.00 to 14.00 from Mondays to Thursdays and from 9.00 to 12.00 on Fridays and Saturdays, except during public holidays. English is the spoken language of the staff.

Bibliographies

A list of publications of the Central Statistics Division is compiled and published annually by the Government Printer.

Statistical publications

¶ A – General

558
Statistical summary (Central Statistical Division, Ministry of Economic Planning and Industrial Development).
Government Printer, MacCarthy Square, Banjul.
1964- 1967/68. 3s6d. 34p.
Contains statistical data on population, manpower, prices and wages, finance, external trade, internal trade, education, medical and health, judicial, police and fire services, electricity and water services, external transport, posts and telecommunications, election, agriculture, meteorology.
Time factor: the 1967/68 issue, published 1969, has data for the fiscal year 1967/68 and for some earlier years.
§ En.

559
The Gambia: reports for the years... (Gambia: Government).
Government Printer, MacCarthy Square, Banjul.
1946- 1966 & 1967. not priced.
Includes tables in the text on population, agriculture, industry, etc.
Time factor: the 1966 & 1967 edition was published in 1967.
§ En.

¶   A,   continued

560   Bulletin   (Central Bank of the Gambia).
           Central Bank of the Gambia, Banjul.
           1971-   quarterly.   not priced.
           Contains data on banking, money, public finance, foreign trade, tourism, balance of payments, gross
               domestic product, prices, and the retail price index.
           Time factor: each issue has monthly data to the last month of the quarter of the issue, and is published
               two or three months later.
           §   En.

¶   B - Production

ii. Agriculture, fisheries, forestry, etc.

561   Annual report of The Gambia Produce Marketing Board
           The Gambia Produce Marketing Board, 6th Floor, Carolyn House, Dingwall Road, Croydon CR9,
               England, and Government Printer, MacCarthy Square, Banjul.
           1949/50-   1974/75.   D 11.00 (D 11.50 abroad).   53p.
           Includes some statistics on trade, production, prices, sales, shipments, etc, of palm kernel and
               groundnuts, as well as the accounts of the Board.
           The 1974/75 issue, published in 1976, has data for the crop year 1974/75.
           §   En.

562   Annual report   (Department of Agriculture).
           Government Printer, MacCarthy Square, Banjul.
           1926/27-   1971/72.   not priced.   20p.
           Includes some agricultural statistics in the text.
           Time factor: the 1971/72 report, published in 1973, has data for the year 1971/72.
           §   En.

           Refer also to 558, 559.

iii. Industry

           Refer to 559, 560.

v. Energy

           Refer to 558.

¶   C - External trade

563   External trade statistics of The Gambia   (Central Statistics Division).
           Government Printer, MacCarthy Square, Banjul.
           1972-   1971/72-1973/74.   D 15 (D 16 abroad).   no pagination.
           Main tables show statistics of imports and exports arranged by commodity and sub-divided by countries
               of origin and destination.
           Time factor: the 1971/72-1973/74 edition, published in September 1974, has data for the fiscal years
               1971/72, 1972/73 and 1973/74.
           §   En.

           Note: earlier annual trade statistics were included in the "Report of the Customs Department",
               published by the Government Printer.

¶   C,   continued

564   Monthly summary of external trade statistics   (Central Statistics Division).
           Government Printer, MacCarthy Square, Banjul.
           1965-   D 1.00 (D 1.50 abroad) each issue.
           Main tables show statistics of imports and exports arranged by commodity and sub-divided by countries
               of origin and destination.
           Time factor: each issue has cumulated figures for the year to date and is published two or three months
               after the end of the period covered.
           §   En.

           Note: early issues were quarterly and issued by the Customs Department.

           Refer also to 558, 560.

¶   D - Internal distribution and service trades

565   Tourist statistics   (Central Statistics Division).
           Government Printer, MacCarthy Square, Banjul.
           1966/67-1972/73-   1974/75.   D 10.00 (D 11.00 abroad).   no pagination.
           Contains data on tourists entering and leaving the country, hotel beds, travel agents, etc.
           Time factor: the 1974/75 issue, published in 1975, has data for the fiscal year 1974/75.
           §   En.

           Note: a monthly "Summary of tourist statistics" is also issued, price D 1.00 (D 1.50 abroad).

           Refer also to 558, 560.

¶   E - Population

566   Population census   (Central Statistical Division).
           Government Printer, MacCarthy Square, Banjul.
           1881-   1973.   3 vols.
           Contents:
               Vol. I   Statistics for settlements & enumerative areas (population)   (D 16.00).
                      II   Statistics for settlements & enumerative areas (housing)   (D 16.00).
                     III   General report   (D 35.00).
           Also available are transcripts of recorded interviews   (D 21.00).
           Time factor: the results of the 1973 census were published in 1974.
           §   En.

567   Quarterly survey of employment and earnings and hours of work   (Central Statistical Division).
           Government Printer, MacCarthy Square, Banjul.
           1973-   D 5.00 (D 5.70 abroad).
           Contains detailed statistics by employer and employee.
           Time factor: each issue has data to the quarter of the issue and is published about six months later.
           §   En.

568   Urban labour force survey, 1974/75   (Central Statistics Division).
           Government Printer, MacCarthy Square, Banjul.
                       D 3.00 (D 3.70 abroad).
           Time factor: the report was published in May 1975.
           §   En.

           Refer also to 558, 559.

GAMBIA, continued

¶   F - Social

i. Standard of living

569   Household budget survey: Banjul area, 1968/69   (Central Statistics Division).
            Government Printer, MacCarthy Square, Banjul.
                        D 6.00.   various paginations.
            Time factor: issued as Statistical Working Paper No.12 in May 1974.
            §   En.

570   Monthly bulletin of retail prices   (Central Statistics Division).
            Government Printer, MacCarthy Square, Banjul.
            1974-   D 1.00 (D 1.50 abroad) each issue.
            Average retail prices in selected markets/areas.
            §   En.

571   Consumer price index   (Central Statistics Division).
            Government Printer, MacCarthy Square, Banjul.
            monthly.   D 1.00 (D 1.50 abroad) each issue.
            §   En.

        Refer also to 558, 560.

ii. Health and welfare

        Refer to 558.

iii. Education and leisure

572   Education statistics   (Education Department and Central Statistics Division).
            Government Printer, MacCarthy Square, Banjul.
            1976/77-   1976/77.   D 2.50.   no pagination.
            Contains data on enrolments in primary and secondary schools, vocational training, teacher training,
                educational facilities in the regions, size of classes, numbers of teachers, finances, etc.
            Time factor: the 1976/77 issue, published early 1977, has data for the academic year 1976/77.
            §   En.

        Note: earlier education statistics were published in the "Report of the Education Department".

        Refer also to 558.

iv. Justice

        Refer to 558.

¶   G - Finance

        Refer to 558, 560.

¶   H - Transport and communications

        Refer to 558.

¶ H, continued

iv. Air

573 Air transport statistics, 1966/67-1972/73 (Central Statistics Division).
Government Printer, MacCarthy Square, Banjul.
D 3.00. no pagination.
A working paper with statistics of air traffic, passengers, cargoes, mail carried, etc.
Time factor: published in 1974, the paper has data for the years 1966/67 to 1972/73.
§ En.

Refer also to 558.

GHANA

Central statistical office

574   Central Bureau of Statistics,
P O Box 1098, Accra.
t Accra 66512-9. cables GHANASTATS.

In 1961 the Office of the Government Statistician became the Central Bureau of Statistics, under the general control and superintendence of the Government Statistician. The Bureau collects, compiles, analyses, abstracts and publishes statistical information relating to the commercial, industrial, agricultural, social, financial, economic and general activities and conditions of the inhabitants of Ghana, including statistical surveys and censuses. To this end it is empowered to collaborate with the public services, other official, quasi-official and non-official organisations in a co-ordinated scheme of economic and social statistics relating to Ghana. Unpublished statistical information can often be supplied and photocopies and other facilities are available to the public.

Libraries

The Economic Library of the Central Bureau of Statistics (see above) was founded in 1949 for use by the staff of the Bureau, other government departments, and research workers in Ghana and from overseas. It has a collection of Ghanaian and other statistical publications, and is open to the public from Monday to Friday, from 8.00 to 12.30 and 13.30 to 17.00, except during public holidays. The language spoken in the library is English.

Libraries and information services abroad

Copies of all publications of the Central Bureau of Statistics, except the Statistical newsletters, are available for reference in Ghana's embassies abroad, including:-

United Kingdom	Ghana High Commission, 102 Park Street, London W.1. t 01-493 4901.
Australia	Ghana High Commission, 131 MuggaWay, Redhill, Canberra. t 95 1122.
Canada	Ghana High Commission, 85 Range Road, Ottawa. t 236 0871.
U.S.A.	Ghana Embassy, 2460 16th Street NW, Washington DC. t 462 0761.

Bibliographies

A duplicated list of the publications of the Central Bureau of Statistics is issued by the Bureau at intervals.

Statistical publications

¶ A - General

575   Statistical yearbook (Central Bureau of Statistics).
Public Relations Department, Central Sales Division, P O Box 745, Accra.
1961- 7th, 1969-70. Cedi 2.10. 192p.
Main sections:

Geography, climate, administration	Foreign trade
Population	Balance of payments estimates
Passenger movement	National income estimates
Public health	Banking and currency
Agriculture, forestry, fishing	Public finance
Industrial statistics	Education
Public supply of electricity, fuel, water	Culture and entertainment
Transport and communication	Justice and crime
Internal trade	Transactions in land
Labour and wages	Housing
Prices	International tables

Time factor: the 1969-70 edition, published in 1973, contains data for several years to 1970.
§ En.

¶   A,   continued

576   Economic survey   (Central Bureau of Statistics).
            Public Relations Department, Central Sales Division, P O Box 745, Accra.
            1955-   1969-71.   Cedi 6.00.   143p.
            Tables are included throughout the text; there are chapters on economic conditions, external trade and
                balance of payments, money and banking, agriculture, industrial production, transport and
                communication, employment, wages and earnings, prices.
            Time factor: the 1969-71 edition, published in 1976, contains data for the period 1969-71.
            §   En.

577   Statistical handbook   (Central Bureau of Statistics).
            Ministry of Information, Accra.
            1966-   4th, 1970.   Cedi 1.75.   c250p.
            A concise pocketbook of summarised information, including geography and population, passenger
                movements, public health, industrial production, transport and communications, internal trade
                and labour, distributive trade, prices, external trade, national income and balance of payments,
                banking and currency, public finance, education, culture and entertainment, justice and crime.
            Time factor: the 1970 edition, published in 1971, has data for 1970 and for earlier years.
            §   En.

578   Quarterly digest of statistics   (Central Bureau of Statistics).
            Public Relations Department, Central Sales Division, P O Box 745, Accra.
            1952-   Cedi 1.20 per issue.
            Contains data on labour, fuel and power, mining, animals slaughtered, external trade and payments,
                shipping and aircraft movements, inland transport, public finance, prices, banking and currency.
            Time factor: each issue appears about 6 months after the date of the issue, containing data for the last
                three full years and monthly or quarterly figures for the last two years or so up to the date of the
                issue.
            §   En.

579   Quarterly economic bulletin   (Bank of Ghana).
            Bank of Ghana, P O Box 2674, Accra.
            1961-   not priced.
            Includes statistical statements on money and banking, public finance, balance of payments, national
                and Accra consumer price indices, production of raw cotton, and mineral production.
            Time factor: each issue contains the latest data available at the time of publication.
            §   En.

580   Monthly economic bulletin   (Ghana Commercial Bank).
            Ghana Commercial Bank, P O Box 134, Accra; and 60 Cheapside, London EC2, England.
            1970-   not priced.
            A four-page bulletin devoted to the economic scene, economic trends, and selected economic
                indicators.
            §   En.

581   Report...   (Bank of Ghana).
            Bank of Ghana, P O Box 2674, Accra.
            1957/58-   1973/74.   not priced.   69p.
            Part I deals with the operations of the Bank; part II with international developments, internal
                developments, balance of payments, public finance, and monetary and financial developments;
                and part III has statistical statements, including money and banking, public finance, balance of
                payments, and a general section (consumer price indices, etc).
            §   En.

¶ B - Production

i. Mines and mining

582   Annual report   (Ghana Chamber of Mines).
          Ghana Chamber of Mines, P O Box 991, Accra.
          1927-   1974/75.   not priced.   40p.
          Includes statistical data on mineral production of member companies, yearly output of gold from 1880,
              tonnage crushed by individual properties, production of gold by individual properties, estimated
              value of gold produced by largest individual mines, diamond production, diamond exports, licenses
              issued, bauxite produced, manganese produced, and labour employed by mining industry generally.
          Time factor: the 1974/75 report, published late 1975, has data for 1974/75 and some earlier years.
          §   En.

          Refer also to 578, 579.

ii. Agriculture, fisheries, forestry, etc.

583   Report on Ghana sample census of agriculture   (Economic and Marketing Division, Ministry of Agriculture).
          Ministry of Agriculture, P O Box 299, Accra.
          1970-   1970.   not priced.
          Vol. 1 has information on the planning, design and accuracy of the census; data on holders and holdings;
              livestock and poultry; and main cash crops (tree crops, cereals, root crops, pulses and nuts, and
              fruit and vegetables).
          Time factor: Vol. 1 was published in 1972.
          §   En.

584   Annual report   (Ministry of Agriculture).
          Ministry of Agriculture, P O Box 299, Accra.
          1966-   1970.   not priced.   198p.
          Includes the reports of the various divisions of the Ministry, with some statistics in the text - crop
              production, cocoa, mechanisation and transport, irrigation and reclamation, economics and
              marketing, animal husbandry, produce inspection, fisheries, animal health, etc.
          Time factor: the 1970 report, published in 1974, has data for 1970.
          §   En.

585   [Annual report]   (Ghana Cocoa Marketing Board).
          Ghana Cocoa Marketing Board, P O Box 933, Accra.
          1948-   1969/70.   not priced.   77p.
          Contains the trading results of the Board.
          Time factor: the 1969/70 report, published in 1975, has data for the years 1966 to September 1970.
          §   En.

586   Fisheries Department annual report for biennium...   (Ministry of Agriculture).
          Ministry of Agriculture, P O Box 299, Accra.
          1957-   1973/74.   not priced.   26p.
          Contains data on fishery statistics generally, marine fishing, freshwater fishing, the Fishery Research
              Unit, sales of outboard motors, etc.
          Time factor: the 1973/74 report, published in 1975, has data for 1973 and 1974.
          §   En.

          Refer also to 575, 576, 578, 579.

¶   B,   continued

iii. Industry

587   Industrial statistics   (Central Bureau of Statistics).
          Public Relations Department, Central Sales Division, P O Box 745, Accra.
          1958/59-   1969.   Cedi 3.50.   89p.
          Contains data on the gross value and value added of industrial production as a whole; on the number,
              structure and movement of the working labour force engaged in the different industrial production
              activities, and the wages and salaries paid; on gross additions to fixed assets classified by economic
              activity group and type of ownership; and finally, on some important statistical indicators which
              may be used in the study of growth developments and the measurement of productivity in the
              different groups of industrial production activities.
          Time factor: the 1969 issue, published late 1971, contains data for 1969.
          §   En.

          Note: a "Directory of industrial enterprises and establishments" first appeared in 1963 with later
              editions in 1969 and 1970 (Cedi 3.50).

588   Industrial census report   (Central Bureau of Statistics).
          Public Relations Department, Central Sales Division, P O Box 745, Accra.
          1962-   1962.   Cedi 2.00.   640p.
          Contains a comprehensive structural picture of the whole secondary industry of Ghana, including all
              small, medium-sized and large establishments engaged in mining and quarrying, manufacturing,
              construction, electricity, gas and steam.
          Time factor: the report refers to the year 1962 and was published in 1965.
          §   En.

          Refer also to 575, 576, 577.

589   Input-output tables of Ghana: 1968   (Central Bureau of Statistics).
          Public Relations Department, Central Sales Division, P O Box 745, Accra.
                              Cedi 1.00.   19p.
          Time factor: published in October 1973.
          §   En.

  v. Energy

590   Annual report   (Electricity Corporation of Ghana).
          Electricity Corporation of Ghana, P O Box 521, Accra.
          1960/61-   1975.   Cedi 2.00.   55p.
          Includes statistical tables of cost, operations, production and consumption, etc, as well as the
              accounts of the corporation.
          Time factor: the 1975 report, published in 1976, has data for 1975.
          §   En.

          Refer also to 575, 578.

¶   C - External trade

591   Annual report on external trade   (Central Bureau of Statistics).
          Public Relations Department, Central Sales Division, P O Box 745, Accra.
          1952-   1966-68.   Cedi 9.10.   2 vols.
          Contains detailed statistics of imports, exports and re-exports, arranged by commodity sub-divided by
              countries of origin and destination, as well as various summary tables.
          §   En.

¶ C, continued

592   External trade statistics of Ghana   (Central Bureau of Statistics).
            Public Relations Department, Central Sales Division, P O Box 745, Accra.
            1951-   monthly.   Cedi 1.20; Cedi 10.50 yr.
            Contains summary tables; detailed tables of imports, exports and re-exports arranged by commodity and
                sub-divided by countries of origin and destination; imports of motor vehicles; and shipping and
                aircraft cargo statistics.
            Time factor: each issue has data for that month and cumulated figures for the years to date (December
                issue having the annual figures) and is published about two months later.
            §   En.

593   Statistical news letter: Ghana's foreign trade   (Central Bureau of Statistics).
            Central Bureau of Statistics (Information Section), P O Box 1098, Accra.
            monthly, with a supplement.   Cedi 3.60 yr for newsletter; Cedi 3.60 yr for supplement.
            The newsletter contains brief up-to-date totals only; the supplement has more detail and appears later.
            §   En.

            Refer also to 575, 576, 577, 578.

¶   D - Internal distribution and service trades

594   Distribution trade statistics: wholesale and retail trades   (Central Bureau of Statistics).
            Public Relations Department, Central Sales Division, P O Box 745, Accra.
            1967-   1967.   Cedi 3.50.   various paginations.
            Contains summary tables for the whole country and also detailed tables by establishments, kind of
                operation, nationality of owner, numbers employed, wages, etc.
            Time factor: the report of the 1967 census was published in 1971.
            §   En.

            Note: a "Directory of distributive trade establishments" was published in 1968   (Cedi 1.50).

595   Quarterly statistics on tourism   (Ghana Tourist Board).
            Ghana Tourist Board, P O Box 46, Accra.
            1972-   not priced.
            Contains data on tourist movements (arrivals, purpose of visit, mode of travel, port of disembarkation,
                nationality), tourist payments, and the performance of the tourist industry.
            Time factor: each issue is published about three months after the end of the period covered, and
                includes 12 months statistics in some tables.
            §   En.

            Refer also to 575, 577.

¶   E - Population

596   Population census of Ghana   (Central Bureau of Statistics).
            Public Relations Department, Central Sales Division, P O Box 745, Accra.
            1883-   1970.   6 vols, plus special reports.
            Contents:
                1.   Gazeteer   (Cedi 10.00).
                2.   Statistics of localities and enumerative areas   (Cedi 10.00).
                3.   Demographic characteristics   (Cedi 8.00).
                4.   Economic characteristics of local authorities, regions and total country.
                5.   General report.
                6.   Post enumerative survey - statistical summary.
            Special reports:
                A   Statistics of towns with 10,000 population or more.
                B   Socio-economic indices of enumeration areas.
                C   Census data for new regions.
                D   Regions   (Cedi 1.20 for each regional volume).
            §   En.

¶   E,   continued

597   Births and deaths statistical newsletter   (Registrar of Births and Deaths).
         The Registrar of Births and Deaths, P O Box M 270, Accra.
         1965-   quarterly.   not priced.
         Time factor: each issue relates to the quarter ended about six months prior to publication.
         §   En.

598   Migration statistics   (Central Bureau of Statistics).
         Public Relations Department, Central Sales Division, P O Box 745, Accra.
         1953-   no.15, 1971.   Cedi 0.60.   31p.
         Contains data on arrivals and departures by sex, West African and others, month of departure, age,
             country, nationality, frontier posts, etc.
         Time factor: the 1971 issue, with data for 1971, was published late 1974.
         §   En.

599   Labour statistics   (Central Bureau of Statistics).
         Public Relations Department, Central Sales Division, P O Box 745, Accra.
         1957-   no.16, 1971.   Cedi 0.60.   c30p.
         Contains data on employment, including numbers by industry, nationality, and region in all sectors,
             private enterprise sector, and public authorities sector.
         Time factor: the 1971 issue, published in 1973, has data for 1971.
         §   En.

         Refer also to 575, 576, 577, 578.

¶   F - Social

i.   Standard of living

600   Statistical news letter: consumer price index   (Central Bureau of Statistics).
         Central Bureau of Statistics (Information Section), P O Box 1098, Accra.
         monthly.   Cedi 3.60 yr.
         Contains brief up-to-date statistical information.
         §   En.

         Refer also to 575, 576, 577, 579.

ii.   Health and welfare

601   Medical statistics report   (Ministry of Health).
         Ministry of Health, Accra.
         1967-   1967.   not priced.   71p.
         Contains data on population and vital statistics, deaths, hospital residence (in- and out-patients),
             operations, etc.
         Time factor: the 1967 report, published in 1968, has data for 1967.
         §   En.

         Note: earlier data was published in "Report of the Medical Department" from 1937.

         Refer also to 575, 577.

¶   F,   continued

iii. Education and leisure

602   Digest of education statistics (pre-university)   (Ghana Education Service; Ministry of Education).
            Ministry of Education, P O Box M 45, Accra.
            1962/63-   1974/75.   not priced.   159p.
            Contains data on primary, secondary and further education, enrolments, teachers, classes, schools,
                examinations, etc.
            Time factor: the 1974/75 issue, published late 1975, has data for the academic year 1974/75.
            §   En.

            Refer also to 575, 577.

iv. Justice

603   Statistical newsletter: judicial statistics   (Central Bureau of Statistics).
            Central Bureau of Statistics (Information Section), P O Box 1098, Accra.
            monthly.   Cedi 3.60 yr.
            Contains data on judicial and criminal statistics.
            Time factor: each issue has data for several years and months to the latest figures available.
            §   En.

            Refer also to 575, 577.

¶   G – Finance

i. Banking

            Refer to 575, 577, 578, 579, 581.

ii. Public finance

604   Statistical newsletter: public finance   (Central Bureau of Statistics).
            Central Bureau of Statistics (Information Section), P O Box 1098, Accra.
            monthly.   Cedi 3.60 yr.
            Contains data on central government finance, money and banking.
            Time factor: each issue has data for several years and months to the latest figures available.
            §   En.

            Refer also to 575, 576, 577, 578, 579, 581.

v. Insurance

605   Insurance in Ghana...annual report   (Ministry of Finance. Commissioner of Insurance).
            Ministry of Finance, P O Box 202, Accra.
            1966-   1973.   Cedi 2.00.   69p.
            Part II of the report is concerned with insurance statistics (life, fire, motor, accident, marine and
                aviation, employers' liability, etc).
            Time factor: the 1973 report, published in 1976, has data for 1973 and some earlier figures.
            §   En.

¶   H – Transport and communications

            Refer to 575, 576, 577, 578.

¶   H,   continued

ii. Road

06   Motor vehicle statistics   (Central Bureau of Statistics).
          Public Relations Department, Central Sales Division, P O Box 745, Accra.
          1956-   No.15, 1970.   Cedi 0.60.   36p.
          Contains data on new registrations for the past 7 years (cars, public conveyance vehicles, goods
                vehicles, trailers and caravans, special purpose vehicles, timber tugs, tankers, dumpers and
                tippers, tractors and mechanical equipment) and current licences for the year of the issue.
                Issued as Statistical Report Series V.
          Time factor: the 1970 issue was published mid-1973.
          §   En.

07   Statistical newsletter: motor vehicle registrations   (Central Bureau of Statistics).
          Central Bureau of Statistics (Information Section), P O Box 1098, Accra.
                      monthly.   Cedi 3.60 yr.
          Contains data for motor cars, goods and passenger vehicles, special purpose vehicles, tractors and
                mechanical equipment, by class and make of vehicle.
          Time factor: gives provisional figures, and also monthly averages for the past 10 years.
          §   En.

          Refer also to 578.

iii. Rail

608   Administration report of the Ghana Railway, Takoradi Harbour, other ports and lighthouses and Tema
                Harbour...   (Railway and Ports Headquarters).
          Railway and Ports Headquarters, Takoradi.
          1958/59-   1967/68.   not priced.   139p.
          Includes statistics in the text and statistical tables on operations and finances.
          Time factor: the 1967/68 report, published in 1972, has data for 1967/68.
          §   En.

iv. Air

609   Civil aviation statistics   (Central Bureau of Statistics).
          Public Relations Department, Central Sales Division, P O Box 745, Accra.
          1954/56-   no.15, 1972.   Cedi 0.60.   35p.
          Contains data on air traffic by months for the year of the issue (internal and external by port); air
                traffic for the latest four years by port, type of movement, internal and external air traffic,
                origin and destination of aircraft, origin and destination of passengers, commercial freight,
                and mail.   Issued as Statistical Report Series II.
          Time factor: the 1972 issue was published late 1975.
          §   En.

          Refer also to 578.

Central statistical office

610   Service de la Statistique Générale   [General Statistical Office],
B P 221, Conakry.

The office is responsible for the collection, analysis and publication of economic and social statistics of the Republic of Guinea (formerly French Guinea).

Statistical publications

¶   A - General

611   Bulletin spécial de statistique (statistique et économie)   [Bulletin of statistics]   (Service de la Statistique Générale).
Service de la Statistique Générale, B P 221, Conakry.
1962-   /1962 & 1st quarter 1963/   not priced.   32p.
Main sections:

Demography	Public Finance
Transport	Education
Power	Health
Mines and Industry	Agriculture and livestock
Foreign trade	Shipping

Time factor: published in 1965, the tables usually have information for the years 1958 to 1962 and the first quarter of 1963.   It was intended that this should be the first issue of an annual publication.
§   Fr.

612   Etudes agricoles et économiques de quatre villages de Guinée Française   [Agricultural and economic study of four villages in French Guinea]   (Service de la Statistique Générale).
not priced.   4 vols.
Contents:
    I.   Futa Diaion
    II.   Guinée Maritime
    III.   Vallée du Niger
    IV.   Guinée Forestière
Some statistics are included in the text.
Time factor: published from 1955-1957.
§   Fr.

¶   B - Production

Refer to 611, 612.

¶   C - External trade

Refer to 611.

¶   E - Population

613   Etude démographique par sondage en Guinée, 1954-1955: résultats définitifs   [Sample demographic survey of Guinea: final results]   (Service des Statistiques, Administration Générale des Services de la France d'Outre-mer).
Imprimerie Nationale, 2 rue Paul-Hervieu, 75732 Paris Cedex 15, France.
FrF 10 each vol.   2 vols.
Volume 1 contains data on population by sex, age, ethnic group, marital status, births, deaths.
   Volume 2 has data on migration, occupations and educational status.
Time factor: the reports were published in 1959 and 1961.
§   Fr.

Refer also to 611.

¶ F - Social

ii. Health and welfare

Refer to 611.

iii. Education and leisure

Refer to 611.

¶ G - Finance

ii. Public finance

Refer to 611.

¶ H - Transport and communications

Refer to 611.

Central statistical office

614   Direcção Geral de Estatística   [General Department of Statistics],
       Comissariado de Estado de Desenvolvimento Económico e Planificação,
       Bissau.

       The Department compiles and publishes certain statistics, particularly foreign trade statistics, for
Guinea-Bissau, which was Portuguese Guinea until independence.

Libraries

       There is a library in the Commissariat which is open during office hours, and the collection includes
publications of Guinea-Bissau, other countries and international organisations.   Portuguese and French
are the languages best understood by the staff.

Statistical publications

¶   A - General

615   Anuario estatístico   [Statistical yearbook]   (Direcção Geral de Estatística).
       Direcção Geral de Estatística, Bissau.
       1974-   1974.   not priced.
       Contains mainly foreign trade statistics.
       Time factor: the 1974 edition, published in 1977, has data for 1974.
       §   Pt.

616   Boletim trimestral de estatística   [Quarterly bulletin of statistics]   (Direcção Geral de Estatística).
       Direcção Geral de Estatística, Bissau.
       1974-   not priced.
       Includes foreign trade and some other statistics.
       Time factor: each issue is published about twelve months after the period covered.
       §   Pt.

617   Anuário estatístico, vol.II: Território ultramarinos   [Statistical yearbook, vol.II: Overseas territories]
           (Instituto Nacional de Estatística).
       Instituto Nacional de Estatística, Avenida António José de Almeida, Lisboa 1, Portugal.
       1967-   1973.   Esc 100.   264p.
       Main sections:

Area and climate	Manufacturing industry
Demography	Energy
Health	Construction
Labour	Transport and communications
Social security	Tourism
Co-operative organisations	Consumption and internal trade
Education, cultural activities,	Foreign trade
recreation, sport	Wages and prices
Justice	Money and credit
Agriculture, forestry, fisheries	Public finance
Mining industry	

       Covers the territory which is now Guiné-Bissau, but was then Portuguese Guinea.
       Time factor: the 1973 edition has data for several years to 1971 and 1972.   Publication of volume II
           of the yearbook ceased with this edition.
       §   Pt, Fr.

618   Boletim mensal de estatística   [Monthly bulletin of statistics]   (Instituto Nacional de Estatística).
       Instituto Nacional de Estatística, Avenido António José de Almeida, Lisboa 1, Portugal.
       1929-   Esc 30 (Esc 40 abroad) or Esc 300 (Esc 400 abroad) yr.
       Included data on industrial production, construction, transport and communications, tourism, foreign
           trade, and prices for Portuguese Guinea, until it became independent and named Guiné-Bissau.
       §   Pt, Fr.

¶   B - Production

ii. Agriculture, fisheries, forestry, etc.

19   Recenseamento agrícola, 1960-1961   [Agricultural census, 1960-1961]   (Repartição Provincial dos
            Serviços de Economia e Estatística Geral).
            Direcção Geral de Estatística, Bissau.
                                    not priced.
            §   Pt.

        Refer also to 616, 617.

iii. Industry

        Refer to 616, 617, 618.

¶   C - External trade

20   Estatísticas do comércio externo   [Statistics of foreign trade]   (Repartição Provincial dos Serviços
            de Estatística).
            Direcção Geral de Estatística, Bissau.
            1950/51-   1970.   not priced.   190p.
            Main table shows detailed imports arranged by commodity and sub-divided by countries of origin.
            Time factor: the 1970 issue, published in 1974, has data for 1970.
            §   Pt.

21   Boletim mensal de comércio externo   [Monthly bulletin of foreign trade]   (Direcção Geral de Estatística).
            Direcção Geral de Estatística, Bissau.
            1974-   not priced.
            Time factor: each issue is published about six months after the month covered.
            §   Pt.

22   Estatísticas do comércio externo   [Statistics of foreign trade]   (Instituto Nacional de Estatística).
            Instituto Nacional de Estatística, Avenida António José de Almeida, Lisboa 1, Portugal.
            1843-   1967.   2 vols.
            Volume II included a section on the foreign trade of Portugal's overseas provinces, including
                Portuguese Guinea.   Arrangement under each overseas province was by commodities.
            Time factor: the 1967 issue was the last to include this section.
            §   Pt, Fr.

        Refer also to 615, 616, 617, 618.

¶   E - Population

23   Censo da população   [Census of population]   (Repartição Provincial dos Serviços de Economia e
            Estatística Geral).
            Direcção Geral de Estatística, Bissau.
            1940-   1950.   not priced.   2 vols.
            Volume 1 contains data on the non-indigenous population; volume 2 on the indigenous.
            §   Pt.

        Note: a brief report on the indigenous population in 1952 was published in "Boletim cultural da Guiné
            Portuguesa", ano 8, no.29, January 1953.   A census was taken in 1960 but no publications
            have appeared.

        Refer also to 617.

¶   H - Transport and communications

Refer to 617, 618.

Central statistical office

24   Direction de la Statistique   [Department of Statistics],
        B P 222, Abidjan.
        t 32-15-38.

        The Department, which is in the Ministry of Economy and Finance, is responsible for the collection, analysis and publication of regular statistics in the fields of economics and demography, and for undertaking enquiries, surveys and censuses.

Statistical publications

¶   A - General

25   Bulletin mensuel de statistique   [Monthly bulletin of statistics]   (Direction de la Statistique).
        Direction de la Statistique, B P 222, Abidjan.
        1948-   CFA Fr 200 or CFA Fr 2,000 yr. Supplements priced separately.
        Contains data on production (agriculture, livestock, power and mines), construction, climate, transport, foreign trade, wholesale and retail price indices, cost of living indices, and finance. Each year there are supplements on foreign trade, employment, finance, motor vehicle registrations, etc.
        Time factor: each issue includes statistics for about three years including the current year to the date of the issue.
        §   Fr.

26   Situation économique de la Côte d'Ivoire   [Economic situation in the Ivory Coast]   (Direction de la Statistique).
        Direction de la Statistique, B P 222, Abidjan.
        1960- 1972.   not priced.   various paginations.
        Contains data on primary production (agriculture, forestry, fishing, livestock), industrial activity, external trade, transport, labour, education, prices and price indices, public finance, money and credit, and economic accounts.
        Time factor: the 1972 issue, published early 1975, has data for 1972 and also for 1970 and 1971 in some tables.
        §   Fr.

27   Bulletin mensuel   [Monthly bulletin]   (Chambre de Commerce de la République de Côte d'Ivoire).
        Chambre de Commerce de la République de Côte d'Ivoire, 6 avenue Barthe, B P 1399, Abidjan.
        1968-   not priced.
        Contains chapters on the work of commissions, economic questions, information notes (prices of agricultural production, tourism, social affairs and work, foreign trade, etc.), enterprises, offers and orders, traffic at ports, customs revenue, etc.
        §   Fr.

28   Bulletin mensuel   [Monthly bulletin]   (Chambre d'Industrie de Côte d'Ivoire).
        Chambre d'Industrie de Côte d'Ivoire, 11 avenue Lamblin, B P 1758, Abidjan.
        1965-   not priced.
        Mainly an information bulletin, but includes some statistics, such as traffic by rail and at ports, exports of wood, etc.
        §   Fr.

29   Statistiques économiques ivoiriennes   [Economic statistics of Ivory Coast]   (Chambre d'Industrie de Côte d'Ivoire).
        Chambre d'Industrie de Côte d'Ivoire, B P 1758, Abidjan.
        1972- 1974.   not priced.   14p.
        Contains data on national accounts, the infrastructure (population, transport, energy, customs, etc.), foreign trade, agriculture, forestry, fisheries, livestock, industries, construction and public works.
        Time factor: the 1974 issue, published in 1975, has data for 1974.
        §   Fr.

¶   A,   continued

630   Inventaire économique et social de la Côte d'Ivoire   [Economic and social inventory of the Ivory Coast]
              (Ministère des Finances, des Affaires Economiques et du Plan; Service de la Statistique).
              Direction de la Statistique, B P 222, Abidjan.
              1947/56-   1947/58.   not priced.   283p.
              Includes statistical tables on all economic and social subjects.
              Time factor: the 1947/58 edition, published in 1960, has data for the years 1947 to 1958.
              §   Fr.

631   Côte d'Ivoire: faits et chiffres   [Ivory Coast: facts and figures]   (Ministère de l'Information).
              Ministère de l'Information, Abidjan.
              1966-   1970.   not priced.   109p.
              Contains information on the history, geography, law, people, economy and culture of Ivory Coast,
                  and includes a few statistics and statistical tables.
              Time factor: the 1970 issue was published in 1970.
              §   Fr and En eds.

632   Etudes économiques et financières   [Economic and financial studies]   (Bureau d'Etudes et de la
              Coordination, Ministère de l'Economie et des Finances).
              Bureau d'Etudes et de la Coordination, B P 1766, Abidjan.
              1969-   quarterly.   not priced.
              Each issue deals with a different economic or financial subject, and statistical tables are included in
                  the text.
              §   Fr.

633   L'économie ivoirienne   [The economy of Ivory Coast]   (EDIAFRIC).
              EDIAFRIC, 57 avenue d'Iéna, 75783 Paris Cedex 16, France.
                      6th ed, 1977.   FrF 354.   various paginations.
              Contains information, including statistics and statistical tables, on agriculture, forestry, livestock,
                  fisheries, industry, mines, energy, public works, transport, tourism, finance, foreign trade,
                  and regionalisation.
              §   Fr.

¶   B - Production

i. Mines and mining

634   Rapport annuel   [Annual report]   (Ministère de l'Economie et des Finances. Secrétariat d'Etat Chargé
              des Mines).
              Secrétariat d'Etat Chargé des Mines, Ministère de l'Economie et des Finances, Abidjan.
              1970-   1974.   not priced.   97p.
              Contains data on the activities at the mines and their contribution to the national economy, wages and
                  investments, the activities of regional divisions of mines, mining economy (production, value of
                  production and export, finances, taxes, and the export of expertese on uncut diamonds), and
                  geology.
              Time factor: the 1974 issue, published in 1975, has data for 1973 and 1974.
              §   Fr.

              Note: the Secretariat also issues a quarterly press notice.

              Refer also to 625, 633.

¶   B,   continued

ii. Agriculture, fisheries and forestry, etc.

35   Statistiques agricoles   [Agricultural statistics]   (Ministère de l'Agriculture. Direction de la Documentation
            et des Statistiques Rurales. Sous-direction des Statistiques Rurales).
        Ministère de l'Agriculture, Abidjan.
        1970- 1972.   not priced.   131p.
        Contains data on tractors, oils, production, prices, co-operation, and foreign trade.   Crops include
            pineapple, banana, vegetable essences, cocoa, coffee, cotton, nuts, palm oil, tobacco, and
            market-garden crops.
        Time factor: the 1972 issue, published in 1975, has data for 1872.
        §   Fr.

        Refer also to 625, 626, 627, 628.

iii. Industry

36   Recensement des entreprises, 1962   [Census of business, 1962]   (Direction de la Statistique).
        Direction de la Statistique, B P 222, Abidjan.
        The results, in which the data are grouped according to economic activity and kind of power equipment,
            were published in "Bulletin mensuel de statistique: Supplément no.4", 1962.
        §   Fr.

37   Principales industries installées en Côte d'Ivoire   [Principal industries in the Ivory Coast]   (Chambre
            d'Industrie de Côte d'Ivoire).
        Chambre d'Industrie de Côte d'Ivoire, 11 avenue Lamblin, B P 1758, Abidjan.
        1971- 1975.   not priced.   100p.
        Mainly directory information, but also includes statistics of capital, investments, exports, employment,
            wages, etc, for each industry.
        Time factor: the 1975 issue, published in May 1975, has data for the position at 1st January 1975 and
            also earlier years.
        §   Fr.

38   La situation de l'industrie ivoirienne à fin 1970   [The industrial situation in the Ivory Coast at the end of
            1970]   (Ministère du Plan, Direction du Développement Industriel).
        Direction du Développement Industriel, B P 4196, Abidjan.
                            not priced.   33p.
        Concerned with investment in industry, numbers of enterprises, finances, exports, etc.   Statistics and
            statistical tables appear in the text.
        Time factor: includes statistics for two or three years to 1970.
        §   Fr.

        Refer also to 626, 627, 629.

iv. Construction

        Refer to 625, 629.

v. Energy

39   Rapport annuel   [Annual report]   (Energie Electrique de la Côte d'Ivoire).
        Energie Electrique de la Côte d'Ivoire, B P 1345, Abidjan.
        1968- 1975.   not priced.   56p.
        Includes some statistical data on the electricity industry.
        Time factor: the 1975 report, published late 1976, has data for 1975 and 1974.
        §   Fr.

¶   B.v,   continued

640   Statistiques analyriques d'électricité   [Analytical statistics of electricity]   (Energie Electrique de la Côte d'Ivoire).
       Energie Electrique de la Côte d'Ivoire, B P 1345, Abidjan.
       1972-   1975.   not priced.   152p.
       Detailed statistics of production, sales, consumption, etc, of electricity.
       Time factor: the 1975 issue, published in 1976, has data for the years 1972 to 1975.
       §   Fr.

       Refer also to 625.

¶   C - External trade

641   Statistiques du commerce extérieur de la Côte d'Ivoire: commerce spécial: importations   [Foreign trade statistics of Ivory Coast: imports]   (Direction de la Statistique).
       Direction de la Statistique, B P 222, Abidjan.
       1954-   monthly.   not priced.
       Contains detailed statistics of imports arranged by commodity and sub-divided by countries of origin, and also by countries of origin sub-divided by commodities.
       Time factor: each issue has cumulated figures for the year up to the date of the issue, and is published several months later.
       §   Fr.

642   Statistiques du commerce extérieur de la Côte d'Ivoire: commerce spécial: exportations   [Foreign trade statistics of Ivory Coast: exports]   (Direction de la Statistique).
       Direction de la Statistique, B P 222, Abidjan.
       1954-   monthly.   not priced.
       Contains detailed statistics of exports arranged by commodity and sub-divided by countries of destination, and also by countries of destination sub-divided by commodities.
       Time factor: each issue has cumulated figures for the year up to the date of the issue, and is published several months later.
       §   Fr.

643   Commerce extérieur de la Côte d'Ivoire: résultats et évolution   [Foreign trade of the Ivory Coast: results and trends]   (Direction Générale des Affaires Economiques et des Relations Economiques Extérieures).
       Direction Générale des Affaires Economiques et des Relations Economiques Extérieures, Abidjan.
       1962/68-   1973.   not priced.   166p.
       A resumé of the foreign trade of Ivory Coast, with statistical tables in the text.
       Time factor: the 1973 issue, published in 1975, has data for the years 1969 to 1973.
       §   Fr.

       Refer also to 625, 626, 627, 628, 629.

¶   D - Internal distribution and service trades

644   Statistique du tourisme   [Tourist statistics]   (Ministère d'Etat Chargé du Tourism).
       Ministère d'Etat Chargé du Tourism, B P V 184, Abidjan.
       1973-   1975.   not priced.   101p.
       Contains detailed statistics of tourism, including nationality of tourists, reasons for visit, numbers entering the country, etc.
       Time factor: the 1975 issue, published in 1976, has data for 1975.
       §   Fr.

       Refer also to 625, 627, 636.

¶   E – Population

45   Côte d'Ivoire, 1965 population: études regionales 1962, 1965 – synthese   [Ivory Coast, 1965 population:
        regional studies 1962, 1965]   (Ministère du Plan).
      Ministère du Plan, Abidjan.
                         not priced.   208p.
      Contains data on population (history, ethnic, urban and rural), structure (households, etc), individuals
        (age, marital situation, active population, etc), demography and migration.
      Time factor: published in 1967.
      §   Fr.

46   Etude socio-économique de la zone urbaine d'Abidjan, 1963   [Socio-economic study of the urban district
        of Abidjan, 1963]   (Ministère des Finances, des Affaires Economiques et du Plan).
      Ministère des Finances, des Affaires Economiques et du Plan, Abidjan.
      The results of a study published in a series of 8 reports of which 3 contain statistical tables and no.4 an
        analysis of the results.
      Time factor: the reports were published between 1964 and 1966.
      §   Fr.

47   Recensement de la commune de Grand Bassam, avril 1963   [Census of the town of Grand Bassam, April
        1963]   (Ministère des Finances, des Affaires Economiques et du Plan).
      Ministère des Finances, des Affaires Economiques et du Plan, Abidjan.
      Time factor: the report was published in 1966.
      §   Fr.

48   Recensement de la ville de Dabou (1966)   [Census of the town of Dabou (1966)]   (Ministère des Finances,
        des Affaires Economiques et du Plan).
      Ministère des Finances, des Affaires Economiques et du Plan, Abidjan.
      §   Fr.

      Note: censuses of the urban centres at Abengourou, Dimbokro and Man were taken in 1957/58 and of
        Bouake in 1958, the results being published in 1960-1961.

      Refer also to 629.

¶   F – Social

i. Standard of living

      Refer to 625, 626.

iii. Education and leisure

49   Situation de l'enseignement...   [Education situation]   (Ministère de l'Education Nationale).
      Ministère de l'Education Nationale, Abidjan.
      1964-   1970.   not priced.   various paginations.
      Contains data on students, teachers, schools and classes in public and private sector at pre-school,
        primary, secondary, higher and normal level.   Also data on university education.
      Time factor: the 1970 issue contains data as at 1st January 1970 and was published in 1971.
      §   Fr.

¶   G – Finance

      Refer to 625, 626.

IVORY COAST,   continued

¶   G,   continued

ii. Public finance

650   Les comptes de la nation   [National accounts]   (Direction des Etudes de Développement).
            Direction des Etudes de Développement, Abidjan.
            1960/65-   1974.   not priced.   112p.
            Time factor: the 1974 issue, published late 1976, has data for 1974 and some earlier years.
            §   Fr.

651   Evolution du commerce extérieur Ivoirien - balance commercial   [Trends in foreign trade and balance of
                payments]   (Direction des Affaires Economiques et des Relations Economiques Extérieures).
            Direction Générale des Affaires Economiques et des Relations Economiques Extérieures, Abidjan.
            1965/69-   1968/72.   not priced.   142p.
            Time factor: the 1968/72 issue, published in 1972, has data for the years 1968 to 1972.
            §   Fr.

            Note: prior to 1965, published as a supplement to "Bulletin mensuel" (625).

            Refer also to 626, 627, 628.

¶   H - Transport and communications

            Refer to 625, 626, 628, 629.

i. Ships and shipping

652   Port Autonome d'Abidjan: rapport d'exploitation   [Autonomous Port of Abidjan: report of activities]
                (Port Autonome d'Abidjan).
            Port Autonome d'Abidjan, Abidjan.
            1960-   1973.   not priced.   119p.
            Contains data on the activities and traffic of the port.
            Time factor: the 1973 issue, published in 1974, has data for 1972 and 1973.
            §   Fr.

            Refer also to 627.

Central statistical office

53   Central Bureau of Statistics,
      Ministry of Finance and Planning,
      Herufi House, P O Box 30266,
      Nairobi.
      t 333970.   tg HERUFI.

The Central Bureau of Statistics is responsible for the collection, analysis and publication of economic and social statistics of Kenya.

Some other important organisations collecting and publishing statistics

54   East African Statistical Department,
      East African Community,
      P O Box 30462, Nairobi.
      t 26411.

The East African Community was established in December 1967 to provide an institutional and legal framework to strengthen the common market between Kenya, Tanzania and Uganda, and the Statistical Department provides statistical data on an East African basis.

55   Statistics Branch,
      East African Customs & Excise Department,
      Customs House,
      P O Box 90601, Mombasa.

The Statistics Branch is responsible for the collection, analysis and publication of the foreign trade statistics of Kenya, Tanzania and Uganda.   Unpublished statistical information can also be supplied, both to government institutions and to firms.

Libraries

The Central Bureau of Statistics has a library which is available to people conducting personal research. The collection includes statistical publications of Kenya, international organisations, and some other individual countries. It is open from 8.15 to 16.30, and the staff speak English and Swahili.
The East African Statistical Department also has a library which is available to research students and businessmen.

Bibliographies

A sales list of economic and statistical publications is issued at intervals by the Ministry of Finance and Planning.

Statistical publications

¶   A - General

56   Statistical abstract   (Central Bureau of Statistics).
      Central Bureau of Statistics, Ministry of Finance and Planning, P O Box 30266, Nairobi.
      1961- 1975.   K Shg 40.   279p.
      Main sections:

Land and climate	Distribution and services
Population and vital statistics	Financial statistics
Migration and tourism	Transport and communications
National accounts	Education
External and East African trade	Public health
Size distribution of establishments	Public finance
Agriculture	Labour and manpower
Forestry and fishing	Retail prices and consumer expenditure
Industrial production	Justice
Fuel and power	

      Time factor: the 1975 edition, published in 1976, contains data for ten years to 1974.
      § En.

657   Economic survey   (Central Bureau of Statistics).
          Central Bureau of Statistics, Ministry of Finance and Planning, P O Box 30266, Nairobi.
          1961-   1976.   K Shg 25.   164p.
          Main sections:
               Current appraisal and outlook   Agriculture
               The international scene   Natural resources
               The domestic economy   Fuel and power
               Balance of payments   Manufacturing
               Money and banking   Building and construction
               Employment, earnings and consumer   Tourism
                  prices   Transport and communication
               Public finance   Education, health and other social services
               External trade
          Time factor: the 1976 edition, published mid-1976, has data for several years to 1975 with some
               provisional figures for 1975.
          §   En.

658   Kenya statistical digest   (Central Bureau of Statistics).
          Central Bureau of Statistics, Ministry of Finance and Planning, P O Box 30266, Nairobi.
          1963-   quarterly.   K Shg 4; K Shg 16 yr, post free.
          Contains statistical data on population, employment and earnings, migration, tourism, air and sea
               traffic, foreign trade, production, building and construction, financial statistics and consumer
               prices index.
          Time factor: each issue has data for varying periods up to about three months prior to the month of the
               issue.   Many tables have retrospective annual figures for about five years, and monthly or
               quarterly figures for one or two years.
          §   En.

659   Economic and statistical review   (East African Statistical Department).
          East African Statistical Department, East African Community, P O Box 30462, Nairobi.
          1948-   quarterly.   K Shg 10 each issue.
          Contains statistical tables on land and climate, population, migration and tourism, external and
               interstate trade, transport and communication, employment, retail price index numbers, production
               and consumption, banking, currency, insurance, public finance, domestic income and product,
               and balance of payments.
          Time factor: each issue contains figures up to the date of the issue and is published about six months
               later.   Many tables have long runs of annual, monthly and quarterly figures.
          §   En.

660   Economic and financial review   (Central Bank of Kenya).
          Central Bank of Kenya, P O Box 30463, Nairobi.
          1969-   quarterly.   not priced.
          Includes a statistical annex, with data on the Central Bank, commercial banks, monetary survey, private
               financial institutions, balance of payments, foreign trade, government finance, gross domestic
               product, price indices (Nairobi), and economic indicators.
          Time factor: each issue has long runs of figures up to the date of the issue and is published about six
               months later.
          §   En.

661   Annual report   (Central Bank of Kenya).
          Central Bank of Kenya, P O Box 30463, Nairobi.
          1966-   1974/75.   not priced.   78p.
          Includes an appendix of statistical tables on the activities of the Central Bank, commercial banks,
               money, private financial institutions, balance of payments, foreign trade, government finance,
               gross domestic product, main Nairobi price indices, economic indicators, etc.
          Time factor: the 1974/75 report, published late 1975, has long runs of figures for years, quarters and
               months to mid-1975.
          §   En.

¶   A,   continued

561a   Social perspectives   (Central Bureau of Statistics).
        Central Bureau of Statistics, P O Box 30266, Nairobi.
        1976-   quarterly.   free.
        Each issue is on a particular subject and includes appropriate up to date statistics.
        §   En.

¶   B - Production

i. Mines and mining

562   Annual report of the Mines and Geological Department.
        Mines and Geological Department, P O Box 30009, Nairobi.
        1945-   1969.   K Shg 3.50.   18p.
        Contains information on the work of the Department, and on the mining industry (gold, copper, other
            minerals, and oil).   Appendices include statistical data on the Department's finance, the mining
            industry, and explosives.
        Time factor: the 1969 issue, published in 1971, has data for 1969.
        §   En.

        Refer also to 656, 657.

ii. Agriculture, fisheries, forestry, etc.

563   Agricultural census: large farm areas   (Central Bureau of Statistics).
        Central Bureau of Statistics, Ministry of Finance and Planning, P O Box 30266, Nairobi.
        1954-   19th, 1972.   K Shg 11.25.   38p.
        Contains statistical data on holdings, land utilisation, crop acreage, number of livestock, sales and
            farm consumption of livestock, milk production and sales, fertiliser used, tractors, harvestors and
            other farm machinery and implements, and capital expenditure.
        Time factor: the report of the 1972 census was published in February 1974.
        §   En.

564   Annual report of the Department of Agriculture - Vol.I: Report of the Director of Agriculture.
        Department of Agriculture, P O Box 30028, Nairobi.
        1966-   1968.   K Shg 5.   108p.
        Includes tables of rainfall, small-scale farm coffee, quantity and value of agricultural exports,
            quantity and value of the more important products marketed from small-scale areas, and imports
            of fruit.
        Time factor: the 1968 report, published in 1970, has data for five years to 1968.
        §   En.

        Note: Vol.II of the annual report is a record of investigations, including annual reports of research
            sections and stations.

565   Agricultural census of large farms...a brief statistical analysis   (Central Bureau of Statistics).
        Central Bureau of Statistics, P O Box 30266, Nairobi.
        1973/74-   1973 & 1974.   K Shg 20.   73p.
        Time factor: the results of the 1973 and 1974 census analysis, published in 1977, contain data for the
            years 1971 to 1974.
        §   En.

566   Coffee Board of Kenya: annual report.
        Coffee Board of Kenya, P O Box 30566, Nairobi.
        1969/70-   1974/75.   not priced.   24p.
        Contains accounts and balance sheets, and trading figures.
        Time factor: the 1974/75 report, published early 1976, has data for the crop year 1974/75.
        §   En.

¶   B.ii,   continued

667   Annual report   (Department of Veterinary Services).
            Department of Veterinary Services, Veterinary Research Laboratory, P O Kabete, Nairobi.
            1949- 1971.   K Shg 6.   41p.
            Includes statistics in the text and a small statistical section, with information on livestock imports, the
                dairy industry, the meat industry, innoculation and sale of vaccines and drugs, and outbreaks of
                diseases.
            Time factor: the 1971 report, published in 1974, has data for 1971.
            §   En.

668   East African statistics of sugar   (East African Statistical Department).
            East African Statistical Department, East African Community, P O Box 30462, Nairobi.
            1966/74-   1966/74.   K Shg 5.00.   21p.
            Contains data on production, imports, consumption, stocks of sugar in the world and in Kenya,
                Tanzania and Uganda.   Also local sugar prices and world price trends.
            Time factor: the 1966/74 issue, published in 1976, has data for the years 1966 to 1974.
            §   En.

669   Economic review of agriculture   (Development Planning Division, Ministry of Agriculture).
            Ministry of Agriculture, Kilimo House, Cathedral Road, P O Box 30028, Nairobi.
            1969-   quarterly.   not priced.
            Includes statistical data on livestock and products, permanent crops (coffee, team sisal, wattle),
                cereals (maize, wheat), temporary industrial crops (pyrethrum, tobacco), and other crops
                (horticultural).
            §   En.

670   Report on Kenya fisheries   (Fisheries Department).
            Fisheries Department, Ministry of Tourism and Wild Life, P O Box 241, Nairobi.
            1960/61-   1967 & 1968.   K Shg 4.   30p.
            Contains separate reports for the years 1967 and 1968.   For both years there are statistical tables on
                production of fish in Kenya, imports and exports of fish and fishery products, and fisheries staff.
            Time factor: the report was published in 1970.
            §   En.

671   Forest Department annual report.
            Forest Department, P O Box 30513, Nairobi.
            1960-   1969.   K Shg 6.   38p.
            Includes some statistics in the text and also statistical tables on boundaries; fire protection and
                outbreaks; round log sales; exports of timber and forest woods; firewood sales; new planting,
                repairs and maintenance; area of plantations; area of gazetted forest reserves; progress in forest
                reservation; forest communications (roads, firelines); forest offences; regeneration and afforestation;
                sales of other forest products; primary forest industries; trade in timber and timber products; and
                revenue and expenditure.
            Time factor: the 1969 issue, published in 1974, has data for 1969 and from 1960 to 1969 in some tables.
            §   En.

            Refer also to 656, 657.

iii. Industry

672   Census of industrial production   (Central Bureau of Statistics).
            Central Bureau of Statistics, Ministry of Finance & Planning, P O Box 30266, Nairobi.
            1954-   1967.   K Shg 7.50.   31p.
            The report contains an introductory note and appendices I and II.   Appendix I has summarised results of
                the number of establishments; employment; gross product; input and output by sector, by sector and
                main towns, by sector and province, by sector and type of industrial organisation, by sector and
                nationality of share holding/ownership, by sector and industry, and by sector and size group.
                Appendix II is a copy of the census form.
            §   En.

            Note: a Register of manufacturing firms was issued in 1970 and a Directory of industries in 1974.

¶   B.iii,   continued

673   Revised index of manufacturing production   (Central Bureau of Statistics).
          Central Bureau of Statistics, Ministry of Finance and Planning, P O Box 30266, Nairobi.
          1969-   K Shg 2.25.   12p.
          Time factor: published in 1971, it includes index data for 1964 to 1969 (base year 1969).
          §   En.

674   Input-output tables for Kenya   (Central Bureau of Statistics).
          Central Bureau of Statistics, Ministry of Finance and Planning, P O Box 30266, Nairobi.
          1967-   2nd, 1971.   K Shg 40.   18p.
          The tables detail data at 30-sector level of aggregation.
          Time factor: published in 1976.
          §   En.

675   Surveys of industrial production   (Central Bureau of Statistics).
          Central Bureau of Statistics, P O Box 30266, Nairobi.
          1968/71-   1968-71.   not priced.   54p.
          Results derived from annual surveys, including the number of firms, labour costs, gross product, input
              and output, by province, main towns, etc.
          Time factor: the 1968-71 issue has data for the years 1968 to 1971 and was published in 1975.
          §   En.

676   Industrial production surveys of large-scale firms   (Central Bureau of Statistics).
          Central Bureau of Statistics, P O Box 30266, Nairobi.
          1964/66-   1964/66.   K Shg 7.50.   30p.
          Contains data on the number of firms, numbers employed, gross product, input, output, and stocks.
          Time factor: the 1964-66 issue has data for the years 1964 to 1966 and was published in 1971.
          §   En.

677   East African statistics of industrial production   (East African Statistical Department).
          East African Statistical Department, East African Community, P O Box 30462, Nairobi.
          1967-   1970 & 1971.   K Shg 7.50.   c50p.
          Contains data on the number of establishments, persons engaged, labour costs, gross output, imports and
              value added, inputs, and gross fixed capital.   Data is for Kenya, Tanzania and Uganda.
          Time factor: the 1970 and 1971 issue, published in 1976, has data for the years 1970 and 1971.
          §   En.

678   Statistical analysis of industrial production in East Africa (1963-1970)   (East African Statistical Department).
          East African Statistical Department, East African Community, P O Box 30462, Nairobi.
                            K Shg 10.00.   150p.
          A statistical analysis of the size of establishments, employment, gross output, value added, value of
              production, investment, profit and labour.   Data is for Kenya, Tanzania and Uganda.
          Time factor: published in 1974.
          §   En.

          Refer also to 656, 657, 658, 659.

     iv. Construction

679   Construction cost index   (Central Bureau of Statistics).
          Central Bureau of Statistics, Ministry of Finance and Planning, P O Box 30266, Nairobi.
          1975-   K Shg 7.50.   30p.
          Consists of a residential buildings cost index, a non-residential buildings cost index, a civil engineering
              cost index, and an overall construction cost index.
          Time factor: includes monthly data for March 1973 to December 1974 (base month December 1972) and
              was published in December 1975.
          §   En.

          Refer also to 657, 658.

¶   B,   continued

v. Energy

680   East African statistics of energy and power   (East African Statistical Department).
            East African Statistical Department, East African Community, P O Box 30462, Nairobi.
            1966/73-   1966/73.   K Shg 7.50.
            Time factor: published in 1976.
            §   En.

            Refer also to 656, 657.

¶   C - External trade

681   Annual trade report of Tanzania, Uganda and Kenya   (East African Customs & Excise Department).
            East African Customs and Excise Department, P O Box 90601, Mombasa.
            1961-   1975.   K Shg 60.   various pagination.
            Main tables show imports, exports and re-exports of the three countries separately and of East Africa as
                a whole, arranged by commodity and sub-divided by countries of origin and destination.   Also
                included are tables showing the transfer of goods between partner states.
            Time factor: the 1975 issue, containing data for that year, was published early in 1976.
            §   En.

682   Monthly trade statistics for Tanzania, Uganda and Kenya   (East African Customs and Excise Department).
            East African Customs and Excise Department, P O Box 90601, Mombasa.
            1961-   K Shg 5; K Shg 50 yr, post free.
            Contains tables showing direct imports, exports and re-exports arranged by SITC, and trade by country
                for each of the three countries separately.   Also included are tables showing transfer of goods
                between partner states.
            Time factor: each issue has data for the month and cumulated figures for the year to date, and is
                published about two months later.
            §   En.

            Refer also to 656, 657, 658, 659, 660, 661.

¶   D - Internal distribution and service trades

683   Kenya survey of distribution   (Statistics Division, Ministry of Economic Planning and Development).
            Central Bureau of Statistics, P O Box 30266, Nairobi.
            1960-   1960.   not priced.   101p.
            Includes information on type of organisation, labour costs, purchases and stocks of goods, other current
                costs, sales and types of goods sold.   Covered wholesale, retail and part of service trade sector.
            Time factor: the survey was taken in 1961 on data for 1960, and published in 1963.
            §   En.

684   Survey of services   (Statistics Division, Ministry of Finance and Economic Planning).
            Central Bureau of Statistics, P O Box 30266, Nairobi.
            1966-   1966.   K Shg 4.   53p.
            Survey of services by turnover group, kind of service employment, income and expenditure, location, etc
            Time factor: the 1966 survey was published in 1971.
            §   En.

685   Migration and tourism statistics   (Central Bureau of Statistics).
            Central Bureau of Statistics, Ministry of Finance and Planning, P O Box 30266, Nairobi.
            1968/71-   1971/74.   K Shg 30.   72p.
            Contains migration, hotel occupancy, and game park statistics.
            Time factor: the 1971/74 issue, with data for those years, was published in 1976.
            §   En.

¶ D, continued

86   Nairobi airport tourist survey, 1968-1969   (Central Bureau of Statistics).
        Central Bureau of Statistics, Ministry of Finance and Planning, P O Box 30266, Nairobi.
                K Shg 7.50.
        Time factor: the report of the survey was published in 1972.
        § En.

        Refer also to 656, 657, 658, 659.

¶ E – Population

87   Kenya population census   (Central Bureau of Statistics).
        Central Bureau of Statistics, Ministry of Finance and Planning, P O Box 30266, Nairobi.
        1921-   1969.   3 vols.
        Contents:
            Vol. I contains tables of the population by age, sex, area and density for all administrative
                areas (K Shg 15).
            Vol. II has tables of the urban population by education, relationship to head of household, birth
                place and marital status (K Shg 11.25).
            Vol.III has tables of total population by education, relationship to head of household, birth place
                and marital status.
        Time factor: the volumes were published in 1970 and 1971.
        § En.

88   Demographic baseline survey report   (Central Bureau of Statistics).
        Central Bureau of Statistics, Ministry of Finance and Planning, P O Box 30266, Nairobi.
        1973-   K Shg 20.   64p.
        Contains data on the general characteristics of the population, analysis of fertility, and mortality data.
        Time factor: the report was published in 1975.
        § En.

89   Annual report of the Registrar-General.
        Registrar-General's Department, P O Box 300 31, Nairobi.
        1945/50-   1973.   K Shg 7.50.   65p.
        Contains a statistical appendix with data on companies, business names, births and deaths, Public
            Trustee administration, bankruptcy, winding-up, insurance and building societies, hire purchase,
            estate duty, trade unions, revenue and expenditure.
        Time factor: the 1973 report, published in 1975, has data for 1973.
        § En.

90   Immigration Department annual report.
        Immigration Department, P O Box 30191, Nairobi.
        1950-   1971.   K Shg 2.00.   17p.
        Includes statistics of entry, entry permits, passes, visas, registration, naturalisation, finance, etc.
        Time factor: the 1971 issue, published in 1973, has data for 1971.
        § En.

91   Employment and earnings in the modern sector   (Central Bureau of Statistics).
        Central Bureau of Statistics, Ministry of Finance and Planning, P O Box 30266, Nairobi.
        1963/67-   1972/73.   K Shg 30.   173p.
        The report is confined to the 'modern sector', defined as the entire public sector, entire urban sector,
            large scale firms and other large scale enterprises such as sawmills and mines located outside towns.
            Wages, employment and earnings data are analysed by private and public sectors and by sex,
            industry, occupation, location and income group.
        Time factor: the 1972/73 edition was published mid-1976.
        § En.

¶   E,   continued

692   Ministry of Labour annual report.
            Ministry of Labour, P O Box 40326, Nairobi.
            1946-   1974.   K Shg 7.50.   68p.
            Includes statistical tables in the text and covers employment, wages and hours of work, industrial
                relations, industrial court, workmen's compensation, factories inspectorate, national industrial
                training, national social security fund, national youth service, etc.
            Time factor: the 1974 edition, with data for 1974, was published early 1976.
            §   En.

            Refer also to 656, 657, 658, 659, 685.

¶   F - Social

i.   Standard of living

693   Cost of living indices   (Central Bureau of Statistics).
            Central Bureau of Statistics, P O Box 30266, Nairobi.
            1977-   monthly.   not priced.
            Based on January/June 1976 = 100, the indices are Nairobi lower income index, middle income index,
                and upper income index.
            §   En.

            Refer also to 656, 657, 658, 659, 697.

ii.   Health and welfare

694   Annual report   (Ministry of Health).
            Ministry of Health, P O Box 30016, Nairobi.
            1959-   1968.   K Shg 20.   150p.
            Includes data on vital statistics, public health, curative services, labour services, and training.   The
                statistics are included in the text.
            Time factor: the 1968 report, published in 1973, had data for 1968.
            §   En.

            Note: continues the annual report of the Medical Department.

            Refer also to 656, 657.

iii.   Education and leisure

695   Ministry of Education annual report.
            Ministry of Education, Jogoo House, P O Box 30040, Nairobi.
            1960-   1974.   K Shg 7.50.   34p.
            Contains data on enrolments in primary schools, primary school teachers by citizenship and qualifications,
                enrolments in universities, teachers in universities, post-graduate students, enrolments at teacher
                training colleges, and Ministry of Education expenditure.
            Time factor: the 1974 report, published in 1975, had data for 1974.
            §   En.

            Refer also to 656, 657.

iv.   Justice

            Refer to 656.

KENYA, continued

¶   G - Finance

Refer to 656, 657, 658, 659, 660, 661.

i. Banking

Refer to 657, 659, 660, 661.

ii. Public finance

696   Income tax statistics report: year of income...   (Central Bureau of Statistics).
Central Bureau of Statistics, P O Box 30266, Nairobi.
1973-   1973.   not priced.   12p.
Time factor: the 1973 report, published in 1976, has data for the 1973 tax year.
§   En.

Note: prior to 1973 the statistics were published by the East African Income Tax Department, dissolved
in 1974.

Refer also to 656, 657, 659, 660, 661.

iii. Company finance

Refer to 660, 661.

v. Insurance

697   East Africa, insurance statistics   (East African Statistical Department).
East African Statistical Department, East African Community, P O Box 30462, Nairobi.
1959-   1967.   K Shg 3.00.   41p.
Contains data on all kinds of insurance for East Africa, Kenya, Tanzania and Uganda.
Time factor: the 1967 issue has data for 1965, 1966 and 1967.
§   En.

Refer also to 659.

¶   H - Transport and communications

698   Statistical survey of the East African Community institutions   (East African Community).
East African Community, P O Box 30462, Nairobi.
1973-   1973.   K Shg 7.50.   68p.
Contains data on railways, harbours, posts and telecommunications, airways, etc. for Kenya, Tanzania
and Uganda.
Time factor: the 1973 issue, published in 1975, has data for 1973 or the latest data available.
§   En.

Refer also to 656, 657, 658, 659.

¶   H,   continued

ii. Road

699   Motor vehicle registration statistics   (Central Bureau of Statistics).
          Central Bureau of Statistics, P O Box 30266, Nairobi.
          1962–   monthly.   not priced.
          Contains registration statistics of all vehicles by type and type of registration; all new road vehicles by
              make, type and cubic carrying and seating capacity; all vehicles by make, type and area, and
              type of registration; and new motor cycles by make and cubic capacity.
          Time factor: each issue has data for the month of issue and is published two or three months later.

          Refer also to 656, 657, 659, 698.

LESOTHO

Central statistical office

700
Bureau of Statistics,
P O Box MS 455,
Maseru.
t 3852.

The Bureau, which came into existence in 1964, collects, analyses and publishes economic and social statistics mainly for government use.

Statistical publications

¶ A - General

701
Annual statistical bulletin   (Bureau of Statistics).
Bureau of Statistics, P O Box MS 455, Maseru.
1963/64-   1974.   R 4.00 (USA and Europe, R 7.00).   115p.
Main sections:

Meteorology	Prisons
Agriculture	Motor vehicles (registrations)
Foreign trade	Air transport
Health	Post office transactions
Education	Demography

Time factor: the 1974 edition, published late 1975, contains data for 1974 and also for some earlier years in some tables.
§   En.

702
Quarterly statistical bulletin   (Bureau of Statistics).
Bureau of Statistics, P O Box MS 455, Maseru.
1976-   R 2.50 (R 4.85 in USA and Europe) each issue.
§   En.

703
Lesotho: report for the year...   (Department of Information).
Department of Information, Maseru.
1967-   1971.   not priced.   230p.
The contents are mainly text matter but include some statistics on public finance and expenditure, education, health, labour, justice, etc.   Continues the series of reports issued by the British Colonial Office and Commonwealth Relations Office.
Time factor: the 1971 report, published in 1973, has data for 1971.
§   En.

¶ B - Production

i. Mines and mining

704
Annual report of the Department of Mines and Geology.
Department of Mines and Geology, P O Box MS 750, Maseru.
        1971.   not priced.   no pagination.
Includes statistical data on monthly expenditure, monthly comparisons, diamond digging, other minerals, employment, and explosives.
Time factor: the 1971 report, published in 1974, has data for 1971.
§   En.

¶   B,   continued

ii. Agriculture, fisheries, forestry, etc.

705   Agricultural census report   (Bureau of Statistics).
         Bureau of Statistics, P O Box MS 455, Maseru.
         1949/50-   3rd, 1970.   R 7.50 (R 12.00 in USA and Europe).
         Contains details of the methodology of the census and statistical tables on households, population and
              holdings; crops; livestock and poultry; farm population; agricultural power, machinery, general
              transport facilities; fertilisers and soil dressings; etc.
         Time factor: the report of the 1970 census was published in December 1972.
         §   En.

         Refer also to 701, 702.

iii. Industry

706   Census of production   (Bureau of Statistics).
         Bureau of Statistics, P O Box MS 455, Maseru.
         1965-   2nd, 1968 and 1969.   R 1.00 (R 1.75 in USA and Europe).   39p.
         Contents include a summary of operations, analysis of purchases and changes in stocks, payments for
              services rendered by other firms, numbers employed and earnings in industry, sizes of
              establishments by number of employees, and sizes of establishments by gross output.
         Time factor: the results of the 1968 and 1969 census were published in 1971.
         §   En.

¶   C - External trade

707   Quarterly imports for annual subscription   (Bureau of Statistics).
         Bureau of Statistics, P O Box MS 455, Maseru.
                           R 2.00 (R 3.85 in USA and Europe) yr.
              §   En.

708   Imports price indices   (Bureau of Statistics).
         Bureau of Statistics, P O Box MS 455, Maseru.
                           R 1.50 (R 3.75 in USA and Europe) yr.
              §   En.

709   Trade statement   (Bureau of Statistics).
         Bureau of Statistics, P O Box MS 455, Maseru.
         1966-   1966.   R 0.20; (R 0.30 abroad).   9p.
         Contains detailed statistics of imports and exports arranged by commodity for the four quarters of the
              year.
         §   En.

         Refer also to 701, 702.

¶   E - Population

710   Population census report   (Census Officer).
         Bureau of Statistics, P O Box MS 455, Maseru.
         1875-   1966.   R 4.00 (R 7.00 in USA and Europe) each volume.   2 vols.
         Content:
              Vol. I. Part I: Administrative, methodological and financial report
                        Part II: Census tables
                   II.Part III: Village lists, village populations and population densities
         Time factor: the reports of the 1966 census were published in 1970 and 1971.
         §   En.

¶   E,   continued

711   Demographic component of rural household consumption and expenditure survey report, 1967/69
              (Bureau of Statistics).
          Bureau of Statistics, P O Box MS 455, Maseru.
          Contains data on population and vital statistics.   Vol.I has the administrative and methodological
              report (R 1.00; R 1.50 to R 2.00 abroad); Vol.II has presentation and analysis of data (R 3.00;
              R 3.75 to R 5.70 abroad); Vol.III will contain the evaluation and interpretation of the data.
          Time factor: the first two volumes were published in 1973.
          §   En.

          Refer also to 701, 702.

¶   F - Social

  i. Standard of living

712   Urban household budget survey   (Bureau of Statistics).
          Bureau of Statistics, P O Box MS 455, Maseru.
          1972/73-   1972/73.   R 2.00 (R 2.75 to R 3.85 abroad).   57p.
          Includes population data, household income data, household expenditure data, and general data.
          Time factor: the survey covered the period February 1972 to June 1973 and the results were published
              in October 1973.
          §   En.

713   Poverty eats my blanket   (P J Th. Marres and A C A Van der Wiel).
          Bureau of Statistics, P O Box MS 455, Maseru.
          A poverty study, with statistical tables of income, cost of living, etc.
          Time factor: published in 1975.
          §   En.

  ii. Health and welfare

714   Annual report by the Director of Health Services on the state of health   (Ministry of Health, Education and
              Welfare).
          Ministry of Health, Education and Welfare, P O Box MS 514, Maseru.
          1961-   1974.   not priced.   32p.
          Includes statistics of health and health services.
          Time factor: the 1974 report, published in 1976, has data for 1974.
          §   En.

          Refer also to 701, 703.

  iii. Education and leisure

715   Annual report of the Ministry of Education and Culture.
          Ministry of Education and Culture, P O Box 47, Maseru.
          1946-   1973.   R 0.75.   83p.
          Includes a section of statistical tables on primary, secondary, technical, vocational, higher and teacher
              education, with data on schools, pupils, teachers, examinations, finances, etc.
          Time factor: the 1973 report, published late 1974, has data for the academic year 1973/74.
          §   En.

          Refer also to 701, 703.

  iv. Justice

          Refer to 701, 703.

¶   G - Finance

ii. Public finance

716   National accounts   (Bureau of Statistics).
               Bureau of Statistics, P O Box MS 455, Maseru.
               1964/65 & 1965/66-   1972/73.   R 1.75 (R 3.50 in USA and Europe).   14p.
               Contains data on the origin of gross domestic product at factor cost, expenditure on gross domestic
                    product at market prices, percentage structure of gross domestic product, and the growth of the
                    gross domestic product.
               Time factor: the 1972/73 issue, published early 1976, has data for the fiscal year 1972/73.
               §   En.

               Refer also to 703.

¶   H - Transport and communications

               Refer to 701.

Central statistical office

717   Ministry of Planning and Economic Affairs,
        Mechlin and Broad Streets,
        P O Box 9016, Monrovia.
        t 22622 or 22247.

        One of the responsibilities of the Ministry is to collect, analyse and publish economic and social
        statistics for Liberia.

Libraries

        The Ministry of Planning and Economic Affairs has a library where published statistics and unpublished
        detailed machine listings of external trade statistics may be consulted.

Statistical publications

    ¶   A - General

718   Economic survey of Liberia   (Department of Planning and Economic Affairs).
        Ministry of Planning and Economic Affairs, Monrovia.
        1967-   1975.   not priced.   no pagination.
        Includes a statistical abstract as well as statistical tables in the text, and covers:
            National income   Agriculture and forestry
            Foreign trade   Mining
            Investment   Manufacturing
            Prices   Transport and communications
            Public finance   Public utilities
            Population   Education
            Banking   Health
        Time factor: the 1975 edition, published late 1976, contains statistical data for 1975 and some earlier
            years.
        §   En.

719   The Liberia annual review.
        West Africa Publishing Company, P O Box 1303, Monrovia.
        1965-   1973-74.   not priced.   105p.
        Includes some statistical information in the text on the national economy, investment, industry and
            commerce, manufacturing industry, agriculture, foreign trade.   The volume also includes a
            considerable amount of directory information.
        §   En.

720   Quarterly statistical bulletin   (Ministry of Planning and Economic Affairs).
        Ministry of Planning and Economic Affairs, Monrovia.
        1970-   Lib$ 1.75 each issue.
        Contains data on national accounts, public sector accounts, commercial banking, external trade,
            prices, production, agriculture, employment and earnings, construction, shipping and air traffic,
            sales and services, and consumption of electricity.
        Time factor: recent issues have been annual, the "Summary for 1975" being published in June 1976.
        §   En.

721   Annual report of the Ministry of Planning and Economic Affairs.
        Ministry of Planning and Economic Affairs, Monrovia.
        1966/67-   1975.   not priced.   100p.
        Contains chapters on the state of the economy (national accounts, foreign trade, public finance,
            domestic prices), planning and programming, economic cooperation, statistics, administration,
            etc, and includes some figures in the text.
        Time factor: the 1975 report was published in December 1975.
        §   En.

¶   A,   continued

722   Statistical bulletin   (National Bank of Liberia).
          National Bank of Liberia, E G King Plaza, Broad Street, P O Box 2048, Monrovia.
          1977-   monthly.   not priced.
          Includes data on money, banking, foreign trade, consumer price index, and public finance.
          Time factor: each issue has data up to the month of the issue and is issued about three months later.
          §   En.

723   Annual report   (National Bank of Liberia).
          National Bank of Liberia, P O Box 2048, Monrovia.
          1974-   1974.   not priced.   c60p.
          Includes a statistical appendix with data on foreign trade, public finance, banking, and the consumer
              price index.
          Time factor: the 1974 report, published in 1975, has data to 1974.
          §   En.

¶   B - Production

i. Mines and mining

          Refer to 719.

ii. Agriculture, fisheries, forestry, etc.

724   Census of agriculture   (Ministry of Planning and Economic Affairs).
          1971-   1971.
          A "Summary report for Liberia (preliminary)" was published in 1973 (70p), with data on holdings,
              holders, tenure and type of holding; land utilisation; livestock and poultry; crops; employment
              in agriculture; and farm population.
          §   En.

          Refer also to 718, 719, 720.

iii. Industry

725   Industrial production survey   (Bureau of Statistics).
          Ministry of Planning and Economic Affairs, Monrovia.
          1964-   1966.
          The survey included the collection of data on employment; wages and salaries; value and quantity of
              fuels, electricity and materials consumed; payments and receipts for services rendered; value and
              quantity of goods produced; and investments in fixed assets.
          Time factor: the 1964 survey was taken in 1965, and the 1966 survey was taken in 1967.   No
              publications have ensued.
          §   En.

          Refer also to 718, 719, 720.

iv. Construction

          Refer to 720.

v. Energy

          Refer to 720.

¶   C - External trade

726   External trade of Liberia: imports   (Ministry of Planning and Economic Affairs).
           Ministry of Planning and Economic Affairs, Monrovia.
           1965/67-   1975.   not priced.   302p.
           Contains statistical data on imports by SITC groupings, imports by commodities sub-divided by countries
               of origin, and value of imports by continent and country of origin.
           Time factor: the 1975 issue, published in May 1976, has data for 1975.
           §   En.

           Note: from 1957 to 1964 "Imports of merchandise for consumption by country of origin" (FT report
               no.101).

727   External trade of Liberia: exports   (Ministry of Planning and Economic Affairs).
           Ministry of Planning and Economic Affairs, Monrovia.
           1965/67-   1975.   not priced.
           Contains statistical data on exports by SITC groupings, exports by commodities sub-divided by countries
               of destination, and value of exports by continent and country of destination.
           Time factor: the 1975 issue, published in May 1976, has data for 1975.
           §   En.

           Note: from 1957 to 1964 "Exports of domestic and foreign merchandise by country of destination"
               (FT report no.201).

           Refer also to 718, 719, 720, 721, 722, 723.

¶   D - Internal distribution and service trades

           Refer to 719, 720.

¶   E - Population

728   Census of population and housing   (Ministry of Planning and Economic Affairs),
           Ministry of Planning and Economic Affairs, Monrovia.
           1956-   1974.
           Reports published so far are:
               Administration report   (published in 1974).
               Prospectus for the 1974 census   (published in 1973).
               Population bulletin no.1. Provisional population totals and demographic indices   (published
                   December 1975).
               Population bulletin no.2. Final population totals and related percentages with some salient
                   demographic characteristics   (published September 1976).
           §   En.

           Note: the final results were to be published in 1976.

729   Demographic annual of the population growth survey   (Ministry of Planning and Economic Affairs).
           Ministry of Planning and Economic Affairs, Monrovia.
           The survey was started in 1969 to provide the government with accurate and current estimates of births
               and deaths, yearly data on fertility patterns, population movements, age and sex distribution,
               marital status, literacy, and school attendance.   The survey was planned to be conducted over
               five years and several reports have appeared, including:
                   D - 1   Patterns of mortality   N - 1   Patterns of natality
                   D - 2   Mortality profiles   N - 2   Natality profiles
                   M - 1   Patterns of migration   P - 2   Population profiles
                   M - 2   Migration profiles   S - 1   Demographic patterns
               and also bulletins of selected demographic indices.
           §   En.

           Refer also to 718, 720.

¶   F - Social

i. Standard of living

Refer to 720, 722, 723.

ii. Health and welfare

Refer to 718.

iii. Education and leisure

730   Statistics of education in Liberia   (Ministry of Education).
          Ministry of Education, Monrovia.
          1972-   1974.   not priced.   55p.
          Contains data on schools, teachers, enrolment, etc, for primary, secondary and higher education.
              Also data for those sent abroad for education, and regional statistics.
          Time factor: the 1974 issue, published late 1974, has data for that year.
          §   En.

731   Annual report of the Minister of Education.
          Ministry of Education, Monrovia.
          1968/69-   1975.   not priced.   80p.
          Includes four pages of statistics on schools, teachers, enrolment, kindergarten and elementary education,
              secondary education, and teacher training.
          Time factor: the 1975 report, published late 1975, has data for that year.
          §   En.

          Refer also to 718.

¶   G - Finance

i. Banking

Refer to 721, 723, 724.

ii. Public finance

732   National income in Liberia   (Ministry of Planning and Economic Affairs).
          Ministry of Planning and Economic Affairs, Monrovia.
          1966-   1973.   not priced.
          Time factor: the 1973 edition, published in 1974, has data for 1973.
          §   En.

733   Public sector accounts of Liberia   (Ministry of Planning and Economic Affairs).
          Ministry of Planning and Economic Affairs, Monrovia.
          1965-   1973.   not priced.   46p.
          Time factor: the 1973 issue, published in mid-1974, has data for 1973.
          §   En.

LIBERIA, continued

¶   G.ii,   continued

734   Annual report   (Ministry of Finance).
           Ministry of Finance, Monrovia.
           1969/70-   1975.   not priced.   110p.
           Includes statistical data in the text which is devoted to a review of the international and national
                situation, revenues, fiscal affairs, concessions, and public corporations.
           Time factor: the 1975 report, published in December 1975, has data for the fiscal year 1974/75.
           §   En.

           Refer also to 718, 720, 721, 722, 723.

       iv. Investment

           Refer to 718, 719.

¶   H - Transport and communications

           Refer to 718.

     i. Ships and shipping

           Refer to 720.

     iv. Air

           Refer to 720.

Central statistical office

735   Census and Statistical Department,
        Ministry of Planning and Scientific Research,
        Tripoli.
        t 31731.

        The Department has the responsibility for conducting, processing and publishing the results of periodical
population and industrial censuses; the collection, collation and publication of statistics of external trade
and balance of payments; undertaking surveys on a regular or ad hoc basis on petroleum, mining,
manufacturing establishments, construction activity, family budgets, etc, and the publication of results;
and the collection and publication of information on wholesale and retail prices.   The Department also
co-ordinates the statistical activities of various Ministries, Departments and financial institutions.
Unpublished statistical information is not supplied as a rule, but a request for specific data may be provided
if not confidential.

Libraries

        There is a library in the Census and Statistical Department which has statistical publications of Libya,
the United Nations and its specialised agencies, and also certain publications on trade, industry and the
like which are received from other countries, as well as some material on economics and statistics.

Libraries and information services abroad

        Publications of the Census and Statistical Department are available for reference in Libyan Embassies
abroad, including:
        United Kingdom   Libyan Arab Republic Embassy, 58 Prince's Gate, London SW7.   t 01-589 5235.
        USA   Libyan Arab Republic Embassy, 1118 22nd Street NW, Washington DC.
                               t 452-1290.

Statistical publications

¶   A - General

736   Statistical abstract   (Census and Statistical Department).
        Census and Statistical Department, Ministry of Planning and Scientific Research, Tripoli.
        1958/62-   1974.   not priced.   337p.
        Main sections:
            Climate   Education
            Population   Agriculture
            Vital statistics   Industrial production
            Foreign travel and tourism   Petroleum
            Health   Prices
            Social statistics (family budgets, social   Foreign trade
                insurance, major crimes, co-operative   Transport, communications,
                societies)   road accidents
            Labour (including cost of living index)   Banking and finance
        Time factor: the 1974 edition, published late 1976, contains data for 1973 and 1974.
        §   En & Ar eds.

737   Quarterly bulletin of statistics   (Census and Statistical Department).
        Census and Statistical Department, Ministry of Planning and Scientific Research, Tripoli.
        1950-   not priced.
        Includes data on vital statistics, foreign travel and migration, industrial production, petroleum and
            natural gas production, buildings completed, transport, value of exports, crude oil exports, value
            of imports, banking and finance, cost of living index, retail prices of main food items (Tripoli),
            and wholesale prices (Tripoli town).
        Time factor: each issue has data for that quarter, the separate months of that quarter, and the previous
            quarter, and comparative figures for the quarter of the previous year.   Publication is some months
            later.
        §   En & Ar eds.

¶   A,   continued

38   Economic bulletin   (Central Bank of Libya).
            Central Bank of Libya, P O Box 1103, Tripoli.
            1961-   monthly.   not priced.
            Includes a section of statistical tables on the Central Bank of Libya, commercial banks, money and
                prices, industrial and Real Estate Bank, foreign trade and foreign exchange, public finance, and
                petroleum.
            Time factor: each issue has long runs of annual and monthly figures to about two months prior to the
                date of the issue.
            §   En & Ar eds.

            Note: the "Annual report" of the Bank also has a few statistics.

39   Survey of national economy (covering 1968 and certain main indicators for 1969)   (Census and Statistical
                Department).
            Census and Statistical Department, Ministry of Planning and Scientific Research, Tripoli.
                            not priced.   136p.
            The survey covers population and social development (population, labour force, education, health,
                housing and urban affairs, household budget surveys and prices); national accounts; external trade
                and balance of payments; production, commerce and tourism (agriculture, petroleum industry,
                manufacturing industry, construction, electricity supply, commerce, tourism); transport and
                communications; money and banking; and public finance.   There are statistical tables in the text.
            Time factor: the figures mainly relate to 1968 and 1969, but there are also some long runs of earlier
                figures in some tables.
            §   En.

¶   B - Production

i.   Mines and mining

40   Report of the annual survey of the petroleum industry   (Census and Statistical Department).
            Census and Statistical Department, Ministry of Planning and Scientific Research, Tripoli.
            1966-   1973.   not priced.   31p.
            The survey covers all units holding petroleum mining concession rights and the National Oil Corporation,
                and the report includes statistics on employment, wages, cost of raw materials and other inputs,
                production of goods and services, and value of new additions to fixed capital assets.
            Time factor: the 1973 edition, published in 1974, relates to 1972.
            §   En, Ar.

41   Annual survey of petroleum mining (servicing) units   (Census and Statistical Department).
            Census and Statistical Department, Ministry of Planning and Scientific Research, Tripoli.
            1969-   1972.   not priced.   12p.
            Contains data on number of employees, compensation for employees, value of transactions in fixed
                capital items, value of materials consumed, value of services purchased, miscellaneous current
                costs, value of gross output, value added, for each category of servicing unit.
            Time factor: the 1972 edition, published in 1974, has data for 1972.
            §   En, Ar.

            Refer also to 736, 737, 739.

ii.   Agriculture, fisheries, forestry, etc.

42   Census of agriculture   (Ministry of Agriculture).
            Ministry of Agriculture, Tripoli.
            1960-   1960.   not priced.   573p.
            The report and tables of the census.   Includes detailed statistics of holdings, land tenure, land
                utilisation, arable land, wells, springs and cisterns, irrigation, farm population, power and
                machinery, use of fertilisers, crop production, livestock, livestock products, and wood extraction.
            Time factor: published early 1962.
            §   En.

¶   B.ii,   continued

743   [Statistics on the agricultural sector, 1961-1971]   (Ministry of Agriculture and Agrarian Reform).
                Ministry of Agriculture, Tripoli.
                                    not priced.   various paginations.
                Time factor: published in 1972.
                §   Ar.

            Refer also to 736, 739.

        iii.   Industry

744   Report of the annual survey of large manufacturing establishments   (Census and Statistical Department).
                Census and Statistical Department, Ministry of Planning and Scientific Research, Tripoli.
                1967-   1974.   not priced.   42p.
                Contains data on the number of establishments employing 20 or more persons; employment; wages and
                    salaries; new capital; cost of fuels, packing materials, electricity, water and services; and the
                    value of total output.
                Time factor: the 1974 edition, published in 1976, relates to 1974.
                §   En & Ar eds.

745   Monthly statistics of production and employment in selected large manufacturing establishments   (Census
                and Statistical Department).
                Census and Statistical Department, Ministry of Planning and Scientific Research, Tripoli.
                1970-   issued quarterly.   not priced.
                Contains data on quantity and value of goods produced, number of persons engaged, average number of
                    operatives, and total man-hours worked by operatives.
                Time factor: each issue has data for each of the three months in the quarter of the issue and is published
                    some considerable time later.
                §   En, Ar.

746   [Report of the industrial census of Libya]   (Ministry of Oil and Industry).
                Ministry of Oil and Industry, Tripoli.
                1955-   3rd, 1971.   not priced.   323p.
                Includes data on input costs, value of fixed capital, value of gross output and value added, persons
                    engaged, labour costs, etc, for the petroleum industry, stone quarrying industry, large
                    manufacturing establishments, small manufacturing establishments, the construction industry,
                    and the electricity and gas industries.
                Time factor: the 1971 report, refers to the year 1971.
                §   Ar; the 1955 and 1964 reports were also available in En.

747   [Distribution of industrial installations according to province, municipality, labour and type of industry]
                (Ministry of Oil and Industry).
                Ministry of Oil and Industry, Tripoli.
                                    not priced.   2 vols.
                Time factor: published in 1972.
                §   Ar.

            Refer also to 736, 737, 739.

        iv. Construction

748   Report of the annual survey of large construction units   (Census and Statistical Department).
                Census and Statistical Department, Ministry of Planning and Scientific Research, Tripoli.
                1968-   1974.   not priced.   44p.
                Relates to both national and international large construction units in Libya.   Contains data on number of
                    employees, compensation for employees, value of transactions in fixed capital items, value of
                    materials consumed, value of services purchased, miscellaneous current costs, value of gross output,
                    value added, for each category.
                Time factor: the 1974 edition, published in 1976, has data for 1974.
                §   En & Ar eds.

            Refer also to 737, 739.

¶   B,   continued

v. Energy

749   Oil and gas statistics   (Ministry of Petroleum Economic Affairs. Planning and Following-up Department).
      Ministry of Petroleum Economic Affairs, Planning and Following-up Department, Tripoli.
      1973-   quarterly.   not priced.
      Contains data on wells drilled and rigs operated, crude oil production, gas production, yearly average
         production of crude oil, and crude oil exports by weight and gravity, by group, by destination,
         and by terminal.
      Time factor: each issue has data for the previous quarter and cumulation for the year to the end of that
         quarter.
      §   En, Ar.

750   Libyan oil, 1954-1967   (Ministry of Petroleum Affairs).
      Ministry of Oil and Industry, Tripoli.
                  not priced.   148p.
      Part 1: legal aspects; part 2: economic aspects; part 3: Libyan participation in oil organisations and
         conferences;   part 4: petroleum development; part 5: manpower; part 6: data and statistics
         (section 1: oil concessions, production and exports; section 2: technical data).
      §   En.

      Refer also to 736, 737, 738, 739, 740, 741.

¶   C - External trade

751   External trade statistics   (Census and Statistical Department).
      Census and Statistical Department, Ministry of Planning and Scientific Research, Tripoli.
      1963/64-   1974.   not priced.   616p.
      Main tables show imports, exports, and re-exports arranged by commodity and sub-divided by countries
         of origin and destination; and imports, exports, and re-exports arranged by country of origin or
         destination and sub-divided by commodities.
      Time factor: the 1974 issue, published late 1975, has data for 1974.
      §   En, Ar.

752   External trade statistics   (Census and Statistical Department).
      Census and Statistical Department, Ministry of Planning and Scientific Research, Tripoli.
      1956-   quarterly.   not priced.
      Main tables show imports, exports and re-exports arranged by commodity and sub-divided by countries of
         origin and destination.   There are also summary tables by country, and by commodity sub-divided
         by country.
      Time factor: each issue has cumulated figures for the year to date and is published some months later.
      §   En, Ar.

753   External trade statistics: monthly summary   (Census and Statistical Department).
      Census and Statistical Department, Ministry of Planning and Scientific Research, Tripoli.
      1968-   not priced.
      Contains tables on exports, re-exports and imports by currency area; exports and imports by commodity
         section; crude petroleum exports by countries of destination; exports, re-exports and imports by
         commodity division; and exports, re-exports and imports by country.
      Time factor: each issue has data for the month of the issue and is published some months later.
      §   En, Ar.

      Refer also to 736, 737, 738, 739.

¶   D - Internal distribution and service trades

      Refer to 736, 737, 739.

¶   E - Population

754   General population census   (Census and Statistical Department).
       Census and Statistical Department, Ministry of Planning and Development, Tripoli.
       1931- 1964.   not priced.   117p.
       This final report is a summary of ten detailed volumes and includes statistics of the total population by
            sex, age group, religion and marital status.   There is also information on aliens, educational
            status and school attendance.
       Time factor: the report was published in 1966.
       §   En, Ar.

       Note: a population census was taken in 1973; for which preliminary results were published in 1973
            in English and in Arabic.

755   Housing and establishment census   (Census and Statistical Department).
       Census and Statistical Department, Ministry of Planning and Development, Tripoli.
       1973- 1973.
       Preliminary results were published in English and in Arabic in 1973.

756   Vital statistics   (Census and Statistical Department).
       Census and Statistical Department, Ministry of Planning and Scientific Research, Tripoli.
       1971- 1974.   not priced.   39p.
       Contains data on crude rates of vital events, births, deaths, marriages and divorces.
       Time factor: the 1974 issue, published in 1975, has data for 1974.
       §   En, Ar.

       Refer also to 736, 737, 739.

¶   F - Social

i. Standard of living

757   Household sample survey 1969   (Census and Statistical Department).
       Census and Statistical Department, Ministry of Planning and Scientific Research, Tripoli.
                         not priced.   6 vols.
       Papers 1 and 2 analyse the results by households in Tripoli and Benghazi; papers 3 and 4 report on the
            first phase of the survey; economically active population in Tripoli and Benghazi; paper 5 reports
            on the economically inactive population in the two towns.   The two reports of the second phase
            are concerned with household expenditure in Tripoli and Benghazi towns.
       Time factor: the reports were published in 1970.
       §   En, Ar.

758   Wholesale prices in Tripoli town   (Census and Statistical Department).
       Census and Statistical Department, Ministry of Planning and Scientific Research, Tripoli.
       quarterly.   not priced.
       Monthly wholesale prices of about 150 individual commodity items, industrial raw materials,
            construction materials, fuels, and some items of machinery and transport equipment.
       §   En & Ar eds.

759   Monthly retail prices of selected items of food and other consumer goods in Tripoli town   (Census and
            Statistical Department).
       Census and Statistical Department, Ministry of Planning and Scientific Research, Tripoli.
       1972- issued quarterly.   not priced.
       §   En & Ar eds.

¶ F.i, continued

760 Monthly cost of living index for Tripoli town (Census and Statistical Department).
Census and Statistical Department, Ministry of Planning and Scientific Research, Tripoli.
1966– not priced.
§ En, Ar.

Refer also to 736, 737, 739.

ii. Health and welfare

Refer to 736, 739.

iii. Education and leisure

761 [Statistical bulletin] (Ministry of Education).
Ministry of Education, Tripoli.
1961/62– 1971. not priced. 4 vols.
Separate volumes devoted to the initial stage, preparatory stage, secondary level, and religious
education.
Time factor: the issues for 1971, published in 1972, have data for 1971.
§ Ar.

762 [General statistics of schools in West Tripoli province – primary and upwards, 1943-63] (Ministry of
Education).
Ministry of Education, Tripoli.
not priced. 49p.
Time factor: published in 1963.
§ Ar.

763 [Education – tables, 1960-1970] (Ministry of Education).
Ministry of Education, Tripoli.
not priced. 16p.
§ Ar.

Refer also to 736, 739.

iv. Justice

Refer to 736.

¶ G – Finance

Refer to 736, 737, 738, 739.

i. Banking

Refer to 736, 737, 738, 739.

¶   G,   continued

ii. Public finance

764   Balance of payments   (Central Bank of Libya).
             Central Bank of Libya, P O Box 1103, Tripoli.
             1953-   1973 (1392-1393 Hijjri).   not priced.   18p.
             Time factor: the 1973 issue, published December 1974, has the balance of payments statement for
                 1973 and revised figures for 1971 and 1972.
             §   En & Ar eds.

             Note: published by the Census and Statistical Department until 1969.

765   National accounts of the Libyan Arab Republic   (Ministry of Planning).
             Ministry of Planning and Scientific Research, Tripoli.
             1962/69-   1962-1971.   not priced.   132p.
             Time factor: published in October 1972.
             §   En.

             Refer also to 736, 737, 738, 739.

¶   H - Transport and communications

         Refer to 736, 737, 739.

Central statistical office

766   Institut National de la Statistique et de la Recherche Economique, [National Institute for Statistics and Economic Research]
B P 485, Tananarive.
t 216-13.

The Institute, which is under the Ministère des Finances et du Plan [Ministry of Finance and Planning] is responsible for the collection, analysis and publication of economic and social statistics and for undertaking censuses and surveys.

Libraries

The Institut National de la Statistique et de la Recherche Economique has a library, which is open to the public during office hours for reference.   The collection includes statistical publications concerning Madagascar, publications of other countries throughout the world received on exchange, and publications of international organisations.   The language spoken is French.

Bibliographies

The Institut National de la Statistique et de la Recherche Economique issues a list of its publications from time to time.

Statistical publications

¶ A - General

767   Bulletin mensuel de statistique   [Monthly bulletin of statistics]   (Institut National de la Statistique et de la Recherche Economique).
Institut National de la Statistique et de la Recherche Economique, B P 485, Tananarive.
1955-   MG Fr 160 or MG Fr 1,600 yr (MG Fr 180 or MG Fr 2,000 yr abroad).
Contains statistical data on climate, production, transport, foreign trade, retail prices, wholesale prices, price indices, money and credit (posts and telecommunications, Central Bank), finance, and employment.
Time factor: each issue has data for the previous month and for a varying number of earlier months, as well as for the corresponding periods for the previous year.   Some tables have cumulative figures.
§   Fr.

768   Situation économique   [Economic situation]   (Institut National de la Statistique et de la Recherche Economique).
Institut National de la Statistique et de la Recherche Economique, B P 485, Tananarive.
1968-   6-monthly.   MG Fr 380 or MG Fr 660 yr.
Contains text and tables on industrial production, prices, transport, money and credit, public finance.
Time factor: each issue is published 3 or 4 months after the end of the period covered, and contains data for that half-year and also for the previous two years.
§   Fr.

¶   A,   continued

769   Annuaire statistique de Madagascar   [Statistical yearbook of Madagascar]   (Institut National de la
            Statistique).
            Institut National de la Statistique et de la Recherche Economique, B P 485, Tananarive.
            Vol.1, 1938/51-   1938/51.   not priced.   186p.
            Main sections:

Area	Transport and communication (road,
Climate	rail, river, sea, air, posts and
Population	telecommunications)
Public health	Foreign trade
Education	Prices
Justice	Public finance
Employment	Money, credit, banking
Production (agriculture, livestock,	
forests, mines, electric energy)	

            Time factor: only one volume was published; it covered the years 1938 to 1951 and was published in
                  1953.
            §   Fr.

770   Economie Malgache: évolution 1950-1960   [Malagasy economy: development 1950-1960]   (Commissariat
            Général au Plan).
            Commissariat Général au Plan, Tananarive.
                              not priced.   277p.
            Contains data on physical geography, political and administrative organisation, population, health,
                  education, employment, wages, cost of living, agriculture, crops, animals, fisheries, forests,
                  mines, energy, industry and crafts, roads and road transport, rail, port and maritime transport,
                  air transport, posts and telecommunications, tourism, foreign exchange, imports, exports, prices,
                  investments, public finance, money and credit, and economic accounts.
            Time factor: published in 1962.
            §   Fr.

771   Rapport d'activité   [Annual report]   (Banque Nationale Malagasy de Développement).
            Banque Nationale Malagasy de Développement, rue de France, Tananarive.
            1963-   1975.   not priced.   68p.
            Contains a few statistics and statistical tables in the text, and deals briefly with the international
                  situation, then the national situation (including agricultural, industrial and mineral production),
                  banking generally, and the activities and finances of the Bank Nationale Malagasy de
                  Développement.
            Time factor: the 1975 report was published mid-1976.
            §   Fr.

772   Bulletin mensuel de statistiques   [Monthly bulletin of statistics]   (Banque Centrale de Madagascar).
            Banque Centrale de Madagascar, B P 550, Tananarive.
            1976-   not priced.
            Contains data on the Bank's financial situation and the situation of other financial institutions and
                  economic statistics, including consumer price index, industrial production, foreign trade,
                  transport indicators.
            Time factor: each issue has long runs of annual and quarterly or monthly statistics to about three months
                  prior to the date of issue.
            §   Fr.

¶   B - Production

773   Mémento des principales données économiques de la République Malgache   [Record of the principal
            economic statistics of the Republic of Malagasy]   (Office Malgache d'Exportation; Ministère
            des Mines, de l'Industrie et de Commerce).
            Office Malgache d'Exportation, B P 3187, Tananarive.
                              not priced.   335p.
            Contains data on production, exports, quality, etc, of products.
            Time factor: published in 1971, the volume covers the years from 1960 to 1970.
            §   Fr.

¶   B,   continued

i. Mines and mining

Refer to 767, 768, 769, 770, 771, 773.

ii. Agriculture, fisheries, forestry, etc.

774   Annuaire statistiques agricoles   [Statistical yearbook of agriculture]   (Service de la Statistique Agricole).
Service de la Statistique Agricole, 38 Route Circulaire, Tananarive.
1968-   1974.   not priced.   345p.
Main sections:

General	Forests
Hydro-agriculture	Export, import
Principal crops, by province and	Prices
by product	Commercialisation of products
Livestock	Agricultural credit
Means of production (fertilisers, etc)	Agricultural education
Fisheries	

Time factor: the 1974 edition, published in July 1976, has data for 1974 and provisional data for 1975.
§   Fr.

Note: issued as "Série statistique courant".

775   Enquête agricole (exploitations agricoles de type traditionnel)   [Agricultural survey (traditional agricultural
cultivation)]   (Institut Nationale de la Statistique et de la Recherche Economique).
Institut National de la Statistique et de la Recherche Economique, B P 485, Tananarive.
not priced.   99p.
Time factor: the results of the survey were published in 1966.
§   Fr.

Refer also to 767, 769, 770, 771.

iii. Industry

776   Recensement industriel   [Industrial census]   (Institut National de la Statistique et de la Recherche
Economique).
Institut National de la Statistique et de la Recherche Economique, B P 485, Tananarive.
1967-   1971-1972 and 1973-1974.   not priced.   2 vols.
The results of two censuses taken in 1973 and 1975, relating to the periods 1971-1972 and 1973-1974.
Vol.I contains data on the earlier census and vol.II on the later.   Contains data on production,
by industry; capacity for production; sales; gross profit margin; value added; personnel;
building; etc.
Time factor: the results were published in 1976.
§   Fr.

777   Recensement des entreprises de Madagascar   [Census of enterprises in Madagascar]   (Institut National de
la Statistique et de la Recherche Economique).
Institut National de la Statistique et de la Recherche Economique, B P 485, Tananarive.
1959-   1959.   not priced.   14p.
Lists the number of enterprises in Antananarivo and 5 other towns, by an economic activity classification.
§   Fr.

Note: the census was repeated in 1963 but the results were not published.

Refer also to 767, 768, 769, 770, 771, 772, 773, 785.

v. Energy

Refer to 769.

¶   C - External trade

778   Commerce extérieur de Madagascar   [Foreign trade of Madagascar]   (Institut National de la Statistique
          et de la Recherche Economique).
          Institut National de la Statistique et de la Recherche Economique, B P 485, Tananarive.
          1957-   1974.   not priced.   2 vols.
          Fascicule 1 includes statistics of imports and exports arranged by commodity and sub-divided by countries
              of origin and destination; fascicule 2 includes statistics of imports and exports arranged by countries
              of origin and destination and sub-divided by commodities.
          Time factor: the 1974 issues, published in 1976, have data for 1974.
          §   Fr.

          Note: there is also an issue titled "Séries retrospectives, 1949-1961" covering those earlier years.

          Refer also to 767, 769, 770, 772, 773, 785.

¶   D - Internal distribution and service trades

779   Recensement des entreprises de Madagascar   [Census of enterprises in Madagascar]   (Institut National de
          la Statistique et de la Recherche Economique).
          Institut National de la Statistique et de la Recherche Economique, B P 485, Tananarive.
          1959-   1959.   not priced.   14p.
          Lists the number of enterprises in Antananarivo and 5 other towns, by an economic activity classification.
          §   Fr.

          Note: the census was repeated in 1963 but the results were not published.

780   Les 415 premiers établissements commerciaux de Madagascar (vente en gros et importations)   [The 415
          most important commercial establishments in Madagascar (wholesale and importers)]   (Institut
          National de la Statistique et de la Recherche Economique).
          Institut National de la Statistique et de la Recherche Economique, B P 485, Tananarive.
          1968/69-   1968/69.   not priced.   100p.
          Contains statistical data by size, speciality, etc, of the establishments.
          §   Fr.

          Refer also to 770, 773, 777, 785.

¶   E - Population

781   Recensement...   [Census of population]   (Institut National de la Statistique et de la Recherche
          Economique).
          Institut National de la Statistique et de la Recherche Economique, B P 485, Tananarive.
          1946-
          The most recent censuses are:-
              Recensement des communes de: Faratsiho (Sous-Préfecture de Faritsiho), d'Ambano et de Belazao
                  (Sous-Préfecture d'Antsirabe) - Janvier 1971.
              Recensement urbains: chefs-lieux de province, effectués en 1959-1960 (Tananarive, Fianarantsoa,
                  Tamatave, Majunga, Tuléar, Diégo-Suarez).
              Recensement urbains: province de Tananarive (1962): Antsirabe, Ambatolampy, Arivonimamo.
              Recensement urbains: province de Fianarantsoa (1962 à 1964): Ambositra, Ambalavao, Mananjary,
                  Manakara, Farafangana.
              Recensement urbains: province de Diégo-Suarez, de Majunga, et de Tuléar: Antalaha, Hell-Ville,
                  Sambava, Marovoay, Morondava, Morombe, Fort-Dauphin (1962 à 1964).
              Recensement urbains: province de Tamatave (1962-1963): Ambatondrazaka, Fénérive,
                  Maroantsetra, Moramanga.
              Recensement de la commune urbaine de Vohémar: avril 1967. [restricted circulation].
              Recensement de la commune rurale d'Antanetibe (Sous-Préfecture d'Anjozorobe): juin 1967.
                  [restricted circulation].
              Recensement de la Sous-Préfecture de Maroantsetre (septembre 1967).
              Recensement: bâtiment - logement - population: commune urbain de Mandritsara (mai 1968).
          §   Fr.

¶ E, continued

82 Population de Madagascar [Population of Madagascar] (Institut National de la Statistique et de la
Recherche Economique).
Institut National de la Statistique et de la Recherche Economique, B P 485, Tananarive.
1965- 1972. not priced. 155p.
Contains data on population by province, demography, and international migration.
Time factor: the 1972 issue, published in 1973, has data for the situation as at 1st January 1972.
§ Fr.

83 Etude de la population de Madagascar (Study of the population of Madagascar] (Institut National de
la Statistique...).
Institut National de la Statistique et de la Recherche Economique, B P 485, Tananarive.
not priced. 90p.
Contains data on demography, its structure, internal migration, active population, and projections.
Time factor: published in 1974, with data for 1966.
§ Fr.

84 Enquête démographique: Madagascar 1966 [Demographic survey: Madagascar 1966] (Institut National
de la Statistique et de la Recherche Economique).
Institut National de la Statistique et de la Recherche Economique, B P 485, Tananarive.
not priced. 169p.
Time factor: published in 1967 in connection with the development plan.
§ Fr.

Refer also to 767, 769, 770, 785, 786.

¶ F - Social

85 Inventaire socio-économique [Socio-economic inventory] (Institut National de la Statistique et de la
Recherche Economique).
Institut National de la Statistique et de la Recherche Economique, B P 485, Tananarive.
1938/51- 3rd, 1964-1968. not priced. 2 vols.
Vol.I contains data on physical geography and climate, population and social evolution, and
production; vol.II contains data on internal trade, transport and communications, enterprises,
foreign trade, money and credit, investments, public finance, and economic accounts.
Time factor: the 1964-1968 edition, published in 1972, has data for the years 1964 to 1968.
§ Fr.

86 Inventaire des statistiques sociales [Inventory of social statistics] (Institut National de la Statistique
et de la Recherche Economique).
Institut National de la Statistique et de la Recherche Economique, B P 485, Tananarive.
not priced. 119p.
Contains data on demography, education, employment, justice, health and religion.
Time factor: data is for 1971 or 1970 and four or more earlier years.
§ Fr.

i. Standard of living

87 Enquête sur les budgets des ménages en milieu rural (1968-69) [Survey of household budgets in rural areas
(1968-69)] (Institut National de la Statistique et de la Recherche Economique).
Institut National de la Statistique et de la Recherche Economique, B P 485, Tananarive.
not priced. 124p.
§ Fr.

¶   F.i,   continued

788   Enquête sur les dépenses des ménages étrangers à Tananarive-ville (1969)   [Survey of expenditures of
              foreign households in Antananarive town (1969)]   (Institut National de la Statistique et de la
              Recherche Economique).
          Institut National de la Statistique et de la Recherche Economique, B P 485, Tananarive.
                              not priced.   48p.
              §   Fr.

789   Enquête sur les vacances (1968-1969): ménages Malgaches à Tananarive   [Survey of holidays (1968-1969):
              Madagascan households in Antananarivo]   (Institut National de la Statistique et de la Recherche
              Economique).
          Institut National de la Statistique et de la Recherche Economique, B P 485, Tananarive.
                              not priced.   9p.
              §   Fr.

          Refer also to 767, 770, 772.

    ii.   Health and welfare

              Refer to 769, 770, 786.

    iii. Education and leisure

              Refer to 769, 770, 786.

    iv.   Justice

              Refer to 769, 786.

¶   G - Finance

              Refer to 767, 768, 769, 770, 785.

    i. Banking

              Refer to 767, 769, 771, 772.

    ii. Public finance

              Refer to 768, 769, 770, 771, 785.

    iv. Investment

              Refer to 770, 785.

¶   H - Transport and communications

     Refer to 767, 768, 769, 770, 772, 785.

ii.   Road

'90   Répartition des véhicules neufs, usagés immatriculés pour la première fois à Madagascar et des véhicules reconstruits par genre, marque, province   [Distribution of new vehicles, used vehicles registered for the first time in Madagascar and of reconstructed vehicles by kind, make, province] (Institut National de la Statistique et de la Recherche Economique).
Institut National de la Statistique et de la Recherche Economique, B P 485, Tananarivo.
1964-   1976.   not priced.   c70p.
Time factor: the 1976 issue, published early 1977, has data for 1976.
§   Fr.

Central statistical office

791   National Statistical Office,
P O Box 333, Zomba.
t 558.   tg PRESMIN, Zomba.

The Office is responsible for the collection, analysis and publication of statistics of industrial production, commerce, agriculture, finance, transport, employment and earnings, balance of payments, external trade, etc. It also undertakes censuses and surveys and publishes the results.

Libraries

Copies of publications of the National Statistical Office are available for reference in the National Archives of Malawi, P O Box 62, Zomba.

Libraries and information services abroad

Copies of publications of the National Statistical Office are available for reference in Malawi's embassies abroad, including:
United Kingdom   High Commission for Malawi, 47 Gt Cumberland Place, London W.I.
                    t 01-723 6021.
USA   Malawi Embassy, 1400 20th Street NW, Washington DC.   t 296-5530.

Bibliographies

The National Statistical Office issues a list of current publications monthly.

Statistical publications

¶   A - General

792   Malawi statistical yearbook   (National Statistical Office).
          National Statistical Office, P O Box 333, Zomba.
          1965-   1976.   K 6.00 (K 6.50 abroad).   192p.
          Main sections:

Population	Building and construction
Housing	Prices
Climate	Electricity
Employment and earnings	External trade
Education	Balance of payments
Health	Transport
Agriculture	Posts and telecommunications
Forestry	Banking and finance
Fisheries	Public finance
Industrial production	National accounts
Tourism	

          Time factor: the 1976 edition, containing data for several years to 1975, was published late 1976.
          §   En.

793   Monthly bulletin of statistics   (National Statistical Office).
          National Statistical Office, P O Box 333, Zomba.
          1971-   K 12.00 (K 14.00 yr abroad).
          Contains current information on external trade, government revenue, transport, money and banking, agriculture, building, electricity, tourism, manufacturing output, and price indices. A quarterly supplement contains more detailed external trade data and information on employment and earnings, construction output, and retail sales.
          Time factor: each issue is published during the current month and contains data for the preceding month, cumulated figures for the year to date, and totals for the last 12 months, compared with the same periods for the previous year.
          §   En.

¶　A,　continued

794　　　Economic report　　(Office of the President and Cabinet, Economic Planning Department).
　　　　　　Office of the President, Zomba.
　　　　　　1966-　1977.　　K 3.00.　　77p.
　　　　　　Contains tables on external trade, agricultural and natural resources, transport and communications,
　　　　　　　　commerce and industry, employment and social services, banking and finance, public finance,
　　　　　　　　and the development programme.
　　　　　　Time factor: the 1977 issue, published early 1977, has long runs of figures to 1976.
　　　　　　§　En.

795　　　Mid-year economic review　　(Office of the President and Cabinet, Economic Planning Department).
　　　　　　Office of the President, Zomba.
　　　　　　1971/72-　1976/77.　　K 0.70.　　27p.
　　　　　　Contains similar information to 794 above.
　　　　　　Time factor: the 1976/77 review was published in 1976.
　　　　　　§　En.

796　　　Economic and financial review　　(Reserve Bank of Malawi).
　　　　　　Reserve Bank of Malawi, P O Box 565, Zomba.
　　　　　　1969-　quarterly.　　not priced.
　　　　　　Includes a statistical annex of about 60 pages, with data on the banking system, other financial
　　　　　　　　institutions, central government finance, balance of payments, national accounts, and general
　　　　　　　　economic indicators.
　　　　　　§　En.

797　　　Annual report and statement of accounts　　(Reserve Bank of Malawi).
　　　　　　Reserve Bank of Malawi, P O Box 565, Zomba.
　　　　　　1966-　1974.　　not priced.　　52p.
　　　　　　Includes a statistical section covering the same subjects as item 796 above.
　　　　　　Time factor: the 1974 issue, published in 1975, has data from 1969 to 1973 or 1974.
　　　　　　§　En.

¶　B　-　Production

ii.　Agriculture, fisheries, forestry, etc.

798　　　Compendium of agricultural statistics　　(National Statistical Office).
　　　　　　National Statistical Office, P O Box 333, Zomba.
　　　　　　1968-　2nd, 1971.　　K 5.00 (K 5.50 abroad).　　91p.
　　　　　　A detailed historical record of Malawi's agriculture, including livestock, forestry and fishing, and
　　　　　　　　purchases by the Farmers' Marketing Board.
　　　　　　Time factor: the 1971 edition, published in 1971, contains long runs of statistics to 1969.
　　　　　　§　En.

799　　　National sample survey of agriculture　　(National Statistical Office).
　　　　　　National Statistical Office, P O Box 333, Zomba.
　　　　　　1967/68-　1968/69.　　K 8.00 (K 8.50 abroad).　　185p.
　　　　　　A sample survey of the whole country, giving acreage, yield, income and expenditure, and livestock.
　　　　　　§　En.

800　　　Annual report　　(Department of Veterinary Services and Animal Industry).
　　　　　　Department of Veterinary Services and Animal Industry, Zomba.
　　　　　　1961-　1972.　　not priced.　　68p.
　　　　　　Contains data on numbers of livestock, animal diseases, animal health, etc.
　　　　　　Time factor: the 1972 report, published in 1973, has data for 1972.
　　　　　　§　En.

¶   B.ii,   continued

801   Annual report   (Department of Agriculture, Ministry of Natural Resources and Surveys).
        Ministry of Agriculture, P O Box 303, Zomba.
        1963-   1969/70.   not priced.   c40p.
        Includes a statistical appendix on rainfall, purchase of trust land, produce, trust land tobacco statistics,
             tobacco leaf sold, tea statistics, seed cotton production, tung statistics, main agricultural exports,
             and fish catches.
        Time factor: the 1969/70 report, published in 1971, has data for the year 1969/70.
        §   En.

802   Annual report of the Department of Agriculture   (Animal Husbandry Research).
        Ministry of Agriculture, P O Box 303, Zomba.
        1963-   1970/71.   K 0.65.   52p.
        Includes statistics and statistical tables in the text on cattle herds, calving, milk yield, etc.
        Time factor: the 1970/71 report, published in 1974, has data for 1970/71.
        §   En.

        Refer also to 792, 793, 794, 795.

    iii.   Industry

803   Annual survey of economic activities   (National Statistical Office).
        National Statistical Office, P O Box 333, Zomba.
        1967-   1973.   K 3.00 (K 3.50 abroad).   60p.
        Contains a summary of output, employment and capital, and more detailed information of the
             derivation of gross output, the purchase and consumption of goods and services, employment
             and earnings, the book value of assets and capital formation and depreciation.
        Time factor: the 1973 issue, containing data for that year, was published in 1976.
        §   En.

        Refer also to 792, 793, 794, 795.

    iv.   Construction

        Refer to 792, 793.

    v.   Energy

804   Annual report and statement of accounts   (Electricity Supply Commission of Malawi).
        Electricity Supply Commission of Malawi, Zomba.
        1964-   1975.   not priced.   44p.
        Apart from financial data the report contains data on production and sales, operating costs, consumer
             statistics, plant capacity, generating statistics, etc.
        Time factor: the 1975 report, published mid-1976, has data for 1975.
        §   En.

        Refer also to 792, 793.

¶   C - External trade

305   Annual statement of external trade   (National Statistical Office).
             National Statistical Office, P O Box 333, Zomba.
             1964-   1975.   K 6.50.   286p.
             Includes tables of trade with principal countries, detailed statistics of imports and exports and re-exports
                  arranged by commodity and sub-divided by countries of origin and destination, and trade indices.
             Time factor: the 1975 issue, containing data for that year, was published late 1976.
             §   En.

             Refer also to 792, 793, 794, 795.

¶   D - Internal distribution and service trades

306   Tourist report   (National Statistical Office).
             National Statistical Office, P O Box 333, Zomba.
             1970-   1974.   K 1.00; K 1.50 abroad.   c10p.
             Detailed report on departing visitors, reasons for visit, country of permanent residence, places visited,
                  and average daily expenditure.
             Time factor: the 1974 issue, published in 1975, has data for 1974.
             §   En.

307   Zomba town market survey, 1970/71   (National Statistical Office).
             National Statistical Office, P O Box 333, Zomba.
                           K 2.00; K 2.50 abroad.   70p.
             A detailed report on the origin of agricultural produce offered for sale.
             Time factor: published in 1971.
             §   En.

308   Lilongwe town market survey, 1971/72   (National Statistical Office).
             National Statistical Office, P O Box 333, Zomba.
                           K 3.00; K 3.50 abroad.   82p.
             A report on the origin, means of transport, type of seller and prices of agricultural produce offered for
                  sale.
             Time factor: published in 1973.
             §   En.

             Refer also to 792, 793.

¶   E - Population

309   Malawi population census   (National Statistical Office).
             National Statistical Office, P O Box 333, Zomba.
             1911-   1966.   2 vols.
             The final report (K 8.00; K 8.50 abroad) contains data on population by land, area, region, etc;
                  population by age and sex; population by race and sex; places of birth; school attendance;
                  languages spoken; personal income; wages and salaries.   The methodological report (K 2.00;
                  K 2.50 abroad) contains the history of population counts in Malawi as well as description of the
                  methods used for the 1966 census.
             §   En.

             Note: the next census is scheduled for October 1977.   A pilot census, based on 10% sample, for
                  9 districts was taken between 1973 and 1974 (K 1.00; K 1.50 abroad for each report) and
                  for Blantyre City in 1972 (K 3.00; K 3.50 abroad).

¶   E,   continued

810   Population changes survey report 1970-1972   (National Statistical Office).
         National Statistical Office, P O Box 333, Zomba.
                           K 4.00; K 4.50 abroad.
         The report contains data on fertility, mortality, natural rate of growth, life tables, migration and
             general demographic characteristics.
         §   En.

811   Blantyre city population sample census   (National Statistical Office).
         National Statistical Office, P O Box 333, Zomba.
         1972.   K 3.00; K 3.50 abroad.
         The report contains population statistics by age, sex, race and ward; data on place of birth, school
             attendance, employment, unemployment, income, and dwelling units.
         §   En.

812   Chiradzulu pilot census   (National Statistical Office).
         National Statistical Office, P O Box 333, Zomba.
         1973/74.   K 1.00; K 1.50 abroad.
         Contains population statistics for Chiradzulu on a 10% sample basis by age, sex, marital status, place
             of birth, school attendance, fertility, mortality, labour force, income and dwelling unit facilities.
         §   En.

         Note: this report is the first of a series of nine districts covered by the pilot census.

813   Employment and earnings annual report   (National Statistical Office).
         National Statistical Office, P O Box 333, Zomba.
         1967- 1974.   K 3.00; K 3.50 abroad.   23p.
         Contains data on employment and earnings in government and private sectors.   For the private sector
             only large establishments (i.e. with 20 or more employees) are included.
         Time factor: the 1974 issue, published late 1975, has data for 1970 to 1974.
         §   En.

814   Manpower survey 1971: results of the survey and analysis of requirements 1971-1980   (Office of the
             President and Cabinet, Economic Planning Division).
         Office of the President, Zomba.
                           not priced.   99p.
         Time factor: published late 1972.
         §   En.

815   Reported employment and earnings...annual report   (National Statistical Office).
         National Statistical Office, P O Box 333, Zomba.
         1967- 1971.   K 2.00 (K 2.50 abroad).   14p.
         The report of a quarterly employment enquiry.
         Time factor: the 1971 issue, published in May 1972, has data for 1971.   Prior to the 1971 issue the
             report was published quarterly.
         §   En.

         Refer also to 792, 793, 794, 795.

      ¶   F - Social

      i. Standard of living

816   Household income and expenditure survey   (National Statistical Office).
         National Statistical Office, P O Box 333, Zomba.
         1968- 1968.   K 8.00; K 8.50 abroad.   259p.
         Household income and expenditure by detailed commodities for four main towns and other urban centres.
         Time factor: the report was published in 1970.
         §   En.

¶   F.i,   continued

817   Malawi Broadcasting Corporation radio listenership survey   (National Statistical Office).
            National Statistical Office, P O Box 333, Zomba.
            1970-   1975.   K 1.50.   18p.
            Contains data on radio ownership, listening habits, wave bands, peak listening times, etc, for African
                households in both rural and urban areas.
            Time factor: the survey covers several months and the results of the 1975 survey were published in 1976.
            §   En.

            Refer also to 793.

    ii.   Health and welfare

            Refer to 792.

    iii.   Education and leisure

818   Annual report of the Ministry of Education.
            Ministry of Education, BB 328, Capital City, Lilongwe 3.
            1926-   1965.   3s6d.   21p.
            Includes statistical appendices on professionally qualified staff, staff without qualifications, number of
                classes and pupils in classes, general education enrolment by levels and by districts, teacher
                training, technical and vocational courses, examinations, finances, scholarships and bursaries.
            Time factor: the 1965 report, published in 1966, has data for 1965.
            §   En.

            Refer also to 792.

¶   G - Finance

            Refer to 792, 793, 794, 795, 796, 797.

    i.   Banking

            Refer to 792, 793, 794, 795, 796, 797.

    ii.   Public finance

819   National accounts report   (National Statistical Office).
            National Statistical Office, P O Box 333, Zomba.
            1964/67-   1964/71.   K 3.00; K 3.50 abroad.   34p.
            A comprehensive report on the structure and growth of Malawi's economy.
            Time factor: the 1964/71 issue, published in 1972, has data for the years 1964 to 1971.
            §   En.

820   Balance of payments   (National Statistical Office).
            National Statistical Office, P O Box 333, Zomba.
            1964/65-   1974.   K 2.00; K 2.50 abroad.   24p.
            Contains detailed data on Malawi's economic transactions with foreign institutions, governments and
                individuals.
            Time factor: the 1974 issue, published in 1976, has data for 1974.
            §   En.

MALAWI,   continued

¶   G.ii,   continued

821   Public sector financial statistics   (Ministry of Finance).
           Ministry of Finance, Zomba.
           1969-   1976.   K 2.00.   71p.
           Statistics of public enterprises and government accounts.
           Time factor: the 1976 issue, published in 1977, has data from 1968 to 1976/77.
           §   En.

822   Annual report of the Commissioner of Taxes   (Department of Taxation, Ministry of Finance).
           Ministry of Finance, Zomba.
           1967/68-   1974/75.   K 0.60.   31p.
           Includes statistical tables of analysis on taxes of individuals, companies, etc.
           Time factor: the 1974/75 report, published in 1976, has data for the fiscal year 1974/75.
           §   En.

           Refer also to 792, 793, 794, 795, 796, 797.

¶   H - Transport and communications

           Refer to 792, 793, 794, 795.

ii. Road

823   Annual report of the Road Traffic Commissioner.
           Road Traffic Commission, Ministry of Transport and Communications, Box 30177, Chichiri, Blantyre 3.
           1967-   1969.   4s.0d.   38p.
           Includes data on government and privately owned vehicles; new and secondhand vehicles imported;
               taxis, by area of operation; goods vehicles permits; vehicles licensed by districts.
           Time factor: the 1969 report, published in 1970, has data for 1969.
           §   En.

iv. Air

824   Annual report of statistics   (Department of Civil Aviation).
           Department of Civil Aviation, Zomba.
           1969/70-   1975.   K 1.20.   21p.
           Contains data on air traffic, passengers, cargoes, etc.
           Time factor: the 1975 report, published in 1976, has annual figures from 1972 to 1975 and monthly
               figures for 1975.
           §   En.

           Note: from 1964 to 1968/69 the data were published in the annual report of the Department of
               Civil Aviation.

v. Telecommunications and postal services

           Refer to 792, 794, 795.

Central statistical office

825   Direction Nationale de la Statistique [National Office of Statistics],
B P 12, Bamako.
† 227 53.

     The rôle of the Office is to collect statistical information and to put it at the disposal of users in the various forms of activity in the country.   The data are analysed and published in regular statistical publications.   The Office also undertakes censuses and surveys and publishes the results.   Unpublished statistical information is provided on request whenever possible.

Libraries

     The Direction Nationale de la Statistique has no library, but its publications may be consulted in the Office.

Statistical publications

¶   A - General

826   Annuaire statistique de la République Mali   [Statistical yearbook of Mali]   (Service de la Statistique).
     Direction Nationale de la Statistique, B P 12, Bamako.
     1960-   1973.   FrM 5,000 or US$25.00 by air.   214p.
     Main sections:
         Introduction - history - geography
         Climate, hydrography
         Population
         Economic resources (agriculture, livestock, water, forests, energy, industry)
         Foreign trade and communications (transport, posts and telegraphs, foreign trade)
         Prices (retail, production)
         Finance (money and credit, public finance)
     Time factor: the 1973 edition, published in 1976, has data for 1972/73 and 1973.
     §   Fr.

827   Annuaire statistique   [Statistical yearbook]   (Direction Régionale du Plan et de la Statistique, Gouvernorat de Bamako).
     Direction Régionale du Plan et de la Statistique, Bamako.
     1970-   1971.   not priced.   102p.
     Similar in content to 826 above, but concerned only with the region of Bamako.
     Time factor: the 1971 edition, published in December 1976, has data for 1971.
     §   Fr.

828   Annuaire statistique   [Statistical yearbook]   (Direction Régionale du Plan et de la Statistique, Gouvernorat de Gao).
     Direction Régionale du Plan et de la Statistique, Gao.
     1969-   2nd, 1973.   not priced.   181p.
     Similar in content to 826 above, but concerned with the region of Gao.
     Time factor: the 1973 edition, published in December 1974, has data for 1973.
     §   Fr.

829   Annuaire statistique   [Statistical yearbook]   (Gouvernorat de la Région de Kayes).
     Gouvernorat de la Région de Kayes, Kayes.
     1967-   3rd, 1970.   not priced.   95p.
     Similar in content to 826 above, but concerned with the region of Kayes.
     Time factor: the 1970 edition, published in January 1973, has data for 1970.
     §   Fr.

¶ A, continued

830 Annuaire statistique [Statistical yearbook] (Direction Régionale du Plan et de la Statistique, Gouvernorat de Mopti).
Direction Régionale du Plan et de la Statistique, Mopti.
1971 & 1972- 2nd, 1973. not priced. 122p.
Similar in content to 826 above, but concerned with the region of Mopti.
Time factor: the 1973 edition, published in March 1977, has data for 1973.
§ Fr.

831 Annuaire statistique [Statistical yearbook] (Gouvernorat de la Région de Segou).
Gouvernorat de la Région de Segou, Segou.
1971- 1971. not priced. 107p.
Similar in content to 826 above, but concerned with the region of Segou.
Time factor: the 1971 edition, published in January 1973, has data for 1971.
§ Fr.

832 Troix ans d'expérience... [Three years experience...] (Gouvernorat de la Région de Sikasso).
Gouvernorat de la Région de Sikasso, Sikasso.
1969-1971. not priced. 39p.
Similar in content to 826 above, but concerned with the region of Sikasso.
§ Fr.

833 Bulletin mensuel de statistique [Monthly bulletin of statistics] (Service de la Statistique).
Direction Nationale de la Statistique, B P 12, Bamako.
1959- FrM 6,000 yr; US$25.00 yr by air.
Contains data on climate, demography, transport, production, prices, public finance, money and credit.
Time factor: each issue has data for the month of the issue and cumulated figures for the year to date, and is published some months later.
§ Fr.

¶ B - Production

i. Mines and mining

Refer to 826.

ii. Agriculture, fisheries, forestry, etc.

834 Enquête agricole [Agricultural survey] (Service de la Statistique).
Direction Nationale de la Statistique, B P 12, Bamako.
1964/65- 1973/74. FrM 3,000; US$18.00 by air. 96p.
Contains a short general section, then data on active population, agricultural development, cultivation, yield and production, and livestock.
Time factor: the 1973/74 issue, published in 1976, has data for 1973 and 1973/74, and earlier figures. The survey is made annually.
§ Fr.

Refer also to 826, 827, 828, 829, 830, 831, 832, 833.

MALI, continued

  B, continued

  iii. Industry

835   Evolution des activités du secteur économique organisé d'après les résultats des enquêtes auprès des
            entreprises,   [Development of activities in the economic sector...results of a survey of enterprises]
            (Direction Nationale du Plan et de la Statistique).
         Direction Nationale de la Statistique, B P 12, Bamako.
         1960/70-   2nd, 1968-1974.   Fr 3,000 or US$18.00 by air.   c130p.
         Covers enterprises with an annual turnover of 10 million francs or more, and includes data on
            employment, wages and salaries, cost of inputs, value of output, stocks, turnover, work and
            services rendered by others, etc.
         Time factor: the results for 1968 to 1974 were published in December 1976.
         §   Fr.

         Refer also to 826, 827, 828, 829, 830, 831, 832, 833.

  v. Energy

         Refer to 826, 827, 828, 829, 830, 831, 832, 833.

  ¶   C - External trade

836   Statistiques douanières du commerce extérieur   [Customs statistics of external trade]   (Service de la
            Statistique).
         Direction Nationale de la Statistique, B P 12, Bamako.
         1967-   1974.   FrM 25,000 or US$65.00 by air.   not paged.
         Computer print-out. Data are detailed statistics of imports and exports arranged by commodities sub-
            divided by countries of origin and destination, and arranged by countries sub-divided by
            commodities.
         Time factor: the 1974 issue, published late 1975, has data for 1974.
         §   Fr.

837   Associés: commerce extérieur: République Mali: annuaire 1959-1966. Associates: foreign trade: Mali
            Republic: yearbook 1959-1966   (European Communities).
         Office des Publications Officielles des Communautés Européennes, C P 1003, Luxembourg; or from
            sales agents.
                         £0.90 or FrB 100.   128p.
         One of a series of retrospective publications on the foreign trade of African states associated with the
            European Communities.   Main tables show imports and exports arranged by commodity and sub-
            divided by countries of origin and destination.   Values are in US $.
         Time factor: published early 1969.
         §   De, En, Fr, It, Nl.

         Refer to 826.

  ¶   D - Internal distribution and service trades

         Refer to 826.

¶ E - Population

838 Enquête démographique du Mali [Demographic survey of Mali] (INSEE, Paris).
INSEE, 18 boulevard Adolphe Pinard, 75675 Paris Cedex 14, France.
1956/58- 1960-1961. not priced. 349p.
Time factor: the results of the 1960-1961 survey were published in 1967.
§ Fr.

Refer also to 826, 827, 828, 829, 830, 831, 832, 833.

¶ G - Finance

839 Comptes économiques du Mali [Economic accounts of Mali] (Service de la Statistique).
Direction Nationale de la Statistique, B P 12, Bamako.
1956- 1971. FrM 5,000; US$25.00 by air. 112p.
Time factor: the 1971 issue, published in 1974, has data for 1971 and 1970/71.
§ Fr.

Refer also to 826, 827, 828, 829, 830, 831, 832, 833.

¶ H - Transport and communications

Refer to 826, 827, 828, 829, 830, 831, 832, 833.

MAURITANIA - MAURITANIE - MAURETANIEN

Central statistical office

840   Direction de la Statistique et des Etudes Economiques   [Department of Statistics and Economic Studies],
B P 240, Nouakchott.
† 514.77 and 526.59.

      The Department, which is attached to the Ministry of Planning and Research, is responsible for the collection of all official statistics and for the organisation of surveys and enquiries.   Unpublished statistical information may be supplied on request if available.

Statistical publications

¶ A - General

841   Annuaire statistique [Statistical yearbook]   (Direction de la Statistique).
        Direction de la Statistique, B P 240, Nouakchott.
        1968- 1974.   200 UM.   143p.
        Main sections:

Economic and social chronology	Mines
Geography	Energy
Climate	Transport
Population	Posts and telecommunications
Health	Internal trade
Justice	Prices
Labour	Foreign trade
Agriculture	Money and credit
Tourism	Insurance
Livestock	Public finance
Fisheries	Foreign aid
Forestry	

        Time factor: the 1974 edition, published late 1975, has data for 1974 and some earlier years in some
           tables.
        §   Fr.

        Note: the yearbook supercedes "Bulletin statistique et économique" which was issued at irregular
           intervals from 1960 to 1967.

842   Bulletin mensuel statistiques   [Monthly bulletin of statistics]   (Direction de la Statistique).
        Direction de la Statistique, B P 240, Nouakchott.
        1968-   400 UM yr.
        Contains data on climate, population, tourism, health, production, transport, foreign trade, prices,
           money and credit, and public finance.
        Time factor: each issue has data for that month and corresponding month and year for the previous year,
           and is published about four months later.
        §   Fr.

¶ B - Production

i. Mines and mining

      Refer to 841, 842.

ii. Agriculture, fisheries, forestry, etc.

      Refer to 841, 842.

¶   B,   continued

iii. Industry

843   Recensement industrial et commercial   [Industrial and commercial census]   (Direction de la Statistique).
        Direction de la Statistique, B P 240, Nouakchott.
        1968-   1969-70.   200 UM.   c60p.
        The census covered all enterprises with an annual turnover of CFA Fr 10 M or more.
        Time factor: the 1969/70 census report was published in 1974.
        §   Fr.

        Refer also to 841, 842.

v. Energy

        Refer to 841.

¶   C - External trade

844   Statistiques du commerce extérieur de la Mauritanie: commerce special: importations, exportations:
            résultats provisoires   [Foreign trade statistics of Mauritania: imports, exports, provisional results]
            (Direction de la Statistique).
        Direction de la Statistique, B P 240, Nouakchott.
        1970-   1973.   200 UM.   291p.
        Contains detailed data on imports and exports arranged by commodity sub-divided by countries of origin
            and destination, and arranged by countries sub-divided by commodities.
        Time factor: the 1973 issue, published in 1974, has data for 1973.
        §   Fr.

845   Associés: commerce extérieur: République Islamique de Mauritanie: annuaire 1959-1966.   Associates:
            foreign trade: Mauritania: yearbook 1959-1966   (European Communities).
        Office des Publications Officielles des Communautés Européennes, C P 1003, Luxembourg; or from
            sales agents.
                        £0.90 or FrB 100.   94p.
        One of a series of retrospective publications on the foreign trade of African states associated with the
            European Communities.   Main tables show imports and exports arranged by commodity and sub-
            divided by countries of origin and destination.   Values are in US $.
        Time factor: published early in 1969.
        §   De, En, Fr, It, Nl.

        Refer also to 841, 842.

¶   D - Internal distribution and service trades

        Refer to 841, 842.

¶   E - Population

846   Recensement démographique des agglomérations (enquête 1961-1962)   [Demographic census of collectives
            (survey 1961-1962)]   (Service de la Statistique).
        Direction de la Statistique, B P 240, Nouakchott.
        1936-   1961-1962.   not priced.   91p.
        Time factor: published in 1964.
        §   Fr.

¶   E,   continued

847   Enquête démographique, 1965: résultats définitifs   [Demographic survey, 1965: final results]   (Ministère
          des Finances, du Plan, et de la Fonction Publique <u>and</u> INSEE, Paris).
          Ministère des Finances, Nouakchott.
                              not priced.   327p.
          Time factor: published in 1972.
          §   Fr.

          Refer also to 841, 842.

¶   F - Social

i. Standard of living

          Refer to 841, 842.

ii. Health and welfare

          Refer to 841, 842.

iv. Justice

          Refer to 841.

¶   G - Finance

ii. Public finance

848   Comptes économiques de la Mauritanie   [National accounts of Mauritania]   (Direction de la Statistique).
          Direction de la Statistique, B P 240, Nouakchott.
          1964-   1973.   100 UM.   32p.
          Time factor: the 1973 issue, published in April 1975, has data for 1973.
          §   Fr.

          Refer also to 841, 842.

v. Insurance

          Refer to 841.

¶   H - Transport and communications

          Refer to 841, 842.

Central statistical office

849   Central Statistical Office,
           Rose Hill, Port Louis.
           † 4-2088.

Created in 1945 to collect and compile accurate information regarding the remuneration of labour, the number and types of employment in various industries, the level of prices and the computation of cost of living statistics, the Office has gradually extended its functions to include the periodical statistical survey of every branch of economic activity in the island; industrial, financial and commercial. It is also responsible for the compilation and analysis of demographic, vital, health, educational and other social statistics.   The statistical branch of the Customs and Excise Department has been transferred to the Central Statistical Office, and all trade statistics are processed in the Office although their publication is still the responsibility of the Comptroller of Customs.   Unpublished statistical information can be supplied to enquirers if available; unpublished statistics of foreign trade may be supplied by the Customs and Excise Department at Port Louis.

Another important organisation collecting and publishing statistics

850   Customs and Excise Department,
           Port Louis.
           † 2-0521.

One of the responsibilities of the Department is the collection, collation and publication of foreign trade statistics.   Unpublished statistical information can be supplied to enquirers if it is available, but a charge may be made for this service to cover cost of time spent on the work.

Libraries

The Central Statistical Office possesses a small library containing a collection of statistical publications of other countries and of international organisations as well as those of Mauritius, together with books dealing with statistical theory and methods.   The library is, in principle, for the sole use of the staff of the office, but anyone wishing to consult a publication would be welcome.   The language spoken by the staff is English.

Statistical publications may also be consulted at the Mauritius Archives, Sir William Newton Street, Port Louis.

Bibliographies

A list of the publications of the Central Statistical Office is published in the annual report of the Office.

Statistical publications

¶ A - General

851   Bi-annual digest of statistics   (Central Statistical Office).
           Government Printer, Port Louis.
           1961-   Rs 25.00 each issue.
           Includes data on population and vital statistics, public health, public finance and banking, national
              accounts, consumer price index, external trade, employment and wages, social assistance,
              education, transport and communication, land utilisation, local production, and climate.
           Time factor: was quarterly until 1967.   Issued about 6 months after the end of the period covered, the
              June issue has data for the first half-year and the December issue for the whole year.   Each issue
              also contains some quarterly figures and retrospective figures for about 5 years.
           §   En.

           Note: a "Yearbook of statistics" was published from 1946 to 1959.

¶   A,   continued

852   Mauritius: report for the year   (Commonwealth Office).
            H M Stationery Office, P O Box 569, London SE1 9NH, England.
            1946-   1967.   £1.25.   212p.
            Part 1 of the report is a general review; part 2 deals in more detail with various aspects of the island's
                life and work; part 3 contains more general observations on the history, geography and
                administration of Mauritius.   Tables occur throughout the text and include population, occupations,
                wages, currency and banking, commerce and industry, production, social services, justice, police,
                prisons, public liabilities, public works, and communications (including transport and tourism).
            Time factor: the 1967 report, published in 1970, contains data for 1967 and sometimes for one or two
                earlier years.   It is the final report by the Commonwealth Office as Mauritius became independent
                in 1967.
            §   En.

853   Mauritius economic review   (Ministry of Economic Planning and Development).
            Government Printer, Port Louis.
            1970/72-   1971/75.   Rs 15.   108p.
            Concerned with the main trends in the economy (output, income, external trade, balance of payments;
                capital flow; public finance; money, banking and financial institutions; population, labour force
                and employment; wages and prices), development by sector (rural development programme,
                fisheries, cooperatives, transport and communications, water, electricity, sewerage, manufacturing,
                construction, housing, health, tourism, educational training and manpower, youth and sports), and
                Rodrigues.   Statistical tables are included in the text.
            Time factor: the 1971/75 review, published mid-1976, has data up to 1974.
            §   En.

            Note: earlier issues are titled "Mauritius economic survey".

854   Annual report . (Bank of Mauritius).
            Bank of Mauritius, P O Box 29, Port Louis.
            1967/68-   1974/75.   not priced.   91p.
            Includes statistical tables on selected economic indicators, activities of the bank, activities of
                commercial banks, money, public finance, employment, consumer price indices, sugar production
                and yields and disposal, foreign trade, tourism, balance of payments, gross national product,
                capital formation.
            Time factor: the 1974/75 report, published in 1976, has long runs of monthly figures to June 1975.
            §   En.

¶   B - Production

ii. Agriculture, fisheries, forestry, etc.

855   Livestock statistics, 1950, 1956 and 1964   (Department of Agriculture).
            Government Printer, Port Louis.
                            Rs 3.00.   12p.
            The results of an enquiry.
            Time factor: published in 1966.
            §   En.

856   Annual report of the Ministry of Agriculture.
            Government Printer, Port Louis.
            1962-   1973.   Rs 12.00.   c150p.
            Includes some statistics and statistical tables in the text on crop results, exports of agricultural produce,
                fisheries, etc.
            Time factor: the 1973 report, published in 1975, has data for 1973.
            §   En.

¶ B.ii, continued

857 The President's report... (Mauritius Chamber of Agriculture).
Mauritius Chamber of Agriculture, Plantation House, Place d'Armes, P O Box 312, Port Louis.
1967/68- 1975/76. free. 77p.
Includes an annual statistical bulletin with data on meteorology, cane production, sugar production, sugar prices and sugar insurance fund, secondary industries (molasses, alcohol and alcohol products, tea, tobacco and cigarettes, aloe fibre, foodcrops), and miscellaneous subjects (import of fertilisers, employment by estates with factories and large plantations).
Time factor: the 1975/76 report, published late 1976, has data for 1975 and also for earlier years in some tables.
§ En.

858 Annual report of the Forestry Service.
Government Printer, Port Louis.
1962/63- 1974. Rs 5.00. 16p.
Contains some statistics in the text on forest policy, administration, management, forest protection, surveys, roads and buildings, silviculture, exploitation and utilisation. There are also statistical appendices on offences against forest laws, silviculture operations in plantations, main imports of forest products, and summary of revenue and expenditure.
Time factor: the 1974 report, published in March 1976, has data for 1974.
§ En.

859 Mauritius sugar news bulletin (Mauritius Chamber of Agriculture).
Mauritius Chamber of Agriculture, Place d'Armes, Port Louis.
monthly. not priced.
Single sheets giving details of crop production, export, etc.
§ En.

Refer also to 851, 852, 853, 854.

iii. Industry

860 The census of industrial production (Central Statistical Office).
Government Printer, Port Louis.
1964- 2nd, 1967-68. Rs 10.00. 51p.
Contents:
    Part I Characteristics of all manufacturing industries
           II Characteristics of large industrial establishments
          III Characteristics of small industrial establishments
          IV Industry tables
Data includes the number of establishments by industry and size, employment, gross output, cost of materials, net output, labour costs, etc.
Time factor: data for the 1967-68 census was collected for either the year 1967 or the accounting year 1967/68, and the report was published in 1970.
§ En.

Refer also to 851, 852, 853, 854.

iv. Construction

Refer to 853.

v. Energy

Refer to 853.

¶ C – External trade

861   Annual report of the Customs and Excise Department.
       Government Printer, Port Louis.
       1967-   1974.   Rs 160.00.   387p.
       The appendix to the report contains detailed trade statistics, the main tables being imports and exports
          arranged by commodity and sub-divided by countries of origin and destination.   There is also a
          table showing trade with dependencies.
       Time factor: the 1974 edition, published in December 1975, contains data for 1974 and comparative
          data for 1973.
       §   En.

862   Quarterly statistical report of the Customs and Excise Department.
       Government Printer, Port Louis.
       1967-   not priced.
       Contains detailed tables of trade arranged by commodities imported and exported, also direction of trade.
       Time factor: each issue contains data for the period of the issue and is published 5 or 6 months later.
       §   En.

       Refer also to 851, 852, 853, 854.

¶ D – Internal distribution and service trades

863   International travel and tourism   (Central Statistical Office).
       Government Printer, Port Louis.
       1974-   two a year.   Rs 15.00 each issue.
       Time factor: published in June and December.
       §   En.

       Refer to 852 for internal distribution and also to 852, 853, 854 for tourism.

¶ E – Population

864   Housing and population census of Mauritius and its dependencies   (Central Statistical Office).
       Government Printer, Port Louis.
       1786-   1972.   6 vols.
       Contents:
          Vol.   I   Population – preliminary report   (Rs 25.00)
               II   Housing – preliminary report   (Rs 15.00)
               III   Rodrigues   (Rs 25.00)
               IV   Housing. Island of Mauritius   (Rs 40.00)
                V   General tables. Island of Mauritius   (Rs 40.00)
               VI   Population in constituencies   (Rs 5.00)
       Time factor: published between 1974 and 1976.
       §   En.

865   Annual report of the Registrar-General's Department.
       Government Printer, Port Louis; or Registrar-General's Department, Sir William Newton Street,
          Port Louis.
       1888-   1975.   Rs 7.00.   50p.
       Includes demographic statistics.
       Time factor: the 1975 report, published in 1976, has data for the year 1975.
       §   En.

¶   E,   continued

866   Natality and fertility in Mauritius, 1825-1955   (Central Statistical Office).
            Government Printer, Port Louis.
                              not priced.   58p.
            Includes tables and graphs in the text.
            Time factor: published in 1976.
            §   En.

867   Bi-annual survey of employment and earnings   (Central Statistical Office).
            Government Printer, Port Louis.
            1966-   Rs 5.00 each issue.
            Contains data on employment by establishment, industry, sex, and age; salaries and wages; job
                vacancies; sugar industry employment; and government service employment.
            Time factor: published in March and September, each issue has data for the six months to the date of the
                issue and is issued about six months later.
            §   En.

868   Annual report of the Ministry of Labour.
            Government Printer, Port Louis.
            1962-   1974/75.   Rs 4.00.   31p.
            Includes statistical tables on industrial stoppages, trade unions, industrial accidents, workmen's
                compensation, employment, hours of work, wages and earnings, etc.
            Time factor: the 1974/75 report, published in May 1977, has data for 1974/75 and also earlier figures
                in some tables.
            §   En.

            Refer also to 851, 852, 853, 854.

¶   F - Social

i.   Standard of living

            Refer to 851, 852, 853, 854.

ii.   Health and welfare

869   Annual report of the Ministry of Health.
            Government Printer, Port Louis.
            1957-   1972.   Rs 27.00.   c200p.
            Includes a section of general statistics, and statistics of pharmaceuticals and supplies, hospitals and
                clinics, public health, diseases, family planning, dental treatment, etc.
            Time factor: the 1972 report, published in 1976, has data for 1972.
            §   En.

870   Report of the Ministry of Social Security.
            Ministry of Social Security, Port Louis.
            1964-   1970.   Rs 3.00.   38p.
            Includes a statistical appendix on relief payments, pensions, etc.
            Time factor: the 1970 report, issued in 1971, has data for 1970.
            §   En.

            Refer also to 851, 852, 853.

¶ F, continued

iii. Education and leisure

871 Annual report on education   (Ministry of Education and Cultural Affairs).
Government Printer, Port Louis.
1960-   1971.   Rs 6.50.   30p.
Includes statistical tables on Mauritius students abroad, number and description of schools and
enrolments by educational level, teachers by level and qualifications, general education enrolment
by level and age, examinations, and expenditure on education.
Time factor: the 1971 report, published in 1973, has data for 1971.
§   En.

872 Triennial survey of education in Mauritius   (Ministry of Education).   ·
Government Printer, Port Louis.
1961/63-   3rd, 1967/69.   Rs 4.25.   47p.
Includes statistics in the text and tables on schools and enrolment, teachers and teacher training,
general education, and examinations.
Time factor: the 1967/69 survey was published in 1970 and covers the years 1967 to 1969.
§   En.

Note: it was intended to issue a further survey report for 1970, 1971 and 1972 in 1973.

Refer also to 851, 852, 853.

iv. Justice

873 Annual report of the Judicial Department.
Government Printer, Port Louis.
1971-   1975.   Rs 5.00.   11p.
Includes statistics of courts and crimes, civil cases, divorce cases, and bankruptcy.
Time factor: the 1975 report, published in 1976, has data for 1975.
§   En.

Refer also to 852.

¶ G - Finance

i. Banking

Refer to 851, 852, 853, 854.

ii. Public finance

874 Financial report for the year...   (Ministry of Finance).
Government Printer, Port Louis.
1956/57-   1974/75.   Rs 55.00.   c125p.
Time factor: the 1974/75 issue was published in 1976.
§   En.

875 Annual report of the Income Tax Department.
Government Printer, Port Louis.
1951/52-   1970/71.   Rs 7.00.   13p.
Includes statistical tables on the state of the work, yield of tax, analysis of tax collected, assessments,
rates of tax, reliefs and allowances, etc.
Time factor: the 1970/71 report, published in 1974, has data for 1970/71.
§   En.

Refer also to 851, 853, 854.

MAURITIUS, continued

¶ H - Transport and communications

Refer to 851, 852, 853.

i. Ships and shipping

876   Annual report of the Ministry of Communications...part IV: marine services.
       Government Printer, Port Louis.
       1961-   1972/73.   Rs 5.00.   13p.
       Includes statistical data on revenue and expenditure, tonnage inwards and harbour dues, vessels calling
           at ports by nationalities and types, etc.
       Time factor: the 1972/73 report, published in 1975, has data for 1972/73.
       §   En.

ii. Road

877   Annual report of the Ministry of Works: part II - road transport.
       Government Printer, Port Louis.
       1961-   1974/75.   Rs 5.00.   c15p.
       Includes statistics in the text on staff, organisation, expenditure, revenue, etc, of the Road Transport
           Commission; registration and licensing of motor vehicles; examination of motor vehicles; bus
           services, fares, licenses, etc; and taxis.   Also includes statistical appendices on revenue of motor
           vehicle licensing, registration, examination and conductor's license fees; applications for licenses;
           motor vehicles registered; and motor vehicles examined.
       Time factor: the 1974/75 report, published in February 1976, has data for 1974/75.
       §   En.

v. Communications

878   Annual report of the Ministry of Communications...part II: Posts and Telegraphs Department.
       Government Printer, Port Louis.
       1957/58-   1974/75.   Rs 5.00.   19p.
       Includes statistics in the text and also has statistical tables on revenue, expenditure, transactions,
           postal services and telegraphic traffic.
       Time factor: the 1974/75 report, published in June 1976, has data for 1974/75.
       §   En.

879   Annual report of the Ministry of Communications...part V: Telecommunications Department.
       Government Printer, Port Louis.
       1962-   1973/74.   Rs 5.00.   12p.
       Includes statistics of subscribers, calls, overseas calls, coast station radio service, radio and television
           licenses, maintenance, finances, etc.
       Time factor: the 1973/74 report, published late 1974, has data for 1973/74.
       §   En.

Central statistical office

880   Direction de la Statistique et des Etudes Démographiques
              [Department of Statistics and Demographic Studies],
           B P 178, Rabat.
           t   315 30.   tx   31065.

              The Department, which is a part of the Secrétariat d'Etat au Plan et au Développement Regional
           [Secretariat of State for Planning and Regional Development], is responsible for the collection, analysis
           and publication of economic statistics of Morocco.   Unpublished statistical data may be supplied to
           enquirers if available.

Libraries

           The Direction de la Statistique has a library where statistical publications may be consulted.

Bibliographies

           The Direction de la Statistique issues a list of its publications from time to time.

Statistical publications

¶   A - General

881   Annuaire statistique du Maroc   [Statistical yearbook of Morocco]   (Direction de la Statistique).
              Direction de la Statistique, B P 178, Rabat.
              1925-   1975.   not priced.   212p.
              Main sections:
                  Climate   Foreign trade
                  Population   Companies, insurance, youth,
                  Education   labour, sport, cinema
                  Public health   Prices, wages
                  Justice   Money and budget
                  Agriculture, forestry, fisheries   National accounts
                  Energy, mines and industry
                  Transport, communications and
                      migratory movements
              Time factor: the 1975 edition, published in 1977, has data for 1975 or for 1973 or 1974.
              §   En, Ar.

              Note: there are also statistical yearbooks for some provinces, i.e. for Fez.

882   Bulletin mensuel: statistiques   [Monthly bulletin of statistics]   (Direction de la Statistique).
              Direction de la Statistique, B P 178, Rabat.
              1957-   not priced.
              Contains statistical data on climate, energy, mines, industrial production index, carpet manufacture,
                  construction, transport, motor vehicle registration, migration, prices, money, the budget,
                  internal trade, agriculture and fisheries, and foreign trade.
              Time factor: each issue has data for several months or quarters up to the date of the issue, and some
                  tables also contain retrospective annual figures.
              §   Ar, Fr.

¶   A,   continued

883   Statistiques rétrospectives de 1970 à 1975   [Retrospective statistics for 1970 to 1975]   (Direction de la
              Statistique).
              Direction de la Statistique, B P 178, Rabat.
                              not priced.   39p.
              Main sections:
                   Mines   Tourism
                   Phosphates   Wholesale price index
                   Coal   Cost of living index
                   Electricity   Livestock slaughter
                   Petroleum production   Sea fishing
                   Indices of industrial production   Foreign trade
                   Construction permits   Money
                   Transport
              Time factor: published in 1976.
              §   Fr.

884   Le Maroc en chiffres   [Morocco in figures]   (Direction de la Statistique; and Banque Marocain du
              Commerce Extérieur).
              Direction de la Statistique, B P 178, Rabat.
              1961-   1975.   not priced.   85p.
              Contains data on climate, area and population, public health, education, justice, internal trade and
                   prices (retail and wholesale prices, cost of living and wholesale price indices, and registration of
                   motor vehicles), agriculture, forestry, fisheries, industry, mines, energy, tourism, transport,
                   foreign trade, money and budget, and economic accounts.
              Time factor: the 1975 edition, published in 1976, has data for 1975, 1974 and 1973.
              §   Fr.

885   La situation économique du Maroc   [The economic situation in Morocco]   (Direction de la Statistique).
              Direction de la Statistique, B P 178, Rabat.
              1958-   1974.   not priced.   109p.
              Statistical tables are included in the text, covering population, education, agriculture, industry,
                   foreign trade, transport, prices and finance.
              §   Fr & Ar eds.

886   Monthly information review   (Banque Marocaine du Commerce Extérieur).
              Banque Marocaine du Commerce Extérieur, 241 boulevard Mohamed V, Casablanca.
              1970-   not priced.
              Includes social, economic and financial briefs, foreign trade statistics, and other statistics such as those
                   for fertilisers and phosphates.
              §   En & Fr eds.

              Note: replaces both "Bulletin bimestriel d'information" and "Revue bimensuelle".

887   Annual report   (Banque Marocaine du Commerce Extérieur).
              Banque Marocaine du Commerce Extérieur, 241 boulevard Mohamed V, Casablanca.
              1960-   1974.   not priced.   52p.
              Includes statistics on the activities of the Bank, and also foreign trade statistics by commodity groups,
                   sub-divided by continents and countries.
              Time factor: the 1974 report, published in 1975, has data for 1974.
              §   En, Ar.

888   Etudes et statistiques   [Studies and statistics]   (Banque du Maroc).
              Banque du Maroc, 287 avenue Mohamed V, Rabat.
              1958-   quarterly.   not priced.
              Contains data on monetary statistics, structure of interest rates, financial establishments, public finance,
                   price indices (wholesale and cost of living in Casablanca), production (industry, mining, energy,
                   crops, agriculture), exchange rates, foreign trade (by principal products, by groups of commodities,
                   and by principal countries), balance of payments, and national accounts.
              Time factor: each issue has long runs of annual and quarterly figures to six or nine months prior to the
                   date of the issue.
              §   Fr.

¶   A,   continued

889   Rapport   [Report]   (Banque du Maroc).
           Banque du Maroc, 287 avenue Mohamed V, Rabat.
           1958-   1974.   not priced.   169p.
           Includes data on banking, production (mining, agriculture, industry), investment, trade, cost of living
                indices, finance, etc.
           Time factor: the 1974 report, published in 1975, has data for 1974 and some earlier years.
           §   Fr.

890   Rapport annuel   [Annual report]   (Banque Nationale pour le Développement Economique).
           Banque Nationale pour le Développement Economique, Place des Alaouites, Rabat.
           1960-   1975.   not priced.   no pagination.
           The report is in three parts – Fascicule 1 is on the activities of the bank; Fascicule 2 on Moroccan
                economy in 1975; and Fascicule 3 contains résumés in English and French.   Includes statistical
                data on resources, employment, prices, public finance, money, balance of payments, agriculture,
                energy, mines, industry, tourism, and transport.
           Time factor: the 1975 report, published in 1976, has data for 1972 to 1975, on the economy.
           §   Fr; résumés in En.

¶   B – Production

891   Etude de structure sur l'industrie, les mines, l'énergie, le bâtiment, les travaux publics, les transports et
                le commerce en gros, 1969   [Study of the structure of industry, mines, energy, construction,
                public works, transport and wholesale trade, 1969]   (Direction de la Statistique).
           Direction de la Statistique, B P 178, Rabat.
                             ·   not priced.   15 volumes.
           Each of the reports deals with a specific part of the whole subject coverage.
           §   Fr.

i.   Mines and mining

892   Etat des statistiques minières   [Mining statistics]   (Direction des Mines et de la Geologie: Division des
                Mines).
           Direction des Mines et de la Geologie, Rabat.
           1970-   1973.   not priced.   30p.
           Time factor: the 1973 issue, published in 1974, has data for 1973.
           §   Fr.

893   Etat des statistiques de production, des exportations et des ventes locales minérales   [Statistics of
                production, exports and local sales of minerals]   (Direction des Mines et de la Geologie:
                Division des Mines).
           Direction des Mines et de la Geologie, Rabat.
           1967-   monthly.   not priced.
           Time factor: each issue has data for the month of the issue and cumulated figures for the year to date,
                and is published a few months later.
           §   Fr.

           Refer also to 881, 882, 883, 884, 888, 889, 890, 891.

ii.   Agriculture, fisheries, forestry, etc.

894   Résultats par culture de la campagne agricole   [Results of agricultural cultivation]   (Direction de la
                Statistique).
           Direction de la Statistique, B P 178, Rabat.
           1964/64-   1971/72.   not priced.   187p.
           Includes statistics of principal crops and fruit plantations.
           Time factor: the 1971/72 report, published in 1973, has data for the crop year 1971/72.
           §   Fr.

¶   B.ii,   continued

895   Notes rapides sur les résultats de la campagne agricole   [Rapid results of agriculture]   (Direction de la
              Statistique).
              Direction de la Statistique, B P 178, Rabat.
              1969/70-   1972/73.   not priced.   26p.
              Time factor: the 1972/73 issue, published in December 1973, relates to the crop year 1972/73.
              §   Fr.

              Refer also to 881, 882, 883, 884, 885, 888, 889, 890.

     iii.   Industry

896   Etudes et conjoncture: perspective pour...l'industrie marocaine   [Perspectives for...of Moroccan industry]
              (Direction de la Statistique).
              Direction de la Statistique, B P 178, Rabat.
              1964-   irregular.   not priced.
              Includes data on production, prices, wages, etc.
              §   Fr.

897   Rapports sur l'enquête de structure sur l'industrie   [Reports on the survey on the structure of industry]
              (Direction de la Statistique).
              Direction de la Statistique, B P 178, Rabat.
              1967-   1967.   not priced.
              The survey covered establishments with 50 or more employees and 50% of establishments with 10 to 49
                  employees (a sample).   Data includes employment, wages and salaries, gross output, value added,
                  expenditure and sales of fixed assets.
              §   Fr.

              Refer also to 881, 882, 883, 884, 885, 888, 889, 890, 891.

     iv.   Construction

              Refer to 882, 883, 891.

     v.   Energy

898   Activité du secteur pétrolier   [Activities of the petroleum industry]   (Division de l'Energie: Ministère du
              Commerce et d'Industrie).
              Ministère du Commerce et d'Industrie, Rabat.
              1970-   1975.   not priced.   111p.
              Includes a statistical section with data on production, refining, prices, exports, etc.
              Time factor: the 1975 report, published in 1976, has data for 1975 and also for earlier years in some
                  tables.
              §   Fr.

              Refer also to 881, 882, 883, 884, 890, 891.

¶   C - External trade

899   Statistiques du commerce extérieur du Maroc   [Statistics of foreign trade of Morocco]   (Ministère des
              Finances: Office des Changes).
              Ministère des Finances, Office des Changes, Rabat.
              1967-   1975.   DH 50.   855p.
              Main tables show statistics of imports and exports arranged by commodity and sub-divided by countries of
                  origin and destination, and imports and exports by countries of origin and destination sub-divided by
                  commodities.   There are also less detailed tables showing total trade, trade by groups of commodities
                  balance of payments, trade by mode of transport, and trade by customs area.
              Time factor: the 1975 issue, published in 1976, has data for 1975.
              §   Fr.

¶ C, continued

900 Bulletin mensuel d'information [Monthly bulletin of information] (Office de Commercialisation et
d'Exportation).
Office de Commercialisation et d'Exportation, 45 avenue des F.A.R., Casablanca.
1960- not priced.
Includes summary foreign trade statistics arranged by commodity and sub-divided by countries of origin
and destination.
§ Fr.

Refer also to 881, 882, 883, 884, 885, 886, 887, 888, 889, 890.

¶ D - Internal distribution

901 Statistiques touristiques [Tourist statistics] (Ministère de l'Habitat, de l'Urbanisme, du Tourisme et de
l'Environnement).
Ministère de l'Habitat, de l'Urbanisme, du Tourisme et de l'Environnement, Rabat.
1971- 1973. not priced. 45p.
Contains data on entry of tourists, cruise tourists, receipts, hotels, travel agencies, guides, etc.
Time factor: the 1973 issue, published in 1975, has data for 1973 and 1972.
§ Fr.

902 Exercice (Crédit Immobilier et Hôtelier).
Crédit Immobilier et Hôtelier, 159 avenue Hassan II, Casablanca.
1970- 1973. not priced. no pagination.
Includes data on the economy generally, and on the activities of Crédit Immobilier et Hôtelier, and a
statistical annex with data on comparisons of tourist entries, number of tourists by months, number
of tourists by frontier post, number of beds, construction authorisations, number of apartments,
number of purchases (villas, flats, etc) and amounts of money invested, etc.
Time factor: the 1973 issue, published in 1975, has data for 1972 and 1973.
§ Fr.

Refer also to 882, 883, 884, 889, 890, 891.

¶ E - Population

903 Recensement générale de la population et de l'habitat [General census of population and housing]
(Direction de la Statistique).
Direction de la Statistique, B P 178, Rabat.
1921- 1971.
Contents:
Série S - results of the 10% sample census
Vol. I Results of the 10% sample. National level.
II Active population.
III Cultural characteristics of the population.
IV Housing.
V Housing by provinces and regions.
VI Work of analysing the figures.
Série E - exhaustive results
Vol. I Population of Morocco after the 1971 census.
II Rural population.
III Population by sex, age, marital state, place of birth, place of residence, duration of
residence, households.
IV Cultural characteristics of the population.
V Active population.
VI Population by province and region.
VII Work of analysis of the census results.
VIII Methodological report.
Time factor: the report of the 1971 census was published between 1971 and 1974.
§ Fr.

Refer also to 881, 882, 884, 885, 890.

¶   F - Social

i. Standard of living

904   Note rapide sur les indices de prix à Casablanca   [Price indices at Casablanca]   (Direction de la
              Statistique).
              Direction de la Statistique, B P 178, Rabat.
              1970-   monthly.   not priced.
              §   Fr.

905   Note rapide indice du coût de la vie   [Cost of living index]   (Direction de la Statistique).
              Direction de la Statistique, B P 178, Rabat.
              1966-   monthly.   not priced.
              Gives indices by town in Morocco, based on 210 articles.
              §   Fr.

906   Indice de la coût de la vie (210 articles): base 100: Mai 1972 – Avril 1973   [Cost of living index (210
              articles): base year 100: May 1972 to April 1973]   (Direction de la Statistique).
              Direction de la Statistique, B P 178, Rabat.
                            not priced.   36p.
              The construction on which the monthly index is based.
              Time factor: published July 1975.
              §   Fr.

907   La consommation et des dépenses des ménages du Maroc   [Consumption and expenditure in Moroccan
              households]   (Direction de la Statistique).
              Direction de la Statistique, B P 178, Rabat.
                            not priced.   4 vols.
              Volume I gives brief results on a national basis, volume II is on methodology, volume III deals with
                    housing, and volume IV with food and nutrition.
              Time factor: the survey was carried out between April 1970 and April 1971, and the reports were
                    published between 1972 and 1973.
              §   Fr.

              Refer also to 881, 883, 884, 888, 889.

ii. Health and welfare

              Refer to 881, 884.

iii. Education and leisure

              Refer to 881, 884, 885.

iv. Justice

              Refer to 881, 884.

¶   G - Finance

i. Banking

              Refer to 887, 888, 889, 890.

    ¶   G,   continued

    ii. Public finance

908   Comptes de la nation   [National accounts]   (Direction de la Statistique).
          Direction de la Statistique, B P 178, Rabat.
          1960/68-   1964-1974.   not priced.   11p.
          Time factor: the 1964-1974 issue, published in 1975, has data for the fiscal years from 1964 to 1974.
          §   Fr.

909   Statistiques des échanges extérieurs du Maroc   [Statistics of the balance of payments of Morocco]
          (Office des Changes).
          Office des Changes, B P 71, Rabat.
          1968-   monthly.   DH 5 or DH 50 yr; special issues DH 10.
          Contains data on balance of payments and brief foreign trade figures.
          Time factor: each issue has data for the month of the issue and cumulated figures for the year to date,
             and is published about six months later.
          §   Fr.

          Refer also to 881, 882, 884, 885, 888, 890.

    iv. Investment

          Refer to 889.

    v. Insurance

          Refer to 881.

    ¶   H - Transport and communications

910   20 années d'indépendance   [20 years of independence]   (Ministère des Travaux Publics et des
          Communications).
          Ministère des Travaux Publics et des Communications, Rabat.
                      not priced.   3 vols.
          The volumes are devoted to road transport, port equipment, and instruction and improvement.   A few
             figures, graphs, etc, are included in the text.
          Time factor: published in 1976.
          §   Fr.

          Refer also to 881, 882, 883, 884, 885, 890, 891.

    ii. Road

911   Parc automobile du Maroc   [Vehicle registration in Morocco]   (Direction de la Statistique).
          Direction de la Statistique, B P 178, Rabat.
          1963-   1975.   not priced.   28p.
          Contains data on the registration of motor vehicles, motorcycles, motor cars, tractors, etc.   Also data
             on imports of vehicles and on accidents.
          Time factor: the 1975 issue gives the situation at 31st December 1975 and was published in 1976.
          §   Fr.

          Refer also to 882, 884.

¶   H.ii,   continued

912   Les P.T.T. ... activité, réalisations, perspectives   [The PTT...activities, achievements, prospects]
              (Ministère des Postes, des Télégraphes et des Téléphones).
         Ministère des Postes, des Télégraphes et des Téléphones, Rabat.
         1972-   1973.   not priced.   96p.
         Contains data on the financial results of the Ministry, postal services, telecommunications, etc.
         Time factor: the 1973 report, published in 1975, has data for 1972 and 1973.
         §   En & Ar eds.

         Refer also to 881.

Central statistical office

913 Direcção Nacional de Estatística   [National Department of Statistics],
Praça 7 de Março,
C P 493, Maputo.
t 25550.   tx 2478/25550/25950.

The Department compiles and publishes current and base statistics, and carries out surveys and studies.
Unpublished statistical information may be supplied to enquirers when available.   Statistical data, even
when published, will be supplied to enquirers who have difficulty in consulting the publications.

Libraries

Statistical publications of Mozambique may be consulted in the Bibliotéca Nacional [National Library]
at Maputo.   The library of the Direcção Nacional de Estatística also has a collection of statistical
publications.

Bibliographies

The Direcção Nacional de Estatística lists the titles of its publications on the back covers of all its
publications.   New publications are also listed at the end of each issue of "Boletim mensal de estatística".
(915).

Statistical publications

¶ A - General

914 Anuário estatística   [Statistical yearbook]   (Instituto Nacional de Estatística).
Direcção Nacional de Estatística, C P 493, Maputo.
1928- 1973.   Esc 200.   469p.
Main sections:

Area and climate	Mining industries
Demography	Manufacturing industries
Health	Energy
Labour	Construction
Housing	Transport and communications
Social security	Tourism
Cooperatives	Consumption and internal trade
Education, cultural activities,	Foreign trade
recreation, sport	Organisations
Justice	Revenue, wages and prices
National accounts	Money, credit and insurance
Agriculture, forestry, fisheries	Public finance

Time factor: the 1973 edition, published in January 1976, has data for 1973.
§   Pt, Fr.

915 Boletim mensal de estatística   [Monthly bulletin of statistics]   (Direcção Nacional de Estatística).
Direcção Nacional de Estatística, C P 493, Maputo.
1960-   Esc 25 (Esc 30 abroad); Esc 250 (Esc 300 abroad) yr.
Includes data on area and climate, demography, health, employment, housing, social security, education,
    cultural activities, recreation, sport, justice, national accounts, agriculture, forestry, fisheries,
    mining industry, manufacturing industry, energy, construction, transport and communications, tourism,
    consumption and internal trade, foreign trade, organisations, revenue, wages and prices, money,
    credit, insurance, and public finance.
Time factor: each issue appears 10 or 11 months after the month covered, and there are also earlier
    figures in some tables.
§   Pt, Fr.

¶ A, continued

916   Anuário estatístico, vol.II: Territórios ultramarinos   [Statistical yearbook, vol.II: Overseas territories]
            (Instituto Nacional de Estatística).
        Instituto Nacional de Estatística, Avenida António José de Almeida, Lisboa 1, Portugal.
        1967-   1973.   Esc 100.   264p.
        Main sections:

Area and climate	Manufacturing industry
Demography	Energy
Health	Construction
Labour	Transport and communications
Social security	Tourism
Co-operative organisations	Consumption and internal trade
Education, cultural activities,	Foreign trade
recreation, sport	Wages and prices
Justice	Money and credit
Agriculture, forestry, fisheries	Public finance
Mining industry	

        Covers Mozambique and other territories that were Portuguese at the time.
        Time factor: the 1973 edition has data for several years to 1971 or 1972.   Publication of the volume II
            of the yearbook ceased with this edition.
        §   Pt, Fr.

917   Boletim mensal de estatística   [Monthly bulletin of statistics]   (Instituto Nacional de Estatística).
        Instituto Nacional de Estatística, Avenida António José de Almeida, Lisboa 1, Portugal.
        1929-   Esc 30 (Esc 40 abroad) or Esc 300 (Esc 400 abroad) yr.
        Included data on industrial production, construction, transport and communications, tourism, foreign
            trade, and prices for Mozambique until it became independent.
        §   Pt, Fr.

918   Indicadores economico-sociais   [Economic and social indicators]   (Direcção Nacional de Estatística).
        Direcção Nacional de Estatística, C P 493, Maputo.
        1965-   monthly.   not priced.
        Contains data on demography, housing, fishing, mining, manufacturing, energy, transport and
            communications, tourism, consumption and internal trade, foreign trade, company finance, wages
            and prices, money and credit, and public finance.
        Time factor: each issue includes data for 7 months to the date of the issue, and is published about 6
            months later.
        §   Pt.

¶   B - Production

i. Mines and mining

        Refer to 914, 915, 916, 918.

ii. Agriculture, fisheries, forestry

919   Estatísticas agrícolas de Moçambique   [Agricultural statistics of Mozambique]   (Direcção dos Serviços de
            Estatística).
        Direcção Nacional de Estatística, C P 493, Maputo.
        1941-   1963.   Esc 80.   452p.
        Contents include general information such as climate, land, production, consumption, prices, and
            foreign trade in agricultural products; also more detailed data on agricultural enterprises, land
            improvements, cultivation, harvests, consumption, cattle, other animals, wage rates of agricultural
            workers, and the sale of agricultural products, including prices.
        Time factor: the 1963 issue was published in 1968.
        §   Pt.

¶ B.ii, continued

920 Recenseamento agrícola de Moçambique, 1970 [Census of agriculture of Mozambique] (Missão de
Inquérito Agrícola de Moçambique).
Direcção Nacional de Estatística, C P 493, Maputo.
not priced. 83p.
The report of an enquiry into Mozambique agriculture, including utilisation of land, crops – ground,
crops – trees, crops – industrial (oils, etc), livestock, labour, energy, machinery, transport,
fertilisers and insecticides, etc.
Time factor: the report was published in 1973.
§ Pt.

Refer also to 914, 915, 916.

iii. Industry

921 Estatísticas industriais [Industrial statistics] (Direcção dos Serviços de Estatística).
Direcção Nacional de Estatística, C P 493, Maputo.
1947– 1972. Esc 150. 440p.
Contains data on the number of establishments, production, consumption, power used, and personnel in
the extractive industries (minerals and metals), transformation industries, manufacturing industries,
construction industry, electricity, gas and water industries.
Time factor: the 1972 issue, published in 1974, has data for 1972 and some earlier years.
§ Pt.

Refer also to 914, 915, 916, 917, 918.

iv. Construction

Refer to 914, 915, 916, 917.

v. Energy

Refer to 914, 915, 916, 918.

¶ C – External trade

922 Estatísticas do comércio externo [Statistics of external trade] (Direcção dos Serviços de Estatística).
Direcção Nacional de Estatística, C P 493, Maputo.
1957– Vol. 1, 1970.
Vol. 2, 1961. Esc 80 each volume. 2 vols.
Volume 1 contains detailed statistics of imports, exports and transit trade, arranged by commodities
and sub-divided by countries of origin and destination. Volume 2 contains tables of imports,
exports and transit trade arranged by countries of origin and sub-divided by commodities.
Time factor: Vol.1 for 1970 was published in 1973; vol.2 for 1963 was published in 1964 and is no
longer issued.
§ Pt.

923 Estatísticas do comércio externo [Statistics of foreign trade] (Instituto Nacional de Estatística).
Instituto Nacional de Estatística, Avenida António José de Almeida, Lisboa 1, Portugal.
1843– 1967. 2 vols.
Volume II included a section on the foreign trade of Portugal's overseas provinces, including Mozambique.
Arrangement under each overseas province was by commodities.
Time factor: the 1967 issue was the last to include this section.
§ Pt, Fr.

Refer also to 914, 915, 916, 917, 918.

MOZAMBIQUE,   continued

¶   D - Internal distribution and service trades

Refer to 914, 915, 916, 917, 918.

¶   E - Population

924   Recenseamento geral da população   [General census of population]   (Direcção Provincial dos Serviços de
           Estatística).
           Direcção Nacional de Estatística, C P 493, Maputo.
           1928-   4th, 1970.   Esc 200.00 each volume.
           Volumes published are:-
              1. Distrito de Lourenço Marques
              2. Distrito de Manica e Sofala
              3. Distrito de Tete
              4. Distrito de Niassa
              5. Distrito de Gaza
              6. Distrito de Cabo Delgado
              7. Distrito de Inhambane
              8. Distrito de Zambézia
              9. Distrito de Moçambique
              Censo resumo da população da província   [Summary volume]
           Time factor: publication of the reports commenced in 1973.
           §   Pt.

Refer also to 914, 915, 916, 918.

¶   F - Social

i. Standard of living

Refer to 914, 915, 918.

ii. Health and welfare

Refer to 914, 915, 916.

iii. Education and leisure

925   Estatísticas da educação   [Educational statistics]   (Direcção dos Serviços de Estatística).
           Direcção Nacional de Estatística, C P 493, Maputo.
           1963/64-   1973.   Esc 50.00.   166p.
           Covers education generally, infants, primary, secondary, higher, giving data for numbers of children,
              teachers, schools, etc.   Also data on examinations, grants, cultural activities, recreation, and
              sports activities.
           Time factor: published every two years, the 1973 edition was issued in October 1976 and covers the
              academic year 1972/73.
           §   Pt, Fr.

Refer also to 914, 915, 916.

iv. Justice

Refer to 914, 915, 916.

212

¶ G - Finance

Refer to 914, 915, 916, 918.

ii. Public finance

26   Contas da gerência e do exercício   [Accounts of the public sector]   (Direcção dos Serviços de Finanças).
        Direcção dos Serviços de Finanças, Maputo.
        1929/30-   1972.   not priced.   468p.
        Contains detailed accounts of the various government departments and public authorities.
        Time factor: the 1972 issue, published in 1973, has data for 1972.
        §   Pt.

27   Estatísticas das contribuições e impostos   [Statistics of contributions and taxes]   (Direcção dos Serviços
            de Estatística).
        Direcção Nacional de Estatística, C P 493, Maputo.
        1960/1961/1962-   1970/71.   Esc 80.   190p.
        Time factor: the 1970/71 issue, published in 1974, has data for the fiscal year 1970/71.
        §   Pt.

        Refer also to 914, 915, 916, 918.

iii. Company finance

Refer to 918.

v. Insurance

Refer to 914, 915.

¶ H - Transport and communications

28   Estatísticas dos transportes   [Statistics of transport]   (Direcção dos Serviços de Estatística).
        Direcção Nacional de Estatística, C P 493, Maputo.
        1971-   1971.   not priced.   96p.
        Contains data on international transport, ground transport (rail, road, accidents), water transport (sea
            and river), and air transport.
        Time factor: the 1971 issue, published in 1973, has data for 1971.
        §   Pt.

        Refer also to 914, 915, 916, 917, 918.

i. Ships and shipping

29   Cabotagem   [Coastal trade]   (Direcção dos Serviços de Estatística).
        Direcção Nacional de Estatística, C P 493, Maputo.
        1962-   1967.   not priced.   49p.
        Contains data on movement of goods, by commodity group, from port to port.
        Time factor: the 1967 issue, published in 1970, has data for 1967.
        §   Pt.

¶ H.i, continued

930 Boletim mensal [Monthly bulletin] (Direcção dos Serviços dos Portos, Caminhos de Ferro e Transportes de Moçambique).
Direcção dos Serviços dos Portos, Caminhos de Ferro e Transportes de Moçambique, C P 19, Maputo.
1972- not priced.
The monthly bulletin of the Moçambique Harbours, Railways and Transport Administration includes statistics on movements at ports, movements of trucks and traffic handled on railways, and air traffic.
§ En, Fr, Pt.

iii. Road

931 Estatísticas dos veículos automóveis [Statistics of motor vehicles] (Direcção dos Serviços de Estatistica).
Direcção Nacional de Estatística, C P 493, Maputo.
1957- 1970. not priced. 66p.
Contains statistics of registrations by province, numbers of motor vehicles in circulation, road accidents, and miscellaneous data (petrol sales, numbers of petrol pumps, etc).
Time factor: the 1970 issue, published in 1972, has data for 1970.
§ Pt.

The territory is still being administered by the Republic of South Africa, although the International Court of Justice ruled that South Africa's presence is illegal and against the United Nations instructions.

Reference should be made to the publications of South Africa, which sometimes show separate figures for South West Africa.

Central statistical office

932   Direction de la Statistique et des Comptes Nationaux
         [Department of Statistics and National Accounts],
       Ministère du Développement et de la Coopération,
       Niamey.
       t 72 27 79.

       The rôle of the Department is to assemble all statistical data in the fields of demography and economics for the whole of the Republic of Niger, and to analyse them for use in the elaboration of the financial, social and economic policy of the country.   It is also responsible for the publication of regular and ad hoc statistical publications.   Unpublished statistical information may be supplied if requested.

Libraries and information services abroad

       Official publications of Niger are available for reference in the embassies abroad, including:-
         U.S.A.   Embassy of the Republic of Niger, 2204 R Street NW, Washington DC.   t 483 4224.

Statistical publications

¶   A - General

933   Annuaire statistique   [Statistical yearbook].   (Direction de la Statistique).
         Direction de la Statistique, Niamey.
         1962-   1969.   not priced.   191p.
         Main sections:

Climate	Fishing
Demography	Mines
Health	Energy
Education	Industry
Work and employment	Transport
Wages	Public finance
Agriculture	Foreign trade
Livestock	

         Time factor: the 1969 edition, has detailed statistics for 1969 and brief ones for the years 1963 to 1969.
         §   Fr.

934   Bulletin de statistique   [Statistical bulletin]   (Direction de la Statistique).
         Direction de la Statistique, Niamey.
         1959-   quarterly.   Fr 300 or Fr 1,200 yr.
         Contains data on climate, production, transport, foreign trade, prices, finance, money and credit.
         Time factor: each issue includes data for one or more quarters prior to the date of the issue, the corresponding period for the previous year, and annual figures for the last complete year.
         §   Fr.

935   Rapport annuel...   [Annual report]   (Banque de Développement de la République du Niger).
         Banque de Développement de la République du Niger, B P 227, Niamey.
         1968-   1975.   not priced.   72p.
         Contains general information on the economy of Niger and specifically on agriculture, livestock, trade (internal and external), mines and energy, financial resources, and the activities of the Bank.
         Time factor: the 1975 report, published in 1976, has data for 1975 or 1974 and some earlier years.
         §   Fr.

¶   B - Production

i. Mines and mining

936   Rapport annuel   [Annual report]   (Ministère des Mines et de l'Hydraulique).
              Ministère des Mines et de l'Hydraulique, Niamey.
              1967- 1974.   not priced.   56p.
              Contains data on the production of mines, mining research, and hydraulics, and includes some
                   statistics and statistical tables in the text.
              Time factor: the 1974 report, published in 1976, has data for 1974.
              §   Fr.

              Refer also to 933, 934, 935.

ii. Agriculture, fisheries, forestry, etc.

937   Enquête agricole au Niger: rapport...   [Agricultural survey of Niger: report...]   (INSEE).
              INSEE, 18 boulevard Adolphe Pinard, 75675 Paris Cedex 14, France.
              Time factor: the report was published in 1970.
              §   Fr.

              Refer also to 933, 934, 935.

iii. Industry

         An annual industrial and commercial survey has been taken since 1962, covering all establishments and
         collecting data on employment, wages and salaries; value and quantity of materials, electricity and water
         consumed; stocks; fixed assets; goods produced and sold; etc.   The results are not published.

              Refer to 933, 934.

v. Energy

              Refer to 935.

¶   C - External trade

938   Commerce extérieur   [External trade]   (Direction de la Statistique).
              Direction de la Statistique, Niamey.
              1961- 1973.   not priced.   64p.
              Contains summary tables and main tables showing imports and exports arranged by countries and sub-
                   divided by commodities, and imports and exports arranged by commodities.
              Time factor: the 1973 issue, published in 1976, has data for the three, six, nine and twelve months
                   of 1973.
              §   Fr.

              Refer also to 933, 934, 935.

¶   D - Internal distribution and service trades

              Refer to 935.

¶   E - Population

939   Etude démographique du Niger: Résultats définitifs   [Democratic study of Niger: final results]   (Service
             de la Statistique, Niamey <u>and</u> INSEE, Paris).
          Imprimerie Nationale, 2 rue Paul-Hervieu, 75732 Paris Cedex 15, France.
                         Fr 10 each volume.   2 vols.
          Fascicule 1 contains the collective statistics for the whole country, and fascicule 2 the data for
             individual areas.
          Time factor: the survey was carried out in 1960 and the results published in 1962 and 1963.
          §   Fr.

940   Etude démographique et économique en milieu nomade   [Demographic and economic survey of the nomad
             communities]   (Service de la Statistique, Niamey and INSEE, Paris).
          Imprimerie Nationale, 2 rue Paul-Hervieu, 75732 Paris Cedex 15, France.
                         Fr 10 each volume.   3 vols.
          Volume 1 is concerned with generalities and methodology, volume 2 with the data collected on
             demography, and volume 3 on crops.
          Time factor: the reports were published in 1966.
          §   Fr.

          Refer also to 933.

¶   F - Social

i. Standard of living

          Refer to 933, 934.

ii. Health and welfare

          Refer to 933.

iii. Education and leisure

941   Annuaire des statistiques scolaires   [Yearbook of education statistics]   (Ministère de l'Education).
          Ministère de l'Education, Niamey.
          1972/73-   1972/73.   not priced.   92p.
          Contains data on primary, secondary and higher education, including enrolments, schools, teachers,
             classes, finances, etc.
          Time factor: the 1972/73 issue, published in 1974, has data for the academic year 1972/73.
          §   Fr.

          Note: prior to this publication, education statistics were issued as an annex to the annual report of
             the Ministry.

          Refer also to 933.

¶   G - Finance

i. Banking

          Refer to 935.

NIGER, continued

  ¶ G, continued

  ii. Public finance

942   Balance des paiements du Niger   [Balance of payments of Niger]   (Direction de la Statistique).
         Direction de la Statistique, Niamey.
         1968-   1972.   not priced.   17p.
         Time factor: the 1972 issue, published in 1974, has data for 1972.
         § Fr.

         Refer also to 933, 934, 935.

  ¶ H - Transport and communications

943   Rapport   [Report]   (Direction des Transports).
         Direction des Transports, Niamey.
         1965-   1969.   not priced.
         The report deals with road, air, rail, sea, river transport and statistics are included in the text.
         Time factor: the 1969 report, published in 1970, has data for 1969 and earlier years also in some
            tables.
         § Fr.

         Refer also to 933, 934.

Central statistical office

944   Federal Office of Statistics,
Ministry of Economic Development,
Administrative Headquarters,
7 Okotis-Eboh Road,
P M Bag 12528, Lagos.
t 26651.

The Federal Office of Statistics is responsible for national accounts, research and planning; economic statistics; demographic and social statistics; the rural economic survey; the urban consumer survey; statistics coordination; and statistical servicing units.   Unpublished statistical information may be supplied to enquirers if available.

Libraries

The Federal Office of Statistics has a library where statistical publications may be consulted by the public.   The National Library at Lagos also has valuable statistical and other publications on Nigeria. The Library of the Federal Ministry of Trade is also open to businessmen as a reference library.

Libraries and information services abroad

Copies of publications of the Federal Office of Statistics are available for reference in Nigerian embassies abroad, including:-
United Kingdom   High Commissioner for Nigeria, 9 Northumberland Avenue, London WC2.
                    t 01-839 1244.
U.S.A.   Nigerian Embassy, 2201 M Street NW, Washington DC.   t 223-9300.

Bibliographies

945   Nigerian government publications, 1966-1973: a bibliography, by Janet Stanley.
University of Ife Press, Ile-Ife, Nigeria.
Published in 1975.
§   En.

Statistical publications

¶   A - General

946   Annual abstract of statistics   (Federal Office of Statistics).
Federal Office of Statistics, 7 Okotie-Eboh Street, Ikoyi, Lagos.
1960-   1973.   N1.25.   233p.
Main sections:

Area and climate	Prices (including retail price index)
Population and migration	Public finance
Manpower; employment	Finance
Agriculture	National accounts
Mining, manufacturing & electricity	Education
Transport	Health
Communications	Other social statistics (crime & justice)
External trade	2nd national development plan statistics
Balance of payments	

Time factor: the 1973 edition, published in 1975, contains data for several years up to 1973.
§   En.

Note: see also items 948 to 954 for regional data.

¶ A, continued

947 Digest of statistics   (Federal Office of Statistics).
         Federal Office of Statistics, 7 Okotie-Eboh Street, Ikoyi, Lagos.
         1952-   quarterly.   N 0.50 each issue.
         Includes data on area, population, migration, manpower, agricultural products, mining, manufacturing,
             electricity, external trade, balance of payments, transport, prices, public finance, finance,
             savings, national accounts, and national development plan statistics.
         Time factor: each issue, published in the month of issue, contains data for the previous month, and
             usually some annual figures, together with monthly figures for the last two years.
         §   En.

948 Western State of Nigeria statistical abstract   (Statistics Division: Ministry of Economic Planning and
             Construction).
         Ministry of Economic Planning and Construction, Ibadan.
         1959-   1972.   N1.50.   226p.
         Similar subject coverage to 946 above but for the Western State of Nigeria only.
         Time factor: the 1972 edition, published in 1973, has data for several years to 1971.
         §   En.

949 Statistical yearbook   (Ministry of Economic Planning and Rural Development).
         Ministry of Economic Planning and Rural Development, Kaduna.
         1969-   1975.   N0.50.   196p.
         Similar subject coverage to 946 above but for Kaduna State (North Central State of Nigeria) only.
         Time factor: the 1975 edition, published in 1976, has long runs of figures to the latest available
             (1970/71, 1973, or 1974).
         §   En.

950 Kano State statistical yearbook   (Military Governor's Office).
         Military Governor's Office, Kano.
         1970-   1970.   N0.50.   156p.
         Similar subject coverage to 946 above but for Kano State only.
         Time factor: the 1970 edition, published in 1972, has long runs of data to 1970.
         §   En.

951 North Western State statistical hand book   (Economic Planning Division, Military Governor's Office).
         Military Governor's Office, Sokoto.
         1968-   1973.   N0.50.   178p.
         Similar subject coverage to 946 above but for the North Western State of Nigeria only.
         Time factor: the 1973 edition, published in 1975, has data to 1973.
         §   En.

952 Statistical digest   (Ministry of Economic Development and Reconstruction).
         Ministry of Economic Development and Reconstruction, Calabar.
         1968 & 1969-   1968 & 1969.   not priced.   90p.
         Similar subject coverage to 946 above but for the South Eastern State of Nigeria only.
         Time factor: the 1968 and 1969 edition, published in 1972, has data for the years 1968 and 1969.
         §   En.

953 Statistical digest...East-Central State of Nigeria   (Ministry of Economic Development and Reconstruction).
         Ministry of Economic Development and Reconstruction, Enugu.
         1970-   2nd, 1972.   not priced.   100p.
         Similar subject coverage to 946 above but for the East-Central State of Nigeria only.
         Time factor: the 1972 edition, published in 1974, has data for 1971.
         §   En.

954 Kwara State statistical digest   (Ministry of Economic Development).
         Ministry of Economic Development, Ilorin.
         1968-   1974/75.   N1.00.   100p.
         Similar subject coverage to 946 above but for Kwara State only.
         Time factor: the 1974/75 edition, published in 1976, has data for 1974/75.
         §   En.

¶   A,   continued

955   Economic indicators   (Federal Office of Statistics).
            Federal Office of Statistics, 7 Okotie-Eboh Street, Ikoyi, Lagos.
            1965-   monthly.   N0.35 each issue.
            Contains economic indicators on agriculture, industry, distribution, external trade, transport, prices,
                public finance, banking, savings, national accounts, education, and labour.
            Time factor: each issue contains data for the month of issue or the previous month and earlier figures;
                publication is about 3 months after the date of the issue.
            §   En.

956   Economic and statistical review   (Central Planning Office; Federal Ministry of Economic Development and
                Reconstruction).
            Central Planning Office, Federal Ministry of Economic Development and Reconstruction, Lagos.
            1970-   1973.   N0.30:   24p.
            Includes tables in the text on gross domestic product, capital formation, exports, imports, balance of
                payments, money and banking, consumer price indices, public finance, etc.
            Time factor: the 1973 edition, published in 1974, has data for various periods up to 1973.
            §   En.

957   Developments in the Nigerian economy   (Central Bank of Nigeria).
            Central Bank of Nigeria, P.M.B. 12194, Lagos.
                        2 a year.   not priced.
            Includes tables and charts in the text, on domestic production and prices, the financial system, public
                finance, balance of payments, and international economic developments.
            Time factor: each issue has statistics for 12 months, and for the last two years in some tables, to the
                date of the issue, which is published a few months later.
            §   En.

958   Economic and financial review   (Central Bank of Nigeria).
            Central Bank of Nigeria, P.M.B. 12194, Lagos.
            1963-   quarterly.   not priced.
            Includes articles and a statistical section on central banking, commercial banking, currency in
                circulation, external assets, international trade, money and capital markets, money supply,
                national savings, agricultural production, electrical production, mineral production, consumer
                prices, public debt, and public finance.
            Time factor: each issue contains long runs of annual and monthly figures up to the date of the issue,
                and is published a month or two later.
            §   En.

959   Annual report and statement of accounts   (Central Bank of Nigeria).
            Central Bank of Nigeria, P.M.B. 12194, Lagos.
            1963-   1973.   not priced.
            Reviews the current development plan being implemented, and economic policies.   Gives information
                on domestic production and prices, financial system, public finance and balance of payments.
                Also the statement of accounts of the bank.
            Time factor: the 1973 report, published in 1974, has data for 1973 and some earlier years.
            §   En.

960   Monthly report   (Central Bank of Nigeria).
            Central Bank of Nigeria, P.M.B. 12194, Lagos.
            1972-   not priced.
            Includes statistical data on production, prices, money and banking, customs and excise revenue,
                external trade and reserves, unemployment and labour relations.
            Time factor: each issue contains data for the month 8 weeks earlier than the date of the issue, and also
                includes data for several earlier months in most tables.
            §   En.

NIGERIA, continued

¶ B - Production

i. Mines and mining

961 Mining and mineral resources in Nigeria (Mines Department).
Mines Division, Broad Street, Lagos.
N0.50. 15p.
Contains data on metalliferous minerals, non-metallic minerals, precious stones, precious metals, radio-active minerals, and mineral fuels.
Time factor: data is for 1956/57 and publication was in 1957.
§ En.

962 Annual report of the Mines Division.
Federal Ministry of Mines and Power, Broad Street, Lagos.
1948- 1968/69. N0.50. 48p.
Includes statistics in the text on prospecting, production, exports, etc.
Time factor: the 1968/69 report has data for the year 1968/69.
§ En.

Refer also to 946, 947, 958.

ii. Agriculture, fisheries, forestry, etc.

963 Agricultural development in Nigeria, 1973-1985 (Federal Ministry of Agriculture and Natural Resources, Joint Planning Committee).
Federal Ministry of Agriculture and Natural Resources, Lagos.
not priced. 590p.
Includes statistical tables in the text.
Time factor: published in 1974.
§ En.

Note: an earlier edition, covering 1965-1980, was published in 1966 by FAO.

964 Rural economic survey of Nigeria (Federal Office of Statistics).
Federal Office of Statistics, 7 Okotie-Eboh Street, Ikoyi, Lagos.
1963/64 & 1964/65. N0.50 each vol. 7 vols.
Contents:
Farm survey, 1963/64)
Farm survey, 1964/65) Include data on areas cultivated by farmers.
Livestock enquiry, 1963/64
Livestock enquiry, 1964/65
Household enquiry, 1963/64
Household enquiry, 1964/65
Rural consumption enquiry: food items, 1963/64
§ En.

965 Annual report of the Federal Department of Fisheries.
Federal Department of Fisheries, Lagos.
1970- 1973. N0.50. 111p.
Includes a section of statistics, on imports, fleets, catch, landings, etc.
Time factor: the 1973 report, published in 1974, has data for 1973.
§ En.

966 Annual report on the Forest Administration of North-Central State.
Forest Administration, Kaduna.
1967/68- 1967/68. not priced. 13p.
Includes statistics in the text on the forest estate, management and surveys, forest protection, silviculture, production and trade, rural planning and development, and finance.
Time factor: the 1967/68 report, published in 1972, has data for 1967/68.
§ En.

¶   B.ii,   continued

967   Annual report on the Forestry Administration of the Western State of Nigeria.
         Ministry of Agriculture and Natural Resources, Ibadan.
         1967/68-   1967/68.   N0.35.   39p.
         Includes statistics on forest area, production, exports, of various types of timber, etc.
         Time factor: the 1967/68 report, published in 1970, has data for 1967/68.
         §   En.

         Refer also to 946, 947, 955, 958.

      iii. Industry

968   Census of industrial production and distributive trades   (Federal Office of Statistics).
         Federal Office of Statistics, 7 Okotie-Eboh Street, Ikoyi, Lagos.
         1958/59-   1970.   N2.00.   270p.
         Contains data for establishments with 10 or more employees on gross output, employment, labour costs,
             non-labour costs, value added, capital expenditure, ownership of establishments, size of
             establishments, paid up capital, etc.
         Time factor: the report of the 1970 census was published in 1976.
         §   En.

969   Industrial survey   (Federal Office of Statistics).
         Federal Office of Statistics, 7 Okotie-Eboh Street, Ikoyi, Lagos.
         1962-   1964 & 1965.   N0.50.   156p.
         Contains data on gross output, employment, labour costs, non-labour costs, value added, capital
             expenditure, ownership of establishments, size of establishments, paid up capital, etc.   The data
             is for Nigeria as a whole and for the Lagos Federal Territory, Western Region, Mid-Western
             Region, Eastern Region and Northern Region.
         Time factor: the 1964 and 1965 edition, published in 1968, has data for 1964 and 1965.
         §   En.

         Refer also to 946, 947, 955, 960.

      iv. Construction

         A survey of building and construction was taken for 1973 on a 10% sample of large-scale registered
         building contractors and a 10% sample of small-scale registered building contractors.   No publication
         has been seen by the compiler on the results of the survey.

      v. Energy

970   Annual report and accounts   (National Electric Power Authority).
         National Electric Power Authority, 24/25 Marina, Lagos.
         1951/52-   1975/76.   not priced.   35p.
         Contains data on system operations, distribution and sales, rural electrification, manpower, finances,
             etc.
         Time factor: the 1975/76 report, published late 1976, has data for the year 1975/76.
         §   En.

971   Monthly petroleum information   (Ministry of Petroleum and Energy).
         Ministry of Petroleum and Energy, P.M.B. 12701, Lagos.
         1965-   not priced.
         Contains data on drilling, production, utilisation, exports, refining, consumption, imports, prices, etc.
         Time factor: each issue has data for the month of the issue and is published some months later.
         §   En.

         Refer also to 946, 947, 958.

NIGERIA,   continued

¶   C - External trade

972   Review of external trade   (Federal Office of Statistics).
             Federal Office of Statistics, 7 Okotie-Eboh Street, Ikoyi, Lagos.
             1963-   1975.   K 50.   41p.
             A statistical study, which does not contain very detailed information.
             Time factor: the 1975 edition, published mid-1976, covers the period from 1971 to 1975.
             §   En.

973   Nigeria trade summary   (Federal Office of Statistics).
             Federal Office of Statistics, 7 Okotie-Eboh Street, Ikoyi, Lagos.
             1965-   monthly.   K 50 each issue.
             Main tables show imports and exports arranged by commodity, sub-divided by countries of origin and
                 destination.   Other tables show shipping at ports, sea-borne cargo loaded at each port, transit
                 trade and direction of trade.
             Time factor: each issue includes data for the month of the issue and cumulated figures for the year to
                 date.   Issues are published about six months after the end of the period covered.
             §   En.

             Refer also to 946, 947, 955, 956, 958, 960.

¶   D - Internal distribution and service trades

             An annual survey of distributive trades has been taken since 1969 on establishments employing 10 or
             more persons.   No publications devoted solely to the reports of the surveys have been published, but
             the results may be found in 946, 947 and 955.

             Refer also to 946, 955.

¶   E - Population

974   The population census of...Nigeria   (Federal Office of Statistics).
             Federal Office of Statistics, 7 Okotie-Eboh Street, Ikoyi, Lagos.
             1866-   1963.   N 2.10 each volume.   10 vols.
             Includes data on age, sex, ethnic origin, religion and occupations.   Two volumes each are devoted to
                 the population of Lagos Territory, the Northern Region, the Western Region, the Eastern Region,
                 and the Mid-Western Region.
             §   En.

975   Annual report of the Federal Ministry of Labour, Labour Division.
             Federal Ministry of Labour, 5 Oil-mill Street, Lagos.
             1963/64-   1968/69.   N 0.08.   61p.
             Includes a statistical appendix on unemployed, vacancies, placings, trade test returns, stoppages of
                 work, accidents, compensation, etc.
             Time factor: the 1968/69 report, published in 1974, has data for the year 1968/69.
             §   En.

976   Quarterly review   (Federal Ministry of Labour).
             Federal Ministry of Labour, 5 Oil-mill Street, Lagos.
             1964-   N 0.08 each issue.
             Includes data on manpower and employment, inspections, training, Nigerian labour abroad, trade
                 unions, and social security.
             §   En.

             Refer also to 946, 947, 955, 960.

¶   F - Social

i. Standard of living

977   Urban consumer surveys in Nigeria   (Federal Office of Nigeria).
      Federal Office of Statistics, 7 Okotie-Eboh Street, Ikoyi, Lagos.
      1957-   N 1.50 each issue, except for Lagos volume which is N 2.00.
      A periodical report on enquiries into the income and expenditure patterns of lower and middle income
          households.   Reports are published for each town or group of towns where surveys have been
          conducted.   Reports have been issued for Lagos (1959/60), Enugu (1966), Ibadan (1967),
          Kaduna (1966), Onitsha (1967), Oshogba/Ife/Ilesha (1967), and Akure/Ondo/Owo (1967).
      §   En.

978   Retail market prices of foodstuffs in the East Central State, Nigeria   (Ministry of Finance and Economic
          Development).
      Ministry of Finance and Economic Development, Enugu.
      1972-   monthly.   not priced.
      Time factor: each issue has data for the month of the issue and several earlier months, and is published
          a month or two later.
      §   En.

      Refer also to 946, 956, 958.

ii. Health and welfare

979   Annual digest of medical and health statistics   (Statistics Division; Ministry of Economic Planning and
          Development, Ibadan).
      Ministry of Economic Planning and Development, Ibadan.
      1968-   1969.   N 0.35.   108p.
      Contains data for the Western State of Nigeria on numbers and proprietorship of medical institutions,
          medical and health staff, beds, births, diseases and deaths, expenditure on medical and health
          services.   There is also a list of medical institutions.
      Time factor: the 1969 issue, published in 1970, has data for 1969 and also some earlier figures in some
          tables.
      §   En.

      Refer also to 946.

iii. Education and leisure

980   Statistics of education in Nigeria   (Federal Ministry of Education).
      Federal Ministry of Education, Lagos.
      1957-   1971.   N 0.75.   94p.
      Contains data on schools, classes, teachers, pupils enrolled in primary and secondary schools;
          enrolments, staff, etc. in universities; teacher training colleges; examinations, degrees, etc.
          Data is sub-divided by State.
      Time factor: the 1971 issue, published in 1974, has data for 1971.
      §   En.

      Note: prior to 1961 title was "Digest of education statistics".

981   Statistics of education in Lagos State   (Ministry of Education and Community Development, Lagos State).
      Ministry of Education and Community Development, 216 Broad Street, Lagos.
      1964-   1968.   not priced.   130p.
      Contains similar data to 980 above, but relating only to Lagos State.
      Time factor: the 1968 issue, published in 1971, has data for 1968.
      §   En.

¶   F.iii,   continued

982   Annual digest of education statistics   (Statistics Division, Ministry of Economic Development, Ibadan).
                Ministry of Economic Development, Ibadan.
                1961-   1972.   N 1.00.   145p.
                Contains similar data to 980 above, but relating only to the Western State of Nigeria.
                Time factor: the 1972 issue, published in 1973, has data for 1972.
                §   En.

983   Education statistics for Kano State   (Ministry of Education).
                Ministry of Education, Kano.
                1969-   1973/74.   not priced.   49p.
                Contains similar data to 980 above, but relating to Kano State only.
                Time factor: the 1973/74 issue, published late 1974, has data for the academic year 1973/74.
                §   En.

                Refer also to 946, 955.

iv. Justice

984   Annual report of the Federal Prison Department.
                Federal Prison Department, Lagos.
                1960/61-   1965-66.   N 0.45.   39p.
                Contains statistics of staff, prison population, committals, sentences, recidivism, female prisoners, and
                    lunatics.
                Time factor: the 1965-66 report, published in 1973, has data for 1965/66 and one or two earlier years.
                §   En.

                Refer also to 946.

¶   G - Finance

            Refer to 946, 947, 955, 956, 957, 958, 959, 960.

i. Banking

            Refer to 955, 956, 957, 958, 959, 960.

ii. Public finance

985   Digest of income tax statistics   (Ministry of Economic Planning and Reconstruction).
                Ministry of Economic Planning and Reconstruction, Ibadan.
                                N 0.15.   69p.
                Includes data on the numbers of taxpayers and PAYE payers by income group, area, occupation group,
                    etc, and tax reliefs.
                Time factor: published in 1971, the digest contains data for the years 1964/65 to 1968/69.
                §   En.

                Note: a "Summary of current income tax statistics, 1973" has also been published.

                Refer also to 946, 947, 955, 956, 957, 958, 959, 960.

NIGERIA, continued

    ¶ G, continued

  v. Insurance

986   Insurance statistics: a report on insurance companies' operations in Nigeria   (Federal Office of Statistics).
             Federal Office of Statistics, 7 Okotie-Eboh Street, Ikoyi, Lagos.
             1963/64-   1968.   N 0.30.   22p.
             Time factor: the 1968 issue, published in 1970, has data for 1967 and 1968.
             §   En.

    ¶ H - Transport and communications

987   Annual report of the Government Coastal Agency.
             Government Coastal Agency, Marina, Lagos.
             1955/56-   1971/72.   N 0.15.   42p.
             Contains data on imports through sea and air ports, freight, and sea and air passages.
             Time factor: the 1971/72 report, published in 1973, has 12 months figures from April 1971 to March
                1972 and totals.
             §   En.

             Refer also to 946, 947, 955.

  i. Ships and shipping

988   Annual report   (Nigerian Ports Authority).
             Nigerian Ports Authority, 26/28 Marina, Lagos.
             1955/56-   1970/71.   not priced.   98p.
             Includes a section of general statistics, on traffic, imports and exports, ships handled, etc.
             Time factor: the 1970/71 report, published in 1972, has data for 1970/71.
             §   En.

  ii. Road

989   Motor vehicle statistics   (Federal Office of Statistics).
             Federal Office of Statistics, 7 Okotie-Eboh Street, Ikoyi, Lagos.
             1953/58-   1967.   not priced.   27p.
             A report on the analysis of motor vehicle licenses reissued.
             Time factor: the 1967 issue, published in 1970, has data for 1967.
             §   En.

  iii. Rail

990   Report and accounts   (Nigerian Railway Corporation).
             Nigerian Railway Corporation, Ebute Metta.
              1955/56-   1973/74.   not priced.   164p.
             As well as financial statistics of the Corporation, the report includes general statistics on railway
                finances; combined passenger, freight train and engine statistics; passenger statistics; freight
                statistics; particulars of sidings laid and removed; sleepers used for renewals; stone ballast;
                washouts and floodings; lists and conditions of rolling stock; aggregate capacity of rolling stock;
                analysis of accidents; statement of passengers, livestock and goods traffic; and repairs to rolling
                stock.
             Time factor: the 1973/74 report, published late 1975, has data for the fiscal year 1973/74.
             §   En.

Central statistical office

991   Service Départemental de Statistique de la Réunion   [Departmental Statistical Service for Réunion],
        B P 52, 97487 St Denis CEDEX.
        t 21.36.81.

The Service is a departmental statistical office of the Institut National de la Statistique et des Etudes Economiques (INSEE) of France.   It collects, analyses and publishes statistical information on Réunion.

Libraries

The Service Départemental de Statistique has a library, which includes economic and statistical publications, and is open to the public for reference.

Libraries and information services abroad

The Service Départemental de Statistique de la Réunion issues a catalogue of its publications from time to time, the latest being dated 1977.   INSEE in Paris also issue a sales list of their publications from time to time and this includes some publications concerning Réunion.

Bibliographies

The Service Départemental de Statistique de la Réunion issues a catalogue of its publications from time to time, the latest being issued in 1977.

Statistical publications

¶   A - General

992   Memento statistique   [Statistical handbook]   (Service Départemental de Statistique de la Réunion).
        Service Départemental de Statistique de la Réunion, B P 52, St Denis.
        1974- 1974.   FrF 10.00.   157p.
        Main sections:

General (area, climate, administration)	Trade (internal)
Population	External trade
Education	Communications (roads, road transport,
Health	vehicle registrations, port traffic,
Justice	airport traffic, posts and
Employment	telecommunications)
Wages and salaries	Tourism
Income and expenditure	Prices (and price indices)
Production (agriculture, livestock,	Money and credit (including balance
fisheries, oils, tobacco, sugar	of payments)
and derivatives)	Public finance
Housing	Economic accounts

        Time factor: the 1974 edition, published in 1976, has data for 1974 or the latest available, and
            earlier years in some tables.
        §   Fr.

        Note: supersedes "Annuaire statistique de la Réunion" published by INSEE, Paris, from 1952/55 to
            1969/72 issues.

¶ A, continued

993 Bulletin de statistiques [Statistical bulletin] (Service Départemental de Statistique de la Réunion).
Service Départemental de Statistique de la Réunion, B P 52, St Denis.
1964- quarterly. FrF 6.00 each issue.
Includes data on climate, demography, production, transport, cost of living, incomes, employment, social security, money and credit, public finance, and foreign trade. There are also supplements issued from time to time dealing with one particular subject.
Time factor: each issue is published two or three months after the date of the issue.
§ Fr.

994 Annuaire statistique de la France [Statistical yearbook of France] (INSEE).
Imprimerie Nationale, 2 rue Paul-Hervieu, 75732 Paris Cedex 15, France.
1885- 1976. FrF 150. c800p.
Main sections:
Geography and climate   Transport, communications, internal trade
Population   Prices, incomes, consumption
Economic resources (including   Finance
agriculture, forestry, fisheries   Overall economic figures
and industry)   International data
Includes data for Réunion.
Time factor: the 1976 edition, published early 1976, contains data for 1974 and for several earlier years.
§ Fr.

995 Tableaux relatifs aux D.O.M. [Tables relative to the overseas departments] (INSEE).
INSEE, 18 boulevard Adolphe Pinard, 75675 Paris Cedex 14, France.
1961- 1974. FrF 10.00. 63p.
Contains extracts relative to Réunion and other overseas departments of France from "Annuaire statistique de la France" (994).
§ Fr.

996 Bulletin de conjoncture (Secrétariat Général pour les Affaires Economiques. Mission Régionale. Service Administratif de la Région).
Secrétariat Général pour les Affaires Economiques, Saint-Denis.
1969- quarterly. not priced.
Includes a statistical annex with data on agricultural, fisheries and industrial production; machinery; employment, income and prices; and finance.
§ Fr.

997 Statistiques et indicateurs économiques: mise à jour... [Economic and statistical indicators...] (Secretariat Général pour les Affaires Economiques. Mission Régionale. Service Administratif de la Région).
Secrétariat Général pour les Affaires Economiques, Saint-Denis.
1971- 1975. not priced. 154p.
Contains data on population, the active population, agriculture, sea fishing, industry and services, balance of payments with France, foreign trade, communications, construction and housing, education, tourism, income, consumption, health, prices, money and credit, public finance, and economic accounts.
Time factor: the 1975 issue, published in 1976, has data for 1975 or the fiscal year 1975/76 and earlier years.
§ Fr.

¶ B - Production

ii. Agriculture, fisheries, forestry, etc.

998 Inventaire forestier du Département de la Réunion en 1958 [Forest inventory of Réunion in 1958] (INSEE).
INSEE, 18 boulevard Adolphe Pinard, 75675 Paris Cedex 14, France.
not priced. 24p.
§ Fr.

¶   B.ii,   continued

'99   Enquête sur le cheptel dans le Département de la Réunion (fin 1961)   [Survey of livestock in Réunion
              (end of 1961)]   (INSEE).
          INSEE, 18 boulevard Adolphe Pinard, 75675 Paris Cedex 14, France.
                              not priced.   31p.
          §   Fr.

          Refer also to 992, 993, 994, 995, 996, 997.

    iii. Industry

          Refer to 992, 993, 994, 995, 996, 997.

    iv. Construction

          Refer to 997.

¶   C - External trade

000   Statistiques du commerce extérieur de la Réunion   [Statistics of foreign trade of Réunion]   (Service
              Départemental de Statistique de la Réunion).
          Service Départemental de Statistique de la Réunion, B P 52, St Denis.
          1946/68-   1960-72.   CFA Fr 300.   49p.
          Published as a supplement to "Bulletin de statistique" (993).
          Time factor: the 1960-72 issue was published in 1972.
          §   Fr.

001   Statistiques du commerce extérieur: départements d'outre-mer: importations, exportations en NGP   [Statistics
              of foreign trade: overseas departments: imports, exports by BTN]   (Direction Générale des Douanes).
          Centre de Renseignements Statistiques, 182 rue Saint-Honoré, 75001 Paris, France.
          1949-   1971.   not priced.   949p.
          Contains detailed statistics of imports and exports arranged by commodity and sub-divided by countries of
              origin and destination, for each of the overseas departments of France, including Réunion.
          Time factor: the 1971 issue, published in 1973, contains data for 1971.
          §   Fr.

          Refer also to 992, 993, 997.

¶   D - Internal distribution and service trades

002   Une enquête sur les établissements commerciaux à la Réunion et à la Martinique (recensement de la
              distribution) 1967-1968   [Survey of commercial establishments in Reunion and Martinique (census
              of distribution) 1967-1968]   (INSEE, Paris).
          Service Départemental de Statistique de la Réunion, B P 52, St Denis, Reunion.
                              FrF 5.00.   43p.
          Contains data for both Reunion and for Martinique, on numbers employed, numbers of enterprises, wages,
              investments, trade, stocks, etc.
          Time factor: published in 1971.
          §   Fr.

          Refer also to 992, 994, 995, 997.

¶   E - Population

1003   Résultats statistiques du recensement général de la population des Départements d'Outre-mer...Réunion
           [Results of the general census of population of overseas departments...Réunion]   (INSEE).
       INSEE, 18 boulevard Adolphe Pinard, 75675 Paris Cedex 14, France.
       1840-   1967.   not priced.
       Part 1 contains statistical tables.
       §   Fr.

1004   Recensement démographique de la Réunion du 16 octobre 1967: principaux résultats (provisoires)
           [Demographic census of Réunion on 16th October 1967: principal results (provisional)]   (INSEE).
       INSEE, 18 boulevard Adolphe Pinard, 75675 Paris Cedex 14, France.
                       not priced.   37p.
       Time factor: published in 1969.
       §   Fr.

       Note: a census of population was taken by Service Départemental de Statistique de la Réunion in 1974.

1005   Tendances démographiques dans les Départements insulaires d'Outre-mer - Martinique, Guadeloupe et la
           Réunion   [Demographic tendencies in the overseas departments - Martinique, Guadeloupe and
           Réunion]   (INSEE).
       INSEE, 18 boulevard Adolphe Pinard, 75675 Paris Cedex 14, France.
                   FrF 18.00.   261p.
       Following the 1967 census, an analysis of the characteristics of the population was made with the aid of
           the appropriate demographic indicators.
       Time factor: figures are for 1967 and graphs go to 1970.
       §   Fr.

1006   Recensement des agents de l'Etat et des collectivités locales des Départements d'Outre-mer   [Census of
           central government and local government servants in overseas departments]   (INSEE).
       INSEE, 18 boulevard Adolphe Pinard, 75675 Paris Cedex 14, France.
       1950-   7th, 1969.   not priced.   43p.
       Includes data for Réunion.
       §   Fr.

1007   Le logement dans le Département de la Réunion en 1961   [Housing in Réunion in 1961]   (INSEE).
       INSEE, 18 boulevard Adolphe Pinard, 75675 Paris Cedex 14, France.
                       not priced.   73p.
       Housing and construction by type, area, etc.
       §   Fr.

1008   Statistique du mouvement naturel de la population dans les départements d'outre-mer: Martinique -
           Guadeloupe - Guyane - Réunion   [Demographic statistics of the population of French overseas
           departments...]   (INSEE, Paris).
       Imprimerie Nationale, 2 rue Paul-Hervieu, 75732 Paris Cedex 15, France.
       1951/56-   1965 à 1970.   FrF 45.00.   187p.
       Contains statistics of marriages, births and deaths for each of the four overseas departments of France.
       Time factor: the 1965/1970 issue, published in 1973, has data for each of the years 1965 to 1970.
       §   Fr.

1009   Les causes de décès dans les Départements d'Outre Mer   [Causes of death in the overseas departments]
           (INSEE).
       INSEE, 18 boulevard Adolphe Pinard, 75675 Paris Cedex 14, France.
       1951-   1971.   FrF 8.00.   86p.
       Includes data for Réunion.
       Time factor: the 1971 issue, with data for 1971, was the last to be published.
       §   Fr.

¶   E,   continued

010   Enquête sur l'emploi à la Réunion   [Survey of employment in Réunion]   (INSEE).
            INSEE, 18 boulevard Adolphe Pinard, 75675 Paris Cedex 14, France.
            1967-   2nd, 1971.   FrF 10.00.   37p.
            §   Fr.

            Refer also to 992, 993, 994, 995, 997.

¶   F - Social

i. Standard of living

        Refer to 992, 993, 994, 995, 996, 997.

ii. Health and welfare

        Refer to 992, 993, 997.

iii. Education and leisure

011   Statistiques de l'enseignement dans les départements d'outre-mer: année scolaire...   [Statistics of
            education in the overseas departments: school year...]   (INSEE).
            INSEE, 18 boulevard Adolphe Pinard, 75675 Paris Cedex 14, France.
            1968/69-   1972/73.   FrF 8.00.   36p.
            Contains data on numbers of schools and classes, both public and private; enrolments, standards, and
                examinations, etc, for overseas departments of France, including Réunion.
            Time factor: the 1972/73 issue, published in 1976, has data for the school year 1972/73.
            §   Fr.

            Refer also to 992, 997.

iv. Justice

        Refer to 992.

¶   G - Finance

        Refer to 992, 993, 994, 995, 996, 997.

ii. Public finance

1012   Comptes économiques de la Réunion   [Economic accounts of Réunion]   (INSEE).
            Service Départemental de Statistique de la Réunion, B P 52, St Denis or INSEE, 18 boulevard Adolphe
                Pinard, 75675 Paris Cedex 14, France.
            1965/67-   1972/73.   FrF 5.00.   19p.
            Time factor: the 1972/73 issue, published in 1975, has data for several years to 1972/73.
            §   Fr.

            Refer also to 992, 993, 997.

¶   H – Transport and communications

Refer to 992, 993, 994, 995, 997.

ii. Road

1013   Parc des véhicules automobiles des départements d'outre-mer au ler janvier...   [Motor vehicle
registrations in the overseas departments of France at 1st January...]   (INSEE).
Imprimerie Nationale, 2 rue Paul-Hervieu, 75732 Paris Cedex 15, France.
1959-   1972.   FrF 6.00.   52p.
Contains data on the distribution of private cars, commercial vehicles, autocars and buses; vans,
lorries, tractors, etc, by make and power; motor vehicles by profession of owner; motor vehicles in
circulation by year of production.   Data are for overseas departments of France, including Réunion
Time factor: the 1972 issue, published in 1973, has data for 1972.
§   Fr.

Central statistical office

14   Central Statistical Office,
      P O Box 8063,
      Causeway,
      Salisbury.
      t 26681.

   The Central Statistical Office is responsible for the production of all statistics relating to Rhodesia. It promotes such large-scale exercises as the censuses of population, agricultural production, distribution, industrial production, the estimates of national accounts, employment and external trade, and such social surveys as are requested from time to time. In addition it collates information produced by other government departments and public bodies. The main function of the Office is to provide reliable and up-to-date statistics to government, scientists, industry and commerce, international bodies and the public in general. Unpublished statistical information may be supplied to enquirers upon request.

Libraries

   The Central Statistical Office, Earl Grey Building, 4th Street, Salisbury, has a library where statistical publications may be consulted by the public. Other libraries in Salisbury where statistical publications may be consulted are the Parliamentary Library, Corner Third Street and Baker Avenue, P O Box 8055, Causeway, Salisbury; the Queen Victoria Memorial Public Library, Civic Centre, Rotten Row, P O Box 1087, Salisbury, and the University of Rhodesia Library, Mount Pleasant Drive, P O Box M 167, Mount Pleasant, Salisbury. In Bulawayo, the National Free Library of Rhodesia (Dugald Niven Library), 12th Avenue, P O Box 1773, Bulawayo, also provides this facility.

   Hours of opening are: Central Statistical Office - 8.00 to 13.00 and 14.00 to 17.00, Monday to Friday; Parliamentary Library - 8.00 to 13.00 and 14.00 to 16.45, Monday to Friday (and until 19.00, and also 8.00 to 12.00 on Saturdays when the house is sitting); Queen Victoria Memorial Public Library and the National Free Library - 9.30 to 18.00, Monday to Friday, and 9.30 to 13.00 on Saturdays; University of Rhodesia Library - 8.00 to 22.00, Monday to Friday, and 8.00 to 12.00 on Saturdays. During vacations the hours are 8.00 to 12.45 and 14.00 to 17.00, Monday to Friday, and 8.00 to 12.00 on Saturdays. The Library is closed from Christmas Day to 2nd January.

   English and Shona are spoken by the staff of the Central Statistical Office Library; English, Greek, French, Afrikaans and local African dialects at the University of Rhodesia Library; and English at the other libraries.

   The Central Statistical Office Library and the University of Rhodesia Library receive statistical publications from other countries and from international organisations, and the Parliamentary Library receives publications from international organisations aswwell as those of Rhodesia. The other libraries receive statistical publications of Rhodesia.

Bibliographies

   A list of the currently available statistical publications of the Central Statistical Office is published in the "Monthly digest of Statistics" (1016).

Statistical publications·

¶   A - General

15   Economic survey of Rhodesia   (Ministry of Finance).
        Ministry of Finance, Salisbury.
        1965-   1975.   Rh$ 0.50.   23p.
        Presented to Parliament annually by the Minister of Finance, this survey includes statistical tables of
            balance of payments; national income; gross domestic product; index of industrial production;
            construction output; banking; government finance; population; migration; employment and earnings
            of Africans, Europeans, Asians and coloured persons; index of consumer prices; and public sector
            investment (published separately). The tables are prepared by the Central Statistical Office.
        Time factor: published in April 1976, the 1975 survey includes 10-year runs of figures to 1975.
        §   En.

¶   A,   continued

1016   Monthly digest of statistics   (Central Statistical Office).
         Central Statistical Office, P O Box 8063, Causeway, Salisbury.
         1964-   Rh $ 0.60; Rh$ 7.20 yr inclusive for monthly digest and quarterly supplements.
         The monthly digest contains data on migration, visitors, road accidents and occupational injuries,
              consumer price indices, agriculture, mining, manufacturing index, electrical energy, construction,
              retail trade index, Rhodesia railways, commercial banks, other banks and building societies, money
              property sales and mortgage bonds.   The quarterly supplement contains data on population,
              education, labour, national accounts, agriculture, manufacturing, electrical energy, construction,
              air transport, external trade and balance of payments, public debt and government finance,
              banking, interest rates, company registrations and increases in capital, insolvencies and liquida-
              tions, and stock exchange indices.
         Time factor: most tables in both issues have data for 13 years and monthly figures for the last 2 years,
              up to 1 or 2 months prior to the date of issue of the digest; and quarterly figures for the past 2
              years and up to the previous quarter prior to the date of issue of the supplement.
         §   En.

1017   Rhodesia in brief: some basic facts about Rhodesia   (Ministry of Information).
         Ministry of Information, Immigration and Tourism, P O Box 8232, Causeway, Salisbury; and Rhodesia
              Information Office, 2852 McGill Terrace NW, Washington DC, USA.
                  1973/74.   not priced.   78p.
         Textual information, including a few statistics, on the land and its people, history and governments,
              economic and general development, industries and production, services and communications,
              transport, tourism, broadcasting and television, immigration, and banking.
         Time factor: the 1973/74 edition was published in January 1977.
         §   En.

1018   Economic survey of Rhodesia   (Ministry of Finance).
         Ministry of Finance, P B 705, Causeway, Salisbury.
         1967-   1975.   not priced.   23p.
         Includes statistical tables on balance of payments, national income, industrial origin of gross domestic
              product, index of industrial production, construction output, banking, public finance, estimated
              population, migration, employment and earnings of Africans, Europeans, Asians and Coloured
              persons, and index of consumer prices.
         Time factor: the 1975 issue, published in April 1976, has data from 1966 to 1975, the 1975 figures often
              being preliminary ones.
         §   En.

¶   B - Production

1019   Census of production: mining, manufacturing, construction, electricity and water supply   (Central
              Statistical Office).
         Central Statistical Office, P O Box 8063, Causeway, Salisbury.
         1960-   1973/74.   Rh$ 0.85.   116p.
         Statistical tables include summaries of operations and industry from 1938 to 29th June 1974; derivation
              of gross output; analysis of purchases and changes in stocks; payments for services rendered by
              other firms; numbers employed and earnings; stock and work in progress; net capital expenditure
              on fixed assets, plant and equipment; book values of fixed assets of the manufacturing sector;
              summary of operations by size of enterprise according to number of employees and according to
              gross output in the mining and manufacturing sectors; summary of manufacturing operations by area;
              sales of Rhodesian-made products; analysis of construction work done by sector and type of work;
              analysis of cost of materials and fuels used.
         Time factor: the 1973/74 edition, published in 1976, contains data for the years 1964 to 1973,
              including provisional summary data for 1974/75.
         §   En.

    i. Mines and mining

         Refer to 1016, 1019.

¶ B, continued

ii. Agriculture, fisheries, forestry, etc.

20   Report of the census of livestock in European areas; Part 1 - National and provincial totals   (Central
            Statistical Office).
        Central Statistical Office, P O Box 8063, Causeway, Salisbury.
        1967-   1975.   Rh$ 0.25.   32p.
        Includes statistics of national and provincial totals of livestock for the 1971-1975 (poultry 1970-1975),
            number of cattle and livestock other than cattle on European farms, and a summary of European-
            owned livestock for the years 1914-1975.
        Time factor: the census was taken in June 1975 and the report published in 1976.
        §   En.

21   Agricultural production in African Purchase Lands; Part 1 - National and provincial totals   (Central
            Statistical Office, jointly with the Department of Conservation and Extension).
        Central Statistical Office, P O Box 8063, Causeway, Salisbury.
        1971-   1975.   Rh$ 0.30.   37p.
        Statistical tables include summaries of area and production of crops for 1972, 1973 and 1974 and
            livestock for those years, in addition to details of agricultural production and of cattle and other
            livestock (including goats and poultry) for 1975.
        Time factor: the census was taken in November 1975 and the report published in 1976.
        §   En.

22   Agricultural production in Tribal Trust Land and irrigation schemes, national and provisional totals
            (Central Statistical Office, jointly with the Ministry of Internal Affairs).
        Central Statistical Office, P O Box 8063, Causeway, Salisbury.
        1970-   1974.   Rh$ 0.25.   23p.
        Includes a summary of crop production and livestock for the years 1971-1974, in addition to detailed
            tables of production for 1974.
        Time factor: the census was taken in November 1974 and the report published in 1975.
        §   En.

23   Agricultural production in European areas...   (Central Statistical Office).
        Central Statistical Office, P O Box 8063, Causeway, Salisbury.
        1967-   1976.   Rh$ 0.30.   38p.
        The 1976 issue contains the results of the 1976 census of livestock.
        Time factor: published in 1977.
        §   En.

24   Census of deciduous fruit   (Central Statistical Office).
        Central Statistical Office, P O Box 8063, Causeway, Salisbury.
        1974-   1976.   Rh$ 0.10.   9p.
        Time factor: the report of the 1976 census was published in September 1976.
        §   En.

25   Agricultural economics and markets report   (Ministry of Agriculture, Economics and Markets Branch).
        Ministry of Agriculture, P B 7701, Causeway, Salisbury.
        1971-   twice a year.   not priced.
        §   En.

        Refer also to 1017.

iii. Industry

        Refer to 1015, 1016, 1017, 1018, 1019.

¶   B,   continued

iv. Construction

1026   Monthly construction bulletin   (Central Statistical Office).
         Central Statistical Office, P O Box 8063, Causeway, Salisbury.
         1972-   Rh$ 0.30 each issue.
         Contains data on building activity and demands by town.
         §   En.

         Refer also to 1015, 1016, 1018, 1019.

v. Energy

         Refer to 1016, 1019.

¶   C - External trade

1027   Annual statement of external trade   (Central Statistical Office).
         Central Statistical Office, P O Box 8063, Causeway, Salisbury.
         1964-   1965.   out of print.   176p.
         Main tables show imports and exports arranged by commodity and sub-divided by countries of origin and
             destination; and principal articles imported from and exported to certain countries, sub-divided by
             commodities.
         §   En.

         Note: due to the imposition of sanctions, no subsequent issue has been made.

1028   External trade statistics   (Central Statistical Office).
         Central Statistical Office, P O Box 8063, Causeway, Salisbury.
         1963-   quarterly.   10s6d each issue.
         Contains detailed statistics of imports and exports arranged by commodity and sub-divided by countries
             of origin and destination; re-exports arranged by commodities; and summary tables.
         Time factor: only two issues were published – January-March 1964 and January-June 1964.
         §   En.

         Note: prior to 1964 the quarterly foreign trade statistics of Southern Rhodesia, Northern Rhodesia and
             Nyasaland were combined.

         Refer also to 1016.

¶   D - Internal distribution and service trades

1029   Census of distribution: wholesale and retail trade, hotels and restaurants   (Central Statistical Office).
         Central Statistical Office, P O Box 8063, Causeway, Salisbury.
         1962-   2nd, 1969/70.   Rh$ 0.40.   44p.
         Data for the wholesale trade include turnover, commodities sold, repair revenue, commodities sold on
             commission, personnel and earnings, credit and debt; all by type of business.   For retail trade
             data include tables of type of business, number of units and turnover, labour force, commodities
             sold and repair revenue, personnel and earnings, creditors and debtors; all by types of business.
             There is also a summary by area.   For the service trades the information is the number of units and
             turnover by type of business and by size of labour force, and personnel and earnings by type of
             business.
         Time factor: the census covers the financial years of establishments which ended anywhere between 30th
             June 1969 and 29th June 1970, and was published in May 1972 (with comparative data for 1962).
         §   En.

RHODESIA, continued

¶ D, continued

1030   Annual report   (Rhodesia National Tourist Board).
        Rhodesia National Tourist Board, Salisbury.
        1963/64-   1972.   not priced.   23p.
        Includes statistical data on hotel occupancy, an analysis of tourist traffic, and arrivals by month.
        Time factor: the 1972 report, published in 1973, has data for 1972 and one or two earlier years.
        §   En.

        Note: previously it had been the annual report of the Southern Rhodesia Tourist Board.

        Refer also to 1016, 1017.

¶   E - Population

1031   Census of Africans, Europeans, Asians and Coloured population   (Central Statistical Office).
        Central Statistical Office, P O Box 8063, Causewdy, Salisbury.
        1901-   1969.   Rh$ 7.50.   210p.
        The final report of the 1969 census of population includes data on the growth of the population, its
            geographical distribution, fertility and mortality of the African population, marital status,
            birthplaces, nationality and citizenship, length of residence, religion, transport to work,
            economically active and inactive population, housing, and residents being educated outside
            Rhodesia.
        Time factor: the report was published in 1976.   Interim reports were published during the intervening
            years.
        §   En.

1032   Monthly migration and tourist statistics   (Central Statistical Office).
        Central Statistical Office, P O Box 8063, Causeway, Salisbury.
        1969-   Rh$ 0.10 each issue.
        Contains data on migration of Europeans, Asians and Coloured, by destination, age, industry, and
            occupations; visitors and returning residents; and immigration of African men by country of birth.
        Time factor: each issue has long runs of annual and monthly figures to the date of the issue and is
            published two or three months later.
        §   En.

        Refer also to 1015, 1016, 1017, 1018.

¶   F - Social

i. Standard of living

1033   Reports of the European and urban African budget surveys   (Central Statistical Office).
        Central Statistical Office, P O Box 8063, Causeway, Salisbury.
        1957/58-   ·   , Rh$ 0.25 each.
        The surveys are taken at intervals and are published separately.   Recent surveys are:-
            European budget survey in Rhodesia, 1968
            European budget survey in Salisbury, 1969-71
            Urban African budget survey in Bulawayo, 1968
            Urban African budget survey in Salisbury, 1969
            Urban African budget survey in the Midlands (Gwelo, Que Que and Gatooma), 1970
            Urban African budget survey in Umtali, 1971
        The reports include information on household size and composition, standards of education, occupations,
            income distribution, average monthly income and savings and expenditure, details of expenditure
            on food, consumer durables, etc.
        §   En.

¶   F.i,   continued

1034   Consumer price index for Europeans   (Central Statistical Office).
          Central Statistical Office, P O Box 8063, Causeway, Salisbury.
                    monthly.   not priced.
          Time factor: each issue has data for several years and months to the date of the issue.
          §   En.

1035   Consumer price index for Africans   (Central Statistical Office).
          Central Statistical Office, P O Box 8063, Causeway, Salisbury.
                    monthly.   not priced.
          Time factor: each issue has data for several years and months to the date of the issue.
          §   En.

          Refer also to 1015, 1016, 1018.

   iii.   Education and leisure

1036   Report on education   (Ministry of Education).
          Ministry of Education, P O Box 8022, Causeway, Salisbury.
          1964-   1975.   Rh$ 1.05.   60p.
          Contains information on education for Europeans, Asians and Coloureds.   There are chapters on primary
             and secondary education; teaching service; examinations and higher education; further education;
             inspectorate and regional offices; audio-visual services; finance, legislation, and administration;
             building; personnel; and a final chapter giving statistics of expenditure, examination results,
             leavers, enrolments, number of schools, teaching staff, and age grade classification.
          Time factor: the 1975 report, published in 1976, has data for 1975.
          §   En.

1037   Annual report of the Secretary for African Education
          Ministry of Education, P O Box 8022, Causeway, Salisbury.
          1971-   1975.   Rh$ 0.50.   53p.
          Includes statistics of education for Africans in Rhodesia.
          Time factor: the 1975 report, published in 1976, has data for several years to 1975.
          §   En.

          Refer also to 1016, 1017.

   iv.   Justice

1038   Report of the Secretary for Justice
          Secretary for Justice, Private Bag 7704, Causeway, Salisbury.
          1957-   1972.   Rh$ 1.05.   36p.
          Includes statistical data on courts, prisons, companies and patents, etc.
          Time factor: the 1972 report, published in 1973, has data for 1972 and also some earlier years.
          §   En.

¶   G - Finance

          Refer to 1015, 1016, 1018.

i. Banking

          Refer to 1015, 1016, 1017, 1018.

¶ G, continued

ii. Public finance

1039   National accounts and balance of payments   (Central Statistical Office).
       Central Statistical Office, P O Box 8063, Causeway, Salisbury.
       1954-   1974.   Rh$ 1.00.   c40p.
       Time factor: the 1974 issue, published in 1975, has data for 1974 and one or two earlier years in some
          tables.
       §   En.

1040   Income tax statistics, analysis of assessments and loss statements issued during the fiscal year...   (Central
       Statistical Office).
       Central Statistical Office, P O Box 8063, Causeway, Salisbury.
       1953/54-   1975/76.   Rh$ 0.50.   31p.
       Deals with taxation of both individuals and companies.
       Time factor: the 1975/76 issue, published in December 1976, has data for 1974, 1975 and 1976.
       §   En.

1041   Report of the Commissioner of Taxes
       Commissioner of Taxes, P O Box 8126, Causeway, Salisbury.
       1964/65-   1972/73.   Rh$ 0.50.   17p.
       Includes statistics of the number of taxpayers, taxable incomes, etc.
       Time factor: the 1972/73 report, published in 1974, has data for the fiscal year 1972/73.
       §   En.

       Refer also to 1015, 1016, 1018.

iii. Company finance

       Refer to 1016.

v. Insurance

1042   Report of the Registrar of Insurance
       Registrar of Insurance, Ministry of Finance, P B 7705, Causeway, Salisbury.
       1967-   1972.   Rh$ 1.50.   49p.
       Includes some insurance statistics, which have been compiled by the Central Statistical Office from
          returns lodged with the Registrar, on the number of companies operating, their business, etc;
          revenue and disbursements of life insurance; and revenue and disbursements of non-life insurance.
       Time factor: the 1972 report, published in 1974, has data for 1972.
       §   En.

1043   Insurance statistics   (Registrar of Insurance).
       Registrar of Insurance, Ministry of Finance, P B 7705, Causeway, Salisbury.
       1964-   1969.   not priced.
       Time factor: the 1969 issue, published in 1971, has data for 1969.
       §   En.

¶ H - Transport and communications

       Refer to 1017.

RHODESIA,   continued

¶   H,   continued

ii. Road

1044   Report of the Secretary for Roads and Road Traffic
              Ministry of Roads and Road Traffic, P O Box 8109, Causeway, Salisbury.
              1920-   1973.   not priced.   65p.
              Includes some tables in the text, mainly of an administrative nature.
              Time factor: the 1973 report, published in 1974, has data for 1973.
              §   En.

        iii. Rail

              Refer to 1016.

        iv. Air

              Refer to 1016.

Central statistical office

045   Direction Générale de la Statistique, [General Statistical Office],
B P 46, Kigali.
t 5402.

The Direction Générale de la Statistique is a service of the Ministère du Plan [Planning Ministry], and is responsible for the collection, co-ordination, analysis and publication of economic, social, financial, technical, demographic and administrative statistics. It is also responsible for the national economic accounts. Statistical information which is available but not published may be obtained from the organisations listed below.

Other important organisations collecting statistical information

046   Ministère de l'Agriculture et de l'Elevage [Ministry of Agriculture & Crops]
B P 621, Kigali.

047   Ministère des Finances et de l'Economie [Ministry of Finance and the Economy]
B P 720, Kigali.

048   Banque Nationale du Rwanda [National Bank of Rwanda]
B P 351, Kigali.

049   Office Rwandais du Tourisme et des Parcs Natioanaux [Rwanda Office of Tourism and National Parks]
B P 905, Kigali.

Libraries

The Direction Générale de la Statistique has a library which is open to the public from 7.00 to 12.00 and from 14.00 to 17.30 from Monday to Friday, except for holidays. The library has a large number of economic and social publications of Rwanda and of foreign countries. The staff speak French and Kinyarwanda.

Statistical publications

¶   A - General

050   Bulletin de statistique   [Statistical bulletin]   (Direction Générale de la Statistique).
Direction Générale de la Statistique, B P 46, Kigali.
1964-   quarterly, with an annual supplement.   In Rwanda   R Fr 400 or R Fr 1,800 yr.
                                Africa   US$ 6 or US$ 24 yr.
                                  Europe   US$ 7 or US$ 28 yr.
                                  Elsewhere   US$ 8 or US$ 32 yr.
Contains data on prices (retail, wholesale, & construction materials), climate, demography, migration, mining production, water and energy, building authorisations, foreign trade (by countries, and by commodities) public finance, money and credit, and transport. The annual supplement also covers population, education, public health, social security, agriculture, and crops.
Time factor: each quarterly issue has data for that quarter and earlier figures and is published some months later; the annual issue contains data for the two previous years.
§   Fr.

¶   A,   continued

1051   Situation économique de la République Rwandaise   [Economic situation of the Republic of Rwanda]
                (Direction Générale de la Statistique).
            Direction Générale de la Statistique, B P 46, Kigali.
            New series, no.1, 1973-   1973.   In Rwanda R Fr 400, Africa US$ 6,   66p.
                                            Europe US$ 7, elsewhere US$ 8.
            Contains data on production, foreign trade, transport, retail prices, public finance, money and credit,
                foreign aid, public health, and education.
            Time factor: the 1973 issue, published in October 1974, has data for 1973 and some earlier years.
                Prior to 1973, the old series was issued quarterly.
            §   Fr.

¶   B - Production

1052   Rapport annuel   [Annual report]   (Ministère du Commerce, des Mines, et de l'Industrie).
                Ministère du Commerce, des Mines, et de l'Industrie, Kigali.
                1967-   1971.   not priced.   96p.
                Contains the annual reports of the departments of internal trade, foreign trade, mines and geology.
                    Some statistics and statistical tables are included in the text.
                §   Fr.

    i. Mines and mining

            Refer to 1050, 1052.

    ii. Agriculture, fisheries, forestry, etc.

1053   Rapport annuel   [Annual report]   (Ministère de l'Agriculture et de l'Elevage).
                Ministère de l'Agriculture et de l'Elevage, Kigali.
                1972-   1973.   not priced.   111p.
                Contains data on agronomy, agriculture generally, agriculture, water and forests, small-holdings,
                    climate, animal health, and animal production.   Statistical tables are included in the text.
                Time factor: the 1973 report, issued in 1974, has long runs of statistical data to 1973.
                §   Fr.

            Refer also to 1050, 1051.

    iii. Industry

            Refer to 1051.

    iv. Construction

            Refer to 1050.

    v. Energy

            Refer to 1050.

¶   C - External trade

            Refer to 1050, 1051, 1052.

¶   D - Internal distribution and service trades

      Refer to 1051, 1052.

¶   E - Population

054   Enquête démographique, 1970   [Demographic survey, 1970]   (Direction Générale de la Statistique and
          Secrétariat d'Etat aux Affaires Etrangères, Paris).
       Direction Générale de la Statistique, B P 46, Kigali.
                not priced.   2 vols.
       Time factor: the report of the survey was published in 1973.
       § Fr.

       Note: censuses of the non-indigenous population only were taken in 1952 and 1958.   The results of the
          1958 census were published in "Bulletin mensuel des statistiques générales du Congo Belge et du
          Ruanda-Urundi", série spéciale, no.1, 1959.

       Refer also to 1050.

¶   F - Social

i. Standard of living

      Refer to 1050, 1051.

ii. Health and welfare

      Refer to 1050, 1051.

iii. Education and leisure

055   Statistiques de l'enseignement   [Statistics of education]   (Service de la Statistique; Ministère de
          l'Education Nationale).
       Ministère de l'Education Nationale, Kigali.
       1972/73-   1972/73.   not priced.   120p.
       Contains data on primary, secondary, higher and university education, including enrolments, schools,
          teachers, classes, finances, etc.
       Time factor: the 1972/73 issue, published late 1973, has data for the academic year 1972/73.
       § Fr.

       Refer also to 1050, 1051.

¶   G - Finance

      Refer to 1050, 1051.

¶   H - Transport and communications

      Refer to 1050, 1051.

There is no central statistical office for St Helena, but some economic and social statistics are collected by its government.

Statistical publications

¶   A - General

1056   St Helena: report for the years...
          H M Stationery Office, P O Box 569, London SE1.
          1947-   1970 to 1973.   £1.70.   122p.
          The report is divided into five sections and appendices:-
              Part I General review.
                   II Population; occupations, wages and labour organisations; public finance and taxation;
                       currency and banking; commerce; production; social services; legislation; justice,
                       police and prisons; public utilities and public works; communications; press and
                       information services.
                  III Geography and climate; history; administration; weights and measures.
                   IV Ascension Island.
                    V Tristan da Cunha.
              Appendices   Colony budgets; taxation; expenditure; development projects; import statistics; vital
                       statistics; incidence of income tax on individuals; cases reported to and dealt with
                       by police; offences reported to and persons dealt with by courts; retail price index;
                       statistics of schools; medical statistics; rainfall figures and meteorological
                       observations.
          Some statistical tables are included in the text and the appendices are all statistical.
          Time factor: the 1970 and 1973 report, covering those years, was published in 1976.
          §   En.

¶   B - Production

          Refer to 1056.

¶   C - External trade

1057   Imports and exports   (Collector of Customs).
          Colonial Treasurer's Office, The Castle, Island of St Helena, South Atlantic Ocean.
          annual.   1976/77.   not priced.   10p.
          Contains a detailed table showing imports arranged by commodities sub-divided by countries of origin,
              and also summary tables of imports by country or origin, imports by commodity, and main duty
              producing items.   (There were no exports in 1976/77).
          Time factor: the 1976/77 issue was published mid-1977 and contains figures for that fiscal year.
          §   En.

          Refer also to 1056.

¶   D - Internal distribution and service trades

          Refer to 1056.

¶   E - Population

1058   Census of the population of St Helena Island and Ascension Island   (Census Supervisor).
            Government Printing Office, St Helena.
            1861-   1966.   not priced.   no pagination.
            Contains statistics of population by sex, marital status, age, literacy, sickness and informit,
                nationality, birthplace, religion, occupation, etc.
            §   En.

            Refer also to 1056.

¶   F - Social

            Refer to 1056.

¶   G - Finance

            Refer to 1056.

There is no central statistical office on St Thomas & Prince islands, which became independent of Portugal in July 1975.

Statistical publications

¶ A - General

1059   Boletim informativo trimestral da Repartição Provincial dos Serviços de Economia de S.Tomé e Principe
            [Quarterly information bulletin of the Provincial Department of Economics].
            1964-   not priced.
            Includes information, commentary and statistical data on population, demography, health and
                assistance, production and consumption, foreign trade, internal trade, communications, credit
                and money, and public finance.
            Time factor: issues for 1970 are the latest located.
            §   Pt.

1060   Anuário estatístico, vol.II: Territórios ultramarinos   [Statistical yearbook, vol.II: Overseas territories]
            (Instituto Nacional de Estatística).
            Instituto Nacional de Estatística, Avenida António José de Almeida, Lisboa 1, Portugal.
            1967-   1973.   Esc 100.   264p.
            Main sections:

Area and climate	Manufacturing industry
Demography	Energy
Health	Construction
Labour	Transport and communications
Social security	Tourism
Co-operative organisations	Consumption and internal trade
Education, cultural activities,	Foreign trade
recreation, sport	Wages and prices
Justice	Money and credit
Agriculture, forestry, fisheries	Public finance
Mining industry	

            Covers São Tomé e Principe and other territories that were Portuguese at the time.
            Time factor: the 1973 edition has data for several years to 1971 or 1972.   Publication of volume II of
                the yearbook ceased with this edition.
            §   Pt, Fr.

1061   Boletim mensal de estatística   [Monthly bulletin of statistics]   (Instituto Nacional de Estatística).
            Instituto Nacional de Estatística, Avenido António José de Almeida, Lisboa 1, Portugal.
            1929-   Esc 30 (Esc 40 abroad) or Esc 300 (Esc 400 abroad) yr.
            Included data on industrial production, construction, transport and communications, tourism, foreign
                trade, and prices for São Tomé e Principe until they became independent in July 1975.
            §   Pt, Fr.

¶ B - Production

ii. Agriculture, fisheries, forestry, etc.

1062   Recenseamento agrícola de São Tomé e Principe   [Agricultural census of St Thomas & Prince]   (Missão
            de Inquérito de Cabo Verde, Guiné, S Tomé e Principe).
                1961-1964.   not priced.   2 vols.
            Detailed results of the census of agriculture.
            Time factor: published in 1968.
            §   Pt.

Refer also to 1059, 1060.

¶   B,   continued

iii. Industry

> Refer to 1059, 1060, 1061.

¶   C - External trade

063   Comércio externo e navegação maritime   [Foreign trade and shipping]   (Repartição Provincial dos
              Serviços de Economia).
              1967.   not priced.
              §   Pt.

064   Estatísticas do comércio externo   [Statistics of foreign trade]   (Instituto Nacional de Estatística).
              Instituto Nacional de Estatistica, Avenida António José de Almeida, Lisboa 1, Portugal.
              1843-   1967.   2 vols.
              Volume II included a section on the foreign trade of Portugal's overseas provinces, including St Thomas
                   & Prince.   Arrangement under each overseas province was by commodities.
              Time factor: the 1967 issue was the last to include this section.
              §   Pt, Fr.

> Refer also to 1059, 1060, 1061.

¶   D - Internal distribution and service trades

> Refer to 1059, 1060, 1061.

¶   E - Population

065   Censo da população...   [Census of population]   (Repartição Provincial dos Serviços de Economia).
              1921-   1960.
              A one-page report was published in St Thomas & Prince in 1963; the report is also included in volume
                   6 of the Portuguese census of population.
              §   Pt.

> Note: the first data to be published on the 1970 census of population was in the Oct/Dec 1970 issue of
>   "Boletim informativo".

> Refer also to 1059, 1060.

¶   F - Social

i. Standard of living

> Refer to 1060.

ii. Health and welfare

> Refer to 1059, 1060.

ST THOMAS & PRINCE, continued

¶ F, continued

iii. Education and leisure

Refer to 1060.

¶ G - Finance

Refer to 1059, 1060.

¶ H - Transport and communications

Refer to 1059, 1060, 1061.

Central statistical office

1066   Direction de la Statistique [Department of Statistics],
        Boulevard de l'Est, Point E,
        B P 116, Dakar.
        t 242.31.

   The Department is responsible for the collection, analysis and publication of current economic and
social statistics for the whole country and for its regions, the conduct of censuses and surveys, and for
national accounts, as well as theoretical studies.   It is a department of the Ministry of Finance and Economic
Affairs.

Libraries

   The Direction de la Statistique has a library where statistical publications may be consulted.

Statistical publications

¶   A - General

1067   Situation économique du Sénégal   [Economic situation in Senegal]   (Direction de la Statistique).
        Direction de la Statistique, B P 116, Dakar.
        1962- 1975.   CFA Fr 2,000 (CFA Fr 2,500 abroad).   260p.
        Main sections:

Population	Industrial production
Education	Construction
Health	Transport and communications
Employment	Foreign trade
Justice	Prices
Fishing	Money
Agriculture	Banking and credit
Crops	State budget
Energy	Economic accounts

        Time factor: the 1975 edition, published late 1976, contains data for several years to 1975.
        §   Fr.

068   Bulletin statistique et économique mensuel   [Monthly economic and statistical bulletin]   (Direction de la
            Statistique).
        Direction de la Statistique, B P 116, Dakar.
        1959-   CFA Fr 150; double issues CFA Fr 300; CFA Fr 1,500 yr.
        Contains statistical data on climate, demography, agriculture and livestock, building, industry
            (production indices), electric energy, transport, foreign trade by commodities, foreign trade by
            countries, prices (wholesale, retail, price indices), and finance.
        Time factor: each issue contains data for the month of issue, and many tables have cumulated figures
            with previous cumulations for comparison.   Published about three months after the end of the
            period covered.
        §   Fr.

069   Le Sénégal en chiffres: annuaire statistique du Sénégal   [Senegal in figures: statistical yearbook of
            Senegal]   (Sylvie Berniard & Hedwige Levenant).
        Société Africaine d'Edition, B P 1877, Dakar.
        1976- 1976.   not priced.   352p.
        Main sections:

Geography	Business (transport, posts & telecommunications,
Population	internal trade, foreign trade, tourism, press &
Resources (economic accounts,agriculture,	information, prices & revenues, money and
crops, fisheries, mines, water, energy,	credit, public finance)
industry, construction, public works)	Investment
	Manufacturing costs

        Time factor: the 1976 edition, published in 1976, has data for 1974 and a number of earlier years.
        §   Fr.

¶   A,   continued

1070   Comptes économiques   [Economic accounts]   (Direction de la Statistique).
        Direction de la Statistique, B P 116, Dakar.
        1959-   1971 & 1972.   CFA Fr 1,500.   133p.
        Includes some tables in the text and deals with production and services, administration, finance and
            banking, households, and foreign trade.
        Time factor: the 1971 & 1972 edition, published late 1975, has data for 1971 and 1972.
        §   Fr.

1071   L'économie sénégalaise   [The Senegal economy]   (Ediafric - La Documentation Africaine).
        Ediafric, 57 avenue d'léna, 75783 Paris CEDEX 16, France.
        1970-   3rd, 1975.   FrF 324.   various pagings.
        Issued as a special number of the journal "Bulletin de l'Afrique Noire", the main sections are:
            General information   Foreign trade
            Agriculture, crops, fisheries   Finance and credit
            Industry, energy, mines   4th 4-year plan (1973-1977)
            Transport and communications
        Time factor: the 1975 edition, published early 1976, has data for several years to 1974.
        §   Fr.

¶   B - Production

i. Mines and mining

1072   Rapport annuel: tome 1; partie administrative et statistique   [Annual report: vol.1; administrative and
            statistical part]   (Ministère du Développement Industriel et de l'Environnement. Direction des
            Mines et de la Géologie).
        Direction des Mines et de la Géologie, rue de l'Université, Dakar.
        1967-   1973.   not priced.   70p.
        Includes statistical sections on mines, mining personnel, production, investments, explosives, etc.
        Time factor: the 1973 report, published in 1975, has data for 1973 and some 1972 figures.
        §   Fr.

        Refer also to 1069, 1071.

ii. Agriculture, fisheries, forestry, etc.

        Refer to 1067, 1068, 1069, 1071.

iii. Industry

1073   Les industries du Sénégal   [Industries of Senegal]   (Ministère de la Coopération, Paris).
        Ministère de la Coopération, Paris.
            not priced.   69p.
        The results of an inventory of Senegal's industries, the report contains a general survey, reviews by
            sector, and statistical data of factories and workshops, sales by type of product, local consumption,
            and foreign trade.
        Time factor: the survey was taken in 1963 on activities in 1962 and the results were published in 1965.
        §   Fr.

        Refer also to 1067, 1068, 1069, 1070, 1071.

iv. Construction

        Refer to 1067, 1068, 1069.

SENEGAL, continued

¶ B, continued

v. Energy

Refer to 1067, 1068, 1069, 1071.

¶ C - External trade

1074   Exportations: commerce spécial   [Exports: foreign trade]   (Direction de la Statistique).
        Direction de la Statistique, B P 116, Dakar.
        1962-   twice a year.   not priced.
        Main tables show detailed exports arranged by commodity and sub-divided by countries of destination,
            and by countries of destination sub-divided by commodities.
        Time factor: the issues show the first six months trade and the annual trade, and are published several
            months after the end of the period covered.
        §   Fr.

        Note: originally published monthly, then quarterly, and half-yearly from 1970.

1075   Importations: commerce spécial   [Imports: foreign trade]   (Direction de la Statistique).
        Direction de la Statistique, B P 116, Dakar.
        1962-   twice a year.   not priced.
        Main tables show detailed imports arranged by commodity and sub-divided by countries of origin, and
            by countries of origin sub-divided by commodities.
        Time factor: the issues show the first six months trade and the annual trade, and are published several
            months after the end of the period covered.
        §   Fr.

        Note: originally published monthly, then quarterly, and half-yearly from 1970.

1076   Associés: commerce extérieur: République du Sénégal: annuaire 1959-1966. [Associates: foreign trade:
            Senegal: yearbook 1959-1966]   (European Communities).
        Office des Publications Officielles des Communautés Européennes, C P 1003, Luxembourg; or from
            sales agents.
                        £0.90 or FrB 100.   182p.
        One of a series of retrospective publications on the foreign trade of African states associated with the
            European Communities.   Main tables show imports and exports arranged by commodity and sub-
            divided by countries of origin and destination.   Values are in US$.
        Time factor: published early 1969.
        §   De, En, Fr, It, Nl.

        Refer also to 1067, 1068, 1069, 1070, 1071.

¶ D - Internal distribution and service trades

        Refer to 1068, 1069, 1070.

¶   E - Population

1077   Enquête démographique nationale   [National demographic enquiry]   (Direction de la Statistique).
            Direction de la Statistique, B P 116, Dakar.
            1955-   3rd, 1970-1971.
            Content:
                Provisional results of first round   (CFA Fr 1,500)
                Methodology and annexed documents   (CFA Fr 1,500)
                Results for villages   (CFA Fr 2,500)
                Final results:
                Vol. I by age   (CFA Fr 1,500)
                    II by matrimonial situation   (CFA Fr 1,500)
            §   Fr.

            Refer also to 1067, 1068, 1069.

¶   F - Social

i. Standard of living

        Refer to 1067, 1068.

ii. Health and welfare

        Refer to 1067.

iii. Education and leisure

1078   Annuaire statistique   [Statistical yearbook]   (Ministère de l'Enseignement Technique et de la Formation
            Professionnelle).
            Ministère de l'Enseignement Technique et de la Formation Professionnelle, Building Administratif, Dakar.
            1966/67-   1970/71.   not priced.   61p.
            Contains data on technical and professional education, including schools and colleges, pupils, teachers,
                classes, etc.
            Time factor: the 1970/71 issue, published in 1974, has data for the academic year 1969/70 and some
                earlier years.
            §   Fr.

            Refer also to 1067.

iv. Justice

        Refer to 1067.

¶   G - Finance

        Refer to 1067, 1068, 1069, 1070, 1071.

¶   H - Transport and communications

        Refer to 1067, 1068, 1069, 1071.

SEYCHELLES - SEYCHELLEN

Central statistical office

079   Central Statistical Office,
       P O Box 206,
       Victoria, Mahé.
       t 22041.

       The Central Statistical Office forms part of the Economic and Statistics Division of the Office of the President, and is responsible for the collection, analysis and publication of all official statistics.

Libraries

       The only public library in the Seychelles is the Carnegie Library, which does not have a very wide range of international publications.

Libraries and information services abroad

       The Seychelles High Commission, 2 Mill Street, London W 1 (t 01-499 9951) has copies of publications about the Seychelles which may be consulted by the public.

Statistical publications

¶   A - General

080   Seychelles handbook, incorporating the...statistical abstract   (Central Statistical Office).
       Central Statistical Office, P O Box 206, Victoria, Mahé.
       1976-   1976.   Rs 10.00.   159p.
       A general publication with a statistical appendix, the main sections of which are:
           Land and climate   Transport and communications
           Population   Prices, wages and employment
           Migration and tourism   Education
           External trade   Crime
           Electricity supply   Government finance
       Time factor: the 1976 edition, published in June 1976, has data to 1975.
       §   En.

       Note: this statistical abstract is intended to replace the various official department reports as a source of government statistics.

081   A review of the economy   (Central Statistical Office).
       Central Statistical Office, P O Box 206, Victoria, Mahé.
                   Rs 20.00.   70p.
       Time factor: published in December 1975.
       §   En.

082   Quarterly statistical bulletin   (Central Statistical Office).
       Central Statistical.Office, P O Box 206, Victoria, Mahé.
       1975-   Rs 5.00 each issue.
       Includes data on retail price indices, external trade, tourism, and employment.
       Time factor: each issue is published about two months after the end of the period covered.
       §   En.

083   Seychelles: report for the year...   (Commonwealth Office).
       H M Stationery Office, P O Box 569, London SE1.
       1946-   1967 & 1968.   £0.40.   72p.
       Contains information on the geography, population and development of the Seychelles, including a few statistical tables on finance and taxation, imports and exports, production and population.
       Time factor: the report for 1967 and 1968, containing data for those years, was published in 1970.
       §   En.

¶   B - Production

ii. Agriculture, fisheries, forestry, etc.

1084   Annual report   (Department of Agriculture).
        Department of Agriculture, Botanical Gardens, Victoria, Mahé.
        1913- 1971.   Rs 5.00.   39p.
        Includes statistics in the text and also an appendix of statistical tables.   Subjects covered are climate,
            industry (cinnamon, cocoanut, vanilla, patchouli, tea, etc), livestock, land settlement, forestry,
            fisheries, etc.
        Time factor: the 1971 report, published in December 1974, has data for the years 1965 to 1971.
        §   En.

        Refer also to 1083.

iii. Industry

        Refer to 1083.

v. Energy

        Refer to 1080.

¶   C - External trade

1085   Trade report for the year   (Central Statistical Office).
        Central Statistical Office, P O Box 206, Victoria, Mahé.
        1961- 1975.   Rs 25.00.   81p.
        Detailed statistics of imports and exports arranged by commodity and sub-divided by countries of origin
            and destination.
        Time factor: the 1975 issue, published mid-1976, has data for 1975.
        §   En.

        Refer also to 1080, 1082, 1083.

¶   D - Internal distribution and service trades

        Refer to 1080, 1082.

¶   E - Population

1086   Population census of the Seychelles Colony: report and tables   (Office of the Census Commissioner).
        Office of the Census Commissioner, Seychelles.
        1803- 1960.   not priced.   68p.
        Contains statistical tables of the geographical location of the population, their personal characteristics,
            economic characteristics, cultural characteristics, educational characteristics, fertility, and
            household information.
        Time factor: the 1960 census results were published in 1961.
        §   En.

        Note: a census was taken in 1971 and the final report is to be available shortly.

¶   E,   continued

1087   Annual report of the Registrar General's Department
            Registrar General's Department, Victoria, Mahé.
            1960-   1974.   Rs 7.00.   30p.
            Includes statistical tables in the text and also a section of tables on estimated population by population
                group, sex, and geographical district; arrivals and departures; abstracts of births, marriages and
                deaths; deaths from principal causes; statement of causes of death; and data for Rodrigues.
            Time factor: the 1974 report, published December 1975, has data for 1974.
            §   En.

1088   Biennial report of the Labour Department
            Labour Department, Victoria, Mahé.
                    1969-70.   Rs 3.00.   31p.
            Includes statistical tables on agricultural labour, employment and earnings, rough estimates of
                employment, rates of pay, etc.
            Time factor: the 1969-70 report, published in 1974, has data for 1969 and 1970.
            §   En.

1089   Annual report on the civil status and vital statistics and the Registry of Deeds Department
            Registrar General's Department, Victoria, Mahé.
            1960-   1970.   Rs 3.00.   30p.
            Includes statistics of population, demographic statistics, arrivals and departures of visitors, immigrants
                and residents.
            Time factor: the 1970 report, published in 1972, has data for 1970 (population statistics for 1965 to
                1970).
            §   En.

            Refer also to 1080, 1082, 1083.

¶   F - Social

i. Standard of living

        Refer to 1080, 1082.

iii. Education and leisure

1090   Annual summary   (Department of Education).
            Department of Education, Victoria, Mahé.
            1971-   1973.   not priced.   18p.
            Includes statistical tables on the education salary scale; primary, junior secondary and secondary
                grammar enrolment by management of school; enrolment by level of education and ages - primary,
                junior secondary, secondary grammar, and technical and vocational courses; employment of
                school leavers; teachers at schools and colleges classified by qualification; enrolment in teacher
                training; examination results; and public expenditure on education.
            Time factor: the 1973 report, published in April 1975, has data for 1973.
            §   En.

            Note: from 1960 to 1970 title was "Annual report of the Department of Education".

            Refer also to 1080.

SEYCHELLES, continued

   ¶ F, continued

   iv. Justice

1091   Annual report of the Judicial Department
          Judicial Department, Victoria, Mahé.
          1960- 1970. Rs 2.00. 15p.
          Contains statistical data on cases in civil courts, magistrates courts, supreme courts, and criminal
             cases and appeals.
          Time factor: the 1970 report, published in 1971, has data for 1970.
          § En.

          Refer also to 1080.

   ¶ G - Finance

1092   Annual report of the Income Tax Department
          Income Tax Department, Victoria, Mahé.
          1960- 1974. Rs 3.00. 11p.
          Includes some statistics in the text on cost of administration, taxes collected, income tax, duties, and
             property tax.
          Time factor: the 1974 report, published in 1975, has data for 1974.
          § En.

          Refer also to 1080, 1083.

   ¶ H - Transport and communications

          Refer to 1080.

SIERRA LEONE

Central Statistical office

1093   Central Statistics Office,
        Ministry of Finance,
        Tower Hill, Freetown.
        † 23898.

Set up in 1963 with responsibility for the organisation and implementation of a coordinated scheme of economic and social statistics relating to Sierra Leone.   Its activities are in the fields of population and vital statistics, external trade statistics, agricultural statistics, business and industry statistics, national accounts statistics, and household income and expenditure statistics.   Unpublished statistical data are supplied on request when available, and limited data-processing facilities are offered to the public.

Libraries

Copies of all publications of the Central Statistics Office are available for reference in the National Library, Freetown, and statistical documents not in the library may be consulted at the Central Statistics Office.

Libraries and information services abroad

Copies of all statistical publications of the Central Statistics Office are available for reference at Sierra Leone embassies abroad, including:

United Kingdom   Sierra Leone High Commission, 33 Portland Place, London W.1.   † 01-580 7854.
U.S.A.   Sierra Leone Embassy, 1701 17th Street NW, Washington DC.   † 265-7700.

Statistical publications

¶   A - General

1094   Annual statistical digest   (Central Statistics Office).
        Central Statistics Office, Ministry of Finance, Tower Hill, Freetown.
        1968- 1971.   Leone 0.50.   136p.
        Main sections:
            Geography   External trade
            Population and vital statistics   Balance of payments
            Migration   Air traffic
            Public health   National accounts
            Employment and industrial relations   Prices and public finance
            Agriculture   Electricity and industry
            Education
        Time factor: the 1971 issue, published in 1973, has data for 1971 and also for earlier years in some
            tables.
        §   En.

1095   Statistical bulletin   (Central Statistics Office).
        Central Statistics Office, Ministry of Finance, Tower Hill, Freetown.
        1963-   quarterly.   Leone 0.50 each copy.
        Contains data on demography, foreign trade, transport, agriculture, electricity, wages and hours
            worked, etc.
        Time factor: copies for 1971 are the latest located.
        §   En.

¶   A,   continued

1096   Economic review   (Bank of Sierra Leone).
              Bank of Sierra Leone, Westmoreland Street, Freetown.
              1966–   quarterly.   not priced.
              Includes a statistical section on central banking, money supply, commercial banking, central
                   government finances, external assets – balance of payments and international trade, industry
                   and mining, agriculture, employment, prices, national income and expenditure.
              Time factor: each issue has long runs of annual, quarterly and monthly figures to about six months
                   prior to publication.
              §   En.

1097   Sierra Leone economic trends   (Bank of Sierra Leone).
              Bank of Sierra Leone, Westmoreland Street, Freetown.
              1969–   quarterly.   not priced.
              Contains data on money, banking, government finance, foreign trade, mining, industrial production,
                   agriculture, employment, and consumer price indices (Freetown).
              Time factor: each issue has data to the end of the period of the issue and is published some six months
                   later.
              §   En.

1098   Annual report and statement of accounts...   (Bank of Sierra Leone).
              Bank of Sierra Leone, Westmoreland Street, Freetown.
              1964–   1974.   not priced.   116p.
              Includes a statistical section on money supply; central banking; commercial banking; central
                   government finances; balance of payments, external assets, and international trade; agriculture,
                   mining and industry; employment; prices; and national income and expenditure.
              Time factor: the 1974 report, published late 1974, contains runs for several fiscal years, quarters and
                   months to June 1974.
              §   En.

¶   B – Production

i. Mines and mining

1099   Report of the Mines Division, Ministry of Lands and Mines
              Mines Division, Ministry of Lands and Mines, Freetown.
              1962–   1972.   Leone 0.35.   25p.
              Contains data on mineral exports, approximate expenditure in Sierra Leone by the mining industry
                   (exclusive of the alluvial diamond mining scheme), comparative statement on annual mineral
                   production, direct revenue from the mining industry, record of purchases by the government
                   diamond office, average staff and labour engaged in mining prospecting, prosecutions and
                   diamonds confiscated, as well as mining licenses issued.
              Time factor: the 1972 report, published in 1975, has data for 1972.
              §   En.

              Refer also to 1096, 1097, 1098.

ii. Agriculture, fisheries, forestry, etc.

1100   Agricultural statistical survey, 1965/66   (Central Statistics Office).
              Central Statistics Office, Ministry of Finance, Tower Hill, Freetown.
                       Leone 1.00.
              An ad hoc survey, which was intended to become the base for an annual or biennial one.
              §   En.

¶   B.ii,   continued

1101   Report on the Fisheries Division, Ministry of Agriculture and Natural Resources
         Fisheries Division, Ministry of Agriculture and Natural Resources, Freetown.
         1958-   1967-1973.   Leone 0.50.   50p.
         Includes statistics on the finances of the Division, licensed vessels, trawler landings, landings by
              species, purse seine landings, tuna landings and exports, and loan scheme returns.
         Time factor: the 1967-1973 report, published in 1975, was an attempt to bring the reports up-to-date
              and later ones will be annual.
         §   En.

         Refer also to 1094, 1095, 1096, 1097, 1098.

     iii.   Industry

1102   Report on the survey of business and industry   (Central Statistics Office).
         Central Statistics Office, Ministry of Finance, Tower Hill, Freetown.
         1966/67-   1966/67.   Leone 0.50.   89p.
         Contains data by province and by kind of business.
         Time factor: the report of the 1966/67 survey was published in 1970.
         §   En.

         Refer also to 1094, 1096, 1097, 1098.

     v. Energy

         Refer to 1094, 1095.

¶   C - External trade

1103   Sierra Leone quarterly trade statistics   (Central Statistics Office).
         Central Statistics Office, Ministry of Finance, Tower Hill, Freetown.
         1921-   Leone 0.70; Leone 3.50 yr.
         Main tables show imports and exports arranged by commodity, sub-divided by countries of origin and
              destination.   Other tables include summary of trade, direction of trade, shipping, air traffic,
              revenue and excise.
         Time factor: each issue contains figures for the latest and previous quarters; delay in publication can
              be a year or more.
         §   En.

         Note: an annual "Trade report" covering the years 1964 & 1965 in one volume was issued in 1967, but
              no subsequent issues appeared.

         Refer also to 1094, 1095, 1096, 1097, 1098.

¶   D - Internal distribution and service trades

         Refer to 1097, 1098.

¶   E - Population

1104   Population census of Sierra Leone   (Central Statistics Office).
          Central Statistics Office, Ministry of Finance, Tower Hill, Freetown.
          1802-   1963.   Leone 3.00 each volume.   3 vols.
          Volume 1 contains data on the total population by sex, age and area, and rank of chieftains; volume 2
             contains data on social characteristics such as place of birth, nationality, tribal affiliation,
             education, literacy in English, Mende, Tomne and Arabic, and household composition; volume 3
             contains data on economic characteristics such as labour force and occupations.
          Time factor: published in 1965.
          §   En.

          Refer also to 1094, 1095, 1096, 1097, 1098.

¶   F - Social

i.   Standard of living

1105   Household survey of the rural areas of the provinces, 1969-1970: final report; household expenditure and
             income and economic characteristics   (Central Statistics Office).
          Central Statistics Office, Ministry of Finance, Tower Hill, Freetown.
                         Le 1.00.   126p.
          Includes statistics of household expenditures, individual earnings, and labour force participation.
          Time factor: the report was published in 1972.
          §   En.

1106   Household survey of the...urban areas, 1968-1969: final report; household expenditure and income and
             economic characteristics   (Central Statistics Office).
          Central Statistics Office, Ministry of Finance, Tower Hill, Freetown.
          Separate reports have been issued for each province:-
               Eastern Province   (Le 1.00)
               Northern Province   (Le 1.00)
               Southern Province   (Le 1.00)
               Western Province   (Le 1.00)
          Time factor: the reports were published between 1969 and 1972.
          §   Fr.

          Refer also to 1095, 1097.

ii. Health and welfare

1107   Statistics of the health services and of their activities   (Ministry of Health. Medical Statistics Unit).
          Medical Statistics Unit, Ministry of Health, Freetown.
          1969-   1969.   not priced.   128p.
          Contains general statistical data on area, population and vital statistics; more detailed statistics on
             staff training; health resources; health activities; and special private services.
          Time factor: the 1969 issue, published in 1970, has data for 1969.   It was hoped this would become an
             annual publication.
          §   En.

          Refer also to 1094.

¶ F, continued

iii. Education and leisure

1108   Report of the Ministry of Education...including educational developments and statistics
              Ministry of Education, Freetown.
              1942-   1972/73.   Leone 0.75.   69p.
              Includes statistical data on primary, secondary, technical and vocational education; teacher education;
                   university education; finance; and examination results.
              Time factor: the 1972/73 report, published in 1976, has data for the academic year 1972/73.
              §   En.

              Refer also to 1094.

¶   G - Finance

              Refer to 1094, 1096, 1097, 1098.

i. Banking

              Refer to 1096, 1097, 1098.

ii. Public finance

1109   National accounts of Sierra Leone   (Central Statistics Office).
              Central Statistics Office, Ministry of Finance, Tower Hill, Freetown.
              1963/64 and 1964/65-   1963/64-1971/72.   Leone 1.00.   69p.
              Time factor: the 1963/64-1971/72 issue, published mid-1973, has data for the fiscal years from 1963/64
                   to 1971/72.
              §   En.

1110   Balance of payments   (Bank of Sierra Leone).
              Bank of Sierra Leone, Westmoreland Street, Freetown.
              1963/68-   1971/75.   not priced.   22p.
              Time factor: the 1971/75 issue, published in 1976, covers the years 1971 to 1975.
              §   En.

              Refer also to 1094, 1096, 1097, 1098.

¶   H - Transport and communications

              Refer to 1094, 1095.

SOMALI DEMOCRATIC REPUBLIC - REPUBBLICA DEMOCRATICA SOMALIA -
JAMHURIYADDA DIMOQRAADIGA SOOMAALIYEED

Central statistical office

1111   Waaxda Dhexe ee Istatistikada, [Central Statistical Department]
            Guddiga Qorsheynta Qaranka, [State Planning Commission]
            Mogadisho.
            † 8384, 8385, 8387, 8388, & 838.

   The Department collects, processes, analyses and publishes statistics, including foreign trade statistics, prices and industrial statistics. It also conducts surveys and publishes the results.   Unpublished statistical information may be supplied if available, on payment of a fee.

Libraries

   There is a library in the Central Statistical Department of the State Planning Commission, where statistical publications may be consulted.   The staff speak Somali, Italian, English and Arabic.

Libraries and information services abroad

   Copies of the publications of the Central Statistical Department are available for reference in Somali embassies abroad, including:-
   United Kingdom   Embassy of the Somali Republic, 60 Portland Place, London W.1.   † 01-580 7148.
   U.S.A.   Embassy of the Somali Republic, 600 N H Avenue NW, Washington DC. † 234 3261.

Statistical publications

¶   A - General

1112   Statistical abstract   (Central Statistical Department).
            Central Statistical Department, State Planning Commission, Mogadishu.
            1964-   1973.·   not priced.   140p.
            Main sections:

Meteorology	Development programme
Population	Banking
Migration	Prices
Education	Transport and communications
Health	Industry
Agriculture and livestock	Crime
Foreign trade	

            Time factor: the 1973 edition, published December 1975, has data for 1973 and also earlier years in some tables.
            §   En, Somali.

1113   Monthly statistical bulletin   (Central Statistical Department).
            Central Statistical Department, State Planning Commission, Mogadishu.
            1966-   not priced.
            Contains data on exports by destination, exports by commodity, imports by countries of origin, imports by commodity, shipping statistics, index numbers of cost of living in Mogadishu, and major wholesale and retail prices.
            §   En, Somali.

1114   Somali statistics   (Central Statistical Department).
            Central Statistical Department, State Planning Commission, Mogadishu.
            1967-   monthly.
            Each issue includes data on external trade, turnover statistics, transport and communications, revenue, agriculture, livestock and prices.   Other subjects are included from time to time on an ad hoc basis.
            Time factor: issues for 1972 are the latest to be published.
            §   En, It.

¶   A,   continued

1115   Somalia in figures   (Central Statistical Department).
        Central Statistical Department, State Planning Commission, Mogadishu.
        1967-   1973.   not priced.   10-fold leaflet.
        Contains brief statistics on population, resources, fisheries, minerals, manpower, budget, exports and
            imports, roads, shipping, cost of living index, loans and savings, balance of payments, etc.
        Time factor: the 1973 issue was published in 1974.
        §   En.

1116   Five-year development plan, 1974-1978   (Ministry of Planning and Coordination).
        State Planning Commission, Mogadishu.
                            not priced.   298p.
        Statistics and statistical tables are included in the text, and the plan is in two sections.   Section A has
            a review of the economy, objectives and strategy, and financing and implementation of the plan;
            Section B has data on livestock and related activities, agriculture, forestry, wildlife, fisheries,
            water resources, mining, electricity and power, industry, transport and communications, education,
            health, housing, labour, employment, training, statistics and cartography, tourism, and other
            information.
        Time factor: the plan was published in 1974.
        §   En.

1117   Bulletin   (Central Bank of Somalia).
        Central Bank of Somalia, P O Box 11, Mogadiscio.
        1965-   quarterly.   not priced.
        Contains the national bank accounts, accounts of other banks, data on the banking system, and a
            section relating to foreign trade and payments (consumer price index, balance of trade, source of
            imports, chief exports and imports, and balance of payments).
        Time factor: each issue has runs of figures to about one month prior to the date of the issue.
        §   En, Somali.

1118   Multipurpose statistical surveys   (Central Statistical Department, Ministry of Planning and Coordination).
        Ministry of Planning and Coordination, Mogadishu.
        1961- ongoing.   So Sh 3 or US$ 1.00 each district survey.
                                  So Sh 7 or US$ 1.00 each town survey.
        The surveys cover households and population, population by age and sex, marital status, education,
            students in schools, economic activity status, labour force, distribution of employed persons,
            municipal registration, population movement and migration, livestock, and births and deaths in
            households.   Towns surveyed include Hargeisa, Erigavo, Borama, Las-Anod, Berbera, Burao,
            Las-Korel, Zeila, Gabileh, Odweina and Afgoi; districts include Afgoi, Merca, Baidoa, Gelib,
            Kisimayu, Afmadou and Giamama.
        §   En.

1119   Annual report...   (Central Bank of Somalia).
        Central Bank of Somalia, P O Box 11, Mogadiscio.
        1962-   1974.   not priced.   56p.
        Contains an international monetary survey and information on the domestic economics of production,
            livestock, industrial production, the development plan and investments, public finance, balance
            of payments, monetary survey, prices, monetary policy, activities of the banking system, and
            activities of the Somali National Bank.   Statistics are included in the text and there are also
            statistical tables.
        Time factor: the 1974 report, published in 1975, has data for 1974 and also for earlier years in some
            tables.
        §   En.

¶   B - Production

i. Mines and mining

        Refer to 1115, 1116.

¶ B, continued

ii. Agriculture, fisheries, forestry, etc.

Refer to 1112, 1114, 1115, 1116, 1118.

iii. Industry

1120   Industrial production   (Central Statistical Department).
        Central Statistical Department, State Planning Commission, Mogadishu.
        1967-   1973.   not priced.   58p.
        Contains data on establishments, employment, earnings, capital formation, costs, value of stocks,
            value of services, etc.
        Time factor: the 1973 issue, published in 1975, has data for 1973.
        §   En.

        Refer also to 1112, 1114, 1116, 1119.

v. Energy

Refer to 1116.

¶ C - External trade

1121   Statistica del commercio con l'estero.   Foreign trade returns.   (Central Statistical Department).
        Central Statistical Department, State Planning Commission, Mogadishu.
        1964-   1974.   not priced.   393p.
        Main tables show imports and exports arranged by commodities and sub-divided by countries of origin
            and destination, and arranged by countries of origin and destination and sub-divided by
            commodities.   There is also a number of summary tables.
        Time factor: the 1974 issue, with data for 1974, was published in December 1975.
        §   En, It.

        Refer also to 1112, 1113, 1114, 1115, 1117.

¶ D - Internal distribution and service trades

Refer to 1113, 1114, 1116.

¶ E - Population

1122   Censimento della popolazione italiana e straniera della Somalia   [Census of Italian and foreign population
            in Italian Somaliland]   (Instituto Centrale di Statistica, Roma).
        Libreria Istat, via A Depretis 82, 00100 Roma, Italy.
        1911-   1953.
        §   It.

1123   Recensement de la population de la Côte Française des Somalis (population non originaire)   [Census of
            population of French Somaliland (foreign population)]   (INSEE).
        INSEE, 18 boulevard Adolphe Pinard, 75675 Paris Cedex 14, France.
        1946-   1956.   40p.
        §   Fr.

        Note: a census of population and livestock was to be taken in 1975, for the Republic of Somalia.

        Refer also to 1112, 1115, 1116, 1118.

¶ F - Social

i. Standard of living

Refer to 1113, 1115, 1116, 1118.

ii. Health and welfare

Refer to 1112, 1116.

iii. Education and leisure

1124   Annual report...and statistics of education   (Ministry of Education).
        Ministry of Education, Mogadishu.
        1971/72-   1973.   not priced.   110p.
        Contains statistical data on grades, classes, classrooms, schools and teachers in elementary,
            intermediary and secondary schools, by district.   Also data on examination results.
        Time factor: the 1973 report includes statistics for the academic year 1973/74.
        §   En.

        Refer also to 1112, 1116, 1118.

¶ G - Finance

Refer to 1112, 1115, 1116, 1117, 1119.

¶ H - Transport and communications

Refer to 1112, 1113, 1114, 1115, 1116.

Central statistical office

1125   Department of Statistics, Departement van Statistiek,
          Steyn's Buildings,
          270 Schoeman Street,
          Private Bag X44, Pretoria 0001.
          t 41 1411.   tg STATUS.   tx 30450, 30523.

The main functions of the Department consist in the collection, processing, analysis and publishing of statistics relating to the agricultural, industrial, commercial, shipping, shipping and other business undertakings, and also to the taking of the decennial census of population. Unpublished statistical data and also photocopies may be supplied to enquirers, but each request is considered on its merits. Until recently the Department was named the Bureau of Statistics.

Another important organisation collecting and publishing statistics

1126   Department of Customs & Excise, Departement van Doeane en Aksyns,
          Franz du Toit Building,
          303 Paul Kruger Street,
          Private Bag 47, Pretoria.
          t 48-4308.   tg CUSTEX

The Department's responsibilities include the collection, processing and analysis for publication of statistics of foreign trade. More detailed information than is published and information in advance of publication can, circumstances permitting, be provided on·payment of a fee to cover the cost of extraction.

Libraries

Libraries where statistical publications may be consulted include the library of the Department of Statistics; the Municipal Library, 159 Andries Street, Pretoria; the Public Library, Market Square, Johannesburg; and the South African Library, Victoria Street, Cape Town.

Libraries and information services abroad

Copies of the publications of the Department of Statistics and the Department of Customs and Excise are available for reference at South African embassies, including:-

United Kingdom   South African Embassy, South Africa House, Trafalgar Square, London WC2.
                   t 01-930 4488.
Australia   South African Embassy, State Circle, Yaralmla.   t 73 2424.
Canada   South African Embassy, 15 Sussex Drive, Ottawa.   t 749 5977.
U.S.A.   South African Embassy, 3051 Massachusetts Avenue NW, Washington, DC.
                   t 232-4400.

Bibliographies

A list of the latest publications of the Department of Statistics is published in "Bulletin of statistics" (1130).

1127   A guide to statistical sources in the Republic of South Africa. Bureau of Market Research,
          University of South Africa, 263 Skinner Street, P O Box 392, Pretoria. Revised edition, 1972.

1128   Bibliography of South African government publications, 1910-1968 (Department of Statistics,
          P B X44, Pretoria. 1969.

Statistical publications

¶   A - General

129   South African statistics.   Suid-Afrikaanse statistieke.   (Department of Statistics).
            Government Printer, Bosman Street, P B X85, Pretoria.
            1964-   1976.   R 9.65 (R 12.00 abroad).
            Main sections:

Population	Construction
Migration	Electricity, gas and steam
Vital statistics	Internal trade
Health	Foreign trade
Education	Transport
Social security	Communication
Labour	Public finance
Prices	Currency, banking and general finance
Agriculture	National accounts
Fisheries	Balance of payments
Mining	Foreign liabilities and assets
Manufacturing	Meteorological statistics

            Time factor: the 1976 edition, published late 1976, has data for 1975 and often for 10 or more earlier
                years.   It is published every two years.
            §   Af, En.

            Note: data was included in "Official yearbook of the Republic and of Basutoland, Bechuanaland
                Protectorate and Swaziland" from 1910 to 1960.

130   Bulletin of statistics.   Bulletin van statistiek.   (Department of Statistics).
            Government Printer, Bosman Street, P B X85, Pretoria.
            1920-   quarterly.   R 3.40 (R 4.25 abroad; R 13.60 (R 17.00 abroad) yr.
            Contains data on demography, labour, prices, agriculture, mining, manufacturing, construction,
                electricity, foreign trade, internal trade, public finance, private finance, transport.
            Time factor: each issue has data for several years and quarters to about 6 months before publication
                date, which is the date of the issue.
            §   Af, En.

131   Quarterly bulletin.   (South African Reserve Bank).
            South African Reserve Bank, Church Square, P O Box 427, Pretoria.
            1947-   not priced.
            Includes statistical tables on money and banking, capital market, government finance, international
                economic relations, national accounts, and general economic indicators of production, labour
                and prices.
            Time factor: each issue contains data for about 10 years, up to three months prior to the date of
                publication, which is the date of the issue.
            §   Af, En.

            Note: the bank also issues an "Annual economic report", covering much the same subjects and with
                graphs and tables in the text.

132   Short-term economic indicators   (Department of Statistics).
            Government Printer, Bosman Street, P B X85, Pretoria.
            1967-   monthly.   not priced.
            Contains advance abstracts of the most important statistical series indicating tendencies in the economic
                development of South Africa on a short-term basis.   Covers labour, prices, mining, manufacturing,
                construction, electricity, foreign trade, internal trade, transport, finance, gross domestic product,
                civil judgements for debt insolvencies and company liquidation, and companies registered.
            Time factor: contains the latest available monthly and quarterly data and some earlier figures.
            §   Af, En.

¶ A, continued

1133   Commerce & industry: monthly journal of the Departments of Commerce and of Industries of the Republic of
            South Africa.
            Government Printer, Bosman Street, P B X85, Pretoria.
            1943-   R 0.05 (R 0.10 abroad); R.O 50 (R 0.65 abroad) yr.
            Includes a statistical section giving data on domestic trade, industrial production, mining production,
                price indices, company registrations, labour, transport, building construction, foreign trade, and
                finance.
            Time factor: tables contain data for 12 months up to two or more months prior to the date of the issue.
            §   Af and En eds.

1134   Union statistics for fifty years   (Bureau of Statistics).
            Government Printer, Bosman Street, P B X85, Pretoria.
                            not priced.   various paginations.
            The Jubilee issue for 1910 to 1960, with data on all aspects of South Africa's social and economic
                development, including population, health, education, crime, labour, agriculture, mining,
                industry, trade, communications and finance.
            Time factor: published in 1960.
            §   En.

1135   State of South Africa: economic, financial and statistical yearbook for the Republic of South Africa.
            Da Gama Publishers (Pty) Ltd, 311 Locarno House, Loveday Street, Johannesburg.
            1964-   1976.   not priced.   208p.
            Contains chapters on population, migration, employment, salaries and wages, construction, foreign
                trade, transport, finance, etc.   Statistics and statistical tables are included in the text.
            Time factor: the 1976 edition, published in 1976, has data for several years to 1974 or 1975.
            §   En.

1136   Information digest   (South Africa Foundation).
            South Africa Foundation, P O Box 7006, Johannesburg 2000.
                    1977.   not priced.   87p.
            A pocket-book which includes general statistical tables on population, industry, education, foreign
                trade, balance of payments, transport, mining, agriculture, fisheries, manufactures, national
                income, gross domestic product, etc.
            §   En.

1137   Standard Bank review.
            Standard Bank Investment Corporation Ltd, P O Box 3862, Johannesburg 2000.
                    monthly.   not priced.
            Includes key economic indicators, interest rates and yields, and financial indicators.
            §   En.

1138   Statistical news releases   (Department of Statistics).
            Department of Statistics, Steyn's buildings, 270 Schoeman Street, P B X44, Pretoria 0001.
                    not priced.
            A series of news releases issued on a monthly, quarterly or other periodic basis, according to subject.
                Subjects covered include mining, manufacturing, construction, energy, wholesale and retail trade,
                migration, labour, consumer price index, motor vehicle licenses, road traffic accidents, judiciary,
                and financial statistics.
            Time factor: as press releases, the issues are published very quickly.
            §   Af, En.

        ¶   B - Production

        i. Mines and mining

1139   Mineral resources of the Republic of South Africa   (Department of Mines).
            Government Printer, Bosman Street, P B X85, Pretoria.
                    5th ed, 1976.   R 5.30 (R 6.65 abroad).   470p.
            Contains a general section, and then sections on precious metals and stones, base metallic minerals, and
                non-metallic minerals.   Some statistics are included in the text.
            §   En.

¶ B.i, continued

1140 Minerals: a report for the Republic of South Africa and South West Africa (Department of Mines).
Government Printer, Bosman Street, P B X85, Pretoria.
1969- quarterly. R 0.75 (R 1.00 abroad) each issue.
Contains data on production, local sales, and exports of gold, diamonds, silver, metalliferous minerals, non-metallic minerals, semi-precious stones, and ornamental, building stone, clay and sundries.
Time factor: each issue has data for the quarter of the issue and the corresponding quarter of the previous year, and is published one or two months later.
§ Af, En.

1141 Mining - financial statistics (Department of Statistics).
Government Printer, Bosman Street, P B X85, Pretoria.
1966/69- 1973. R 2.75 (R 3.75 abroad). 39p.
The results of an annual census, the report relates to private establishments and private corporations (but not government undertakings) for South Africa as a whole. Data include numbers of establishments, ownership, employees, houses and flats provided, expenditure and income, accounts and balance sheets, fixed assets, capital expenditure, depreciation, etc.
Time factor: the 1973 report, published in 1976, has data for 1973.
§ Af, En.

1142 Annual report (Department of Mines).
Government Printer, Bosman Street, P B X85, Pretoria.
1966- 1974. R 6.70 (R 8.35 abroad). 51p.
Contains the reports of the Secretary of Mines, the Government Mining Engineer, and the Director of the Geological Survey Division. Includes statistical data on output and sales of minerals and output of manufacturers.
Time factor: the 1974 report, published in 1975, has data for 1974.
§ En.

1143 Annual report (Chamber of Mines of South Africa).
Chamber of Mines of South Africa, 5 Holland Street, Johannesburg.
1890- 1974. not priced. 102p.
The report includes a section of statistical tables on coal production, coal dividends, gold production, gold dividends, labour (accidents, average numbers of employees, salaries and wages), mining taxation, silver output in South Africa since 1910, stores consumed, and uranium production.
Time factor: the 1974 report, published in 1975, has data for 1974.
§ En.

Note: the Chamber also publishes a "Summary of quarterly statements of working results".

Refer also to 1129, 1130, 1132, 1133, 1134, 1136, 1138.

ii. Agriculture, fisheries, forestry, etc.

1144 Handbook of agricultural statistics, 1904-1950 (Department of Agricultural Economics and Marketing).
Government Printer, Bosman Street, P B X85, Pretoria.
not priced. 201p.
Contains statistics on land use, farm labour, livestock, agricultural crops, forestry, imports and exports, prices and price indices.
Time factor: published in 1961.
§ En.

1145 Report on agricultural and pastoral production (Department of Statistics).
Government Printer, Bosman Street, P B X85, Pretoria.
1960/61- 1974. R 2.75 (R 3.75 abroad). 254p.
Results of the annual agricultural census. Contains a summary of the principal statistics, and data on holders and holdings; employment, salaries and wages, etc; agricultural crops; hay crops; livestock and poultry; motor vehicles (tractors, combines, electric motors and other engines); expenditure incurred in connection with farming operations; value of farm products sold and farming debt; and the Agricultural Control Board.
Time factor: the 1974 report, published in 1976, has data for 1974.
§ Af, En.

¶   B.ii,   continued

1146   Census of veterinary services...1961/62 and 1962/63   (Bureau of Statistics).
            Government Printer, Bosman Street, P B X85, Pretoria.
            §   Af, En.

1147   Census of the fishing industry   (Department of Statistics).
            Government Printer, Bosman Street, P B X85, Pretoria.
            1960/61-   1975.
            Time factor: the only results of the 1975 census published so far are in a statistical news release,
                P.9 (1138).
            §   Af, En.

            Refer also to 1129, 1130, 1134, 1136.

        iii. Industry

1148   Census of manufacturing.   Sensus van Fabriekswese   (Department of Statistics).
            Government Printer, Bosman Street, P B X85, Pretoria.
            1960/61-   1967/68.
            Contents:
                Principal statistics according to major groups and groups - South Africa.   60c (75c abroad).
                Statistics according to major groups and groups - South Africa.   R2.75 (R3.75 abroad).
                Census of manufacturing, 1967-68, 1965-66, and 1963-64 - principal statistics on a regional basis.
                    R2.75 (R3.75 abroad).
                The following reports contain data on materials purchase and manufactures sold:
                Food, beverages, tobacco.   75c (95c abroad).
                Textiles, clothing, footwear & made-up textile goods.   R2.75 (R3.75 abroad).
                Wood and cork products (excluding furniture), furniture, cabinetmaking, etc.   R2.75 (R3.75 abroad)
                Paper and paper products, printing, bookbinding, etc.   R2.75 (R3.75 abroad).
                Leather and leather products, excluding footwear, rubber products.   R2.75 (R3.75 abroad).
                Chemicals to miscellaneous manufacturing industries.   R2.75 (R3.75 abroad).
                Manufactured articles sold.   R2.75 (R3.75 abroad).
            Time factor: published between 1971 and 1974.
            §   Af, En.

            Note: the results of the 1970 census are now being published.

1149   Input-output tables, 1967   (Department of Statistics).
            Government Printer, Bosman Street, P B X85, Pretoria.
                            R 2.75 (R 3.75 abroad).
            §   En.

            Refer also to 1129, 1130, 1131, 1132, 1133, 1134, 1136, 1138.

        iv. Construction

1150   Census of construction   (Bureau of Statistics).
            Government Printer, Bosman Street, P B X85, Pretoria.
            1963/64-   1969/1970.   R 0.75 (R 0.95 abroad).   41p.
            Devoted to private construction in South Africa, the census report is divided into I, Construction
                establishments, excluding separate head offices, and II, Head Offices.   Data includes numbers of
                establishments, employment, remuneration of employees, construction account - debits,
                construction account - credits, book value of physical assets, appropriation accounts and balance
                sheets.
            Time factor: the census is taken every two years, and the report for 1969/70 was published in 1973.
            §   Af, En.

¶   B.iv,   continued

1151   Census of architects and quantity surveyors   (Department of Statistics).
            Government Printer, Bosman Street, P B X85, Pretoria.
            1963/64-   1974.   R 2.00 (R 2.50 abroad).
            Time factor: the report of the 1974 census was published in 1975.
            §   Af, En.

1152   Building plans passed and buildings completed   (Department of Statistics).
            Government Printer, Bosman Street, P B X85, Pretoria.
            1964/66-   1974.   R 2.75 (R 3.75 abroad).   238p.
            Contains data on building plans passed, by type of building; and on buildings completed, value,
                additions, and alterations for residential buildings, non-residential buildings, by town and area.
            Time factor: the 1974 issue, published in 1976, has data for 1974 and 1973.
            §   Af, En.

            Refer also to 1129, 1130, 1132, 1133, 1135, 1138.

    v. Energy

1153   Census of electricity, gas and steam   (Department of Statistics).
            Government Printer, Bosman Street, P B X85, Pretoria.
            1963/64-   1974.   R 2.00 (R 2.50 abroad).   30p.
            Contains a general review and data on public supply undertakings and self-producers undertakings,
                employment, salaries and wages, expenditure, income, fixed assets, motive power employed and
                electricity consumed, installed capacities, gross production of electricity supply available,
                production and consumption of electricity, gas and steam, and finances.
            Time factor: the 1974 report, published late 1976, has data for 1974.
            §   Af, En.

            Refer also to 1129, 1130, 1132, 1138.

¶   C - External trade

1154   Foreign trade statistics.   Buitenlandse handelstatistieke.   (Customs and Excise).
            Government Printer, Bosman Street, P B X85, Pretoria.
            1906-   1975.   Vol.I R 4.60 (R 5.70 abroad).   2 vols.
                                            Vol.II R 4.60 (R 5.70 abroad).
            Vol.I includes statistical data on imports and exports arranged by country of origin and destination and
                sub-divided by commodities, imports by commodities and certain countries, and exports by
                commodities only.   Vol.II includes statistical data of imports of principal commodities from certain
                countries, and excise tables.   Data is for the common customs area of Botswana, Lesotho, South
                Africa and Swaziland.
            Time factor: the 1975 issues, published late 1976, have data for 1975 and 1974.
            §   En, Af.

1155   Monthly abstract of trade statistics.   Maandelikse uittreksel van handelstatistieke.   (Customs and Excise).
            Government Printer, Bosman Street, P B X85, Pretoria.
            1947-   R 4.60 (R 5.70 abroad) each issue.
            Contains detailed statistics of imports and exports arranged by commodities.
            Time factor: each issue contains data for the month of the issue, cumulated figures for the year to date,
                and comparative figures for the previous year.
            §   En, Af.

¶   C,   continued

1156   Preliminary statement of trade statistics for the Republic of South Africa   (Department of Customs and Excise).
             Department of Customs and Excise, 303 Paul Kruger Street, Private Bag 47, Pretoria.
                       monthly.   not priced.
             Contains summary figures of imports and exports by continent and by main commodity sections.
             Time factor: each issue has cumulated figures for the year to date and for the corresponding period
                  for the previous year.
             §   Af, En.

             Refer also to 1129, 1130, 1132, 1133, 1134, 1135, 1136.

¶   D - Internal distribution and service trades

1157   Census of wholesale and retail trade   (Bureau of Statistics).
             Government Printer, Bosman Street, P B X85, Pretoria.
             1946/47-   1970/71.
             Final reports are:-
                  Wholesalers: summary   (R 5.00 (R 6.25 abroad))
                  Retailers: summary   (R 5.00 (R 6.25 abroad))
                  Commercial agents and allied services   (R 2.75 (R 3.75 abroad))
             Each contains data on establishments, ownership, revenue size groups, employee size groups, kind of
                  business, salaries and wages, trading profit and loss, fixed assets, accounts and balance sheets.
             There are also other more specific reports, dealing with groups of products, etc:-
                  Wholesale:
                       Foodstuffs, beverages, tobacco.
                       Agricultural and pastoral products, including livestock, textiles, footwear and clothing;
                            furniture, household requisites and household appliances.
                       Books, stationery and office and shop equipment; precious stones, jewellery and silverware;
                            industrial and heavy chemicals; pharmaceuticals and toiletry.
                       Construction and building materials; mining, industrial and agricultural machinery and
                            equipment; general merchandise; miscellaneous commodities.
                       Repair of typewriters and other office equipment; repair of agricultural machinery and
                            implements and farm tractors.
                  Retail:
                       Butchers; dairies and dealers in dairy products; grocers and other dealers in foodstuffs; bottle
                            stores.
                       Men's outfitters; ladies' outfitters; general outfitters and dealers in piece goods and textiles;
                            shoe stores.
                       Dealers in furniture, household requisites and household appliances; book stores and stationers;
                            jewellers.
                       Chemists; building material and hardware merchants; bicycle and motor cycle dealers; fuel and
                            coal merchants.
                       Dealers in sport and entertainment requisites; general department stores; general dealers;
                            dealers in miscellaneous goods.
                       Repair of footwear and other leather goods; repair, servicing and installation of electric and
                            non-electric household and personal appliances; blacksmiths shops; watch, clock and
                            jewellery repairs; other repair and servicing establishments.
             Time factor: the reports of the 1970-71 census were published in 1976 and 1977.
             §   Af, En.

1158   Census of motor trade and repair services   (Bureau of Statistics).
             Government Printer, Bosman Street, P B X85, Pretoria.
             1963/64-   1970.   R 2.75 (R 3.75 abroad).   167p.
             The report is in three sections; Part I: Garage: franchise holders, dealers in used vehicles, service
                  stations and workshops; part II: Other motor trade establishments: motor scrap yards and dealers
                  in spares, accessories and tyres; part III: Wholesale trade in motor vehicles and accessories.
             Time factor: the 1970 report, published in 1976, has data for 1970.
             §   Af, En.

¶ D, continued

159 Catering services (Department of Statistics).
Government Printer, Bosman Street, P B X85, Pretoria.
1946/47- 1971. R 2.75 (R 3.75 abroad). 27p.
Results of a census of catering services, the report includes numbers of establishments, employees,
salaries and wages, services, purchases, sales, profit and loss, fixed assets, capital expenditure,
depreciation, and other financial data.
Time factor: the 1971 report, published in 1975, relates to a census taken during September 1971.
§ En.

160 Census of cinemas, café-bioscopes and drive-in theatres (Bureau of Statistics).
Government Printer, Bosman Street, P B X85, Pretoria.
1946/47- 1969/70. R 2.75 (R 3.75 abroad). 55p.
Time factor: the report of the 1969/70 census was published in 1975.
§ Af, En.

161 Licensed hotels, 1969 (Department of Statistics).
Government Printer, Bosman Street, P B X85, Pretoria.
R 0.60 (R 0.75 abroad). 18p.
The results of a census of hotels licensed to sell liquor, which includes data on trading revenue, beds
and bednights sold, percentage occupancy, employment and remuneration of employees, stocks, etc.
Time factor: the results of the census were published in 1971.
§ Af, En.

162 Census of accommodation establishments (Department of Statistics).
Government Printer, Bosman Street, P B X85, Pretoria.
1964/65- 1969-70. R 2.75 (R 3.75 abroad).
Time factor: the results of the census were published in 1971.
§ Af, En.

Refer also to 1129, 1130, 1132, 1134, 1138, 1176.

¶ E - Population

163 Population census (Department of Statistics).
Government Printer, Bosman Street, P B X85, Pretoria.
1865- 1970.
Final reports are:
Geographical distribution of the population (R 2.75 (R 3.75 abroad))
Dwellings - geographical district (R 2.75 (R 3.75 abroad))
Dwellings - provinces and metropolitan areas (R 2.75 (R 3.75 abroad))
Age, marital status and type of dwelling by districts and economic region (R 2.75 (R 3.75 abroad))
Families - geographical district (R 2.75 (R 3.75 abroad))
Families - provinces and metropolitan areas (R 2.75 (R 3.75 abroad))
Single ages, 1941-1970 (R 2.75 (R 3.75))
Occupations: age, level of education, marital status, citizenship, birthplace, national unit
(R 2.75 (R 3.75 abroad))
Occupations (income, industry and identity) (R 2.75 (R 3.75 abroad))
Occupations and industry by industry and economic region (R 2.75 (R 3.75 abroad))
Income and work status by industry and economic region (R 2.75 (R 3.75 abroad))
Industry (R 2.75 (R 3.75 abroad))
Personal income (R 2.75 (R 3.75 abroad))
Nature of education (R 2.75 (R 3.75 abroad))
Level of education (R 2.75 (R 3.75 abroad))
Metropolitan areas - Capetown (R 5.00 (R 6.25 abroad))
Metropolitan areas - East London (R 5.00 (R 6.25 abroad))
Xhosa (R 2.75 (R 3.75 abroad))
Zulu (R 5.00 (R 6.25 abroad))
Seshoeshoe (R 2.75 (R 3.75 abroad))
South Ndebele (R 2.75 (R 3.75 abroad))

[continued next page]

275

¶ E, continued

1163, continued

       North Ndebele (R 3.50 (R 4.50 abroad))
       Venda (R 2.75 (R 3.75 abroad))
       Tswana (R 2.75 (R 3.75 abroad))
       Sepedi (R 5.00 (R 6.25 abroad))
       Swazi (R 3.50 (R 4.50 abroad))
       Foreign Bantu (R 5.00 (R 6.25 abroad))
       South African Bantu with home language other than a South African Bantu Language
          (R 3.50 (R 4.50 abroad))
   Time factor: the reports were published between 1975 and 1977.
   §   Af, En.

1164   Population of South Africa, 1904-1970   (Department of Statistics).
       Government Printer, Bosman Street, P B X85, Pretoria.
            R 2.75 (R 3.75 abroad).   454p.
       Related to the 1970 census of population, this volume gives population statistics for 1904, 1911, 1921,
          1936, 1946, 1951, 1960 and 1970 for Whites, Coloureds, Asians, Bantu, by cities, towns,
          regions, etc.
       Time factor: published in 1976.
       §   Af, En.

1165   Population projections for the Republic of South Africa, 1970 to 2020   (Department of Statistics).
       Government Printer, Bosman Street, P B X85, Pretoria.
            R 2.75 (R 3.75 abroad).   20p.
       Projections of the population of Whites, Coloureds, Asians and South African Bantu, with the results of
          the 1970 population census taken as a base.
       Time factor: published in 1976.
       §   Af, En.

1166   Urban and rural population of South Africa, 1904 to 1960   (Department of Statistics).
       Government Printer, Bosman Street, P B X85, Pretoria.
            R 0.50 (R 0.65 abroad).   280p.
       Detailed statistics of the geographical distribution of the population.
       Time factor: published in 1968.
       §   Af, En.

1167   Migration statistics: tourists, immigrants and emigrants   (Department of Statistics).
       Government Printer, Bosman Street, P B X85, Pretoria.
       1924/64-   1970/71.   R 2.75 (R 3.75 abroad).   141p.
       Contains data on Whites (arrivals, departures, foreign and South African tourists), non-Whites,
          Whites - immigrants, Whites and non-Whites - migrants, and South African visitors to other
          countries.
       Time factor: the 1970/71 issue, published in 1974, has data for 1970/71.
       §   Af, En.

1168   Report on births...South Africa   (Department of Statistics).
       Government Printer, Bosman Street, P B X85, Pretoria.
       1964/71-   1972/74.   R 3.50 (R 4.40 abroad).   85p.
       Time factor: the 1972/1974 issue, published in 1977, has data for the years 1972 to 1974.
       §   Af, En.

1169   Report on marriages and divorces...South Africa   (Department of Statistics).
       Government Printer, Bosman Street, P B X85, Pretoria.
       1958-   1974.   R 2.75 (R 3.75 abroad).   79p.
       Time factor: the 1974 issue, published in 1976, has data for 1974.
       §   Af, En.

¶ E, continued

170   Report on deaths - Whites, Coloureds and Asians... South Africa   (Department of Statistics).
       Government Printer, **Bosman** Street, P B X85, Pretoria.
       1972-   1973.   R 5.00 (R 6.25 abroad).   167p.
       Time factor: the 1973 issue, published in 1977, has data for 1973.
       § Af, En.

171   Report on Bantu deaths in selected magisterial districts   (Department of Statistics).
       Government Printer, Bosman Street, P B X85, Pretoria.
       1968/71-   1974.   R 2.75 (R 3.75 abroad).   114p.
       Time factor: the 1974 issue, published in 1976, has data for 1974.
       § Af, En.

172   Labour statistics: wage rates, earnings and average hours worked...   (Department of Statistics).
       Government Printer, Bosman Street, P B X85, Pretoria.
       1965-   irregular.   R 2.75 (R 3.75 abroad).
       Each issue deals with one or more industries, i.e. commerce, printing and newspapers, engineering,
            building.
       Time factor: data is given for about five years and is published about 18 months to two years later.
       § Af, En.

173   Labour statistics: labour relations, trade unions   (Bureau of Statistics).
       Government Printer, Bosman Street, P B X85, Pretoria.
       1959/60-   1968/69.   R 0.60 (R 0.75 abroad).   25p.
       Results of the annual survey of trade unions, including statistical data on unions, membership,
            employment, revenue, expenditure, and assets.
       Time factor: the results of the 1968/69 survey were published in 1971.
       § Af, En.

       Refer also to 1129, 1130, 1132, 1133, 1134, 1135, 1136, 1138.

‘ F - Social

i. Standard of living

174   Survey of family expenditure   (Bureau of Statistics).
       Government Printer, Bosman Street, P B X85, Pretoria.
       1955-   1966.   3 vols.
       Content:
            Detailed expenditure of families   (R 0.50 (R 0.65 abroad))
            Family income   (R 0.50 (R 0.65 abroad))
            Detailed expenditure of families according to occupational groups, income groups and family
                 composition   (R 0.60 (R 0.75 abroad))
       § Af, En.

175   Statistics of houses and domestic servants...and of flats: eleven principal urban areas of South Africa
            (Department of Statistics).
       Government Printer, Bosman Street, P B X85, Pretoria.
       1938/65-   1975.   R 2.00 (R 2.50 abroad).   46p.
       Contains statistics of houses and flats occupied by Whites, and of domestic servants, from information
            collected for the annual survey.
       Time factor: the 1975 issue, published late 1976, has data for 1975 and also for several earlier years.
       § Af, En.

¶   F.i,   continued

1176   Report on prices   (Department of Statistics).
            Government Printer, Bosman Street, P B X85, Pretoria.
            1973-   1975.   R 2.75 (R 3.75 abroad).   115p.
            Contains data on wholesale prices of commodities, retail prices of commodities, and prices of services.
                Data collected for use in compilation of the wholesale and retail price indices, etc.
            Time factor: the 1975 issue, published in 1976, has data for 1975 and for 1974 in some tables.
            §   Af, En.

            Note: prior to 1973 there were two separate publications, "Wholesale prices of commodities" and
                "Retail prices of commodities and services".

            Refer also to 1131, 1135, 1137.

     ii.   Health and welfare

1177   Census of health services...medical practitioners and dentists   (Department of Statistics).
            1963-   2nd, 1972-1973.   R 2.75 (R 3.75 abroad).   122p.
            Time factor: the report of the 1972-1973 census was published late 1976.
            §   Af, En.

            Refer also to 1129, 1134.

    iii.   Education and leisure

1178   Education - principal statistics   (Department of Statistics).
            Government Printer, Bosman Street, P B X85, Pretoria.
            1968-   1972.   R 0.75 (R 0.95 abroad).   20p.
            An early release of certain statistics relating to schools for Whites, Coloureds, Indians and Chinese,
                Bantu, including numbers of schools, pupils and teachers for South Africa as a whole and for
                each state.
            Time factor: the 1972 issue, published in 1973, has data for 1972.
            §   Af, En.

1179   Education of Whites   (Department of Statistics).
            Government Printer, Bosman Street, P B X85, Pretoria.
            1957/63-   1974.   R 3.50 (R 4.00 abroad).   63p.
            Contains statistics for the whole range of education for Whites, including pre-primary, primary, and
                secondary ordinary education, tertiary education, special education, and other schools.   Statistical
                tables are included in the text.
            Time factor: the 1974 report, published in 1977, has data for 1974 and some earlier years.
            §   Af, En.

1180   Education: Coloured and Asians   (Department of Statistics).
            Government Printer, Bosman Street, P B X85, Pretoria.
            1957/63-   1973.   R 2.75 (R 3.75 abroad).   71p.
            Contains data on State and State-aided schools, private schools, and teacher training colleges,
                including enrolments, staff, etc.
            Time factor: the 1973 report, published in 1976, has data for the years 1969 to 1973.
            §   Af, En.

            Refer also to 1129, 1134.

¶   F,   continued

iv. Justice

1181   Statistics of offences and of penal institutions   (Bureau of Statistics).
         Government Printer, Bosman Street, P B X85, Pretoria.
         1949/62-1963/64-   1967/68.   R 0.60 (R 0.75 abroad).   145p.
         Time factor: the 1967/68 issue, published in 1971, has data for the year 1967/68.
         §   Af, En.

         Refer also to 1132, 1134, 1138.

¶   G - Finance

1182   Monthly release of money and banking statistics   (South Africa Reserve Bank).
         South Africa Reserve Bank, Church Square, P O Box 427, Pretoria.
         1967-   not priced.
         A two-page leaflet of up-to-date statistics of money and banking.
         §   En.

         Refer also to 1129, 1131, 1132, 1133, 1134, 1135, 1137, 1138.

i. Banking

         Refer to 1129, 1131.

ii. Public finance

1183   Local government statistics   (Department of Statistics).
         1959/60-   1974/75.   2 vols.
         The results of a survey of financial statistics of local authorities, the reports are:
              Part I: Orange Free State; part II: Transvaal   (R 2.75 (R 3.75 abroad))
              Part III: Natal; part IV: Cape   (R 3.50 (R 4.40 abroad))
         Time factor: the reports of the 1974/75 survey were published in June and December 1976.
         §   Af, En.

1184   Divisional council statistics   (Department of Statistics).
         Government Printer, Bosman Street, P B X85, Pretoria.
         1964/66-   1975.   R 2.75 (R 3.75 abroad).
         A complete survey of financial statistics of divisional councils.
         Time factor: the 1975 issue, published 1977, has data for 1975.
         §   Af, En.

1185   Anticipated capital expenditure of the public sector   (Department of Statistics).
         Department of Statistics, Steyn's Buildings, 270 Schoeman Street, P B X44, Pretoria.
         1968/70-   1976 to 1977.   R 0.75 (R 0.95 abroad).   c30p.
         Time factor: the 1976 to 1977 issue, published in 1976, has actual expenditure data for 1975 and
              anticipated expenditure for 1976 and 1977.
         §   Af, En.

1186   Statistics of Bantu Affairs Administration Boards   (Department of Statistics).
         Government Printer, Bosman Street, P B X85, Pretoria.
         1973/74-   1974/75.   R 2.75 (R 3.75 abroad).   25p.
         A complete survey of the financial statistics of the Boards.
         Time factor: the 1974/75 issue, published in 1976, has data for 1974/75.
         §   Af, En.

1187   National accounts of the Bantu homelands   (Department of Statistics).
          Government Printer, Bosman Street, P B X85, Pretoria.
          1969/70-   2nd, 1971 to 1974.   R 3.50 (R 4.40 abroad).   67p.
          Official estimates of the gross domestic product and public expenditure for each homeland in South
              Africa.   Excludes Transkei - to be published separately.
          Time factor: the 1971 to 1974 issue, published early 1977, has data for the years 1971 to 1974.
          §   Af, En.

1188   Gross domestic product at factor cost, 1911-1968   (Bureau of Statistics).
          Government Printer, Bosman Street, P B X85, Pretoria.
                          R 0.60 (R 0.75 abroad).   59p.
          Official estimates of gross domestic product at factor costs.
          Time factor: published in 1970, the work covers the years 1911 to 1968.
          §   Af, En.

1189   Gross geographical product by magisterial district, 1968   (Bureau of Statistics).
          Government Printer, Bosman Street, P B X85, Pretoria.
                          R 2.75 (R 3.75 abroad).   25p.
          Contains data on gross domestic product at factor incomes by magisterial district, and remuneration of
              employees by magisterial district.
          Time factor: data relates to the year 1968.
          §   Af, En.

          Refer also to 1129, 1130, 1131, 1136.

    iii. Company finance

1190   Transfers of rural immovable property   (Department of Statistics).
          Government Printer, Bosman Street, P B X85, Pretoria.
          1962/63-   1974/75.   R 2.75 (R 3.75 abroad).   37p.
          Time factor: the 1974/75 issue, published mid-1976, has data for the year ended 31st March 1975.
          §   Af, En.

1191   Mortgage bond statistics   (Department of Statistics).
          Government Printer, Bosman Street, P B X85, Pretoria.
          1946/63-   1975.   R 2.75 (R 3.75 abroad).   21p.
          Statistics of mortgage bonds registered, increased and cancelled.
          Time factor: the 1975 issue, published mid-1976, has data for 1975.
          §   Af, En.

1192   Census of accounting, auditing and bookkeeping   (Department of Statistics).
          Government Printer, Bosman Street, P B X85, Pretoria.
          1962-   1970.   R 2.75 (R 3.75 abroad).   15p.
          Time factor: the report of the 1970 census was published in 1974.
          §   Af, En.

1193   Financial statistics of companies   (Department of Statistics).
          Government Printer, Bosman Street, P B X85, Pretoria.
          1970-   1970.   R 2.75 (R 3.75 abroad).   180p.
          The results of a census of companies, including data on number of companies, share capital, assets,
              revenue; public and private companies according to economic activity; public and private
              companies according to years of incorporation.
          Time factor: the results were published in 1975.
          §   Af, En.

¶   G.iii,   continued

194   A survey of the accounts of companies in manufacturing, construction, commerce, real estate, and services,
          including transport   (Department of Statistics).
          Government Printer, Bosman Street, P B X85, Pretoria.
          1965/66-1966/68-   1970/71 & 1969/70.   R 0.75 (R 0.90 abroad).   90p.
          The consolidated accounts of 285 companies whose shares are listed on the Johannesburg stock exchange
              and 137 non-listed companies.
          Time factor: the 1970/71 & 1969/70 issue, published in 1973, has data for the fiscal years 1970/71 and
              1969/70.
          §   Af, En.

195   A survey of the accounts of mining companies...   (Department of Statistics).
          Government Printer, Bosman Street, P B X85, Pretoria.
          1962-   1974/75 & 1973/74.   R 2.75 (R 3.75 abroad).   85p.
          An analysis of the accounts of companies owning mines in the production stage.
          Time factor: the 1974/75 & 1973/74 issue, published in 1976, has data for the fiscal years 1974/75
              and 1973/74.
          §   Af, En.

196   A survey of the accounts of companies in secondary and tertiary industries   (Department of Statistics).
          Government Printer, Bosman Street, P B X85, Pretoria.
          1965/66 & 1964/65-   1974/75 & 1973/74.   R 2.75 (R 3.75 abroad).   94p.
          Summations and analyses of the consolidated accounts of 548 companies engaged in secondary and
              tertiary industries, including 404 whose shares are listed on the Johannesburg stock exchange.
          Time factor: the 1974/75 & 1973/74 issue, published in 1976, has data for the fiscal years 1974/75
              and 1973/74.
          §   Af, En.

197   Census of boards of executors and trust companies   (Department of Statistics).
          Government Printer, Bosman Street, P B X85, Pretoria.
          1963/64-   1973/74 & 1974/75.   R 2.75 (R 3.75 abroad).   c10p.
          Time factor: the 1973/74 & 1974/75 issue, published in 1976, gives results for the two fiscal years.
          §   Af, En.

          Refer also to 1130, 1132, 1133.

   iv. Investment

198   Census of investment companies and other financial enterprises, 1964-65   (Bureau of Statistics).
          Government Printer, Bosman Street, P B X85, Pretoria.
                              R 0.50 (R 0.60 abroad).   22p.
          Time factor: the report of the census was published in 1968.
          §   Af, En.

          Refer also to 1131, 1137.

   v. Insurance

199   Census of insurance services   (Bureau of Statistics).
          Government Printer, Bosman Street, P B X85, Pretoria.
          1964/65-   1969/70.   R 0.75 (R 0.95 abroad).   7p.
          Time factor: the report of the census of 1969/70 was published in 1973.
          §   Af, En.

SOUTH AFRICA, continued

¶   H - Transport and communications

1200   Census of transport and allied services   (Department of Statistics).
          Government Printer, Bosman Street, P B X85, Pretoria.
          1970-   1970.   R 2.75 (R 3.75 abroad).   37p.
          Contains principal statistics by groups, by income size groups, and by economic regions; and detailed
              statistics of employment; income, expenditure and net profit; capital expenditure; fixed assets
              sold and book value of fixed assets; appropriation accounts; nature of transport activities and
              number of establishments; totals (air, sea and coast, passenger, etc); transport of goods by road;
              allied services and other services; number of establishments and total income; stocks of vehicles
              and other mobile equipment by groups.
          Time factor: the census was taken in 1969-70 and the report published in 1975.
          §   Af, En.

          Refer also to 1129, 1130, 1132, 1133, 1135, 1136.

     ii. Road

1201   Statistics of new vehicles licensed   (Department of Statistics).
          Government Printer, Bosman Street, P B X85, Pretoria.
          1966-   1974-76.   R 3.50 (R 4.40 abroad).   45p.
          Includes data on motor cars, minibuses, buses, commercial vehicles, motor cycles, tractors, trailers,
              and other vehicles, mainly construction and farming equipment, by province and licencing district.
          Time factor: the 1974-76 issue, published in 1977, has data from 1st July 1974 to 30th June 1976.
          §   Af, En.

1202   Motor vehicle statistics as at...all vehicles   (Department of Statistics).
          Government Printer, Bosman Street, P B X85, Pretoria.
          1961-   1972.   R 2.75 (R 3.75 abroad).
          Time factor: the 1972 issue, published 1973, has data for the situation on 30th June 1972.
          §   Af, En.

1203   Road traffic accidents   (Department of Statistics).
          Government Printer, Bosman Street, P B X85, Pretoria.
          1962-   1975.   R 3.50 (R 4.40 abroad).   80p.
          Time factor: the 1975 report, published in 1977, has data for 1975.
          §   Af, En.

          Refer also to 1138.

     v. Telecommunications and postal services

          Refer to 1129, 1134.

Central statistical office

1204   Instituto Nacional de Estatística   [National Institute of Statistics],
Avenida del Generalísimo 91,
Madrid 16, Spain.
† 459 07 00/04, 08, 12, 18, 50.

    The Institute is responsible for the collection, analysis and publication of all economic and social statistics for Spain and for Spanish territories overseas.   Spanish North Africa now consists of the two enclaves on the African coast, Ceuta and Melilla, and the Canary Islands.

Statistical publications

¶   A - General

1205   Anuario estadístico de España   [Statistical yearbook of Spain]   (Instituto Nacional de Estadística).
Instituto Nacional de Estadística, Avenida del Generalísimo 91, Madrid 16, Spain.
1912-   1975.   Ptas 1,200.   798p.
Main sections:

Area and climate	External trade
Population	Finance
Agriculture, forestry, livestock	Health service
and fisheries	Education
Industry	Justice and culture
Transport and communications	

Includes data for Ceuta and Melilla, Canary Islands and also the ex-Spanish territories of Sahara, Ifni, and Equatorial Guinea.
Time factor: the 1975 edition, published in 1976, has data for several years to 1974.
§   Es.

1206   Resumen estadístico del Africa Española   [Statistical abstract for Spanish Africa]   (Direccion General de Plazas y Provincias Africanas and Instituto de Estudios Africanos).
Instituto Nacional de Estadística, Avenida del Generalísimo 91, Madrid 16, Spain.
1953/55-   1965/66.   Ptas 250.   538p.
A general pocketbook covering Ceuta and Melilla, Ifni, Sahara, and Equatorial Guinea.   Subjects include area, climate, population, agriculture, forestry, livestock, fisheries, industry, trade and prices, transport and communications, public finance, private finance, employment and social security, health and benefits, culture, justice, and religion.
Time factor: the 1965/66 edition, published in 1967, has data for several years to 1965/66.
§   Es.

1207   Boletín mensual de estadística   [Monthly bulletin of statistics]   (Instituto Nacional de Estadística).
Instituto Nacional de Estadística, Avenida del Generalísimo 91, Madrid 16, Spain.
1918-   Ptas 100 or Ptas 900 yr.
Contains data on population, tourism, radio and television, culture, health, justice, production and consumption, foreign trade, transport, communications, finance, labour, prices, and cost of living.   Includes data for Ceuta, Melilla and the Canary Islands.
Time factor: tables usually include data for the last five years and the last 12 months, the latest figures available varying from three to six months prior to the date of the issue.
§   Es.

¶   B - Production   ₣

ii. Agriculture, fisheries, forestry, etc.

    Refer to 1205, 1206, 1207.

¶ B, continued

iii. Industry

Refer to 1205, 1206, 1207.

¶ C - External trade

1208 Estadística del comercio exterior [Foreign trade statistics] (Camara Oficial de Comercio, Industria y Navegación de la Provincia de Santa Cruz de Tenerife and Instituto Tinerfeño de Expansion Economica).
Camara Oficial de Comercio, Industria y Navegación, Santa Cruz de Tenerife, Canary Islands.
1970- 1975. not priced. 291p.
Contains detailed tables of imports and exports arranged by commodities, and arranged by countries of origin and destination sub-divided by commodities for the province of Santa Cruz de Tenerife. Also imports and exports by commodity and summary imports and exports by countries for the province of Las Palmas.
Time factor: the 1975 issue, published late 1976, has data for 1975.
§ Es.

1209 Estadística del comercio exterior de la Provincia de Las Palmas [Foreign trade statistics for the province of Las Palmas] (Camara Oficial de Comercio, Industria y Navegación, Las Palmas).
Camara Oficial de Comercio, Industria y Navegación, Las Palmas, Canary Islands.
1971- 1975. not priced. 384p.
Contains detailed tables of imports and exports arranged by commodities, and arranged by countries of origin and destination sub-divided by commodities for the province of Las Palmas. Also imports and exports by commodity and summary imports and exports by country for the province of Santa Cruz de Tenerife.
Time factor: the 1975 issue, published late 1976, has data for 1975.
§ Es.

1210 Estadístico del comercio exterior de España: comercio por zonas, admisiones, depósitos y transitos [Statistics of the foreign trade of Spain: trade between Spain and its colonies; temporary imports, free deposits and transit trade] (Dirección General de Aduanas).
Dirección General de Aduanas, Guzmán el Bueno, 137, Madrid 3, Spain.
1922- 1970. Ptas 300. 427p.
Contains data on the trade between the Peninsula, Canary Islands, Spanish Sahara, Ceuta and Melilla, as well as temporary imports, free deposits and transit trade.
Time factor: the 1970 edition, published in 1972, has data for 1970.
§ Es.

Refer also to 1205, 1206, 1207.

¶ D - Internal distribution and service trades

Refer to 1206, 1207.

¶ E - Population

1211 Censo de la población y de las viviendas de España [Population and housing census of Spain] (Instituto Nacional de Estadística).
Instituto Nacional de Estadística, Avenida del Generalisimo 91, Madrid 16, Spain.
1957- 1970. Vol.I costs Ptas 600 (paper) or Ptas 800 (bound).
Volume I of the census contains data for Ceuta and Melilla and the Canary Islands.
§ Es.

Refer also to 1205, 1206, 1207.

¶   F - Social

i. Standard of living

Refer to 1207.

ii. Health and welfare

Refer to 1205, 1206, 1207.

iii. Education and leisure

Refer to 1205, 1206, 1207.

iv. Justice

Refer to 1205, 1206, 1207.

¶   G - Finance

Refer to 1205, 1206, 1207.

¶   H - Transport and communications

Refer to 1205, 1206, 1207.

Central statistical office

1212   Department of Statistics,
        Ministry of Finance and National Economy,
        P O Box 700, Khartoum.
        t Khartoum 77255.
        tx 324 Khartoum Answerback EIMAR KM.

    The Department is responsible for national accounts statistics, foreign trade statistics, demographic statistics, censuses and surveys, and other internal economic and social statistics.   Unpublished statistical information can be supplied if available.

Libraries

    There is a library in the Department of Statistics where statistical publications may be consulted.

Libraries and information services abroad

    Copies of the publications of the Department of Statistics are available for reference in Sudanese embassies abroad, including:
        United Kingdom   Sudanese Embassy, 3-5 Cleveland Row, London SW1.   t 01-839 8080.
        U.S.A.   Sudanese Embassy, 600 N H Avenue NW, Washington, DC.   t 338-8565.

Bibliographies

    The Department of Statistics issues an annual "List of publications".

Statistical publications

¶   A - General

1213   Statistical yearbook   (Department of Statistics).
        Department of Statistics, Ministry of Finance and National Economy, P O Box 700, Khartoum.
        1970-   2nd, 1973.   not priced.   no pagination.
        Mainly devised to summarise and survey the economic, social and cultural statistics of the Sudan.   Main
            sections are:

Maps	Industry
Sudan in brief	Transport and communication
Climate	Foreign trade & balance of payments
Population	Public finance
Labour force, employment and unemployment	Money and credit
	Labour market
Education	Household income and expenditure,
Health	price indices & housing conditions
Agriculture, livestock and forestry	National accounts

        Time factor: the 1973 edition, published in 1974, has data for varying periods up to 1972 or 1973.
        §   En.

¶   A, continued

1214   Sudan facts and figures   (Ministry of Culture and Information).
            Ministry of Culture and Information, P O Box 291, Khartoum.
            irregular.   1974.   not priced.   62p.
            Main sections:

Area	Communications
Climate	Foreign trade
Population	Balance of payments
Economic survey	Banking and finance
Agriculture	Education and culture
Industry	Public health

            Time factor: the 1974 edition, published late 1974, has data for the years 1956 to 1973.
            §   En.

1215   Economic and financial bulletin   (Bank of Sudan).
            Bank of Sudan, Khartoum.
            1960–   quarterly.   not priced.
            Includes a statistical appendix with data on foreign trade, cotton seed production, cotton shipments,
                banking, industrial production, etc.
            §   En.

1216   Economic survey   (National Planning Commission).
            National Planning Commission, Khartoum.
            1959–   1974.   not priced.   246p.
            Contains chapters on world economic conditions, population and social development, development of
                the economy as a whole, production, transport and communication, balance of payments and foreign
                trade, money and credit, public finance, and an evaluation of five-year plan performance.
                Tables are included in the text.
            Time factor: the 1974 edition, published mid-1975, has data to 1973/74.
            §   En.

1217   Annual report   (Bank of Sudan).
            Bank of Sudan, Khartoum.
            1960–   1974.   not priced.   c140p.
            Includes data on the world economic situation, agricultural and industrial production, foreign trade,
                money supply, balance of payments for exchange reserves, bilateral agreement, flow of external
                resources, banking and credit, government finance, currency in circulation, accounts of the Bank
                of Sudan.   There are statistical and graphical appendices.
            Time factor: the 1974 edition, published early 1975, has data for 10 years or more to 1974.
            §   En.

1218   Internal statistics   (Department of Statistics).
            Department of Statistics, Ministry of Finance and National Economy, P O Box 700, Khartoum.
            1960/61–   1972.   not priced.   60p.
            Contains data on retail prices; wholesale prices; production; sales; exports, etc. of cotton, gum,
                groundnuts, animals, etc; transport and communication; public finance; education; medical, etc.
            Time factor: the 1972 edition, published in 1975, has data for 1972 or 1971/72 and some earlier years.
            §   Ar, En.

SUDAN, continued

¶   B - Production

ii. Agriculture, fisheries, forestry, etc.

1219   Yearbook of agricultural statistics   (Department of Agricultural Economics, Ministry of Agriculture, Food
            and Natural Resources).
        Department of Agricultural Economics, Ministry of Agriculture, Food and Natural Resources, Khartoum.
        1974-   1974.   2½ Sudanese pounds.   118p.
        Main sections:
            Summary of crop statistics by provinces   Other crops
            Land utilisation and irrigation   Crop statistics by province
            Cotton   Horticultural crops
            Dura (sorghum)   Livestock
            Dukhn (millet)   Agricultural machinery
            Wheat   Agricultural exports
            Groundnuts   Rainfall, etc
            Sesame
        Time factor: the 1974 edition, published mid-1974, has data for the crop years 1970/71, 1971/72,
            1972/73, and preliminary estimates for 1973/74.
        §   En.

        Note: supersedes the "Bulletin of agricultural statistics".

1220   Current agricultural statistics   (Department of Agricultural Economics, Ministry of Agriculture, Food and
            Natural Resources).
        Department of Agricultural Economics, Ministry of Agriculture, Food and Natural Resources, Khartoum.
        1975-   periodic.   not priced.
        Contains data on crops; estimates of area, production and average yield; sugar; supply and utilisation
            of cereals and oil seeds; prices of agricultural commodities; foreign trade; miscellaneous
            (mechanisation, irrigation, rainfall, etc).
        Time factor: Vol.1, no.1, was dated July 1975 and vol.1, no.2, June 1976.   The second issue has
            data for several years to 1975 or 1974/75.
        §   En.

1221   A report on the census of pump schemes   (Department of Statistics).
        Department of Statistics, P O Box 700, Khartoum.
                1963.   P 100 each vol.   2 vols.
        Vol.I contains a co-ordinated picture of the area irrigated by pump schemes in the Republic of the
            Sudan, and vol.II is in five parts, one for each of the provinces - Blue Nile, Northern, Khartoum,
            Upper Nile, and Kassala.
        Time factor: the census was taken in June-August 1963 and the results were published between 1965 and
            1967.
        §   En.

1222   Census of agriculture   (Department of Statistics).
        Department of Statistics, P O Box 700, Khartoum.
        1965-   1965.   P 40 to P 100 each vol.
        Published results include:-
            Some results of the pilot sample census of agriculture in some councils of the Republic of the
                Sudan, 1963-1964.
            A report of the pilot surveys conducted in 1965-1966 and 1966-1967 for estimating the yield rate
                of wheat in pump irrigation schemes of the Northern province.
            A brief report on the sample census of agriculture...in Kassala province.
            A brief report on the sample census of agriculture...in Darfur province.
            A brief report on the sample census of agriculture...in Kordofan province.
            A brief report on the sample census of agriculture...in Northern and Khartoum province.
            A report on the sample census of agriculture...in the Blue Nile province.
            Instructions to enumerators. Concepts, definitions and procedures.
        Time factor: the reports were published between 1968 and 1969; the instructions in 1964.
        §   En.

¶   B.ii,   continued

1223   Sudan cotton bulletin   (Cotton Public Corporation).
         Cotton Public Corporation, P O Box 1672, Khartoum.
               monthly.   not priced.
         Reviews the Sudan cotton situation and gives statistics of cotton sales for export by country and type.
         Time factor: each issue has data for that month.
         §   En.

1224   Sugar transport study   (Transport and Communications Section, Ministry of Finance, Planning and
           National Economy).
         Ministry of Finance, Planning and National Economy, Khartoum.
               not priced.   108p.
         Includes statistical data on production, import, consumption, etc. of sugar, for varying periods.
         Time factor: published in December 1976.
         §   En.

         Refer also to 1213, 1214, 1215, 1217, 1218.

     iii.   Industry

         Refer to 1213, 1214, 1215, 1216, 1217, 1218.

¶   C - External trade

1225   Foreign trade statistics report   (Department of Statistics).
         Department of Statistics, P O Box 700, Khartoum.
         1947-   1976.   not priced.   306p.
         Main tables show detailed statistics of imports and exports arranged by commodity and sub-divided
           by countries of origin and destination.   Summary tables show trade of commodities by section,
           division and group of the classification system.
         Time factor: the 1976 issue, published early 1977, has data for 1976.
         §   Ar, En.

1226   Foreign trade statistics   (Department of Statistics).
         Department of Statistics, P O Box 700, Khartoum.
         1947-   monthly.   not priced.
         Main tables show detailed statistics of imports and exports arranged by commodity and sub-divided by
           countries of origin and destination.   There are also summary tables.
         Time factor: each issue has data for that month and cumulated figures for the year to date, and is
           published some months later.
         §   Ar, En.

1227   Foreign trade annual statistical digest   (Bank of Sudan).
         Bank of Sudan, Khartoum.
         1968-   1973.   not priced.   53p.
         Contains data on foreign trade by commodity and by countries of origin and destination.
         Time factor: the 1973 issue, published in 1974, has monthly,quarterly and annual figures for 1973.
         §   En.

1228   Foreign trade statistical digest   (Bank of Sudan).
         Bank of Sudan, Khartoum.
         1968-   quarterly.   not priced.
         Contains data on foreign trade by commodity and by countries of origin and destination.
         Time factor: each issue has cumulated figures for the year to date and corresponding comparative
           figures for earlier years; it is published several months after the end of the period covered.
         §   En.

         Refer also to 1213, 1214, 1215, 1216, 1217, 1218, 1220, 1223, 1224.

¶   D - Internal distribution and service trades

     Refer to 1218.

¶   E - Population

1229   Population and housing survey   (Department of Statistics).
       Department of Statistics, P O Box 700, Khartoum.
       1955/56-   1964/66.
       The survey replaces the first population census taken in 1955/56.   Data includes numbers of population
         by sex and age, marital status, place of birth, in-migrants, nationality, educational attainment,
         economic activity and status, labour force, housing conditions, households, average monthly
         income, etc.   There is a general survey of the urban areas and volumes for the urban areas of each
         province (Northern, Kordogan, Blue Nile, Khartoum, Darfur, and Kassala).   There are also
         volumes for each of the main towns (Port Sudan, Khartoum, El Gedaref, Atbara, Kassala,
         Omdurman, Nyala, El Fasher, El Obeid, En Nahoud, Kosti, Wad Medani, and El Geneina).
       Time factor: the reports were published between 1966 and 1968, the surveys for the towns having been
         taken in 1964/65 and for the urban areas in 1964/66.
       §   En.

1230   [Population projections for the six year plan 1977/78-1982/83]   (Department of Statistics).
       Department of Statistics, P O Box 700, Khartoum.
                       not priced.   86p.
       Time factor: published in 1976.
       §   Ar.

       Refer also to 1213, 1214, 1216.

¶   F - Social

i. Standard of living

1231   Household budget survey in the Sudan   (Department of Statistics).
       Department of Statistics, P O Box 700, Khartoum.
       1965-   1967/68.   not priced.
       The survey was confined to the settled population and was designed to yield estimates separately for the
         urban, semi-urban and rural areas.   The investigation covered about 7,000 households
         representing different areas as well as different income groups.
       §   En.

       Refer also to 1213.

ii. Health and welfare

1232   Annual statistical report   (Vital and Health Statistics Division, Ministry of Health).
       Vital and Health Statistics Division, Ministry of Health, Khartoum.
       1969-   1975.   not priced.   113p.
       Contains data on malaria control project, proportional mortality rate by age, National Health
         Laboratory Chemical Pathology Department, paediatric surgery, cancer registry, and cases
         treated in all Health Units (in- and out-patients).
       Time factor: the 1975 edition, published in 1976, has data for 1975.
       §   Ar, En.

       Refer also to 1213, 1214, 1218.

SUDAN, continued

¶   F,   continued

iii. Education and leisure

1233   Educational statistics   (Bureau of Educational Statistics, Ministry of Education).
            Ministry of Education, Khartoum.
            1959/60-   1969/70.   not priced.   c80p.
            Contains data on schools, teachers, pupils and students from elementary to university education, and
                also teacher training.
            Time factor: the 1969/70 issue, published in 1970, has data for the academic year 1969/70.
            §   Ar & En eds.

        Note: from 1928 to 1959/60 statistics of education were published in the annual report of the Ministry
            of Education.

        Refer also to 1213, 1214, 1218.

¶   G - Finance

        Refer to 1214, 1216, 1217.

i. Banking

        Refer to 1214, 1217.

ii. Public finance

1234   National income accounts and supporting tables   (Department of Statistics).
            Department of Statistics, P O Box 700, Khartoum.
            1966/67-   1971/72.   not priced.   188p.
            Includes statistics of production value, value added, indirect taxes, consumption of fixed capital and
                compensation of employees, etc, by kind of industrial activity.
            Time factor: the 1971/72 issue, published April 1974, has data for the fiscal year 1971/72.
            §   Ar, En.

        Refer also to 1213, 1216, 1217, 1218.

¶   H - Transport and communications

1235   Transport statistical bulletin   (Transport and Communications Section, National Planning Commission).
            Transport and Communications Section, National Planning Commission, Khartoum.
            1974-   1974.   LS 1.00.   89p.
            Contains data on trends in the overall transport system, the rail transport system, the road transport
                system, river transport, the air transport system, and ports and shipping.   Also data on the
                pipeline, freight traffic, passenger traffic, financial performance, operations, and inventories.
            Time factor: the 1974 issue, published in 1975, has data for 1973/74 or 1972/73 and also earlier
                figures in some tables.   It is intended to become an annual publication.
            §   En.

        Refer also to 1213, 1214, 1216, 1218.

291

¶   H,   continued

ii. Road

1236   Road traffic survey: origin and destination statistics   (Transport and Communications Section, National
              Planning Commission).
           National Planning Commission, Khartoum.
                          LS 1.00.   228p.
           A research study.
           Time factor: the survey was undertaken and also published in 1975.
           §   En.

iii. Rail

1237   Sudan Railways annual report
           Sudan Railways, Atbara.
           1964/65-   1972/73.   not priced.
           Includes statistics of operations, rolling stock, etc, as well as finances.
           Time factor: the 1972/73 report, published in 1974, has data for 1972/73.
           §   En.

Central statistical office

¶ 238   Central Statistical Office,
        P O Box 456, Mbabane.
        t 2774.

        The Office is responsible for the collection, collation and publication of economic and social statistics for the country.

Library

        The Central Statistical Office is organising a library for the provision of economic and statistical information from the comprehensive collection it aims to build up.

Statistical publications

¶   A - General

¶ 239   Swaziland: annual statistical bulletin   (Central Statistical Office).
            Central Statistical Office, P O Box 456, Mbabane.
            1966-   1975.   E 2.00.   157p.
            Main sections:
                Basic demographic and economic data   Fuel and power
                Land and climate   Employment and earnings
                Population and vital statistics   Industry, commerce & construction
                Migration, tourism   Banking and insurance
                Agriculture   Public finance
                Foreign trade   National accounts
                Transport and communications   Education
                Prices and cost of living   Health
                Mining   Judiciary and police
            Time factor: the 1975 edition, published in 1975, contains data for several years to 1974.
            §   En.

240   Quarterly digest of statistics   (Central Statistical Office).
            Central Statistical Office, P O Box 456, Mbabane.
            1967-   E 1.00 each issue.
            Contains data on foreign trade, mineral production, new registrations of motor vehicles, airport traffic,
                migration, tourism, retail price index, health, agriculture, national income, banking, etc.
            Time factor: each issue contains quarterly statistics for two or three years up to about six months prior
                to the date of the issue.
            §   En.

241   Economic review   (Swaziland Government).
            Swaziland Government, Mbabane.
            1970/71-   1974.   not priced.   25p.
            Contains data on gross domestic product, major exports, paid employment by sector, imports of
                equipment and materials for investment, public finance, and retail price indices.
            Time factor: the 1974 issue, published 1975, has data for the years 1970 to 1974.
            §   En.

242   Swaziland: report for the year...   (Commonwealth Office).
            H M Stationery Office, P O Box 569, London SE1 9NH, England.
            1946-   1966.   £0.75.   149p.
            Includes statistical tables in the text on population, labour and wages, finance and taxation, foreign
                trade, production, and social services.
            Time factor: the 1966 report (the last to be published) contains data for several years to 1966 and was
                published in 1968.
            §   En.

¶   A,   continued

1243   Statistical review and economic indicators   (Central Statistical Office).
            Central Statistical Office, P O Box 456, Mbabane.
            1967-   monthly.   not priced.
            Contains data on imports, exports, production, transport, tourism, retail price index, health, banking,
                etc.
            §   En.

¶   B - Production

i. Mines and mining

1244   Annual report of the Geological Survey and Mines Department...
            Geological Survey and Mines Department, Ministry of Industry, Mines and Tourism, P O Box 9,
                Mbabane.
            1958-   1974.   R 0.75.   51p.
            Includes data on production of about 10 minerals, exports and sales, labour on and below the surface,
                and earnings.
            Time factor: the 1974 edition, published in 1975, has data for 1974.
            §   En.

            Refer also to 1239, 1240.

ii. Agriculture, fisheries, forestry, etc.

1245   Agricultural sample census (Swazi Nation Land)   (Central Statistical Office).
            Central Statistical Office, P O Box 456, Mbabane.
            1970/71-   1971/72.   E 4.00.   2 vols.
            Part I: Swazi Nation Land; part II: Individual tenure farms (adjoining RDA's).
            Time factor: the report of the census was published in 1972.
            §   En.

1246   Census of individual tenure farms   (Central Statistical Office).
            Central Statistical Office, P O Box 456, Mbabane.
            1968/69-   1974/75.   E 0.25.   c50p.
            Time factor: the 1974/75 census results were published late 1976.
            § · En.

1247   Report on annual survey of Swazi Nation Land   (Central Statistical Office).
            Central Statistical Office, P O Box 456, Mbabane.
            1972/73-   1974/75.   E 0.25.   c25p.
            Time factor: the 1974/75 census results were published late 1975.
            §   En.

1248   Report on commercial timber plantation and wood products statistics   (Central Statistical Office).
            Central Statistical Office, P O Box 456, Mbabane.
            1970-   1974.   E 0.25.   c30p.
            Time factor: the 1974 report was published late 1976.
            §   En.

1249   Annual report of the Ministry of Agriculture
            Ministry of Agriculture, Mbabane.
            1963-   1975.   not priced.   224p.
            The report has sections on the various departments of the Ministry (Agriculture, Veterinary, Rural
                Development Areas, Extension and Training, Economy and Farm Management) and a few statistical
                tables are included in the text.
            §   En.

            Refer also to 1239, 1240.

¶   B,   continued

iii. Industry

250   Census of industrial production   (Central Statistical Office).
      Central Statistical Office, P O Box 456, Mbabane.
      1967-   1973.   E 0.25.   31p.
      Contains data on summary of operations by industry group, etc; gross output analysis for mining,
          manufacturing and utilities construction; service output analysis; analysis of employment, wages
          and salaries; analysis of fixed capital formation; and analysis of productivity.
      Time factor: the 1973 report, published in 1975, has data for 1973 and for two or three earlier years.
      §   En.

      Refer also to 1239, 1241, 1242, 1243.

iv. Construction

      Refer to 1239.

v. Energy

251   Annual report and statement of accounts   (Swaziland Electricity Board).
      Swaziland Electricity Board, P O Box 258, Mbabane.
      1962-   1975/76.   not priced.
      Includes a statistical section with the Board's accounts and also operating statistics.
      Time factor: the 1975/76 report, published in 1976, has data for the fiscal year 1975/76.
      §   En.

      Refer also to 1239.

¶   C - External trade

      Refer to 1239, 1240, 1241, 1242, 1243.

      Note: trade statistics are not comprehensive, because of difficulties in compilation and the special
          trade relationship with South Africa.

¶   D - Internal distribution and service trades

252   Survey of markets in Swaziland   (Central Statistical Office).
      Central Statistical Office, P O Box 456, Mbabane.
            5th, 1975.   E 0.15.   6p.
      The survey included all permanent or 'established' markets, and data is given on number of stalls,
          sellers, unpaid family workers in each market.
      Time factor: the report of the 1975 survey was published in 1975.
      §   En.

      Refer also to 1239, 1240, 1243.

¶   E - Population

1253   Swaziland population census   (Central Statistical Office).
             Central Statistical Office, P O Box 456, Mbabane.
             1904-   1966.   Report   E 6.00.   731p.
                     Distribution and density maps.   E 1.00.
         The report contains statistical data on the age and sex of the population, conjugal conditions, birth
             places, places of residence, occupation and employment, income, literacy, languages spoken,
             and religion.
         Time factor: both volumes were published in 1968.
         §   En.

1254   Employment and wages   (Central Statistical Office).
             Central Statistical Office, P O Box 456, Mbabane.
             1969-   1975.   E 0.25.   24p.
             Contains data on total employment, employment and wages in the private sector, and employment and
                 wages in the public sector.
             Time factor: the 1975 issue, published late 1976, has data for 1975.
             §   En.

1255   Swaziland's survey of manpower resources and requirements, April 1969 - March 1974   (Department of
                 Economic Planning and Statistics).
             Central Statistical Office, P O Box 456, Mbabane.
                             not priced.   36p.
             Time factor: published in December 1970.
             §   En.

1256   Survey of housing in Msunduza-Mbabane   (Central Statistical Office).
             Central Statistical Office, P O Box 456, Mbabane.
                             E 0.25.   30p.
             Time factor: the survey was taken and the report published in 1970.
             §   En.

1257   Survey of housing in Manzini and Peru urban area   (Central Statistical Office).
             Central Statistical Office, P O Box 456, Mbabane.
                             E 0.25.   26p.
             Time factor: the survey was taken in 1971 and the report published in 1972.
             §   En.

             Refer also to 1239, 1240, 1242.

¶   F - Social

i.   Standard of living

         Refer to 1239, 1240, 1241, 1242, 1243.

ii.   Health and welfare

1258   Annual medical and sanitary report   (Ministry of Health).
             Ministry of Health, Mbabane.
             1961-   1972.   not priced.   91p.
             Includes statistical data on hospitals, clinics, staffing, work, etc.
             Time factor: the 1972 report, published in 1973, has data for 1972.
             §   En.

             Refer also to 1239, 1240, 1242, 1243.

¶   F,   continued

iii. Education and leisure

259   Education statistics   (Central Statistical Office).
            Central Statistical Office, P O Box 456, Mbabane.
            1968-   1974.   not priced.   40p.
            Contains data on primary, secondary education, including enrolments, schools, pupils, teachers,
                classes, etc.
            Time factor: the 1974 issue, published in 1974, has data for the academic year 1963/64 and some
                earlier years; also estimates.
            §   En.

260   Education report   (Central Statistical Office).
            Central Statistical Office, P O Box 456, Mbabane.
            1968-   1976.   E 0.25.   35p.
            Contains data on primary, secondary education; expenditure, population, pupils and teachers, teacher
                training; enrolment; sex and age distribution; and also district tables as well as tables for the whole
                country.
            Time factor: the 1976 issue, published late 1976, has data to 31st March 1976.
            §   En.

            Note: there are also a few statistics included in the "Annual report summary of the Ministry of
                Education".

261   Census of African schools   (Education Department).
            Education Department, Mbabane.
                    1963.   not priced.   58p.
            Cover title is "African school's census".   Contains data on enrolments, staff, accommodation by
                schools and by district; ages of scholars, teachers, boarding schools; and enrolments by missions.
            Published as HCP R232.
            §   En.

            Refer also to 1239.

iv. Justice

262   Annual report of the Judiciary
            Ministry of Justice, Mbabane.
            1965-   4th, 1968.   not priced.   13p.
            Includes statistical appendices on criminal cases, criminal appeals, civil cases, civil appeals, high
                court criminal statistics, and subordinate court criminal statistics.
            Time factor: the 1968 report, published in 1969, has data for 1968.
            §   En.

            Refer also to 1239.

¶   F - Finance

263   The Monetary Authority of Swaziland: quarterly review   (Monetary Authority of Swaziland).
            Monetary Authority of Swaziland, P O Box 456, Mbabane.
            1974-   not priced.
            Contains banking and financial statistics.
            §   En.

            Note: the Authority also issues an annual report.

            Refer also to 1242.

¶   F,   continued

i. Banking

Refer to 1239, 1240, 1243.

ii. Public finance

1264   National accounts   (Central Statistical Office).
          Central Statistical Office, P O Box 456, Mbabane.
          1965/66 & 1966/67-   1973.   E 0.50.   63p.
          Contains data on national income, government income and expenditure.
          Time factor: the 1973 edition, published late 1975, has data for the fiscal year 1972/73.
          §   En.

1265   Balance of payments   (Central Statistical Office).
          Central Statistical Office, P O Box 456, Mbabane.
          1968/69-   1969/70 & 1970/71.   E 0.25.   11p.
          Time factor: the 1969/70 & 1970/71 issue, published in 1973, has data for both the 1969/70 and the
              1970/71 fiscal years.
          §   En.

1266   Annual report   (Income Tax Department).
          Income Tax Department, Mbabane.
          1968/69-   1973/74.   not priced.   36p.
          Includes statistics of revenue collected, tax payable by category of taxpayer, assessments, etc.
          Time factor: the 1973/74 report, published in 1975, has data for the fiscal year 1973/74.
          §   En.

          Refer also to 1239, 1240, 1241, 1242.

v. Insurance

Refer to 1239.

¶   H - Transport and communications

Refer to 1239, 1243.

ii. Road

Refer to 1240.

iv. Air

1267   Annual report   (Ministry of Works, Power & Communications: Civil Aviation Branch).
          Civil Aviation Branch, Ministry of Works, Power & Communications, P O Box 58, Mbabane.
          1966-   1973.   not priced.   20p.
          Includes statistical data on air traffic (goods and passengers), hours flown, operations, etc.
          Time factor: the 1973 report, published in June 1974, has data for 1973.
          §   En.

          Refer also to 1240.

¶ H, continued

v. Telecommunications and postal services

268   Annual report of the Department of Posts and Telecommunications
         Department of Posts and Telecommunications, Mbabane.
         1964-   1972/73.   not priced.   19p.
         Includes statistical data on telephones, telex, telegraph, posts, staff, etc.
         Time factor: the 1972/73 report, published in 1975, has data for the fiscal year 1972/73.
         §   En.

TANZANIA – TANZANIE – TANSANIA

Central statistical office

1269   Bureau of Statistics,
Ministry of Finance and Planning,
P O Box 796, Dar es Salaam.
t 22722.   tg "STATISTICS".

The Bureau is responsible for the collection, collation and publication of economics and social statistics.

Some other important organisations collecting and publishing statistics

1270   East African Statistical Department,
East African Community,
P O Box 30462,
Nairobi, Kenya.
t 26411.

The East African Community was established in December 1967 to provide an institutional and legal framework to strengthen the common market between Kenya, Tanzania and Uganda, and the Statistical Department provides statistical data on an East African basis.

1271   Statistics Branch,
East African Customs & Excise Department,
Customs House,
P O Box 90601, Mombasa.

The Statistics Branch is responsible for the collection, analysis and publication of the foreign trade statistics of Kenya, Tanzania and Uganda.   Unpublished statistical information can also be supplied, both to government institutions and to firms.

Libraries

The Bureau of Statistics has a library which is open during office hours, from 7.30 to 14.30 (local time) Mondays to Saturdays, and the staff speak English and Kiswahili.

Bibliographies

1272   A guide to Tanzania statistics.   Central Bureau of Statistics, 1963.   T Shg 10.

1273   A bibliography of economic and statistical publications on Tanzania.   Central Bureau of Statistics, 1975.   T Shg 7.50.

A sales list of publications is also issued at intervals by the Central Bureau of Statistics.

Statistical publications

¶   A – General

1274   Statistical abstract   (Bureau of Statistics).
Government Publications Agency, P O Box 1801, Dar es Salaam.
1961– 1970.   T Shg 20.   237p.

[continued next page]

Main sections:

Land and climate	Commerce and industry
Constitution	Cooperative societies
Population	Buildings
Migration	Currency and banking
External and inter-state trade	Public finance
Transport and communication	National accounts of Tanzania
Agriculture and animal husbandry	Retail prices
Forestry	Employment and earnings
Mining	Public health
Water supply	Education
Fuel and power	Judiciary

Time factor: the 1970 edition contains statistics for the years from 1966 to 1969.
§   En.

275   Quarterly statistical bulletin   (Bureau of Statistics).
         Government Publications Agency, P O Box 1801, Dar es Salaam.
         1951-   T Shg 4 per issue.
         Includes statistical information on population, migration, national accounts, agriculture, livestock,
             forestry, mining, industry, transport and communication, external trade, commerce, government
             finance, and prices.
         Time factor: each issue contains about four years' annual figures and the last two years' monthly or
             quarterly figures, up to about 4 or 5 months prior to the date of the issue.
         §   En, Swahili.

276   Economic and operations report   (Bank of Tanzania).
         Bank of Tanzania, P O Box 2939, Dar es Salaam.
         1966-   1974/75.   not priced.
         Includes a statistical section with data on the activities of the Bank of Tanzania, finance, commercial
             banks, foreign trade balance, exports and imports, agricultural and industrial production, price
             indices, etc.
         Time factor: the 1974/75 report, published late 1975, has long runs of annual, quarterly and monthly
             figures to June 1975.
         §   En.

277   Economic survey   (Ministry of Economic Affairs and Development Planning).
         Government Publications Agency, P O Box 1801, Dar es Salaam.
         1970/71-   1975/76.   T Shg 30.   103p.
         Contains data on main trends in the economy (output and income; capital formation; external trade and
             balance of payments; public finance; money, banking and other financial institutions; employment,
             wages and prices; parastatal sector performance; and the international economic situation), and
             development by sector (agriculture; natural resources; mining; industry; trade and tourism;
             construction; housing and urban development; transport and communications; water and power;
             education, training and manpower; health; labour and social welfare; national culture and youth).
         Time factor: the 1975/76 issue, published late 1976, has long runs of figures to 1974 and provisional
             figures for 1975.
         §   En & Swahili eds.

278   Economic and statistical review   (East African Statistical Department).
         East African Statistical Department, East African Community, P O Box 30462, Nairobi, Kenya.
         1948-   quarterly.   K Shg 10 each issue.
         Contains statistical tables on land and climate, population, migration and tourism, external and
             interstate trade, transport and communication, employment, retail price index numbers,
             production and consumption, banking, currency, insurance, public finance, domestic income
             and product, and balance of payments.
         Time factor: each issue contains figures up to the date of the issue and is published about six months
             later.   Many tables have long runs of annual, monthly and quarterly figures.
         §   En.

¶ A, continued

1279 Economic bulletin (Bank of Tanzania).
        Bank of Tanzania, P O Box 2939, Dar es Salaam.
        1969- quarterly. not priced.
        Includes statistical tables on the Bank of Tanzania, commercial banks, banking generally, central
            government finance, balance of payments, foreign trade balance, and foreign trade.
        Time factor: each issue has long runs of annual and monthly statistics to the month of issue, and is
            published some months later.
        § En.

¶ B - Production

1280 An input-output table for Tanzania (Bureau of Statistics).
        Government Publications Agency, P O Box 1801, Dar es Salaam.
        1969- 1969. T Shg 5. 9p.
        Time factor: the 1969 table was published in 1973.
        § En.

i. Mines and mining

1281 Annual report of the Mineral Resources Division, Ministry of Commerce and Industries.
        Government Publications Agency, P O Box 1801, Dar es Salaam.
        1962- 1967. T Shg 8. 104p.
        Statistics are included in the text of the report, and there are also appendices on mineral production,
            exports and local sales, diamond production and export, miscellaneous coloured gem stones
            exported, gold and silver production and sales, salt production and sales, tin production and
            sales, mining concerns operating in Tanzania, accident statistics, labour employed in mining
            and prospecting, explosives imports and consumption, accounts of the Mining (Loan) Board,
            prospecting licences, and mining rights.
        Time factor: the 1967 report, published in 1974, has data for 1967.
        § En.

        Refer also to 1274, 1275, 1277.

ii. Agriculture, fisheries, forestry, etc.

1282 Census of large-scale commercial farming (Bureau of Statistics).
        Government Publications Agency, P O Box 1801, Dar es Salaam.
        1962- 1964. T Shg 5. 41p.
        Time factor: published in 1965, the census results refer to 1964.
        § En.

1283 Market statistical report on Tanzania main agricultural commodities (S T Botros).
        Ministry of Agriculture, P O Box 9192, Dar es Salaam.
                            not priced. 43p.
        Contains data on production, local sales, and exports for each crop.
        Time factor: published in 1973, the report has data for various years to the crop year 1972/73.
        § En.

1284 Monthly market bulletin (Ministry of Agriculture: Marketing Development Bureau: Marketing Information
            Service).
        Ministry of Agriculture, P O Box 9192, Dar es Salaam.
        Contains data on general market trends, including producer and retail prices of staples, vegetables,
            fruits, and livestock products.
        § En.

¶ B,ii, continued

1285 East African statistics of sugar (East African Statistical Department).
    East African Statistical Department, East African Community, P O Box 30462, Nairobi, Kenya.
    1966/74- 1966/74. K Shg 5.00. 21p.
    Contains data on production, imports, consumption, stocks of sugar in the world and in Tanzania,
        Kenya and Uganda. Also local sugar prices and world price trends.
    Time factor: the 1966/74 issue, published in 1976, has data for the years 1966 to 1974.
    § En.

1286 Crop production statistics in Tanzania (Ministry of Agriculture).
    Ministry of Agriculture, P O Box 9192, Dar es Salaam.
    1964/72- 1964-1972. not priced. 92p.
    Contains detailed statistics for each crop.
    Time factor: the 1964-1972 issue, published 1974, has data for the years 1964 to 1972.
    § En.

1287 Annual report (Ministry of Natural Resources and Tourism: Fisheries Division).
    Ministry of Natural Resources and Tourism, P O Box 9372, Dar es Salaam.
    1965- 1971. not priced. 42p.
    Includes data on marine and freshwater fishing, production, marketing and trade.
    Time factor: the 1971 report, published in 1973, has data for 1971.
    § En.

1288 Annual report (Ministry of Agriculture, Food and Co-operation: Forest Division).
    Ministry of Agriculture, P O Box 9192, Dar es Salaam.
    1949- 1967. not priced. 38p.
    Contains information on forest products research, silviculture research, beekeeping, forest crops, staff
        and labour, finance, educational training, etc. A few statistics are included in the text.
    § En.

    Refer also to 1274, 1275, 1276, 1277.

iii. Industry

1289 Annual survey of industrial production (Bureau of Statistics).
    Government Publications Agency, P O Box 1801, Dar es Salaam.
    1958- 1972. T Shg 7.50. c90p.
    Covers manufacturing, motor vehicle repairing, mining, and electricity.
    Time factor: the report of the 1972 survey was published in December 1975. A census of industrial
        production was taken in 1961.
    § En.

    Note: a directory of industries was published in 1968 and in 1975 (T Shg 7.50).

1290 East African statistics of industrial production (East African Statistical Department).
    East African Statistical Department, East African Community, P O Box 30462, Nairobi, Kenya.
    1967- 1970 & 1971. K Shg 7.50. c50p.
    Contains data on the number of establishments, persons engaged, labour costs, gross output, import and
        value added, inputs, and gross fixed capital. Data is for Tanzania, Kenya and Uganda.
    Time factor: the 1970 & 1971 issue, published in 1976, has data for the years 1970 and 1971.
    § En.

¶   B.iii,   continued

1291   Statistical analysis of industrial production in East Africa (1963-1970)   (East African Statistical Department)
          East African Statistical Department, East African Community, P O Box 30492, Nairobi, Kenya.
                    K Shg 10.00.   150p.
          A statistical analysis of the size of establishments, employment, gross output, value added, value of
                production, investments, profit and labour.   Data is for Tanzania, Kenya and Uganda.
          Time factor: published in 1974.
          §   En.

          Refer also to 1274, 1275, 1276, 1277, 1278.

     iv. Construction

          Refer to 1277.

     v. Energy

1292   East African statistics of energy and power   (East African Statistical Department).
          East African Statistical Department, East African Community, P O Box 30462, Nairobi, Kenya.
          1966/73-   1966/73.   K Shg 7.50.
          Time factor: published in 1976.
          §   En.

          Refer also to 1274, 1277.

¶   C - External trade

1293   Annual trade report of Tanzania, Uganda and Kenya   (East African Customs and Excise Department).
          East African Customs & Excise Department, P O Box 90601, Mombasa.
          1961-   1975.   K Shg 60.   various pagination.
          Main tables show imports, exports and re-exports of the three countries separately and of East Africa as
                a whole, arranged by commodity and sub-divided by countries of origin and destination.   Also
                included are tables showing the transfer of goods between partner states.
          Time factor: the 1975 issue, containing data for that year, was published early in 1976.
          §   En.

1294   Monthly trade statistics for Tanzania, Uganda and Kenya   (East African Customs & Excise Department).
          East African Customs & Excise Department, P O Box 90601, Mombasa.
          1961-   K Shg 5; K Shg 50 yr, post free.
          Contains tables showing direct imports, exports and re-exports arranged by SITC, and trade by country
                for each of the three countries separately.   Also included are tables showing transfer of goods
                between partner states.
          Time factor: each issue has data for the month and cumulated figures for the year to date, and is
                published about two months later.
          §   En.

          Refer also to 1274, 1275, 1276, 1277, 1278, 1279.

¶   D - Internal distribution and service trades

1295   Survey of distributive trade, Dar es Salaam, 1970   (Bureau of Statistics).
          Government Publications Agency, P O Box 1801, Dar es Salaam.
                    ,   T Shg 5.   31p.
          Covers all distributive trades establishments with at least one employee.   The survey was taken as a
                pilot survey for a census.
          Time factor: the report was published in 1972.
          §   En.

¶ D, continued

296 Report on tourism statistics in Tanzania (Bureau of Statistics).
    Government Publications Agency, P O Box 1801, Dar es Salaam.
    1968- 1970. T Shg 5. 58p.
    Contains data on migration, aviation, hotel occupancy, and national park statistics.
    Time factor: the 1970 issue, published in 1972, has data for 1970 and also some figures for 1968 and
        1969.
    § En.

297 Report on airport tourism survey (Bureau of Statistics).
    Government Publications Agency, P O Box 1801, Dar es Salaam.
                      T Shg 5.   35p.
    Includes data on monthly arrivals by country of residence, visitors by place of arrival, visitors by
        residence and mode of transport, reasons for trip, etc.
    Time factor: the survey was carried out from March to December 1968 and published in July 1970.
    § En.

    Refer also to 1274, 1275, 1277, 1278.

¶ E - Population

298 Population census (Bureau of Statistics).
    Government Publications Agency, P O Box 1801, Dar es Salaam.
    1921- 1967.   7 vols.
    Content:
        Vol. 1 Statistics for enumeration areas (T Shg 30)
             2 Statistics for urban areas (T Shg 20)
             3 Demographic statistics (T Shg 25)
             4 Economic statistics (T Shg 30)
             5 Census methodology (T Shg 20)
             6 An analysis of the...census (not priced)
        Population census district maps showing enumeration areas (T Shg 5)
    Time factor: the reports of the census were published between 1969 and 1973.
    § En.

299 National demographic survey, 1973 (Bureau of Statistics).
    Government Publications Agency, P O Box 1801, Dar es Salaam.
                      not priced. 5 vols.
    The results of the survey are being published in 5 volumes, of which vol.1 is concerned with regional
        data and vol.4 with methodology.
    § En.

300 Survey of employment and earnings (Bureau of Statistics).
    Government Publications Agency, P O Box 1801, Dar es Salaam.
    1962- 1972. T Shg 7.50. 79p.
    Analysed by sector, by industry, and by region.
    Time factor: the 1972 issue has data for 1972 and also one or two earlier years in some tables, and was
        published mid-1974.
    § En.

301 Migration statistics (Bureau of Statistics).
    Government Publications Agency, P O Box 1801, Dar es Salaam.
    1963- 1970. T Shg 5. 46p.
    Contains data on immigrants and emigrants by type, sex and method of travel; and numbers of visitors
        and persons in transit by length of stay.
    Time factor: the 1970 issue, published in 1972, has data for 1970.
    § En.

    Refer also to 1274, 1275, 1277, 1278.

¶   F - Social

i. Standard of living

1302   Household budget survey   (Bureau of Statistics).
              Government Publications Agency, P O Box 1801, Dar es Salaam.
              1961/62-   1969.   3 vols.
              Content:
                    Vol. 1 Income and consumption   (T Shg 10)
                          2 Housing conditions   (T Shg 10)
                          3 Retail prices. Tanzania mainland   (T Shg 5)
              §   En.

1303   Prices and price index numbers for eighteen towns in Tanzania   (Bureau of Statistics).
              Government Publications Agency, P O Box 1801, Dar es Salaam.
              1968/69-   1972/73.   T Shg 7.50.   not paged.
              Contains data on retail prices.
              Time factor: the 1972/73 issue covers that period and was published in 1974.
              §   En.

1304   National consumer price index, 1969-1973: basic materials, computations and results   (Bureau of Statistics).
              Government Publications Agency, P O Box 1801, Dar es Salaam.
                              T Shg 5.   63p.
              Time factor: published October 1974.
              §   En.

              Refer also to 1274, 1277.

ii. Health and welfare

1305   Annual report of the Health Division   (Ministry of Health and Social Welfare).
              Ministry of Health and Social Welfare, P O Box 9083, Dar es Salaam.
              1965-   1966.   T Shg 5.50.   2 vols.
              Includes statistical data on diseases, health, hygiene, prisons, hospitals, dental, supplies and pharmacy,
                    nurses, etc.   Volume 1 is textual and vol. 2 has statistical tables.
              Time factor: the 1966 report was published in 1969.
              §   En.

              Refer also to 1274, 1277.

iii. Education and leisure

              Refer to 1274, 1277.

iv. Justice

              Refer to 1274.

¶   G - Finance

              Refer to 1274, 1276, 1277, 1278.

TANZANIA,   continued

¶   G,   continued

i. Banking

Refer to 1274, 1276, 1277, 1278, 1279.

ii. Public finance

1306   National accounts of Tanzania   (Bureau of Statistics).
        Government Publications Agency, P O Box 1801, Dar es Salaam.
        1960/62-   1964/72.   T Shg 5.   69p.
        Time factor: the 1964/72 issue, published in 1974, has data for the years 1964 to 1972.
        §   En.

        Refer also to 1274, 1275, 1277, 1279, 1280.

iii. Company finance

1307   Analysis of accounts of parastatals   (Bureau of Statistics).
        Government Publications Agency, P O Box 1801, Dar es Salaam.
        1966/67-   1966/74.   T Shg 7.50.   c30p.
        Contains data on the numbers of parastatal enterprises by industry and numbers of employees, and
            accounts (receipts from sales, government subsidies, etc; expenditure on wages and salaries,
            interest on loans, rent, depreciation, purchases, etc; and taxes).
        Time factor: the 1966/74 issue, published late 1975, has data for the years 1966 to 1974.
        §   En.

        Refer also to 1277.

v. Insurance

1308   East Africa, insurance statistics   (East African Statistical Department).
        East African Statistical Department, East African Community, P O Box 30462, Nairobi, Kenya.
        1959-   1967.   K Shg 3.00.   41p.
        Contains data on all kinds of insurance for East Africa, Kenya, Tanzania and Uganda.
        Time factor: the 1967 issue, has data for 1965, 1966 and 1967.
        §   En.

        Refer also to 1278.

¶   H – Transport and communications

1309   Statistical survey of the East African Community institutions   (East African Community).
        East African Community, P O Box 30462, Nairobi, Kenya.
        1973-   1973.   K Shg 7.50.   68p.
        Contains data on railways, harbours, posts and telecommunications, airways, etc. for Tanzania, Kenya
            and Uganda.
        Time factor: the 1973 issue, published in 1975, has data for 1973 or the latest available.
        §   En.

        Refer also to 1274, 1275, 1277, 1278.

Central statistical office

1310   Direction de la Statistique   [Department of Statistics],
        Ministère du Plan   [Ministry of Planning],
        B P 118, Lomé.
        † 22 87.

   The Department is responsible for the collection, analysis and publication of economic and social statistics.

Statistical publications

¶   A - General

1311   Annuaire statistique du Togo   [Statistical yearbook of Togo]   (Direction de la Statistique Générale).
        Direction de la Statistique, B P 118, Lomé.
        1955/56-   1973.   CFA Fr 3,000.   181p.
        Main sections:
            Area and climate   Industry (Including energy)
            Demography and social   Transport, communications, foreign trade
            Primary production (agriculture,   Prices
               livestock, forestry)   Finance
        Time factor: the 1973 edition, published late 1975, has data for several years to 1973 or 1972/73.
        §   Fr.

        Note: the yearbook supersedes "Inventaire économique".

1312   Bulletin mensuel de statistique   [Monthly bulletin of statistics]   (Direction de la Statistique Générale).
        Direction de la Statistique Générale, B P 118, Lomé.
        1952-   CFA Fr 400; CFA Fr 4,000 yr; special numbers CFA Fr 1,000.
        Contains data on climate, demography, agriculture, building, energy, transport, foreign trade, prices, money and credit.
        Time factor: each issue has data for the month of the issue, cumulation for the year to date, and comparative figures for the previous year.   It is published about six months later.
        §   Fr.

1313   Togo 1960: faits et chiffres   [Togo 1960: facts and figures]   (Banque Centrale des Etats de l'Afrique de l'Ouest).
        Banque Centrale des Etats de l'Afrique de l'Ouest, Paris.
                        not priced.   218p.
        A statistical survey of the newly independent republic.
        Time factor: published in 1960.
        §   Fr.

1314   Indicateurs de l'économie Togolaise   [Indicators of the Togo economy]   (Direction de la Statistique).
        Direction de la Statistique, B P 118, Lomé.
        1970-   half-yearly.   not priced.
        Contains data on production, foreign trade, indices of consumer prices; African families in Lomé, indices of consumer prices: European families in Lomé, transport (port traffic, air traffic), and the financial situation.
        §   Fr.

¶ B - Production

ii. Agriculture, fisheries, forestry, etc.

1315 Enquête agricole générale, 1970 (Recensement mondial de l'agriculture) (resultats provisoires) [General agricultural survey, 1970 (World census of agriculture) (provisional results)] (Direction de la Statistique <u>and</u> Ministère de l'Economie Rurale. Direction Générale de l'Economie Rurale).
Direction de la Statistique, B P 118, Lomé.
                not priced.   114p.
Contains data on production of crops and livestock, employment, cultivation, etc, for the whole country and for each region.
Time factor: the report was published in 1973.
§ Fr.

1316 Rapport annuel [Annual report] (Ministère de l'Equipement Rural: Direction des Services de l'Elevage et des Industries Animales).
Direction des Services de l'Elevage et des Industries Animales, Lomé.
1961- 1974.   not priced.   87p.
Includes tables of production and consumption, diseases, etc, as well as statistics throughout the text.
Time factor: the 1974 report, published in 1977, has data for 1974.
§ Fr.

1317 Rapport annuel [Annual report] (Ministère de l'Economie Rurale: Direction de l'Agriculture).
Direction de l'Agriculture, Lomé.
1966- 1971.   not priced.   various paginations.
Includes an annex of production, distribution, sales, etc, statistics, as well as information on the activities of the division, linked organisations, and regional offices.
Time factor: the 1971 report has data for 1971.
§ Fr.

Refer also to 1311, 1312.

iii. Industry

1318 Enquête sur les entreprises industrielles et commerciales du Togo [Enquiry on the industrial and commercial enterprises of Togo] (Direction de la Statistique).
Direction de la Statistique, B P 118, Lomé.
1970- 1970.   not priced.   276p.
Part 1 contains the introduction and general results by branch of economic activity; part 2 deals with commerce, industry and services; and part 3 contains information on the contribution of public and para-public enterprises. Data is given by branch of activity, on employment, wages, value added, sales, revenue, capital formation, profits, etc.
Time factor: the results of the enquiry relate to 1970 and were published in 1972.
§ Fr.

Refer also to 1311, 1312.

iv. Construction

Refer to 1312.

v. Energy

Refer to 1311, 1312.

¶   C - External trade

1319   Annuaire des statistiques du commerce extérieur   [Statistical yearbook of foreign trade]   (Direction de la
            Statistique Générale).
            Direction de la Statistique Générale, B P 118, Lomé.
            1962- 1974.   CFA Fr 1,000.   379p.
            Contains detailed statistical data on imports and exports arranged by commodities and sub-divided by
                countries of origin and destination, by countries of origin and destination sub-divided by
                commodities, and summary tables.
            Time factor: the 1974 issue, published late 1975, has data for 1974 and 1973.
            §   Fr.

1320   Annuaire rétrospectif des statistiques du commerce extérieur du Togo, 1960 à 1970   [Retrospective
            yearbook of foreign trade statistics of Togo, 1960 to 1970]   (Direction de la Statistique).
            Direction de la Statistique, B P 118, Lomé.
                            not priced.   48p.
            Contains summary statistics of imports and exports arranged by principal countries and regions, and also
                arranged by products.
            §   Fr.

            Refer also to 1311, 1312, 1314.

¶   E - Population

1321   Recensement général de la population   [General census of population]   (Direction de la Statistique).
            Direction de la Statistique, B P 118, Lomé.
            1959-   2nd, 1970.   not priced.   2 vols.
            Vol. 1 contains the first results and information on the methodology of the census; vol. 2 contains
                detailed results of the census.
            Time factor: the results were published in 1975.
            §   Fr.

1322   Enquête sur les agents (salariés) de l'état (résultats de juillet 1972) et des collectives locales et
            para-publiques (résultats de decembre 1971)   [Survey of central government and local government
            servants]   (Direction de la Statistique).
            Direction de la Statistique, B P 118, Lomé.
                            not priced.   53p.
            Time factor: the results were published in June 1973.
            §   Fr.

            Refer also to 1311, 1312.

¶   F - Social

i. Standard of living

1323   Enquête sur les budgets familiaux et la consommation des ménages au Togo   [Enquiry on family budgets and
            household consumption in Togo]   (Société d'Etudes pour le Développement Économique et Social).
            Société d'Etudes pour le Développement Economique et Social, Lomé.
            Contents:
                    Volume I   Family budgets
                                    Part I fasc.1   Presentation of the enquiry
                                            fasc.2   Results for Lomé
                                        II   Secondary urban centres
                                        III   Rural areas. Results for all Togo
                                        IV   Annexes
                    Volume II Nutrition
            §   Fr.

            Refer also to 1314.

¶   F,   continued

ii.   Health and welfare

Refer to 1311.

iii.   Education and leisure

1324   Statistiques scolaires   [Education statistics]   (Ministère de l'Education Nationale),
       Ministère de l'Education Nationale, B P 3221, Lomé.
       1965/66-   1975-1976.   not priced.   164p.
       Contains data on finance; 1st, 2nd and 3rd degree education; technical and professional education;
           higher education; and university education, includes numbers of pupils, teachers, schools, etc.
       Time factor: the 1975-1976 issue, published in 1976, has data for the 1975/76 academic year.
       §   Fr.

1325   Tableau de bord: évolution des effectifs scolaires enseignements primaire et secondaire, 1966-1972
           [Improvement of primary and secondary education, 1966-1972]   (Ministère de l'Education Nationale).
       Ministère de l'Education Nationale, B P 3221, Lomé.
       Basic statistics of numbers of pupils being educated.
       Time factor: published in 1972, the figures relate to the years 1966 to 1972.
       §   Fr.

1326   Rapport sur l'évolution de l'éducation...   [Report on the improvement in education]   (Ministère de
           l'Education Nationale).
       Ministère de l'Education Nationale, B P 3221, Lomé.
       1970/71-   1973-1975.   not priced.
       Time factor: published in 1975.
       §   En & Fr eds.

¶   G - Finance

Refer to 1311, 1312, 1314.

ii.   Public finance

1327   Comptes nationaux   [National accounts]   (Direction de la Statistique).
       Direction de la Statistique, B P 118, Lomé.
       1963-   1970 & 1971.   not priced.   133p.
       Time factor: the 1970 & 1971 issue, published in 1975, has data for 1970 and 1971.
       §   Fr.

¶   H - Transport and communications

Refer to 1311, 1312, 1314.

TRANSKEI

Currently, statistics for Transkei can be found in publications of the Republic of South Africa.

Central statistical office

1328   Institut National de la Statistique   [National Institute of Statistics],
        31 avenue de Paris,
        Tunis.
        t 24 38 27.

        The Institute is a part of the Ministère du Plan [Ministry of Planning] and is responsible for the
collection, analysis and publication of economic and social statistics for Tunisia.

Statistical publications

¶   A - General

1329   Annuaire statistique de la Tunisie   [Statistical yearbook of Tunisia]   (Institut National de la Statistique).
        Institut National de la Statistique, 31 avenue de Paris, Tunis.
        1940/46-   1970 & 1971.   T Din 1.500.   467p.
        Main sections:

Climate	Industry
Population	Tourism
Education	Transport and communication
Public health	Internal trade
Justice	Foreign trade
Employment	Money and banking
Energy	State budget

        Time factor: the 1970 & 1971 edition, published 1975, has data from 1965 or 1969 to 1971 in the tables.
        §   Fr.

1330   Bulletin mensuel de statistique   [Monthly bulletin of statistics]   (Institut National de la Statistique).
        Institut National de la Statistique, 31 avenue de Paris, Tunis.
        1954-   T Din 5.000 yr.
        Contains data on climate, population (births, marriages and deaths), employment, energy, industry,
            tourism, transport, internal trade (including cost of living and retail price index), money and
            banking, public finance, and foreign trade.
        Time factor: each issue has data for 12 months up to the month of issue or one or two months earlier,
            and is published about two months later.
        §   Fr.

1331   L'économie de la Tunisie en chiffres   [The economy of Tunis in figures]   (Institut National de la
            Statistique).
        Institut National de la Statistique, 31 avenue de Paris, Tunis.
        1960-   1972.   T Din 1.000.   115p.
        A pocket-sized volume containing statistical data on:

Climate	Industry
Population	Tourism
Education	Transport and communication
Public health	Internal trade
Employment	Money and banking
Agriculture and fishing	State budget
Energy	Economic accounts

        Time factor: the 1972 edition, published in 1973, has data for 1970, 1971 and 1972.
        §   Fr.

1332   Statistiques financières   [Financial statistics]   (Banque Centrale de Tunisie).
        Banque Centrale de Tunisie, 7 Place de la Monnaie, Tunis.
        1972-   monthly.   not priced.
        Contains data on money, credit and change; and general economic statistics, including prices,
            agricultural production, industrial production, tourism, foreign trade, national accounts, and
            balance of payments.
        Time factor: each issue has long runs of figures to two or three months prior to the date of the issue.
        §   Fr.

¶ A, continued

1333   Rapport annuel   [Annual report]   (Banque Centrale de Tunisie).
        Banque Centrale de Tunisie, 7 place de la Monnaie, Tunis.
        1959–   1975.   not priced.   187p.
        Contains a section on the international economy; on economic activities of Tunisia (agriculture,
            industry and mining, tourism, internal trade, wages, prices, investments, foreign trade, balance
            of payments, and public finance); on money and credit (action of the monetary authorities,
            liquidity and balance of the banking system, monetary resources, and distribution of credit); and
            on the work of the Central Bank itself.
        Time factor: the 1975 edition, published in 1976, has data for 1975 and two or three earlier years in
            some tables.
        §   Fr.

1334   Conjoncture   (Banque Centrale de Tunisie).
        Banque Centrale de Tunisie, 7 place de la Monnaie, Tunis.
        1964–   monthly.   free.
        A 12-page economic bulletin, with some statistics on various subjects but no regular tables.
        §   Fr.

1335   Conjoncture: bulletin d'information économique   [Economic information bulletin]   (Ministère de
            l'Economie Nationale).
        Ministère de l'Economie Nationale, La Kasbah, Tunis.
        1974–   monthly.   T Din 2,300 (T Din 4,000 abroad) yr.
        Includes some statistics and statistical tables in the text.   Includes data on internal trade, foreign
            trade, mining, finances, energy, employment, etc.   Subjects covered vary each month.
        §   Fr.

¶ B – Production

i. Mines and mining

        Refer to 1333, 1335.

ii. Agriculture, fisheries, forestry, etc.

1336   Statistique agricole: enquête agricole annuelle dans le governorat...   [Agricultural statistics: annual
            agricultural survey of the governorate...]   (Direction du Développement Agricole).
        Direction du Développement Agricole, Secrétariat d'Etat au Plan, Tunis.
                    1968.   6 vols.
        Separate volumes are devoted to the agriculture of Beza, Bizerta, Gabes, Jendouba, Nabeul, and Tunis.
        Time factor: the reports of the 1968 surveys were published in 1969.
        §   Fr.

1337   Statistiques agricoles: informations trimestrielles   [Agricultural statistics: quarterly information]
            (Institut National de la Statistique).
        Institut National de la Statistique, 31 avenue de Paris, Tunis.
        1969–   not priced.
        Contains data on internal trade of agricultural products, foreign trade of agriculture and fisheries,
            necessities imported (i.e. machines, oil), investments, etc.
        §   Fr.

        Refer also to 1331, 1332, 1333.

¶ B, continued

iii. Industry

1338   Recensement des activités industrielles: résultats...tableaux statistiques   [Census of industrial activities:
           results...statistical tables]   (Institut National de la Statistique).
           Institut National de la Statistique, 31 avenue de Paris, Tunis.
           1957-   1973.   T Din 0.750 (T Din 1.400 abroad).   179p.
           Includes data on employment; wages and salaries; capacity of power equipment; transport equipment;
               expenditure on fixed assets; inventories; cost of individual materials, fuels and electricity; and
               gross output for individual industries.
           Time factor: the 1973 edition, published 1975, contains data for 1973.
           §   Fr.

           Refer also to 1329, 1331, 1332, 1333, 1334.

iv. Construction

1339   Revue Tunisienne de l'équipement   [Tunisian review of equipment]   (Ministère de l'Equipement).
           Ministère de l'Equipement, Centre de Documentation, Cité-Jardins, Tunis.
           1972-   quarterly.   not priced.
           Includes statistics of building authorisations, etc.
           §   Fr.

v. Energy

           Refer to 1329, 1330, 1331, 1335.

¶ C - External trade

1340   Statistiques du commerce extérieur de la Tunisie   [Statistics of the foreign trade of Tunisia]   (Institut
           National de la Statistique).
           Institut National de la Statistique, 31 avenue de Paris, Tunis.
           1960-   1974.   T Din 2.200.   465p.
           Contains detailed statistics of imports and exports arranged by commodities and sub-divided by
               countries of origin and destination, and trade by country sub-divided by broad commodity
               groupings.
           Time factor: the 1974 issue, published mid-1975, has data for 1974.
           §   Fr.

1341   Statistiques résumées du commerce extérieur de la Tunisie   [Summary statistics of foreign trade of Tunisia]
           (Institut National de la Statistique).
           Institut National de la Statistique, 31 avenue de Paris, Tunis.
           1970-   monthly.   T Din 2.200 yr.
           Contains summary tables on direction of trade, balance of trade, imports and exports by commodity
               group, and principal products imported and exported.
           Time factor: each issue has cumulated figures for the year up to and including that month, and
               corresponding figures for the previous year, and is published about two months after the end of
               the month of the issue.
           §   Fr.

           Refer also to 1329, 1330, 1332, 1333, 1335, 1337.

¶   D - Internal distribution and service trades

1342   Le tourisme en chiffres   [Tourism in figures]   (Office National du Tourisme Tunisien).
Office National du Tourisme Tunisien, avenue Muhamed V, Tunis.
1970-   1975.   not priced.   84p.
Contains data on numbers of arrivals, length of stay, tours offered, entry of non-residents, movements
of non-residents, tourism as foreign trade.   Statistics are given on professionals in the tourist
industry, promotions, air traffic, entry to museums, and climate.
Time factor: the 1975 issue, published in 1976, has data for 1975 or earlier figures.
§   Fr.

1343   Bulletin trimestriel: statistiques   [Quarterly bulletin: statistics]   (Office National du Tourisme Tunisien).
Office National du Tourisme Tunisien, avenue Muhamed V, Tunis.
1954-   not priced.
Contains statistics of numbers of visitors by nationality, by months, by hotel, and numbers of motorists,
etc.
Time factor: each issue has cumulated figures for the year to the end of the quarter of the issue and
corresponding figures for the previous year.
§   Fr.

Refer also to 1329, 1330, 1331, 1332, 1333, 1335.

¶   E - Population

1344   Recensement général de la population et des logements   [General census of population and housing]
(Institut National de la Statistique).
Institut National de la Statistique, 31 avenue de Paris, Tunis.
1896-   1966.   not priced.   4 vols.
Vol. 1, chapter 1. Population by administrative division   (T Din 2.200)
chapter 2. Demographic characteristics
chapter 3. Fecundity
chapter 4. Foreign population
Vol. 2, chapter 5. Migration   (T Din 1.400)
Vol. 3, chapter 6. Educational characteristics   (T Din 2.200)
chapter 7. Economic characteristics
Vol. 4, chapter 8. Households   (T Din 1.400)
chapter 9. Houses
§   Fr.

Note: a census was taken in May 1975 of population and housing, for which preliminary results are now
being published.

1345   Etudes et enquêtes de l'INS: série démographie   [Studies and surveys of INS: demographic series]
(Institut National de la Statistique).
Institut National de la Statistique, 31 avenue de Paris, Tunis.
1974-   irregular.   not priced.
Each issue is on a separate subject, some being issued on an annual basis.   Subjects covered include
sources of demography, migration and employment, a national demographic enquiry, the structure
of the population, vital statistics, marriages and divorces, etc.
§   Fr.

Refer also to 1329, 1330, 1331, 1335.

¶   F - Social

Refer to 1330, 1333.

TUNISIA, continued

¶ F, continued

ii. Health and welfare

1346   Statistiques   [Statistics]   (Ministère de la Santé Publique, Service Centrale des Statistiques).
            Ministère de la Santé Publique, Tunis.
            1969-   1973.   not priced.
            Each issue is devoted to one subject.   The 1969 issue to capacity and activity in hospitals and
                declarable infectious diseases, 1970 to medical statistics, in 1971 one volume was on the state
                of the health of the population and the other on the network and functions of the health services,
                1972 was on the network and functions of the health service and on declarable infectious
                diseases, 1973 on a census of health personnel at 31/12/72.
            §   Fr.

1347   Statistiques de planning familial   [Statistics of family planning]   (Office National de Planning Familial
                et de la Population).
            Office National de Planning Familial et de la Population, Bab Saadoun, Tunis.
            1974-   quarterly.   not priced.
            Time factor: each issue has data for each month and the 4th issue each year has annual statistics.
            §   Fr.

            Refer also to 1329, 1331.

    iii. Education and leisure

            Refer to 1329, 1331.

    iv. Justice

            Refer to 1329.

¶   G – Finance

            Refer to 1329, 1330, 1331, 1332, 1333, 1335.

¶   H – Transport and communications

            Refer to 1329, 1330, 1331.

    i. Ships and shipping

1348   Bulletin annuel de statistiques   [Annual bulletin of statistics]   (Office des Ports Nationaux).
            Office des Ports Nationaux, avenue République, Tunis.
            1969-   1974.   not priced.   24p.
            Contains data on traffic at Tunisian ports, including numbers of ships, value and quantity of cargoes,
                and numbers of passengers.
            Time factor: the 1974 issue, published in 1976, has data for 1974.
            §   Fr.

TUNISIA, continued

1349   Bulletin trimestriel de statistiques   [Quarterly bulletin of statistics]   (Office des Ports Nationaux).
        Office des Ports Nationaux, avenue République, Tunis.
        1973–   not priced.
        Contains data on the traffic at Tunisian ports – ships, merchandise and passengers.
        Time factor: each issue has data for the quarter of the issue and the corresponding quarter for the
            previous year, and is published one or two months later.
        §   Fr.

    ii. Road transport

1350   Parc automobile et parc tracteur de la Tunisie: situation au 31 Decembre...   [Motor vehicle and tractor
            registration in Tunisia: situation at 31 December...]   (Institut National de la Statistique).
        Institut National de la Statistique, 31 avenue de Paris, Tunis.
        1967–   1972.   T Din 1.200.   27p.
        Time factor: the 1972 issue, published in December 1974, has data on the situation at December 1972.
        §   Fr.

Central statistical office

1351   Statistics Division,
            Ministry of Planning,
            P O Box 13, Entebbe.
            t 771.   tg STATISTICS ENTEBBE.

       The Statistics Division carries out the functions of a central statistical office and assists Ministries and Departments.   Its work covers national income estimates, calculation of cost of living indices, industrial production surveys, an annual enumeration of employees, budget surveys, migration, building, trade, etc. Unpublished statistical information may be supplied if requested, depending on its nature and whether or not the Statistics Act would be contravened.

Other important organisations collecting and publishing statistics

1352   East African Statistical Department,
            East African Community,
            P O Box 30462,
            Nairobi, Kenya.
            t 26411.

       The East African Community was established in December 1967 to provide an institutional and legal framework to strengthen the common market between Kenya, Tanzania and Uganda, and the Statistical Department provides statistical data on an East African basis.

1353   Statistics Branch,
            East African Customs and Excise Department,
            Customs House,
            P O Box 90601,
            Mombasa, Kenya.

       The Statistics Branch is responsible for the collection, analysis and publication of the foreign trade statistics of Kenya, Tanzania and Uganda.   Unpublished statistical information can also be supplied, both to government institutions and to firms.

Libraries

       There is a small library in the Statistics Division of the Ministry of Planning where statistical publications may be consulted.

Bibliographies

       A list of the publications of the Statistics Division of the Ministry of Planning is published in the "Statistical abstract" (1354).

Statistical publications

¶   A - General

1354   Statistical abstract   (Statistics Division, Ministry of Planning).
            Government Printer, P O Box 33, Entebbe.
            1957-   1973.   Ug Sh 22.00.   117p.
            Main sections:
                Land and climate   Industry and commerce
                Population   Banking and currency
                Migration   Public finance
                External and inter-community trade Gross domestic product and capital
                Transport and communications   formation
                Agriculture   Prices and cost of living
            [continued next page]

319

¶   A,   continued

1354,   continued

Fishing	Employment and earnings
Forestry	Public health
Mining and water supplies	Education
Fuel and power	Government prisons

Time factor: the 1973 edition, published in 1975, contains data for 1972 or for the fiscal year 1972/73, and some tables have retrospective figures.

§   En.

1355   Quarterly economic and statistical bulletin   (Statistics Division, Office of the President).
Government Printer, P O Box 33, Entebbe.
1965-   Ug Sh 10.00 yr; single issues Ug Sh 3.00.
Includes data on tourism, external and inter-community trade, transport and communications, production and sales, prices and cost of living, public finances, and banking.
Time factor: each issue, published some time after the quarter of the issue, contains runs of annual and quarterly figures up to the quarter of the issue or the previous quarter.
§   En.

1356   Economic and statistical review   (East African Statistical Department).
East African Statistical Department, East African Community, P O Box 30462, Nairobi.
1948-   quarterly.   K Shg 10 each issue.
Contains statistical tables on land and climate, population, migration and tourism, external and interstate trade, transport and communication, employment, retail price index numbers, production and consumption, banking, currency, insurance, public finance, domestic income and product, and balance of payments.
Time factor: each issue contains figures up to the date of the issue and is published about six months later.   Many tables have long runs of annual, monthly and quarterly figures.
§   En.

1357   Quarterly bulletin   (Bank of Uganda).
Bank of Uganda, 37/43 Kampala Road, Kampala.
1968-   not priced.
Includes a statistical appendix on economic events, production, foreign trade, balance of payments, and money.
§   En.

Note: the annual report of the Bank of Uganda also has a statistical appendix with economic statistics as well as information on the finances of the Bank.

¶   B ·- Production

i. Mines and mining

1358   Annual report of the Geological Survey and Mines Department.
Geological Survey and Mines Department, Ministry of Mineral and Water Resources, P O Box 9, Entebbe.
1960-   1971.   Ug Sh 4.00.   38p.
Includes some statistics in the text, which is divided into sections on regional mapping, mineral appraisal and exploration, headquarters services, the Mines Division, the Drilling Division, and staff and general.
Time factor: the 1971 report was published in 1973.
§   En.

Refer also to 1354.

UGANDA, continued

¶ B, continued

ii. Agriculture, fisheries, forestry, etc.

1359 Report of the Uganda census of agriculture (Ministry of Agriculture and Cooperation).
Government Printer, P O Box 33, Entebbe.
1963/65- 1962/66. Ug Sh 5.50 (abroad Ug Sh 6.00) each volume. 4 vols.
Vol.1 contains an explanation of the objectives and organisation, planning and design of the census,
and data on holders, holders' households, labour employed on holdings, and livestock. Vol.2
is the report of a census of livestock in the Karamaja district taken in 1963. Vol.3 is mainly
concerned with the areas of holdings and land under the major crops grown in Uganda. Vol.4
is a general volume covering the whole range of the census and analysing the data.
Time factor: the census was carried out between July 1962 and June 1966 and the reports were
published between 1965 and 1967.
§ En.

1360 Report of agricultural statistics (Department of Agriculture, Ministry of Agriculture and Forestry).
Government Printer, P O Box 33, Entebbe.
1967/68 and 1968. Ug Sh 7.50. 144p.
The report on a study of trends in acreages and yields of crops.
Time factor: the report was published in 1969.
§ En.

1361 Annual report of the Agriculture Department.
Ministry of Agriculture and Forestry, P O Box 102, Entebbe.
1910/11- 1971. Ug Sh 7.00. 44p.
Appendices include statistics on cotton production, crop production, exports of agricultural produce,
plantation crop production, prices paid to farmers, and population and availability of land.
Time factor: the 1971 report, published in 1974, contains data for 1970 and 1971 and the 1970/71 season.
§ En.

1362 East African statistics of sugar (East African Statistical Department).
East African Statistical Department, East African Community, P O Box 30462, Nairobi, Kenya.
1966/74- 1966/74. K Shg 5.00. 21p.
Contains data on production, imports, consumption, stocks of sugar in the world and in Uganda, Kenya
and Tanzania. Also local sugar prices and world price trends.
Time factor: the 1966/74 issue, published in 1976, has data for the years 1966 to 1974.
§ En.

1363 Annual report (Department of Veterinary Services and Animal Industry).
Department of Veterinary Services, Entebbe.
1960- 1971. not priced. 85p.
Includes some statistical tables on production, health and sales.
Time factor: the 1971 report, published in 1973, has data for 1971.
§ En.

1364 Annual report (Forest Department).
Forest Department, Entebbe.
1938- 1964/68. Ug Sh 7.00. c70p.
Includes statistical data on forest land, reserves, timber felled and sold, etc.
Time factor: the 1964/68 report, published in 1970, has data for the years 1964 to 1968.
§ En.

1365 Annual report (Ministry of Animal Industry, Game and Fisheries; Fisheries Department).
Fisheries Department, P O Box 4, Entebbe.
1967- 1970. not priced. 24p.
Includes statistical data on fishery vessel licenses, catch recorded from surveyed areas of lakes and
rivers, and estimated fish production.
Time factor: the 1970 report, published late 1972, has data for 1970.
§ En.

Refer also to 1354.

¶ B, continued

iii. Industry

1366 Survey of industrial production (Statistics Division, Ministry of Planning).
Government Printer, P O Box 33, Entebbe.
1963- 1969. Ug Sh 7.50. 142p.
Contains data on number of establishments, numbers employed, wages and salaries, other current costs, gross output and value added, locations, value added and net capital expenditure, size of establishments, etc.
Time factor: the 1969 survey report was published in December 1972.
§ En.

1367 East African statistics of industrial production (East African Statistical Department).
East African Statistical Department, East African Community, P O Box 30462, Nairobi, Kenya.
1967- 1970 & 1971. K Shg 7.50. c50p.
Contains data on the number of establishments, persons engaged, labour costs, gross output, imports and value added, inputs, and gross fixed capital. Data is for Uganda, Kenya and Tanzania.
Time factor: the 1970 & 1971 issue, published in 1976, has data for the years 1970 and 1971.
§ En.

1368 Statistical analysis of industrial production in East Africa (1963-1970) (East African Statistical Department).
East African Statistical Department, East African Community, P O Box 30462, Nairobi, Kenya.
K Shg 10.00. 150p.
A statistical analysis of the size of establishments, employment, gross output, value added, value of production, investment, profit and labour. Data are for Uganda, Kenya and Tanzania.
Time factor: published in 1974.
§ En.

Refer also to 1354, 1355, 1356, 1357.

v. Energy

1369 East African statistics of energy and power (East African Statistical Department).
East African Statistical Department, East African Community, P O Box 30462, Nairobi, Kenya.
1966/73- 1966/73. K Shg 7.50.
Time factor: published in 1976.
§ En.

Refer also to 1354.

¶ C - External trade

1370 Annual trade report of Tanzania, Uganda and Kenya (East African Customs and Excise Department).
East African Customs and Excise Department, P O Box 90601, Mombasa.
1961- 1975. K Shg 60. various paginations.
Main tables show imports, exports and re-exports of the three countries separately and of East Africa as a whole, arranged by commodity and sub-divided by countries of origin and destination. Also included are tables showing the transfer of goods between partner states.
Time factor: the 1975 issue, containing data for that year, was published early in 1976.
§ En.

1371 Monthly trade statistics for Tanzania, Uganda and Kenya (East African Customs and Excise Department).
East African Customs and Excise Department, P O Box 90601, Mombasa.
1961- K Shg 5; K Shg 50 yr, post free.
Contains tables showing direct imports, exports and re-exports arranged by SITC, and trade by country for each of the three countries separately. Also included are tables showing the transfer of goods between partner states.
Time factor: each issue has data for the month and cumulated figures for the year to date, and is published about two months later.
§ En.

¶   C,   continued

1372   Monthly/quarterly trade bulletin   (Office of the President; Statistics Division).
Office of the President, P O Box 13, Entebbe.
1969-   Ug Sh 4 or Ug Sh 15 yr.
Contains summary data of foreign trade; detailed imports, exports and re-exports arranged by countries
       of origin and destination; detailed imports, exports and re-exports arranged by commodities; and
       revenues collected (import and excise duties).
Time factor: monthly until the end of 1973, the bulletin is now issued quarterly.   Each issue has data
       for 3 months, the quarter and the corresponding periods for the previous year.   Publication is some
       time later.
§   En.

Refer also to 1354, 1355, 1356, 1357.

¶   D - Internal distribution and service trades

1373   Census of distribution   (Statistics Division, Ministry of Planning).
Government Printer, P O Box 33, Entebbe.
1966-   1966.   Ug Sh 5.00 (abroad Ug Sh 6.00) each part.   2 vols.
Part I presents the results of the first stage of the census, including all businesses engaged in wholesale
       trade and commission agency trade, and all retailers employing 10 or more employees.   Part II is
       a survey of retail trade establishments employing fewer than 10 persons and is the result of a sample
       census.   Tables include number of enterprises, number of employees, sales and commissions,
       receipts per enterprise and per employee, purchases and stocks, turnover, gross profit and operating
       costs, and net profit for the wholesale and retail trade, by kind of business.
Time factor: Part I was published in 1967 and Part II in 1969.
§   En.

Refer also to 1356.

¶   E - Population

1374   Report of the...population census   (Ministry of Planning and Economic Development).
Government Printer, P O Box 33, Entebbe.
1948-   3rd, 1969.   4 vols.
Content:
       Vol. 1 The population and administrative areas (Ug Shs 25)
              2 Administrative report (Ug Shs 15)
              3 Additional tables - selection of results of general and sample census (Ug Shs 18)
              4 Analytical report (Ug Shs 18)
Time factor: the reports of the census were published between 1971 and 1974.
§   En.

1375   Enumeration of employees   (Statistics Division, Ministry of Planning).
Government Printer, P O Box 33, Entebbe.
1949-   1970.   Ug Shs 3.   26p.
Contains data on total employees by district and industry, total African employees by district and
       industry, total African employees by industry and country of birth, and by wage group.
Time factor: the 1970 issue, published in December 1971, gives the position at June 1970.
§   En.

Refer also to 1354, 1356.

¶   F – Social

i. Standard of living

1376   Rural food consumption survey 1968   (Statistics Division, Ministry of Planning).
              Office of the President, P O Box 13, Entebbe.
                          Ug Shs 7.50.   94p.
              The survey covered Ankole, Busoga, Masaka and West Nile.
              Time factor: taken in 1968, the results of the survey were published in 1970.
              §   En.

              Refer also to 1354, 1355, 1356.

ii. Health and welfare

1377   Medical services statistical records   (Ministry of Health).
              Ministry of Health, P O Box 8, Entebbe.
              1959–   1968/69.   not priced.   c60p.
              Contains data on hospitals, patients, out-patients, diseases, maternity, leprosy, etc.
              Time factor: the 1968/69 issue, published in 1970, has data for the year 1968/69.
              §   En.

              Refer also to 1354.

iii. Education and leisure

1378   Education statistics   (Ministry of Education).
              Ministry of Education, P O Box 7063, Kampala.
              1965–   1967.   not priced.   various paginations.
              Contains data on primary, secondary, technical and higher education, including the University of
                  East Africa and education abroad.
              Time factor: the 1967 issue, published in 1969, has data for 1967.
              §   En.

              Refer also to 1354.

iv. Justice

              Refer to 1354.

¶   G – Finance

              Refer to 1354, 1356, 1357.

i. Banking

              Refer to 1354, 1355, 1356.

¶ G, continued

ii. Public finance

379   The public accounts of the Republic of Uganda...   (Office of the President).
Office of the President, P O Box 13, Entebbe.
1929-   1967/68.   not priced.   160p.
Time factor: the 1967/68 issue, published in 1969, has data for the fiscal year 1967/68.
§   En.

Refer also to 1354, 1355, 1356.

v. Insurance

380   East Africa, insurance statistics   (East African Statistical Department).
East African Statistical Department, East African Community, P O Box 30462, Nairobi, Kenya.
1959-   1967.   K Shg 3.00.   41p.
Contains data on all kinds of insurance for East Africa, Kenya, Tanzania and Uganda.
Time factor: the 1967 issue, has data for 1965, 1966 and 1967.
§   En.

Refer also to 1356.

¶ H - Transport and communications

381   Statistical survey of the East African Community institutions   (East African Community).
East African Community, P O Box 30462, Nairobi, Kenya.
1973-   1973.   K Shg 7.50.   68p.
Contains data on railways, harbours, posts and telecommunications, airways, etc, for Uganda, Kenya and Tanzania.
Time factor: the 1973 issue, published in 1975, has data for 1973 or the latest available.
§   En.

Refer also to 1354, 1355, 1356.

Central statistical office

1382   Direction de la Statistique et de la Mécanographie   [Department of Statistics],
        B P 374, Ouagadougou.
        t 32-70 and 32-95.   tx 5256 Answerback MIFICOM 5256UV.

   The Department is attached to the Ministry of Commerce and is responsible for the collection, analysis
and publication of economic and social statistics for Upper Volta.

Statistical publications

¶   A - General

1383   Bulletin annuaire d'information statistique et économique   [Annual bulletin of statistical and economic
            information]   (Ministère du Plan, du Développement Rural, de l'Enseignement et du Tourisme and
            Institut National de la Statistique et de la Démographie).
        Ministère du Plan, Ouagadougou.
        1960-   1974.   not priced.   78p.
        Main sections:
            Climate   Foreign trade
            Health   Prices
            Education   Money and credit
            Production   Public finance
            Transport
        Time factor: the 1974 edition, published in 1976, has data for 1973 and four earlier years, and also for
            the 12 months of 1973.   Issued monthly to 1972.
        §   Fr.

1384   L'économie Voltaique   [The economy of Upper Volta]   (EDIAFRIC).
        EDIAFRIC, 57 avenue d'Iéna, 75783 Paris Cedex 16, France.
            1st ed, 1971.   FrF 354.   various paginations.
        Contains information, including statistics and statistical tables, on agriculture, forestry, livestock,
            fisheries, industry, energy, public works, transport, finance, foreign trade, and regionalisation.
        §   Fr.

¶   B - Production

   ii. Agriculture, fisheries, forestry, etc.

1385   Annuaire des statistiques agricoles   [Statistical yearbook of agriculture]   (Ministère du Plan, du
            Développement Rural, de l'Enseignement et du Tourisme. Direction des Services Agricoles).
        Direction des Services Agricoles, Ouagadougou.
        1970-   1972.   not priced.   90p.
        Contains data on climate, demography, land and production, factors of production (intermediate
            consumption, manure, machinery), commercialisation, imports and exports, and sales in Upper
            Volta.
        Time factor: the 1972 issue, published in 1974, has data for 1972 and 1971.
        §   Fr.

1386   Rapport annuel   [Annual report]   (Ministère du Plan, du Développement Rural, de l'Enseignement et du
            Tourisme. Direction des Services Agricoles).
        Direction des Services Agricoles, Ouagadougou.
            1974/75.   not priced.   77p.
        Includes some statistics of production, prices, sales, etc.
        Time factor: the 1974/75 report, published in July 1975, has data for the crop year 1974/75.
        §   Fr.

   Refer also to 1383, 1384.

¶ B, continued

iii. Industry

Refer to 1383, 1384.

¶ C - External trade

1387   Statistiques du commerce extérieur (édition mécanographie trimestrielle)   [Foreign trade statistics
       (quarterly machine compilations)]   (Direction de la Statistique).
       Direction de la Statistique, B P 374, Ouagadougou.
       1960-   quarterly.   price on application.
       Contains detailed statistics of imports and exports arranged by commodities and sub-divided by countries
          of origin and destination.
       Time factor: each issue has cumulated figures for the year to date, so that the last quarter's issue each
          year has annual figures.   The issue with figures for 1971 was published some months later.
       §   Fr.

1388   Balance commerciale et commerce extérieur   [Balance of payments and foreign trade]   (Ministère des
       Finances et du Commerce).
       Ministère des Finances et du Commerce, Ouagadougou.
       1967-   1972.   not priced.   221p.
       A study on imports, exports, balances, etc.
       Time factor: the 1972 issue, published in 1973, has data for 1972.
       §   Fr.

1389   Associés: commerce extérieur: Haute-Volta: annuaire 1959-1966.   [Associates: foreign trade: Upper Volta:
       yearbook 1959-1966]   (European Communities).
       Office des Publications Officielles des Communautés Européennes, C P 1003, Luxembourg; or from
       sales agents.
                £0.90 or FrB 100.   130p.
       One of a series of retrospective publications on the foreign trade of African states associated with the
       European Communities.   Main tables show imports and exports arranged by commodity and sub-
       divided by countries of origin and destination.   Values are in US$.
       Time factor: published in 1969.
       §   De, En, Fr, It, Nl.

Refer also to 1383, 1384.

¶ E - Population

1390   La situation démographique en Haute-Volta, 1960/1961   [The demographic situation in Upper Volta,
       1960/1961]   (Institut National de la Statistique et des Etudes Economiques).
       Imprimerie Nationale, 2 rue Paul-Hervieu, 75732 Paris Cedex 15.
               FrF 8.   54p.
       Published in 1962.
       §   Fr.

1391   Recensement démographique Ouagadougou, 1961-1962: résultats définitifs   [Demographic census of
       Ouagadougou, 1961-1962: final results]   (Institut National de la Statistique et des Etudes
       Economiques).
       Imprimerie Nationale, 2 rue Paul-Hervieu, 75732 Paris Cedex 15.
               FrF 9.   93p.
       Published in 1964.
       §   Fr.

¶ E, continued

1392 Enquête démographique: Ouagadougou, 1968 [Demographic survey: Ouagadougou] (Direction de la Statistique et de la Mécanographique).
Issued as a supplement to "Bulletin mensuel d'information statistique et économique" in 1969.
§ Fr.

¶ F - Social

ii. Health and welfare

Refer to 1383.

iii. Education and leisure

Refer to 1383.

¶ G - Finance

Refer to 1383, 1384.

ii. Public finance

1393 Comptes économiques de la Haute-Volta [Economic accounts of Upper Volta] (Direction de la Statistique).
Direction de la Statistique, B P 374, Ouagadougou.
1954/59- 1968. not priced. 178p.
Contains data on the production sector, administration, accounts of households and domestic consumption, and balance of payments, etc.
Time factor: the 1968 issue, published in 1971, has statistical tables in the text relating to 1968.
§ Fr.

Refer also to 1383.

¶ H - Transport and communications

Refer to 1383, 1384.

ii. Road

1394 Situation de parc automobile [Registration of motor vehicles] (Ministère du Plan et des Travaux Publics).
Ministère du Plan et des Travaux Publics, Ouagadougou.
1957- 1971. not priced. 57p.
Includes data on registration of all vehicles (cars, motorcycles, tractors, buses, lorries, etc), new and secondhand, by origin.
Time factor: the 1971 issue gives the position as at 31st December 1971, and was published in 1972.
§ Fr.

ZAIRE

Central statistical office

1395   Institut National de la Statistique   [National Institute of Statistics],
          B P 20, Kinshasa.
          t   59407/59289.

          The Institute is responsible for the collection, analysis and publication of economic and social
          statistics for the Republic of Zaire.

Statistical publications

¶   A - General

1396   Bulletin trimestriel des statistiques générales   [Quarterly bulletin of general statistics]   (Institut
              National de la Statistique).
          Institut National de la Statistique, B P 20, Kinshasa.
          1955-   not priced.
          Contains data on production, transport, prices, money and credit, public finance, and population.
          Time factor: each issue has data for the period of the issue, several earlier quarters and the last
              complete year, and is published several months after the end of the period covered.
          §   Fr.

1397   Etudes statistiques   [Statistical studies]   (Institut National de la Statistique).
          Institut National de la Statistique, B P 20, Kinshasa.
          1975-   irregular.   not priced.
          Each issue is on a particular economic subject.
          §   Fr.

1398   Bulletin trimestriel   [Quarterly bulletin]   (Banque du Zaire).
          Banque du Zaire, Kinshasa.
          1962-   not priced.
          Contains data on money and credit, public finance, balance of payments and foreign trade, transport,
              production (minerals and metals, electric energy, oil), wages, and price indices.
          Time factor: each issue has data for 1 or 2 years and several quarters to the quarter of the issue, and is
              published six or more months later.
          §   Fr.

1399   Bulletin mensuel de la statistique   [Monthly bulletin of statistics]   (Banque du Zaire).
          Banque du Zaire, Kinshasa.
          1975-   not priced.
          Contains data on money and credit, public finance, foreign trade relations, production, transport, and
              price indices at Kinshasa.
          Time factor: each issue covers several years and months to the month prior to the date of the issue and is
              published about 3 or 4 months later.
          §   Fr.

1400   Rapport annuel   [Annual report]   (Banque du Zaire).
          Banque du Zaire, Kinshasa.
          1967-   1974.   not priced.   309p.
          Contains information on the activities of the Bank and also economic and financial data on gross
              national product, production of principal sectors, investments, prices, labour, public finance,
              balance of payments, money and credit.
          Time factor: the 1974 report, published in 1975, has data for several years to 1974.
          §   Fr.

¶   A,   continued

1401   Conjoncture économique   [Economic bulletin]   (Département de l'Economie Nationale).
         Departement de l'Economie Nationale, Kinshasa.
         1961-   1974.   not priced.   381p.
         Contains data on foreign trade, the Bank of Zaire, public finance, energy, oil, mineral production,
             construction, industrialisation (including tourism), foreign aid, transport and communications.
         Time factor: No.14, the 1974 edition, has data for 1973 and the 1st quarter of 1974, and was
             published in April 1975.
         §   Fr.

¶   B - Production

i. Mines and mining

         Refer to 1398, 1401.

iii. Industry

1402   Enquête sur les entreprises   [Survey of businesses]   (Département de l'Economie Nationale).
         Département de l'Economie Nationale, Kinshasa.
         1968-   1969-70.   not priced.   2 vols.
         Vol.1 contains methodology, document annexes, structure of businesses, study on structure of
             establishments, and employment; vol.2 contains data on wages, sales and stocks, finances,
             investment, value added, and a study on the structure of establishments.
         Time factor: the report of the 1969-1970 survey was published in 1973.
         §   Fr.

1403   Situation de la production de la République Democratique du Congo de 1965 à 1970   [Situation on
             production in the Democratic Republic of Congo from 1965 to 1970]   (Institut National de la
             Statistique).
         Institut National de la Statistique, B P 20, Kinshasa.
                                   not priced.   25p.
         Issued as no.5 in the series "Etudes statistiques".
         Time factor: published in 1970.
         §   Fr.

         Refer also to 1396, 1399, 1400, 1401.

iv. Construction

         Refer to 1401.

v. Energy

         Refer to 1398, 1401.

¶   C - External trade

1404   Annuaire des statistiques du commerce extérieur   [Statistical yearbook of foreign trade]   (Institut
             National de la Statistique).
         Institut National de la Statistique, B P 20, Kinshasa.
         1962-   1970.   not priced.   633p.
         Main tables show imports, exports re-exports and transit trade arranged by commodities and sub-
             divided by countries of origin and destination.
         Time factor: the 1970 issue has data for 1970.
         §   Fr.

¶   C,   continued

1405   Etats mécanographiques des importations   [Machine tabulations of import statistics]   (Institut National de
          la Statistique).
          Institut National de la Statistique, B P 20, Kinshasa.
          1964-   quarterly.   not priced.
          Detailed statistics of imports arranged by commodity groups, by countries of origin, and by commodities
             sub-divided by countries of origin.
          §   Fr.

1406   Etats mécanographiques des exportations   [Machine tabulations of export statistics]   (Institut National
          de la Statistique).
          Institut National de la Statistique, B P 20, Kinshasa.
          1964-   quarterly.   not priced.
          Detailed statistics of exports arranged by commodity groups, by countries of destination, and by
             commodities sub-divided by countries of destination.
          §   Fr.

          Refer also to 1398, 1399, 1401.

¶   D - Internal distribution and service trades

1407   Rapport annuel   [Annual report]   (Office National du Tourisme).
          Office National du Tourisme, Kinshasa.
          1972-   1974.   not priced.   58p.
          Contains data on tourists entering the country, length of stay, accommodation, etc.
          Time factor: the 1974 report, published in 1975, has data for 1974 and also for one or two earlier years
             in some tables.
          §   Fr.

          Refer also to 1401.

¶   E - Population

1408   Résultats officiels du recensement général de la population de la République Démocratique du Congo...
          [Official results of the general census of the Democratic Republic of Congo]   (Institut National
          de la Statistique).
          Institut National de la Statistique, B P 20, Kinshasa.
          1952-   1970.   not priced.   14p.
          Time factor: published in 1970.
          §   Fr.

1409   Recueil des rapports et totaux: calculés à partir des résultats officiels du recensement de la population de la
          R.D.C. en 1970   [Collection of reports and totals: some results of the census of population of
          R.D.C. of 1970]   (Institut National de la Statistique).
          Institut National de la Statistique, B P 20, Kinshasa.
                      not priced.   94p.
          §   Fr.

1410   Perspectives démographiques provisoires pour la République du Zaire, 1970-1980   [Provisional demographic
          forecasts for the Republic of Zaire]   (Bureau du Président, Planification et Développement and
          Institut National de la Statistique).
          Institut National du Statistique, B P 20, Kinshasa.
                      not priced.   31p.
          Time factor: published in April 1972.
          §   Fr.

          Refer also to 1396.

ZAIRE,   continued

¶   F - Social

i. Standard of living

1411   Prix et indice des prix à la consommation familiale   [Prices and price indices of family consumption]
              (Institut National de la Statistique).
           Institut Nationale de la Statistique, B P 20, Kinshasa.
           .1970-   monthly.   not priced.
           §   Fr.

1412   Les enquêtes sur les budgets des ménages en milieu urbain en République du Zaire   [Surveys of household
              budgets in urban Zaire]   (Institut National de la Statistique).
           Institut National de la Statistique, B P 20, Kinshasa.
                           not priced.   67p.
           Issued as no.7 in the series "Etudes statistiques".
           Time factor: published in 1972.
           §   Fr.

           Refer also to 1398.

iii. Education and leisure

1413   Annuaire statistique de l'éducation   [Statistical yearbook of education]   (Ministère de l'Education
              Nationale).
           Ministère de l'Education Nationale, Kinshasa.
           1961/62-   1968/69.   not priced.   unpaged.
           Detailed statistics on all aspects of education in Zaire - schools, pupils, classes, etc.
           Time factor: the 1968/69 issue, published in 1971, has data for the academic year 1968/69.
           §   Fr.

¶   G - Finance

           Refer to 1396, 1398, 1399, 1400, 1401.

¶   H - Transport and communications

1414   Rapport d'activité et comptes financières   [Report of activities and financial accounts]   (Office National
              des Transports).
           Office National des Transports, Kinshasa.
           1973-   1974.   not priced.   30p.
           Covers port, rail, river and sea transport and includes statistics of traffic, cargoes, passengers, and
              finances.
           Time factor: the 1974 report, published in 1976, has data for the years 1973 and 1974.
           §   Fr.

           Refer also to 1396, 1398, 1399, 1401.

ii. Road

1415   Parc automobile   [Motor vehicle registration]   (Institut National de la Statistique).
           Institut National de la Statistique, B P 20, Kinshasa.
                   1972.   not priced.   11 parts.
           Parts 1 to 9 each deal with one region, part 10 is for Zaire as a whole, and part 11 is textual.
           Time factor: the 1972 issue has data for 1972.
           §   Fr.

ZAMBIA - ZAMBIE - SAMBIA

Central statistical office

1416
Central Statistical Office,
P O Box 1908, Lusaka.
t 51922.   tg CENSTAT.

A department of the Zambian Ministry of Finance responsible for the collection, compilation, analysis, coordination and publication of a variety of current and base statistics, censuses and surveys.

Libraries

The Central Statistical Office has a library where Zambian and other statistical publications may be consulted.   The library is open from 08.00 to 13.00 and from 14.00 to 17.00 from Monday to Friday, but is closed during vacations.   The language spoken by staff of the library is English.

The National Archives Library, also in Lusaka, has a collection of statistical publications which may be consulted by the public.

Libraries and information services abroad

Publications of the Zambian Central Statistical Office are available for reference in Zambian embassies abroad, including:-
United Kingdom   High Commission for Zambia, 7-11 Cavendish Place, London W.   t 01-580 0691.
U S A   Zambia Embassy, 1875 Connecticut Avenue NW, Washington, DC.   t 265 9717.

Bibliographies

A list of publications issued by the Central Statistical Office appears every month in the Office's "Monthly digest of statistics" (1421).

Statistical publications

¶ A - General

1417
Statistical yearbook   (Central Statistical Office).
Central Statistical Office, P O Box 1908, Lusaka.
1967-   1971.   K 3.00 (K 3.40 abroad).   203p.
Main sections:

Land, population and housing	Money and banking
Health	Insurance
Education	Public finance
Labour and employment	Second national development plan
Agriculture and forestry	Foreign trade and balance of
Livestock and fisheries	payments
Transport and communications	Prices
Mining, commerce and industry	National accounts
Joint stock companies and	Miscellaneous (climate,
co-operative societies	crime, prisons)

Time factor: the 1971 edition, published in 1972, contains data up to and including 1970.
§   En.

1418
Monthly digest of statistics   (Central Statistical Office).
Central Statistical Office, P O Box 1908, Lusaka.
1965-   K 1.00; K 11.00 yr (K 12.32 yr abroad).
Contains data on population and migration, employment and earnings, agriculture, production (mining, manufacturing, electricity and construction), foreign trade, transport, government accounts, money and banking, prices, national accounts and balance of payments, and miscellaneous (road traffic accidents, student enrolments, average retail prices of selected commodities).
Time factor: each issue, published in the month of the issue, has data for the previous month or quarter and usually for a run of years.
§   En.

1419   Economic report   (Ministry of Development Planning).
        Ministry of Development Planning, Box 3211, Lusaka.
        1968-   1976.   K 1.50.   108p.
        Contains chapters on Zambian economy and prospects, the international economic situation, overall
            performance of the economy, rural development, mining, manufacturing, energy, transport and
            communications, employment and wages, education, and health.   Some statistics are included
            in the text.
        Time factor: the 1976 edition, published early 1977, has data for several years to 1976.
        §   En.

1420   Report...   (Bank of Zambia).
        Bank of Zambia, Lusaka.
        1964/65-   1974.   not priced.   94p.
        Contains an economic report (a general survey; national income, agriculture, mining, industry and
            commerce, transport and communications, energy, employment and prices, balance of payments,
            public finance, money and banking), details of operations and accounts, and monetary and
            financial statistics.
        Time factor: the 1974 report, published in 1975, has data for long periods up to 1974.
        §   En.

1421   Quarterly statistical review   (Bank of Zambia).
        Bank of Zambia, Lusaka.
        1971-   not priced.
        Includes an economic and financial review and statistical tables on money and banking, other financial
            institutions, government finance, trade statistics, prices and production.
        Time factor: each issue has long runs of annual and monthly figures.
        §   En.

1422   Official statistics   (Central Statistical Office).
        Central Statistical Office, P O Box 1908, Lusaka.
        1966-   irregular.   not priced.
        Each issue is devoted to a different topic - insurance, production, fisheries, vital statistics, etc.
        §   En.

¶   B - Production

i. Mines and mining

1423   Annual report of the Mines Safety Department.
        Mines Safety Department, Ministry of Mines and Mining Development, Lusaka.
        1968-   1973.   K 0.30.   28p.
        Time factor: the 1973 report, published in 1975, has data for 1973.
        §   En.

1424   Zambia mining year book   (Copper Industry Service Bureau).
        Copper Industry Service Bureau, P O Box 2100, Kitwe.
        1967-   1975.   not priced.   36p.
        A statistical index includes data on copper production, sales, prices, labour, power, etc, and there is
            also some information on cobalt, lead and zinc.
        Time factor: the 1975 edition, published in 1976, contains data for several years to 1975.
        §   En.

        Refer also to 1417, 1418, 1419, 1420.

¶   B,   continued

ii. Agriculture, fisheries, forestry, etc.

1425   Census of agriculture   (Central Statistical Office).
             Central Statistical Office, P O Box 1908, Lusaka.
             1970/71-   1970/71.   1st report. K 4.00 (K 4.34 abroad).
             The first report contains data on crops, livestock, poultry, and farm employment.
             Time factor: the first report of the 1970/71 census was published in 1974 and a second report was
                  planned to be published in 1977.
             §   En.

1426   Agricultural and pastoral production (commercial farms)   (Central Statistical Office).
             Central Statistical Office, P O Box 1908, Lusaka.
             1964-   1972.   K 1.00 (K 1.20 abroad).   c65p.
             Contains data on areas under cultivation; production and yield of crops; tobacco sales, areas planted,
                  crop production and yield; vegetables sown and produced; number of fruit trees; sale of fruit;
                  livestock; milk and dairy produce production and sales; sales of farm produce; sales of poultry
                  products; farm machinery; investments – for the whole country and for each province.
             Time factor: the 1972 edition, published in 1974, has data for 1972 and also for some earlier years in
                  some tables.
             §   En.

1427   Quarterly agricultural statistical bulletin   (Statistics Section: Ministry of Lands and Agriculture).
             Central Statistical Office, P O Box 1908, Lusaka.
             1969-   K 0.50 (K 0.70 abroad).
             Content varies with each issue, but includes reports of censuses and surveys as well as regular statistics
                  on crops and livestock production, prices, etc.
             §   En.

1428   Quarterly statistical bulletin   (Ministry of Rural Development).
             Ministry of Rural Development, Lusaka.
             1972-   not priced.
             Contains data on crops (producer and input prices, maize, groundnuts, cotton, tobacco, vegetables,
                  fruit, and other (paddy rice, sorghum, sunflower, sugar)), livestock (beef, dairying, pigs, poultry),
                  fisheries, and general agricultural statistics (consumer price indices, retail prices, external trade).
             Time factor: each issue has annual figures for two years and 12 months to the date of the issue, and is
                  published some two or three months later.
             §   En.

1429   Fishery statistics (natural waters)   (Central Statistical Office).
             Central Statistical Office, P O Box 1908, Lusaka.
             1965-   1970.   K 0.35 (K 0.55 abroad).   140p.
             Contains data on lake and river fisheries, catch, species, gear, dried fish, etc.
             Time factor: the 1970 issue, published in 1971, has data for 1970.
             §   En.

1430   Annual report   (Ministry of Lands, Natural Resources and Tourism. Department of Fisheries).
             Department of Fisheries, Ministry of Lands, Natural Resources and Tourism, Box 55, Lusaka.
             1964-   1974.   K 0.30.   41p.
             Includes statistical tables on fish production from Zambian natural fisheries (quantities).
             Time factor: the 1974 report, published in 1976, has monthly data for 1974 and annual for 1973 and 1974.
             §   En.

¶   B.ii,   continued

1431   Annual report of the Forest Department   (Ministry of Lands and Natural Resources).
          Forest Department, Ministry of Lands, Natural Resources and Tourism, Box 55, Lusaka.
          1964-   1971.   K 0.25.   57p.
             Includes appendices with statistics on area of forest land; progress with forest reservation; forest
                management; area under plans; forest regeneration and afforestation; out-turn of timber, poles and
                fuels in reserved and unreserved lands; output and export of minor forest products; domestic
                consumption of forest products; consumption of timber by mining companies; size of forest
                industries; commercial sawmills in western province; analysis of revenue; comparative financial
                statement of forestry expenditure and revenue, etc.
          Time factor: the 1971 report, published in 1973, has data for 1971.
          §   En.

          Refer also to 1417, 1418, 1419, 1420, 1422.

      iii. Industry

1432   Census of industrial production   (Central Statistical Office).
          Central Statistical Office, P O Box 1908, Lusaka.
          1962-   1971.   K 1.00 (K 1.20 abroad).   49p.
             Contains summary statistics of activity; principal indicators of industrial activity; numbers of
                establishments, persons engaged, manhours worked; compensation of employees; gross output and
                related items; intermediate output and related items, value of stocks; income and expenditure;
                fixed capital formation; and depreciation, for all establishments in mining, quarrying and
                manufacturing, electricity, water supply and construction, except for one-man establishments.
          Time factor: the 1971 report, published in 1973, has data for 1971.
          §   En.

1433   Industry monographs   (Central Statistical Office).
          Central Statistical Office, P O Box 1908, Lusaka.
          1975-   irregular.   K 4.00 (K 4.20 abroad) each issue.
          A series on manufacturing in Zambia, showing development over the five-year period from 1968 to 1972.
          Content:
                No. 1   Food, beverages and tobacco industries
                      2   Textile, wearing apparel and leather industries
                      3   Wood, wood products and furniture
                      4   Paper, paper products, and publishing industries
                      5   Chemicals, rubber and plastics
                      6   Non-metallic mineral products
                      7   Metal products, machinery and transport equipment
                      8   Manufacturing
                      9   Electricity and water supply
                     10   Construction
                     11   Non-ferrous metal ore mining
                     12   Other mining and quarrying
          Each report includes some statistics and statistical tables.
          Time factor: published from 1975 onwards, and relate to 1968-1972.
          §   En.

          Refer also to 1417, 1418, 1419, 1420, 1421, 1422.

      iv. Construction

          Refer to 1418.

      v. Energy

          Refer to 1418, 1419, 1420.

¶ C - External trade

1434 Annual statement of external trade (Central Statistical Office).
Central Statistical Office, P O Box 1908, Lusaka.
1964- 1974. K 4.00 (K 4.34 abroad) each volume. 2 vols.
Each volume contains detailed statistics of imports, exports and re-exports by SITC groupings, sub-
divided by countries of origin and destination. Vol.I also includes explanatory notes and summary
tables; vol.II has data according to major trading partners.
Time factor: the 1974 issue, published in 1976, contains data for 1974.
§ En.

1435 Annual report of the Controller of Customs and Excise.
Ministry of Finance, Box RW 62, Lusaka.
1964- 1973. K 0.25. 11p.
Includes statistical data on staffing; collection of revenue by ports, by type of revenue, from excise
duties; trends of consumption and excisable goods; rebates on duties; numbers of bonded
warehouses, licensed sidings and premises.
Time factor: the 1973 report, published in 1975, has data for 1973.
§ En.

Refer also to 1417, 1418, 1421.

¶ D - Internal distribution and service trades

1436 Census of distribution in 1962: wholesale, retail trade and selected services (Central Statistical Office).
Central Statistical Office, P O Box 1908, Lusaka.
K 0.25 (K 0.36 abroad). 22p.
Includes data on the number of units, turnover, employees and wages in main types of retail and
wholesale trades and selected services. Geographical distribution of wholesale trade is also
included.
Time factor: the census report was published in 1965.
§ En.

1437 Annual report (Ministry of Information, Broadcasting and Tourism).
Ministry of Information, Broadcasting and Tourism, Box 20, Lusaka.
1972. K 0.50. 50p.
Includes appendices on tourist statistics, and national park statistics; data on radio and television
licenses appear in the text.
Time factor: the 1972 report, published in 1974, has tourist monthly statistics for the years 1964 to
1972, and radio and television statistics for 1972.
§ En.

Refer also to 1420.

¶ E - Population

1438 Census of population and housing (Central Statistical Office).
Central Statistical Office, P O Box 1908, Lusaka.
1931- 1969.
Content:
Vol. I Final report (K 3.00; K 3.11 abroad)
II Provincial analysis (8 reports at K 3.00 or K 3.34 abroad, each)
III Demographic analysis (K 2.00; K 2.11 abroad)
IV District analysis (35 district reports at K 2.00, K 2.34 abroad, each issue)
Population monograph no.1 (Fertility data... (K 1.00; K 1.11 abroad)
2 Inter-regional variation in fertility (K 0.50; K 0.61 abroad)
3 Projection of labour force, 1969-1984 (K 1.00; K 1.11 abroad)
§ En.

Note: a sample census of population was taken in 1974 and the preliminary report is available
(K 0.50; K 0.61 abroad).

¶   E,   continued

1439   Registered births, marriages and deaths (vital statistics)   (Central Statistical Office).
            Central Statistical Office, P O Box 1908, Lusaka.
            1965-   1975.   K 0.20 (K 0.31 abroad).   17p.
            Time factor: the 1975 issue, published in March 1975, has data for 1975.
            §   En.

1440   Population projections for Zambia 1969-1999   (Central Statistical Office).
            Central Statistical Office, P O Box 1908, Lusaka.
                            K 4.00 (K 4.56 abroad).   454p.
            Population projections for the country as a whole and also for provinces, urban areas, etc.
            Time factor: published in January 1975.
            §   En.

1441   Migration statistics   (Central Statistical Office).
            Central Statistical Office, P O Box 1908, Lusaka.
            1964-   1975.   K 0.30 (K 0.50 abroad).   28p.
            Contains data on date of arrival, port of entry, transport at frontier, nationality, country come from,
                age, sex.   Also ethnic groups of immigrants, and reasons for visit and length of stay of visitors.
            Time factor: the 1975 issue, published mid-1976, has data for 1975.
            §   En.

1442   Employment and earnings   (Central Statistical Office).
            Central Statistical Office, P O Box 1908, Lusaka.
            1964-   3rd, 1969-1971.   K 1.00 (K 1.20 abroad).
            Time factor: the 1969/1971 issue, published in 1975, has data for the years 1969 to 1971.
            §   En.

1443   Survey of occupations, 1969   (Central Statistical Office).
            Central Statistical Office, P O Box 1908, Lusaka.
                            K 0.50 (K 0.61 abroad).   80p.
            Includes data for each industry, of Zambians and non-Zambians.
            Time factor: the 1969 survey was published in 1972.
            §   En.

1444   Annual report of the Department of Labour.
            Ministry of Labour and Social Services, Box 2186, Lusaka.
                        1973.   K 0.60.   65p.
            Includes statistical tables on employment in industry and service, in copper, lead and zinc mining;
                alien African labour in copper mines; labour turnover; rates of pay; strikes; labour inspections;
                employment exchange services; consumer price index; trade unions; employers' associations;
                and accidents.
            Time factor: the 1973 report, published in 1975, has data for 1973.
            §   En.

            Refer also to 1417, 1418, 1419, 1422.

¶   F - Social

i. Standard of living

1445   Urban budget survey   (Central Statistical Office).
            Central Statistical Office, P O Box 1908, Lusaka.
            1960-   2nd, 1966-68.
            Content:
                Urban household budget survey in low cost housing areas (K 3.00 (K 3.56 abroad)
                Some important tables of urban budget survey (K 1.00 (K 1.11 abroad)
            §   En.

            Refer also to 1418, 1419, 1420.

¶ F, continued

ii. Health and welfare

1446   Annual report   (Ministry of Health).
          Ministry of Health, Box 205, Lusaka.
          1964-   1972.   K 1.50.   303p.
          The report includes 26 tables on staffing, hospitals, diseases, maternity, leprosy, dentistry, and
              psychology.
          Time factor: the 1972 report, published in 1976, has data for 1972.
          §   En.

          Refer also to 1417, 1419.

iii. Education and leisure

1447   Educational statistics   (Ministry of Education).
          Ministry of Education, P O Box RW 93, Lusaka.
              1974.   not priced.   104p.
          Contains data on numbers of schools, pupils, classrooms, etc. in primary and secondary education;
              teacher training; university education; technical and vocational education; examination results;
              and finance.   Data are for the whole country and for regions.
          Time factor: the 1974 issue, published mid-1976, has data for 1974 and some earlier years.
          §   En.

1448   Annual report   (Ministry of Education).
          Ministry of Education, P O Box RW 93, Lusaka.
          1964-   1972.   K 0.75.   c60p.
          Includes a statistical appendix of similar, but less detailed data than above for the country as a whole.
          Time factor: the 1972 report, published in 1973, has data for 1972.
          §   En.

1449   Statistical profile of Zambian education   (Ministry of Education).
          Ministry of Education, P O Box RW 93, Lusaka.
          1975-   1976.   not priced.   45p.
          A new annual title started because of the need for more up-to-date statistics, it is less detailed than
              1447 and 1448 above but is issued earlier.
          Time factor: the 1976 issue was published in December 1976, and has data for academic years from
              1972 to 1976.
          §   En.

          Refer also to 1417, 1418, 1419.

iv. Justice

1450   Annual report of the Judiciary and the Magistracy.
          Ministry of Legal Affairs, P O Box 202, Lusaka.
              1969.   K 0.10.   19p.
          Includes an appendix of statistical returns of the high court (criminal, civil, bankruptcy, probate), and
              of subordinate courts, statistics of criminal cases heard and sentences imposed, and a statistical
              return of local courts.
          Time factor: the 1969 report, published in 1976, has data for 1969.
          §   En.

¶   F.iv,   continued

1451   Prisons Department annual report   (Ministry of Home Affairs).
            Ministry of Home Affairs, P O Box 1862, Lusaka.
                    1973.   K 0.35.   13p.
            Includes statistics in the text on prison population, sentences, recidivism, women prisoners, juveniles,
                prison buildings, prison farms and workshops, employment of prisoners, unconvicted prisoners, etc.
                There is also a statistical appendix on committals, length of sentences, fines and canings, previous
                convictions, daily average in prison, daily average on sick list, etc.
            Time factor: the 1973 report, published in 1976, has data for 1973.
            §   En.

            Refer also to 1417.

¶   G - Finance

            Refer to 1417, 1418, 1420, 1421.

i. Banking

            Refer to 1417, 1418, 1420, 1421.

ii. Public finance

1452   National accounts   (Central Statistical Office).
            Central Statistical Office, P O Box 1908, Lusaka.
            1954/64-   1971.   K 2.00 (K 2.20 abroad).   c90p.
            Time factor: the 1971 issue, published in 1974, has data for 1971.
            §   En.

1453   Financial statistics of the government sector (economic and functional analysis)   (Central Statistical
                Office).
            Central Statistical Office, P O Box 1908, Lusaka.
            1964-   1971.   K 1.00 (K 1.34 abroad).   106p.
            Contains financial statistics of both central and local government.
            Time factor: the 1971 issue, published in 1975, has data for the years 1969, 1970 and 1971.
            §   En.

1454   Financial statistics of public corporations   (Central Statistical Office).
            Central Statistical Office, P O Box 1908, Lusaka.
            1964-   1969.   K 0.30 (K 0.50 abroad).   c80p.
            Contains data on 14 public corporations.
            Time factor: the 1969 issue, published in 1970, has data for the years 1964 to 1969.
            §   En.

1455   Balance of payments statistics   (Central Statistical Office).
            Central Statistical Office, P O Box 1908, Lusaka.
            1968/70-   1973.   K 1.00 (K 1.20 abroad).   45p.
            Time factor: the 1973 issue, published mid-1975, has data for 1973.
            §   En.

ZAMBIA, continued

¶ G.ii, continued

1456 Income tax statistics (Central Statistical Office).
Central Statistical Office, P O Box 1908, Lusaka.
1962/63- 1970. K 0.50 (K 0.61 abroad). 13p.
Mainly data on assessments of income tax.
Time factor: the 1970 issue, published in 1973, has data for the tax year to March 1970.
§ En.

Refer also to 1417, 1418, 1420, 1421.

iii. Company finance

Refer to 1418.

v. Insurance

1457 Insurance statistics (Central Statistical Office).
Central Statistical Office, P O Box 1908, Lusaka.
1965- 1969. K 0.25 (K 0.36 abroad). 22p.
Contains data on number of reporting insurers, distribution of insurance business, total insurance
business, growth rates, claims ratio, expenses, and revenue accounts for life, non-life, fire,
motor, personal accident, transport, etc, insurance.
Time factor: the 1969 issue, published in 1971, has data for 1969 and for four earlier years.
§ En.

Refer also to 1417, 1422.

¶ H – Transport and communications

Refer to 1417, 1418, 1419, 1420.

ii. Road

1458 Transport statistics (Central Statistical Office).
Central Statistical Office, P O Box 1908, Lusaka.
1970- quarterly. K 0.40 (K 0.51 abroad) each issue.
Contains data on new registrations of motor vehicles.
Time factor: each issue contains data for the period of the issue and is published about two years later.
§ En.

1459 Report on passenger road transport in Zambia (Central Statistical Office).
Central Statistical Office, P O Box 1908, Lusaka.
1968- 1974. K 0.40 (K 0.51 abroad). c40p.
Contains data on the bus fleet (omnibuses, passengers, traffic, services) and on taxis (numbers,
distances travelled, etc).
Time factor: the 1974 issue, published in 1974, has data for 1974.
§ En.

¶   H.ii,   continued

1460   Annual report of the Roads Branch   (Ministry of Power, Transport and Works).
            Ministry of Power, Transport and Communications, P O Box RW 65, Lusaka.
                    1971.   K 0.40.   23p.
            Includes statistical appendices on expenditure by province; establishment; recruitment and casualties;
                roads classification, maintaining authority and type of surface; road construction by contract;
                construction works – departmental; betterment works; ferries; traffic densities; etc.
            Time factor: the 1971 report, published in 1973, has data for 1971.
            §   En.

            Refer also to 1418.

    iv. Air

1461   Annual report   (Department of Civil Aviation).
            Department of Civil Aviation, P O Box RW 137, Lusaka.
                    1970.   K 0.20.   16p.
            Includes a comparative statistical return of aircraft, passengers, freight, and mail by aerodrome.
            Time factor: the 1970 report, published in 1973, has data for 1969 and 1970.
            §   En.

INDEX OF ORGANISATIONS - INDEX DES ORGANISATIONS - BEHÖRDENVERZEICHNIS

References are to the serial numbers used in the text.

INDEX OF TITLES - INDEX DES TITRES - TITELREGISTER

References are to the serial numbers used in the text.

INDEX OF TITLES

INDEX OF TITLES

Whilst this index refers to the main subjects covered by
the publications listed in the guide, it does not refer to
all the detailed headings included in those publications.

SUBJECT INDEX

Geographical area, continued
    Central African Republic   378
    Comoro Islands   407
    Congo   413
    Djibouti   430
    Ethiopia   516, 518
    Gabon   538
    Ghana   575, 577
    Guinea-Bissau   617
    Kenya   656, 659
    Madagascar   769-770, 785
    Mali   826
    Mauritania   841
    Morocco   884
    Mozambique   914-916
    Nigeria   946-947
    Réunion   992, 994-995
    St Helena   1056
    St Thomas & Prince   1060
    Seychelles   1080, 1083
    Sierra Leone   1094
    Spanish North Africa   1205-1206
    Sudan   1214
    Swaziland   1239
    Tanzania   1274, 1278
    Togo   1311
    Uganda   1354, 1356
    Zambia   1417
Grain crops   090-097, 177
    see also Agriculture
Gross domestic product see National product
Gross national product see National product
Health   016-017, 026, 032, 036, 052, 199,
    205-206
    Algeria   235-238, 240, 242
    Angola   272, 274, 277
    Benin   293
    Botswana   312, 314, 326, 328
    Burundi   335
    Cameroon   346
    Cape Verde Islands   368
    Chad   390
    Comoro Islands   407
    Congo   413-414
    Djibouti   430
    Egypt   438, 440-442, 492-493
    Ethiopia   516, 518, 533-534
    Gabon   538, 541
    Gambia   558
    Ghana   575, 577, 601
    Guinea   611
    Guinea-Bissau   617
    Kenya   656-657, 694
    Lesotho   701, 703, 714
    Liberia   718
    Libya   736, 739
    Madagascar   769-770, 786
    Malawi   792
    Mauritania   841-842
    Mauritius   851, 853, 869
    Morocco   881, 884
    Mozambique   914-916
    Niger   933
    Nigeria   946, 979
    Réunion   992, 997
    Rwanda   1050-1051
    St Helena   1056
    St Thomas & Prince   1059-1060

Health, continued
    Senegal   1067
    Sierra Leone   1094, 1107
    Somalia   1112, 1116
    South Africa   1129, 1134, 1177
    Spanish North Africa   1205-1207
    Sudan   1213-1214, 1218, 1232
    Swaziland   1239-1240, 1243, 1258
    Tanzania   1274, 1277, 1305
    Tunisia   1329, 1331, 1346-1347
    Uganda   1354, 1377
    Upper Volta   1383
    Zambia   1417, 1419, 1446
    see also Social affairs
Hides and skins   117
    see also Industry
Holidays see Leisure; Tourism
Horticulture see Agriculture
Hospitals see Health
Hotels, boarding houses, etc   186
    Angola   273
    Egypt   479
    Gabon   538
    Rhodesia   1029
    South Africa   1161-1162
    see also Catering; Service trades; Tourism
Household income and expenditure   204
    Botswana   325-326
    Cameroon   357-359
    Comoro Islands   407
    Djibouti   430
    Egypt   490
    Gambia   569
    Kenya   659
    Lesotho   711-713
    Libya   736, 739, 757
    Madagascar   787-788
    Malawi   816
    Morocco   907
    Nigeria   977
    Réunion   992-993
    Rhodesia   1033
    Sierra Leone   1105-1106
    Sudan   1213, 1231
    Tanzania   1302
    Togo   1323
    Zaire   1411
    Zambia   1445
Housing and dwellings   016-017, 193-195, 199
    Algeria   235, 237, 240, 242
    Egypt   438, 441-442, 465
    Ethiopia   520
    Ghana   575
    Libya   739, 755
    Malawi   792
    Mauritius   853, 864
    Morocco   903
    Mozambique   914-915, 918
    Réunion   992, 994-995, 997, 1007
    Somalia   1116
    South Africa   1175
    Spanish North Africa   1211
    Sudan   1213, 1229
    Swaziland   1256-1257
    Tanzania   1277
    Zambia   1417, 1438
    see also Construction

Medical   see   Health
Metals   061-062, 064
   South Africa   1139-1140
   Zaire   1398
     see also   Mines and mining;   Non-ferrous metals;
       Industry;   Production;   individual
       metals
Meteorological data   see   Climate
Migration
   Algeria   236
   Angola   273
   Egypt   486
   Ghana   598
   Guinea   613
   Kenya   656-657, 659, 685, 690
   Liberia   729
   Libya   737
   Morocco   881-882
   Nigeria   946-947
   Rhodesia   1015-1018, 1032
   Rwanda   1050
   Seychelles   1080, 1089
   Sierra Leone   1094
   Somalia   1112, 1118
   South Africa   1129, 1135, 1138, 1167
   Swaziland   1239-1240
   Tanzania   1274-1275, 1278, 1301
   Uganda   1354, 1356
   Zambia   1418, 1441
Minerals   024, 045, 059-060, 072-073
   Algeria   238
   Angola   273, 280
   Botswana   313
   Ghana   579, 582
   Madagascar   771
   Morocco   893
   Nigeria   958, 961
   Somalia   1115
   South Africa   1139, 1140
   Swaziland   1240, 1244
   Tanzania   1281
   Zaire   1398, 1401
     see also   Industry;   Mines and mining;
       Production;   individual minerals
Mines and mining   016-018, 033, 036, 038-039,
       059-060, 063-065

   Algeria   243
   Angola   275, 277, 279-280
   Benin   293, 295
   Botswana   316
   Cameroon   348-349
   Cape Verde Islands   368
   Congo   413-414, 418
   Ethiopia   516, 518
   Gabon   538, 541, 544
   Ghana   578, 582
   Guinea   611
   Guinea-Bissau   617
   Ivory Coast   625, 633-634
   Kenya   662
   Lesotho   704
   Liberia   718
   Libya   740, 741
   Madagascar   769-770
   Mauritania   841
   Morocco   881-884, 888-892
   Mozambique   914-916, 918
   Niger   933, 935-936

Mines and mining,   continued
   Nigeria   946-947, 962
   Rhodesia   1016, 1019
   Réunion   1050, 1052
   St Thomas & Prince   1060
   Senegal   1069, 1071-1072
   Sierra Leone   1096-1099
   Somalia   1116
   South Africa   1129-1130, 1132-1134, 1136, 1138,
       1141-1143, 1195
   Swaziland   1239
   Tanzania   1274-1275, 1277, 1281
   Tunisia   1333, 1335
   Uganda   1354, 1358
   Zambia   1417-1420, 1423-1424
     see also   Metals;   Minerals;   individual
       metals and minerals
Money and credit   029-030, 033, 036, 040-043,
       058, 212, 216
   Algeria   235
   Angola   272, 274-277
   Benin   293-294, 296-297
   Burundi   335, 337
   Cameroon   342-344, 346
   Cape Verde Islands   367-368
   Central African Republic   379-380
   Chad   392
   Comoro Islands   407
   Congo   413-415, 418
   Djibouti   430
   Egypt   444
   Ethiopia   517, 519, 522
   Gabon   538-539, 541-542
   Gambia   560
   Ghana   575-579, 581, 604
   Guinea-Bissau   617
   Ivory Coast   626
   Kenya   657, 659-661
   Liberia   722
   Libya   738-739
   Madagascar   767-770, 785
   Malawi   793
   Mali   826, 833
   Mauritania   841-842
   Mauritius   852-854
   Morocco   881-884, 890
   Mozambique   914-916, 918
   Niger   934
   Nigeria   956, 958, 960
   Réunion   992-993, 997
   Rhodesia   1016, 1050
   Rwanda   1051
   St Helena   1056
   St Thomas & Prince   1059-1060
   Senegal   1067, 1069, 1071
   Sierra Leone   1096-1098
   Somalia   1119
   South Africa   1129, 1131, 1182
   Sudan   1213, 1216-1217
   Tanzania   1274, 1277-1278
   Togo   1312
   Tunisia   1329-1333
   Uganda   1354, 1356-1357
   Upper Volta   1383
   Zaire   1396, 1398-1400
   Zambia   1417-1418, 1420-1421
     see also   Finance

SUBJECT INDEX

Population   016-019, 022, 026, 028, 030-039,
              046-047, 052, 188-193, 199
  Algeria   235, 237-238, 258-260
  Angola   272-274, 277, 286
  Benin   293, 304-305
  Botswana   312, 323, 326
  Burundi   335, 339
  Cameroon   346, 354, 355-356
  Cape Verde Islands   367-368, 374
  Central African Republic   378-379, 387
  Chad   390-391, 403
  Comoro Islands   407, 410
  Congo   413-414, 423-425
  Djibouti   430, 432-433
  Egypt   438-444, 480-482, 486
  Equatorial Guinea   512-513
  Ethiopia   516, 518, 520, 524, 529-530
  Gabon   538, 540, 552-553
  Gambia   558-559, 566
  Ghana   575, 577, 596, 601
  Guinea   611, 613
  Guinea-Bissau   617, 623
  Ivory Coast   629, 644, 646-648
  Kenya   656, 658-659, 687-688
  Lesotho   701, 710-711
  Liberia   718, 728-729
  Libya   736, 739, 754, 757
  Madagascar   769-770, 781-786
  Malawi   792, 809-812
  Mali   826, 833, 838
  Mauritania   841-842, 846-847
  Mauritius   851-853, 864-865
  Morocco   881, 884-885, 903
  Mozambique   914-916, 918, 924
  Niger   933, 939-940
  Nigeria   946-947, 974
  Réunion   992-995, 997, 1003-1006
  Rhodesia   1015-1016, 1018, 1031
  Rwanda   1050, 1054
  St Helena   1056, 1058
  St Thomas & Prince   1059-1060, 1065
  Senegal   1067-1068, 1070, 1077
  Seychelles   1080, 1083, 1086-1087, 1089
  Sierra Leone   1094-1095, 1104
  Somalia   1112, 1115, 1118, 1122-1123
  South Africa   1129-1130, 1134-1136, 1163-1166
  Spanish North Africa   1205-1207, 1211
  Sudan   1213-1214, 1216, 1229-1230
  Swaziland   1239, 1242, 1253
  Tanzania   1274-1275, 1278, 1298-1299
  Togo   1311-1312, 1314, 1321
  Tunisia   1329, 1331, 1344-1345
  Uganda   1354, 1356, 1374
  Upper Volta   1390-1392
  Zaire   1396, 1408-1410
  Zambia   1417-1418, 1438, 1440
    see also   Vital statistics
Port traffic   see   Sea-borne shipping;   Ships and
                shipping;   Transport
Postal services   see   Communications
Power   see   Energy
Press   210
  Egypt   497
  St Helena   1056
  Senegal   1069
    see also   Communications

Prices and price indices   016-017, 020-021, 026,
                032-033, 035-036, 045,
                052, 058, 183, 199, 201,
                212
  Algeria   235-236, 239, 255
  Angola   272, 274-278
  Benin   294, 306
  Botswana   312
  Burundi   335-337
  Cameroon   342-344
  Cape Verde Islands   368-369
  Central African Republic   378-380
  Chad   392, 394
  Comoro Islands   407
  Congo   413, 415
  Djibouti   430
  Egypt   444, 463, 491
  Ethiopia   516-518, 521, 532
  Gabon   538-539, 541-542
  Gambia   558, 560
  Ghana   575-578
  Guinea-Bissau   617-618
  Ivory Coast   626-627
  Kenya   660-661
  Lesotho   708
  Liberia   718, 720-721
  Libya   736, 738-739
  Madagascar   767-770
  Malawi   792-793
  Mali   826, 833
  Mauritania   841-842
  Mauritius   853
  Morocco   881-882, 885, 890, 904
  Mozambique   916-918
  Niger   934
  Nigeria   946-947, 955, 957, 959-960
  Réunion   992, 994-997
  Rwanda   1050
  St Thomas & Prince   1060-1061
  Senegal   1067, 1069
  Seychelles   1080
  Sierra Leone   1094, 1096, 1098
  Somalia   1112, 1114, 1119
  South Africa   1129-1133, 1176
  Spanish North Africa   1206-1207
  Sudan   1213
  Swaziland   1239
  Tanzania   1275-1277, 1303
  Togo   1311-1312
  Tunisia   1332-1333
  Uganda   1354-1355
  Upper Volta   1383
  Zaire   1396, 1398-1400
  Zambia   1417-1418, 1420-1421
    see also   Consumer prices and price indices;
                Cost of living;   Retail prices and price
                indices;   Wholesale prices and price
                indices
Prisons
  Mauritius   852
  Nigeria   984
  St Helena   1056
  Tanzania   1305
  Uganda   1354
  Zambia   1417, 1451
    see also   Justice